SOUTHERN NEW ENGLAND

A Sierra Club Naturalist's Guide to

SOUTHERN
NEW ENGLAND

By Neil Jorgensen

DRAWINGS BY
KATHARINE BREWER AND
PRISCILLA KUNHARDT

SIERRA CLUB BOOKS   *San Francisco*

The Sierra Club, founded in 1892 by John Muir, has devoted itself to the study and protection of the nation's scenic and ecological resources—mountains, wetlands, woodlands, wild shores and rivers. All club publications are part of the nonprofit effort the club carries on as a public trust. There are some 50 chapters coast to coast, in Canada, Hawaii, and Alaska. Participation is invited in the club's program to enjoy and preserve wilderness everywhere. Address: *530 Bush Street, San Francisco, California 94108*

Library of Congress Cataloging in Publication Data

Jorgensen, Neil.
   A Sierra Club naturalist's guide to Southern
New England.

   Includes bibliographies and index.
   1. Natural history—New England.   2. Ecology—
New England.   I. Title.
QH104.5.N4J66   500.974   77–28543
ISBN 0–87156–190–5
ISBN 0–87156–183–2 pbk.

Series design by Klaus Gemming, New Haven, Connecticut
Maps by Neil Jorgensen
Printed in the United States of America
10   9   8   7   6   5   4   3   2

TABLE OF CONTENTS

The Pitch Pine, 247

PART VII / WETLAND AND
WATERCOURSE COMMUNITIES

Wetlands: An Introduction, 250

Wetland and Watercourse Communities, 250—Composite and
Transitional Wetlands, 252

The Marsh Community, 252

Marsh Succession, 254—Herbaceous Plants of the Marsh Community, 255

The Wet Meadow Community, 262

Herbaceous Plants of the Wet Meadow Community, 263

The Shrub Swamp Communities, 267

Two Shrub Swamp Communities, 267—Shrubs of the Shrub
Swamp Communities, 269

The Wooded Swamp Community, 274

Travel in Swamps, 274—Characteristics of Wooded Swamps,
275—Mosses and Liverworts, 277—Succession in Wooded
Swamps, 278—Trees of the Wooded Swamp Community, 279—
Shrubs of the Wooded Swamp Community, 282—Herbaceous
Plants of the Wooded Swamp Community, 284

The Flood Plain Community, 285

Natural Levees, 286—Oxbow Lakes, 286—Flood Plain Soils,
287—Trees of the Flood Plain Community, 288—Other Flood
Plain Plants, 297

The Bog Community, 299

Physical Appearance, 299—Bog Development, 301—Shrubs of the
Bog Community, 303—Insectivorous Plants, 305—Bog Orchids,
308

The Conifer Swamp Community, 309

Trees of the Conifer Swamp Community, 310

The Rock Ravine Community, 314

Trees of the Rock Ravine Community, 316—Shrubs of the Rock
Ravine Community, 318—Herbaceous Plants of the Rock Ravine
Community, 320

PHOTO CREDITS

The author thanks the following contributors for the use of photographs indicated (by color plate or caption number) below. All other photographs are by the author.

Jean T. Buermeyer: Plates I (A, B, D), II (A, C, D), III (A, B), IV (B, C, D); *Bill Byrne:* 160, 161, 165, 172; *Robert J. Deptula:* Plate VIII (A, F); *Klaus Gemming:* 159; *Richard A. Jaynes:* Plate V (D); *Jim Lacey:* Plate VI (A, B, C, D); *David Longland:* Plate V (A); *John A. Lynch:* 8, 62, 67, 75, 151, 170, Plates I (C), II (D), III (C), IV (A), V (B, C), VII (B), VIII (B, D, E); *Massachusetts Audubon Society:* 79; *Allen H. Morgan:* 99; *Hal Morgan:* 76; *New England Wildflower Society:* Plate III (D); *Barbara C. Paine:* cover, 44; *Dick Petersen:* Plates VII (A, C, D, F), VIII (C); *Siah St. Clair, Jr.:* Plate VII (E); *Jack Swedberg:* 110, 162, 167, 168, 169, 171.

The diagram on page 59 is reprinted with permission from "Pleistocene Biogeography of Temperate Deciduous Forests" by Margaret Bryan Davis, in *Geoscience and Man* 13 (March 15, 1976).

CONTENTS

ACKNOWLEDGMENTS

A NUMBER OF PEOPLE have given freely of their time, skill, and knowledge in the preparation of this book. Some have read various parts for factual accuracy and have offered excellent suggestions for improving the organization and format. Others have performed great feats of decipherment in translating the drafts into readable typescript and helping in many other ways with the production of the book. Still others have provided me with constant encouragement during times when it seemed the book would never be finished.

To the following, then, I express my deep gratitude: Ray Angelo, Richard J. Clark, Jim Coleman, Dick Cronin, Peter delTredici, Lincoln Foster, Robert Fritsch, Carol Gaskill, Richard Goodwin, Miriam Grunfeld, Charles Heventhal, Joan Irish, Elizabeth Kline, Walter Lyford, Chet McCord, Bill Newbury, Dick Petersen, Hugh Raup, Eugenie Shaw, Dick Walton, Ted Watt, and Hurd Willett.

The trustees and administration of Wheelock College also deserve thanks for providing me with much-needed secretarial help and allowing me a leave of absence to work on the book.

I wish also to acknowledge the outstanding work of the two illustrators, Katie Brewer and Sibby Kunhardt, whose accurate and beautiful drawings of the southern New England plants adorn so many pages of the book. And I thank the people whose names appear in the photo credits for their generosity and help.

A special note of thanks is due my editor, Gail Stewart, for her patience and support, her unending attention to detail, and her many thoughtful suggestions. I am indebted also to Klaus Gemming for the care he put into the design of the book, to Jack Swedberg, whose superb darkroom work appears in many of the photographs, and to William Niering, one of New England's foremost ecologists, for reading the entire manuscript.

I must also thank members of my family: my children, Erik and Laurie Jorgensen, for accompanying me on many of my explorations and for doing things without me while I was writing; my wife, Sue, for typing parts of the manuscript and, more important, for her continuing forbearance and encouragement; and finally, to my parents, Lenora and William Jorgensen, for their invaluable assistance in the preparation of the manuscript. It is to my parents that I gratefully dedicate this book.

N. J.

ACKNOWLEDGMENTS

Introduction

THE LAST DECADE has brought a tremendous resurgence
of interest in the out-of-doors. Tens of thousands of people
have discovered the pleasures of such slow-paced and con-
templative pastimes as walking, canoeing, bicycling, and
cross-country skiing. All of these activities place the partici-
pant in close fellowship with nature; all allow time to savor its
richness and diversity in intimate detail.

Learning about nature is similar to all learning: we sort
recurrent experiences from a constant parade of random
impressions and place these into schemes or patterns constructed in our minds. If you have just begun to look closely
at the natural surroundings, however, the diversity may at
first seem bewildering, complex, and disorderly; making
sense out of what you see can be difficult and frustrating.

An order and pattern—as this guide will show—does
indeed exist in the southern New England countryside, but
to find it you must not only recognize those features and
phenomena that are significant, but also see enough recur-
ring examples to generalize from them. The overall aim of
this guide is to help you on both counts. In Parts II and III
I have pointed out features and phenomena that combine to
give the natural surroundings in any one place their particular flavor. In the later sections, in order to help you
generalize more quickly from your own observations, I have
described some of the more common patterns that you are
likely to see in the southern New England countryside.

The book has been written with the general reader in
mind, who has had no formal training in ecology and perhaps
only limited experience with the out-of-doors. Moreover,
except for the study of birds—which is only lightly touched
upon and for which binoculars are needed—none of the
topics covered here require that you encumber yourself with
special equipment such as rock hammers or insect nets.

Scope of the Book

To such untutored and unaided eyes, then, what patterns
are likely to be most evident? In southern New England, as

indeed throughout the humid parts of the world, the surface of the land is almost mantled by vegetation and its leafy debris. From a close view, the landscape is really a plant-scape, and it is in the vegetation that we see the most obvious patterns.

The vegetation provides the beginner with a splendid entry point into the understanding of nature. Its complexity is for the most part manageable; it is lasting and stationary and therefore may be studied at will; and its study can yield many clues about other aspects of the natural world.

Trees are especially valuable in this regard. Not only do their numbers include the largest and oldest of all living things, but also because of their vast importance as a renew-able resource a great deal is already known about them.

Patterns in other aspects of the natural surroundings—the fauna, the terrain, and the geology—are far less easily seen, especially from the close perspective one has on foot. Let us consider each in turn.

While it is true that animals play several vital roles in the biotic community, they represent only a tiny fraction of the biomass, that is, the total bulk of living things. Because most animals are timid and move from place to place with such rapidity, they are hard to study in the field. Furthermore, patterns in the terrain and vegetation will yield information about the animals; much less often will the reverse be true.

Information about some of the mammals inhabiting the region may be gleaned from studying their winter tracks, but except for squirrels and a few other species, most mammals are abroad only in the evening or are so retiring that the casual observer never sees them.

Among the other vertebrates, birds are, of course, excel-lent subjects for study. They are active during the day and have definite ecological preferences. But the variety of birds found in southern New England is so great that any detailed description of them would double the size of this guide. Moreover, the field has already been well covered by several outstanding books. The other land vertebrates, the reptiles and amphibians, are easier to observe and the number of native species is more manageable.

Insects, spiders, and other invertebrates exist in almost unimaginable variety. Normally their study requires mag-nifiers, nets, and other special equipment plus the mastery of a highly complex and technical vocabulary. Adequate coverage of these creatures would require a whole shelf of books and would be well beyond the capabilities of most amateurs.

The rocks might at first seem to represent a clear source of patterns in the landscape. Like plants they are permanent; there is definite order in their characteristics, and pattern in their distribution. In parts of the world that are too arid to support a thick layer of vegetation, geological patterns are indeed easy to see and study, but in New England the rocks are usually masked by vegetation and buried beneath a jumbled layer of ice age debris. Geologists must make broad inferences about the hidden rocks from studying only scattered spots where they appear on the surface. These outcrops are usually so darkened with age or encrusted with lichens that they yield information only to a highly trained eye. Fresh bedrock exposures occur only in highway cuts or construction sites, places where slow-traveling naturalists are unlikely to be.

But even if the bedrock surface of New England were laid entirely bare, people would still have great difficulty in understanding what they saw. New England's rocks are very old and highly altered by millions of years spent buried in the earth's hot interior. So complex is most of the bedrock geology that it seems almost the result of diabolical intervention during this long period of time in the underworld. Field interpretation of most bedrock exposures therefore requires formal training and much experience.

The surface features of the land are somewhat more intelligible to the amateur. These are related in part to the ups and downs of the underlying bedrock surface and in part to the glacial debris above. Though some features, such as drumlins and eskers, are almost unmistakable in appearance, most of the surficial patterns in the terrain are indistinct at close range and require the aid of topographic and geological maps for their study.

For all these reasons, then, the major part of this book is devoted to patterns in the vegetation, especially the trees. Emphasis is also placed on the ecological factors such as soils, climate, and the former use of the land that have helped to shape these patterns. Information on terrain and bedrock as it relates to ecology is also included. In addition there is a section on the mammals one is likely to encounter, with illustrations of their tracks, sections on reptiles and amphibians, and an abbreviated section on birds.

Geographical Area
Covered by This Volume

In order to make this guide to the New England countryside comprehensive and detailed enough to be a valuable addition to the naturalist's library yet portable enough to use in the field, it was necessary to organize the information into two volumes. Enough differences exist between the northern and southern New England landscape and natural history to warrant dividing the guide geographically into those two regions rather than by subject matter.

It happens that the northern and southern regions have a natural dividing line which separates two great American forest associations: the oak forest, which covers most of the southern three New England states, and the northern hardwood forest, which covers most of the northern three states. Though a number of landscape features are common to both regions, the vegetation, at least, is substantially different.

For clarity, the division is shown on the accompanying map as a line; in fact, the two great forest types intermingle along a zone of varying width—narrow where the Berkshire hills rise abruptly above the Connecticut Valley and wide across southeastern New Hampshire. Not shown on the map are scattered patches of oak forest persisting northward along the Maine coast to the Portland area, and tongues of this forest type extending some distance up the Housatonic, Connecticut, and Merrimack valleys north of the dividing line.

I have found the distribution of two easily recognizable trees, white birch and hemlock, to be useful in delineating these two forest types. In the oak forest white birch and hemlock often grow only on cool north slopes; in the northern hardwood forest they are common throughout the forest.

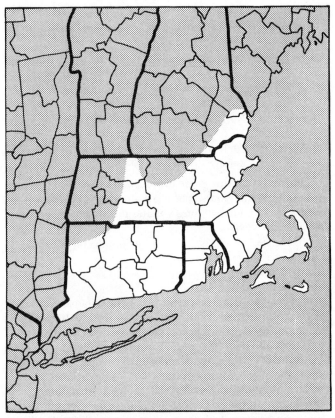

Area covered by this volume, shown in white. This part of New England supports a distinctively different type of woodland vegetation from that of areas to the north and west.

If you spend most of your outdoor time close to the dividing line, you may find both types of forest or a forest with characteristics intermediate between the two. In that case you may need both volumes of this guide.

In addition to the differing forest types, there are several other major geographical differences between southern and northern New England that affect the landscape. The following chart is a summary of these.

	Southern New England	*Northern New England*
Geographical coverage	Southern and eastern New England	Northern and western New England
Forest type	Oak-hickory forest	Northern hardwood and spruce-fir forest
Climate	Relatively warmer climate	Relatively cooler climate
Elevation	No mountainous areas	All of the mountainous areas
Population	High population density	Low population density

Omitted from this guide are saltwater communities such as beaches, tidal pools, and coastal marshes. These will be described in a forthcoming volume in this series, covering the Atlantic coast.

Plant Names

Everyone with a serious interest in the botany and ecology of the region must eventually learn to work with the Latin names of the species, but for obvious reasons beginners will find the colloquial or common names initially more useful. These names originated with country people who came to know the species through day-to-day association.

The problem with colloquial names is that there is no agreement on them. People living in different countries or speaking different languages—sometimes even those living in different parts of the same region—may refer to the same species by several different names. For example, a tree species growing in the southern part of this country, perhaps most commonly known as the Ogeechee tupelo, goes by at least thirteen other colloquial names, even though its entire range is only a few hundred miles. The Ogeechee tupelo is an extreme case, to be sure, but one that clearly illustrates the problem. In this guide I have used what I believe to be the most common New England colloquial names.

Since all the literature of ecology, botany, and natural history—even such mundane publications as most nursery catalogs—uses the Latin names of species as well, those names of course are included here. Unlike the colloquial names, which arise from common usage, the Latin names have been determined by international rules. Thus they provide botanists anywhere in the world with a universal language.

Species are designated by two words: the first, which is always capitalized, refers to the genus to which a plant belongs; the second, generally not capitalized, is the specific name. For example, the Latin names for two common New England trees, the white oak and the black oak, are *Quercus alba* and *Quercus velutina*. Both belong to the same genus and thus share many of the same characteristics, especially in their reproductive morphology; but, as anyone who compares the two will see, they are distinctly different trees and thus rate different specific names.

In scientific literature on botany or ecology the Latin names of species, which are conventionally italicized, are followed by an abbreviation which is not. This abbreviation refers to the person who named the species. Thus, the correct nomenclature for the two oaks in the example above is *Quercus alba*, L., and *Q. velutina*, Lam., the L. standing for Carl Linnaeus and Lam. for Jean Baptiste Lamarck.

Though there is far less confusion over the Latin names than the colloquial, authorities do not always agree even here. Moreover, taxonomic studies sometimes call for the revision of a name. In these cases the author citation becomes important in determining whether or not people are referring to the same species. Since all of the plant nomenclature in this book has come from a single source, *Gray's Manual of Botany, Eighth Edition*, which is regarded by most botanists as the authoritative catalog of northeastern plants, author citations are not needed.

PRONUNCIATION

In the United States scientific Latin is commonly pronounced as if it were English. Because the Latin names for plants are in much more general use than those of the animals, I have included accent marks on the plant names in the descriptive sections of the book as an aid to pronunciation. The accent system, taken from *Gray's Manual of Botany*, indicates which syllable of the word is stressed and the length of the vowel marked. The grave accent (`) indicates the long English sound of the vowel, the acute (ˊ) indicates a shortened or otherwise modified vowel sound. Thus the marking of the Latin name for yellow birch, *Bétula lùtea*, shows that the short *e* (pronounced like the *e* in *end*) is accented in *Betula* and the long *u* (pronounced like the *u* in *prune*) is accented in *lutea*. The diphthongs *oi, au*, and, at the beginning of a name, *ae* are pronounced as they are in English words. At the middle or end of a name *ae* has the sound of long *e*, like the first *e* in *eve*.

You need not labor over memorizing names, either Latin or colloquial. Continued use will soon fix them in your mind.

Metric Measurement

In the descriptive sections of this book, measurements are expressed in the metric system, in most cases with the English equivalents in parentheses. Although the scientific community has been using the metric system for many decades, the United States is among the last countries in the world to abandon the illogical and archaic English system of feet, pounds, and acres for daily use. The long overdue change has now begun and will probably be complete in a few years.

English equivalents should be merely a crutch during this time. Ultimately, you will find that thinking in the metric system is far less cumbersome than converting each metric measurement back to the English system. The following rough equivalencies should be helpful:

LENGTH

Meter (m): About the distance from the floor to the hip on most people.

Centimeter (cm): .01 meter, about the width of the little finger.

Millimeter (mm): .001 meter, about the thickness of a paper match.

Kilometer (km): 1,000 meters, about the length of 11 football fields.

The scales at the end of the book are in inches and centimeters.

A further guide to size is provided in the descriptive sections: the circle accompanying each plant illustration is the size of a penny drawn to scale.

AREA

Hectare: A square 100 meters on a side, or 10,000 square meters. It is used for land measurements like our acre and is about 2½ times as big.

TEMPERATURE

Celsius (C):   A temperature scale in which the freezing point of water is 0°C and the boiling point of water is 100°C. For outdoor activities it is helpful to remember that 0° is freezing, 10° is cool, 20° is pleasant, and 30° is hot. To convert Fahrenheit to Celsius, subtract 32° and multiply by 5/9.

PART I

Looking at the Landscape

Some Tips on Getting Started

NO ONE becomes a competent naturalist overnight. Even within an area as small as southern New England there is a bewildering variety of species, of habitats, and to some extent of natural communities. Moreover, the laws of nature are often hard to discern. If you teach yourself, you can expect to be misled and exasperated many times, and occasionally discouraged. Except perhaps for help from a good teacher, there are no real short cuts to becoming knowledgeable. There are, however, some ways to speed your quest.

Time in the Field

With the possible exception of possessing a good visual memory, there is no single requisite to becoming a competent naturalist that is more important than time spent in the field. Knowledge comes very slowly at first, especially if you are teaching yourself. There is simply no way around spending many hours in the field, a point so obvious that it should scarcely need stating. Yet for most adults, whose spare time is already at a premium, this is probably the greatest obstacle to learning about the natural world.

Books and other aids are useful and often essential adjuncts to field experience. They can help you interpret what you see; their role in helping you develop the all-important skills of recognition is central. But written descriptions, diagrams, or even photographs are little more than meaningless abstractions unless you have had some field experience on which to build and compare.

Clearly, the best way to amass this field experience is to begin as a child. But since few elementary schools include environmental studies in their programs, the responsibility for this facet of a child's education must usually rest with the parent. Of course, burdening a child with formal ecology or natural history lessons on an otherwise enjoyable outing is neither necessary nor desirable, but by taking children into the out-of-doors and capitalizing on their excellent observational powers and innate curiosity you can, over the years, help them become expert naturalists with a minimum of effort.

For readers of this book, however, beginning as a young child is no longer possible. The most efficient and probably the most satisfying way to become knowledgeable is to accompany someone already proficient in ecology and natural history. I have found that the great majority of experienced naturalists enjoy helping interested novices.

You can easily meet such people by taking advantage of the many field trip programs sponsored by various southern New England environmental groups. During the warmer months of the year such organizations as the state Audubon Societies, the Sierra Club, the Appalachian Mountain Club, the New England Wildflower Society, the New England Botanical Club, various local nature centers, some town conservation commissions, and a number of other organizations all run field trips to points of natural interest in the region. Several colleges and adult education organizations are beginning to offer field courses that also provide beginners with an excellent means of basic knowledge, as well as opportunities to meet others who share this interest.

For people truly interested in the out-of-doors, these field trips can be very enjoyable. Several pairs of eyes always see more than one pair. The combined knowledge of a group of people often provides an impressive coverage of several fields, and the enthusiasm of people sharing the same interest is infectious. One great advantage of living in New England is that so many of its residents are already knowledgeable about ecology and natural history.

A Leaf from Thoreau's Journal

You need not travel many miles to unusually interesting natural areas or to large tracts of unoccupied land in order to become an astute naturalist. The best place to concentrate your observation is as close to home as possible. Although southern New England is among the most densely populated parts of the country, much of the terrain is unsuitable for development. As a result there are many tracts of unoccupied land, albeit small ones, often very close to major metropolitan areas. In most cases, just a few acres of varied terrain is a more than adequate training ground; a few square miles of undeveloped land—about the total area of an average New England town—can provide an observant person with enough richness and variety for a lifetime of study and pleasure.

New England's greatest naturalist, Henry David Thoreau, has made this point abundantly clear. Although his prodigious fourteen-volume journal is usually noted for its political and historical content, the greater part is a record of Thoreau's keen observations of nature in the woods and fields around his Concord home. "I have traveled a good deal in Concord . . .," he wrote. Those well-known words still serve as a model for everyone wanting to learn about the natural surroundings.

Aside from sheer convenience, there are several other reasons why a naturalist should begin close to home. All natural communities are far more complex than they first appear to be. In a single visit, even an expert cannot hope to perceive more than a small part of what may be happening there. For the beginner who has not learned to recognize significant details, return visits are especially important.

Moreover, the passage of time itself brings many changes. Those that come with the changing seasons are always interesting to observe; those occurring over a longer period of time are more subtle but often of greater significance. There are, of course, some aspects of the natural world that can only be studied during certain parts of the year, still others that are more noticeable according to the season.

The ever-growing energy crisis may also make areas close to home more attractive for study. Unless you live near the center of a large city or in the middle of one of the unplanned suburban sprawls that sometimes surround cities, there are probably natural areas within walking distance of your home, or at least no more than a short bus ride away.

By using local areas, you also help to relieve the pressures that are starting to affect New England's so-called wilderness areas. Some mountain trails in northern New England, for example, have become so deeply eroded from overuse that new trails—which in turn are now beginning to erode—have had to be built parallel to them. Furthermore, as these two volumes will show, the diversity in the southern New England landscape is far richer than that farther north. Wilderness may provide other benefits, but we do not need it to become good naturalists.

There is no denying, however, that traveling farther afield is also of great value in the education of a naturalist. Many of the broad patterns in the landscape, the fascinating changes in terrain and vegetation that occur from one part of the region to another, cannot be observed in any other way. These broader patterns also contribute greatly to our understanding of the landscape and of the forces that have come to shape it, yet I believe it is by first becoming familiar with the local patterns—those you come to recognize when you have "traveled a good deal" in your own area—that you can best perceive the similarities and differences in the landscape elsewhere.

Growing Native Plants

A splendid way to learn about the native vegetation is to grow it in your own backyard. A collection of native plants is in effect an ecological laboratory that can provide a naturalist with a tremendous amount of information about their characteristics and tolerances.

It is not necessary to do formal scientific research, such as growing control and experimental groups under carefully monitored conditions, in order to gather this information. Merely by keeping a particular species thriving for several years you will learn a great deal about such characteristics as bloom times, growth rates, propagation mechanisms, effects of such climatic factors as drought, summer humidity, or winter cold, and many other ecological requirements.

Another advantage to maintaining your own collection of native plants, especially if you have to travel some distance to a wild area, is that you can study them on a day-to-day basis whenever you have a few spare minutes. Comparing how a particular species grows on your home grounds with how it does in the wild yields still more ecological information.

Most native plants are far tougher than people think. Their survival in the region means that they are already adapted to the rigors of the New England climate; most thrive with the small amount of additional care they would normally receive in a garden. While some of these plants lack the gaudy colors and large blooms of cultivated annuals and perennials, others, such as butterfly weed, *Asclepias tuberosa*, mountain laurel, and the native azaleas, produce impressive floral displays. By using only those species indigenous to the region, it is possible to create a garden of great beauty, variety, and interest. Several books on growing native plants are included in the bibliography at the end of Part I.

Recognizing Species

YOU WILL NOTICE, if you leaf ahead, that much of this book is devoted to descriptions of various species that are native to southern New England. In its concern with patterns and relationships, ecology is much more than the mere identification of species. Yet, because the relationship between a particular species or group of species and the environmental conditions that describe their habitat is the essence of ecological study, being able to tell one species from another is its most important prerequisite.

However, *identification* of species, that is, poring over an identification guide to determine the correct name of a particular plant, is itself insufficient for most ecological studies. If you must tediously track down every species you encounter you will probably never perceive the kinds of patterns and relationships discussed here. It is necessary, therefore, that you learn to *recognize* species, that is, to be able to distinguish one species from another at a glance, much as a person recognizes a friend. Most of the common tree species and many of the shrubs and herbaceous plants that grow in the region are sufficiently distinctive to be recognizable even from some distance away. Experienced naturalists can even recognize many species from a speeding car (a practice that can be dangerous, however, if the naturalist is also the driver).

Recognizing Species by Community

For the beginner, the initial stages of learning the species are difficult and frustrating. Though some regional and local identification guides are appearing, most of the standard identification guides encompass an area of far greater extent than New England and consequently include many species not native to this region.

For this reason I have tried a new scheme to help readers over this barrier: grouping plants by community. Anyone who looks at the natural landscape from one part of southern New England to another will see that habitats with similar ecological conditions look similar because a similar group of plants appears in each. Moreover, only a relatively few species of plants will grow in any one habitat. This community of plants, and to a lesser extent of animals, then, is a natural grouping of organisms living under similar environmental conditions. If the community can be identified, then it is possible to narrow down the number of plants and animals that might be found there, thus greatly simplifying the problem of identification.

Admittedly, community is a concept not embraced by all ecologists. Continuous natural disturbances affect some habitats to such a degree that few recognizable similarities in the plant cover can be seen from one to another, even though the ecological conditions would appear to be alike. Also, even the more stable communities are each in a sense unique: the same species may occur in each, but they will occur in different numbers. But in a region as relatively small and homogeneous as southern New England, these communities are often remarkably similar in appearance and, as such, offer us clearly recognizable patterns in the landscape. They also provide a coherent organizational framework for the descriptive sections of the guide and a key to recognizing many of the common species.

For each of the communities discussed in the book, I have included a description of as many of the usual species found there as space will permit. The descriptive listings are by no means exhaustive, of course. Eventually you will encounter species not covered here. Familiarity with the common species, however, should make identification of the more unusual ones relatively easy.

Fall Foliage Sequence of Common Forest Trees in Southern New England

EARLY (late September)

Species	Site	Colors	Remarks
Red maple *Acer rubrum*	swamp	bright red, bright orange	first swamp tree to lose leaves
White ash *Fraxinus americana*	uplands, stream banks	maroon, rust, dark greenish red	distinctive colors, often very early, trees in dry sites lose leaves first

MIDDLE (early to middle October)

Species	Site	Colors	Remarks
Hickories *Carya* spp.	site varies, often common in lower slopes of upland forest	intense yellow	compound leaves give the foliage a lacy appearance
Black birch *Betula lenta*	most sites except wettest and driest	yellow, though not as intense as the hickories	lustrous black bark also helps in identification
Poison sumac *Rhus Vernix*	swamps and bogs	bright orange	shrub or small tree, compound leaves, excellent time for recognition
Red maple *Acer rubrum*	slopes of upland forest	bright orange, yellow, red	healthy trees will sometimes retain leaves until end of October; light gray bark also aids recognition
Beech *Fagus grandifolia*	somewhat moist shady sites	light green to yellow to brown; tips of branches turn brown first	smooth light gray bark, spreading habit
Tupelo *Nyssa sylvatica*	edges of swamps and ponds	intense dark red	twiggy irregular habit
Sugar maple *Acer saccharum*	lower slopes of upland forests, roadsides	bright orange turning yellow	leaves larger, bark more furrowed than red maple
Quaking aspen *Populus tremuloides*	waste ground, old fields	various shades of yellow	light greenish-gray bark
Sassafras *Sassafras albidum*	old fields, edges of woods, dry sites	pinkish orange becoming yellow	distinctively shaped leaves
Staghorn sumac *Rhus typhina*	old fields, waste ground	brilliant orange becoming brilliant red	often grows in large clumps, dark red furry shrub
Maple-leaved viburnum *Viburnum acerifolium*	upland woods	purplish maroon	common shrub in oak woods

Red oak *Quercus rubra*	upland forest	variable, reddish brown	colors brighter on sapling trees, usually larger than surrounding trees
Black oak *Quercus velutina*	upland forest	variable, yellowish brown	
Norway maple *Acer platanoides*	introduced but naturalized near civilization	bright yellow	last of the maples
Wild cherry *Prunus serotina*	lower slopes of upland woods, old fields	green changing to yellow	one of the last deciduous trees to change color

Recognizing Trees and Shrubs by Their Fall Colors

The deciduous forests of New England present a fall display that is not matched anywhere else in the world. In addition to being a time of splendid scenery, the fall offers a unique opportunity for studying the distribution and ecology of the various forest trees.

Many of the species produce fall foliage of a distinctive color and change color in sequence, though both the brilliance of the colors and the dates the leaves turn vary from year to year. During the dry years of the mid-sixties, for example, the trees lost their leaves earlier than usual and their colors were noticeably muted. But as a general rule, the more familiar you become with the fall colors of the various species, the less difficulty you will have with these yearly differences.

The great advantage in being able to recognize trees by their fall colors is that you are then able to study their distribution from some far vantage point. You are able, for example, to survey a wooded hillside and obtain some idea of what trees—at least to the genus level—are growing there from as far as a kilometer away.

The preceding chart shows the general sequence of foliage in central Massachusetts. Individual trees, of course, may shed their leaves sooner or retain them longer than others. The fall colors are difficult to describe but easy to recognize

Recognizing Species   9

once you have familiarized yourself with the colors from personal observation. Excluded from the chart are those species whose fall foliage is nondescript shades of brown.

Recognition in Winter

Though woody plants can be easy to recognize in winter, they are, paradoxically, hard to identify. Most trees and many shrubs have an overall configuration or "gestalt" that makes them as recognizable in winter as in summer, although the individual characteristics which combine to

1. Shagbark hickory, *Carya ovata*, in winter. The characteristic shape and bark texture of many trees make them as recognizable in winter as in summer.

make winter recognition possible are often hard to describe or illustrate. These may include, for example, the appearance of the bark plus a certain growth habit. Clues from the habitat in which a particular tree or shrub is growing are especially helpful in winter recognition. Of course evergreen species, which also may indicate certain associations and relationships, are easily recognizable in both summer and winter.

Winter identification on the other hand, is ordinarily based on such minute characteristics as the appearance of twigs, winter buds, and leaf scars—and is an even more tedious task than identifying plants in summer. Though winter identification guides such as those listed in the bibliography may be helpful in distinguishing one species from another, the easiest way to become familiar with the appearance of trees and shrubs in winter is to learn to recognize them during the summer and watch them change through the fall.

When snow conditions are right, cross-country skis provide an efficient means of observation. Often you can cover territory by ski more quickly and easily than you can by foot during other seasons. Traveling greater distances sometimes allows you to perceive broader patterns than may be possible at a slower rate of travel, though the cover of snow eliminates some of the clues you might ordinarily obtain from the ground.

Looking for Anomaly

As the beginning naturalist soon discovers, order in the biotic world is quite different from that of Newtonian physics. If, as some have suggested, the first law of ecology is that within any community everything is related to everything else, then the second law must be that these relationships are often subtle, complex, and obscure. Even if it were possible to identify and measure all of the significant variables affecting the dynamics of a particular community, blind chance acting in a myriad of ways would always play an unforeseen role.

Considering all of the likely combinations of events and

factors, each acting to a varying degree, that might have a bearing on the characteristics of a natural community, it is remarkable that order exists to the extent that it does. In this book, therefore, I describe probable patterns, not certain ones. Qualifiers such as "usually," "often," "rarely" appear in many of the statements because they best describe the working of nature.

How much simpler it might seem if the ecologist could predict events in this field with the same certainty as, say, an astronomer can predict an eclipse. I suspect, however, that if ecosystems worked with this degree of precision they would soon lose their fascination for us. It is the anomalies, those inevitable exceptions to the pattern, that provide naturalists with a never-ending source of pleasure and interest.

Anomaly takes many forms. Sometimes it is the appearance of a species that is new to the area or one only rarely encountered. Sometimes it may be a mutant form of a familiar species, such as the beautiful white-flowered form of the familiar pink lady's slipper that is occasionally seen. Anomaly may be a common species in an unexpected habitat, such as the improbable appearance of white pine in the soggy environment of a sphagnum bog. Conversely, it may be the absence of a particular species from a habitat where it should be found.

Anomalies such as these, while vexing to a beginner, provide more experienced observers with a whole new dimension in the natural world. Moreover, they often yield additional and sometimes very subtle information about the ecology of an area, as well as the genetics and physiology of the particular species involved. It is probably the constant possibility of discovering anomaly that keeps naturalists returning again and again to already familiar haunts.

Rare and Local Species

Species vary greatly in the frequency with which they are encountered. Some, like the ubiquitous red maple, *Acer rubrum*, appear in every forest community. At the other end of the scale are species such as the sweetbay magnolia, *Magnolia virginiana*, a common southern tree that appears

2. Sweetbay magnolia, *Magnolia virginiana*, a southern tree species that occurs naturally in New England in only two places in eastern Massachusetts. (*The circle on each drawing in this book is the size of a penny drawn to scale.*)

in this region in only two coastal Massachusetts stations: one in Gloucester and the other in Magnolia (the town named for the plant).

The ultimate in rarity is a species that exists in a population of but a few individuals in a single small area, for example, Ashe's black birch, *Betula uber*, recently rediscovered on one site along a stream in western Virginia. Few of the rare species in our region are so restricted in their distribution. There are a couple of distinct animal species that have evolved in isolation on the islands off Cape Cod, and one species of flowering plant, the Plymouth gentian, *Sabatia Kennedyana* (see color plate III), that is found in only a handful of stations along the southeast coast (as well as a single station in Nova Scotia). But most of the species considered rare in southern New England are more widely distributed or even common elsewhere.

A species with local distribution has a somewhat different status. The stations of local species may be no more numerous than those of rare species, but where that species is found, it is found in great numbers. The climbing fern, *Lygodium palmatum*, is a good example. In southern New England, the distribution of this species is so sparse that few naturalists ever chance upon it by accident. Yet, where it does grow, the fern often forms large spreading mats made up of thousands of individual plants that cover the ground and climb over other vegetation. In spite of this spreading

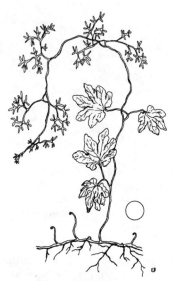

3. Climbing fern, *Lygodium palmatum*, whose vine-like habit makes it distinctive from other ferns, is so rare that it is almost never casually encountered.

tendency, however, the climbing fern grows in so few places that it is now regarded as an endangered species.

If a species is listed as rare or local, the chances that you will casually encounter it are almost nil. This is important to remember, because beginning naturalists often misidentify plants as rare ones or even ones that do not grow in the region at all.

The very existence of these rare and local species adds diversity and interest to the landscape. A study of their distribution and ecology in one habitat and absence from similar habitats nearby raises questions that are not easily answered. Though space does not permit a detailed discussion of rare plant ecology here, the single most plausible explanation for the restricted distribution of these species is that, for one reason or another, they are unable to compete successfully with other species. As a result, rare species are often found in precarious and uncongenial habitats such as shorelines, sandbars, bogs, exposed cliffs, and—in the northern New England mountains—land above the timberline. All of these contain a relatively greater number of rare

plants than the more congenial habitats, where many different species grow and compete with one another and change
occurs more quickly.

Yet the habitats where the rare plants grow do gradually
change. Trees grow taller and cast denser shade; wetlands
tend to dry out while drier areas tend to become more moist.
As a result of these normal successional processes, stations of
rare plants will usually disappear through natural attrition if
the habitat is not managed. Preserving at least some of these
stations of rare plants through careful management of the
habitat seems for now to be the most practicable solution.

Increasing the numbers of these species through propagation and introducing them to new seemingly suitable
habitats may be another method of insuring their continued
survival, one long advocated by conservationists but hardly
ever actually done. Many of these plants, though rare in
nature, are easy to propagate from seed or cuttings. Propagation of these species and introducing them to congenial
habitats would be an excellent conservation project for garden clubs, schools, and other civic organizations. Protected
natural areas such as town conservation land would be ideal
places to establish colonies of rare plants.

In the few thousand years since man has been on the
planet, he has caused the disappearance of hundreds of
species. Hundreds more now face extinction. Increasing the
chances for continued survival of some of these rare and
endangered species in our area therefore seems the least we
can do to make reparations for damage already done.

COLLECTING PLANTS FROM THE WILD

Needless to say, digging up rare plants from their natural
habitats diminishes the environment for all. Though many
will survive in a garden, few will reproduce naturally under
these conditions. By so removing a source of seed from the
natural habitat, plant collectors thus lower the possibility of
the continued survival of the species in the region.

We should not condemn outright all plant collecting,
however. For some common species, especially in rural
areas, no amount of collecting could make the slightest dent
in their numbers. If you would like to bring a particular
species into your garden, a good rule of thumb is to collect

plants only when the colony contains more plants than can easily be counted. In small colonies, the removal of only one or two individuals is sometimes enough to tip the balance toward annihilation. Before collecting any species, however, you should always obtain permission from the landowner.

On balance, the depredations of plant collectors are insignificant in comparison to destruction caused by the bulldozer. Innumerable habitats have been destroyed, especially in the coastal areas, as a result of the growing population. Of course, collecting plants from the path of construction is always desirable. With many acres of open space still disappearing each year, there are many opportunities for gardeners who specialize in native plants to enlarge their collections by this means.

Variant Forms

A careful examination of any large population of a single species of plant or animal is bound to turn up differences between individuals. In a large population of marsh marigolds, *Caltha palustris*, that I have been studying, for example, there are individuals with flowers larger than average and smaller than average, ones with cleft petals (actually petal-like sepals), some with a buttercup-yellow color to their flowers, others with flowers of a sulphur-yellow, some that consistently bloom earlier than average, others that bloom later and hold their flowers for longer than average, plants with leaves larger or smaller, those whose leaves have serrated edges—and the list could go on.

In addition to this "normal" variation, both plants and animals produce occasional mutant forms such as albinos. Often these mutant forms do occur with a certain limited frequency in nature, though they are usually rare. Bloodroot, *Sanguinaria canadensis*, for example, is a common woodland plant across much of the eastern United States. The *multiplex* form of bloodroot, with beautiful peony-like double flowers, has been found only once in nature. A double-flowered form of the hepatica, *Hepatica acutiloba*, has been found perhaps three times.

You should remember, however, that while the chances of finding an unusual form of any one particular species may

4. Bloodroot, *Sanguinaria canadensis*, showing the usual flower form and the rare *multiplex* variant form.

be small, in places where populations of many different species are encountered the chances of finding unusual forms are commensurately greater. Every observant naturalist will come across them from time to time.

COLLECTING AND INCREASING VARIANT FORMS

As regards collecting, the status of these variant forms is somewhat different from that of the rare species described above. It is common knowledge that mutant forms are, in the vast number of cases, at a competitive disadvantage compared to the normal forms; often the chances of their survival in the wild are limited.

Most of the variant forms you find will be merely botanical curiosities. A few, however, could be valuable additions to plant collections where they could be cared for and their numbers increased. Many of the outstanding forms of native plants, as well as such handsome mutants as the double bloodroot and double hepatica described above, originated as chance discoveries in the wild. These mutants, which as garden plants now bring pleasure to many people, would have led a precarious and probably short existence if left in the wild.

In addition to such obvious characteristics as double flowers, some of the following traits might also make particular variant forms worth noting: larger or more numerous flowers; flowers of unusual color; outstanding bud hardiness (plants near the northern limits of their range that consistently bloom no matter how severe the previous winter); dwarf, compact, or unusual growth forms; weeping branches; unusual leaf colors and shapes; variegated leaves; outstanding fall foliage; and many others. The more familiar you become with the usual characteristics of the native species the more easily you will recognize these unusual or variant forms.

If you find a particularly interesting variant form, you should get in contact with one of the several botanical gardens and arboretums in the region. Most of these have skilled horticulturists and the facilities to care for and increase unusual plants. By propagating these plants vegetatively, that is, by grafts or cuttings, propagators are able to grow new plants with the same unusual characteristics. Most botanical gardens and arboretums have a policy of sharing a percentage of these new plants with the discoverer. If the plant is too big or too remote to be moved, or if the discoverer is reluctant to move it, it is often possible to take cuttings directly, to be delivered for propagation. In all cases, you should check with the landowner, as well as with the propagator, before disturbing an unusual plant. Some species are almost impossible to move, others seemingly impossible to propagate. Still others can be moved or propagated only at certain times of the year.

In carefully botanized areas, it is especially important to check with the landowner or other knowledgeable people before collecting any unusual forms. In the woods of Concord, Massachusetts, for example, there is a single clump of the white-flowered form of the fringed polygala, *Polygala paucifolia*, still surviving since its discovery by Thoreau over one hundred years ago. Local naturalists have been studying this colony for many years now; disturbing it would be little less than vandalism. Moreover, an inquiry would reveal that the white-flowered form of polygala does occur in nature with some frequency, so there would be little reason to collect it at any rate.

LOOKING AT THE LANDSCAPE

A Few Precautions

THE New England countryside probably presents fewer hazards to the foot traveler than any other area of comparable size in the United States. If accident statistics can be believed, walking in the woods is several times safer than walking down a city street, many times safer than riding in a car, and even safer than remaining inside the home. The few commonsense precautions that you should take to avoid all of the hazards and pests you are likely to encounter are as simple and straightforward as looking both ways before crossing the street.

Off-Trail Travel in Southern New England

People who try to explore the countryside without ever venturing off roads or trails see only a small part of it. They may not realize that the typical southern New England woodland is usually so open and free of underbrush that off-trail travel, especially at a leisurely pace, is hardly more strenuous than staying on paths or even roads.

One of the few benefits of the closeness of civilization is that getting lost and staying lost in southern New England is practically impossible. There are few places in the region where you will find yourself beyond earshot of highway traffic and fewer still where you can walk for an hour without crossing a road or encountering a house. You might lose your bearings for a time, especially on a cloudy day, but the specter of becoming "lost in the woods," that is, wandering for hours through trackless wilderness, may be safely laid to rest.

Probably the most important advice for the off-trail walker is to learn a little about the terrain in advance. If you are exploring an unfamiliar area, a few minutes spent studying a topographic map of the area will help you plan a route that will keep you away from muddy ground, off steep slopes, and out of people's backyards.

You should also wear proper shoes and clothing. A well-fitting pair of water-resistant hiking boots worn with heavy socks will add immeasurably to your comfort on rough terrain. Sneakers are far less comfortable for off-trail walking. You will also find that long trousers or jeans will lessen the annoyance of prickly underbrush or poison ivy. Carrying a sweater or windbreaker, especially during spring and fall, will protect you from the capricious New England weather.

Traveling Alone

Exploring with an interested companion is usually more enjoyable, but no one should be deterred by the prospect of traveling alone. Many people who are interested in the out-of-doors spend much or even all of their time traveling alone and *never* get into difficulties of any kind. A fall, the only immobilizing accident that might happen to the walker, is highly unlikely to occur if you pay attention to footing and use common sense on steep or rough terrain.

If you are in reasonably good condition, properly clothed and shod, and familiar with the terrain, there is no reason why you cannot travel off-trail alone. Leaving word where you are going and when you plan to return is an added precaution against the infinitely small possibility of an accident.

Impassable Terrain

In southern New England, with its subdued topography, dangerously steep slopes are uncommon and easily avoided. Far more common and less easily avoided are wetlands. As a rule, swamps where trees are growing are passable at all but the wettest times of the year. Marshes are generally impassable, while shrub swamps and bogs usually lie somewhere between these two extremes.

In some upland areas, mountain laurel thickets are very difficult to penetrate and had best be avoided. In lowland areas, greenbrier thickets and bramble patches are as effective barriers to travel as barbed wire.

Poisonous Plants

Though there is a long list of native plants which are poisonous if eaten, less than a handful are poisonous to the touch. Of these few, only poison ivy, *Rhus radicans*, and poison sumac, *Rhus Vernix*, are serious hazards.

Poison Ivy, *Rhùs rádicans*, is an extremely common plant, one that may turn up in almost any habitat and one that all people exploring the region should learn to recognize. Its most important characteristic is its creeping or climbing habit and its compound leaves bearing three leaflets. These have smooth edges or a few coarse notches and usually are glossy. The flowers are inconspicuous, and the fruit, when seen, are small grayish-white berries about 5 mm ($^{3}/_{16}$ in) in diameter, borne in clusters.

Poison ivy is essentially a species peculiar to disturbed land. Though historical records are scanty, apparently poison ivy was not nearly so common prior to and during the agricultural boom. Since that time the plant has become widely distributed, mostly by flickers and other birds that eat the fruit. This may account for the abundance of poison ivy under trees, along fence rows, under telephone lines, and other places where birds are likely to perch. Once established, it persists almost indefinitely, even in deep shade. I have found extensive colonies in the bottoms of rock ravines and in deep woods, though I suspect that in these very shady sites it grows best where the soil is not excessively acidic. As with most other flowering plants, these shaded individuals rarely set seed, though they spread extensively by underground runners.

Poison ivy and its effects have been the subject of more misinformation than any other plant in our flora. Probably the most important and enduring of these myths revolves around how the poison is contracted. Although all parts of the plant contain poisonous sap, it is impossible to be infected unless some parts of the plant are broken or crushed. As long as the leaves and stems remain intact, you cannot get ivy poisoning merely from walking by the plant or brushing up against it.

Once out of the plant, however, the sap is virulent and hard to remove. The compound that causes poisoning seems to remain active indefinitely; people are frequently infected by patting dogs who have rolled in the plant or by handling shoes or other articles of clothing on which the sap has collected. There have even been cases of botanists contracting the poison from working with dried herbarium specimens one hundred or more years old. Another particularly dangerous way of catching ivy poisoning is by breathing tiny droplets of sap adhering to dust and ash from burning poison ivy; these can infect the mucous membranes and cause very serious internal poisoning.

Probably the most egregious piece of misadvice concerning poison ivy in recent years was given by a noted author of wild food books: he recommended eating the young leaves of the plant in spring as a means of developing immunity to the poison! The fact is that cases of internal ivy poisoning caused by eating the leaves as well as breathing the smoke from burning plants have proven to be fatal.

Though there are probably very few people totally immune to poison ivy, the degree of sensitivity varies from person to person. Most people seem to have an allergic threshold, remaining insensitive to the poison until this threshold is passed. People moving to the country for the first time often handle poison ivy with no ill effects for a while, then suddenly come down with a serious case. For some people, subsequent infections seem to make them more sensitive; for others, sensitivity seems to decrease.

There are several poison ivy remedies on the market that seem to offer protection if applied before or shortly after exposure. Since the poison is not as volatile as once thought, it is difficult to remove all traces of it simply with strong soap and water. Once the itchy rash or blisters develop, usually several hours to a day after exposure, it is too late for washing, though some of the newer remedies seem to be quite effective in controlling the itching. The poison cannot be spread by broken blisters on the skin. Serious cases should be treated by a doctor.

Yet poison ivy need not deter people from exploring the countryside. In most places, its distribution is sporadic enough that it can be avoided altogether, and even where it grows, of course, merely walking through patches of the plant does not necessarily mean infection. I am moderately allergic to poison ivy, yet I regularly walk through extensive patches with almost never any ill effects. Although the best

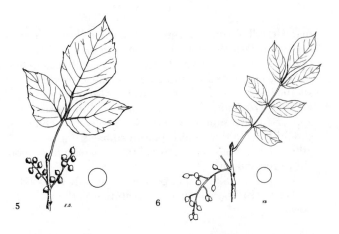

5. Poison ivy, *Rhus radicans*, is easily recognized by its compound leaves bearing three leaflets and its climbing or trailing form. The poisonous sap is only released when some part of the plant is crushed, broken, or burned.

6. Poison sumac, *Rhus Vernix*, is a coarse shrub or tree whose irritating sap is only contracted if the plant is damaged. It is a wetland species, growing only in acidic swamps or bogs.

protection seems to be not crushing the leaves or stems, it is clear that everyone who explores the woods where poison ivy might grow should wear socks and long pants.

Similar species: Poison oak, *Rhus Toxicodendron*, does not grow anywhere in New England. The following nonpoisonous plants in New England are sometimes confused with poison ivy: Virginia creeper, *Parthenocissus quinquefolia*, page 297, dewberry, *Rubus* spp., page 298, box elder, *Acer negundo*, page 296, bladdernut, *Staphylea trifolia*, page 197.

Poison Sumac, *Rhùs Vérnix*, as its generic name suggests, is a close relative of poison ivy. Its poison is, if anything, even more virulent. Fortunately, however, poison sumac is far less common and is practically never found outside acidic wetlands such as swamps and bogs. Poison sumac is often confused with its relatively harmless cousins, staghorn sumac, *Rhus typhina*, or smooth sumac, *Rhus glabra*, which form spreading clumps in dry old fields and waste places.

Poison sumac is a coarse shrub or small tree up to about 6

m (20 ft) tall, reaching its greatest size in full sun but persisting in more shady spots. It has smooth gray bark and compound leaves with seven to thirteen smooth red-stemmed leaflets. In wooded swamps, poison sumac superficially resembles young red ash trees, which also often occupy this habitat. The fruit, clusters of grayish-white berries which appear in late summer, and its coarsely branching habit should help to distinguish poison sumac from red ash and other trees. Its fall foliage, usually a bright orange, is another aid to recognition.

The poison, like that of poison ivy, is only released if its parts are crushed or burned. Treatment is the same as for poison ivy.

Other Poisonous Plants

Among the other externally poisonous plants, nettles, *Urtica* and *Laportea* spp., are the only species with which you are likely to come in contact. *Urtica* grows in river bottomlands and waste places, while *Laportea* grows in rock ravines and other cool habitats. Unlike ivy or sumac poisoning, contact with nettles will be perceived immediately. The rash causes discomfort but does not last long.

The movement toward gathering wild plants for food is not without its hazards. Though many wild species are not only edible but delicious, the considerable number of poisonous species—some of them deadly—should give beginning wild-food gourmets some reason for caution. Wild-mushroom gatherers especially should be sure of correct identification, since several species are poisonous and one, the Destroying Angel, *Amanita verna*, is among the most deadly of all plants. Fatalities allegedly have occurred from handling the plant and ingesting traces left on the hands. Gathering and eating wild food can be an interesting hobby, but it is best learned with the help of someone who is already knowledgeable.

Poisonous Snakes

There is probably nothing that evokes more horror in people unfamiliar with the out-of-doors than the thought of meeting a poisonous snake. Yes, there are poisonous snakes in New England, but in many ways their distribution is like that of rare plants; unless you are directed to where they live you will almost surely never see one. Most naturalists, including those who have traveled the region for years, have yet to encounter one. The reason for this is that their distribution is local and spotty; there are large areas, several whole counties, in fact, where poisonous snakes are known to be absent. Even in areas where they do exist, their retiring habits usually keep them out of human contact.

The chances of being bitten by a poisonous snake are smaller still. Of the 8 million people who live in southern New England, perhaps a dozen receive a snakebite in the space of one year. The probability of being bitten by a poisonous snake, then, is less than that of being struck by lightning. For every person treated for snakebite, there are perhaps 10,000 treated for a serious case of poison ivy.

There are two poisonous species in New England, the timber rattlesnake and the northern copperhead. Both species have elliptical eye pupils, like those of cats, and large nostril-like pits—in addition to the nostrils—below and in front of the eye. The rattlesnake is rarely over a meter in length. It is usually marked with dark brown or black chevron-like cross bands on a yellow or dark brown background, though other color variations exist. The segmented rattle at the tip of the tail is another distinguishing characteristic, though it is important to remember that several harmless snakes may vibrate their tails when alarmed, sometimes making a whirring sound that resembles a rattlesnake's rattle.

The other poisonous species, the northern copperhead, is also variable in ground color, though it usually ranges from beige to tan, with a series of dark brown or reddish hourglass-shaped cross bands on its back. Its head is the color of an old penny. It is a stout snake, rarely exceeding a meter in length. (See color plate VIII).

The venomous water moccasin of the South ranges no closer to New England than coastal Virginia. The harmless northern water snake that inhabits the region's ponds and rivers is sometimes confused with it.

The timber rattlesnake is now rare in southern New England. From the number of Rattlesnake Hills that dot the topographic maps, however, we can assume that the species was more widely distributed when the first European settlers came here. Since that time, rattlesnakes have been ceaselessly hunted down and their habitats destroyed. The only places they now exist are remote rocky areas usually far from human habitation.

Copperheads also prefer rocky habitats, though usually ones near wetlands or watercourses. In areas where copperheads occur, they are also sometimes found in old sawdust piles or around abandoned mines. Though the species remains absent over large areas of the region, in southern New England its distribution is concentrated in the basalt hills of the Connecticut Valley Lowland and along some of the other major river valleys. Most snakebite poisoning cases that occur in the field are from copperhead bites, because this species is more widely distributed within its geographic range and also because it remains fairly close to some heavily urbanized areas in the region. Since its venom is far less potent than that of rattlesnakes, fatalities from copperhead bites are almost unknown.

Both species, however, can deliver a painful bite. Because of their potential danger to people and pets, both should be killed if they enter thickly settled neighborhoods, as there is no safe method for untrained persons to remove them. On the other hand, hunting either species down in their native haunts, where contact with humans is unlikely, would be as senseless as destroying rare plants. At a time when hundreds of species of animals are facing extinction, perhaps we should keep in mind that all creatures have the right to exist irrespective of benefit or detriment to man.

TRAVEL IN SNAKE COUNTRY

In areas where poisonous snakes may be found, a few commonsense precautions will keep you safe.

1. High leather boots should be worn. Most recorded snakebites are on the extremities: the foot or lower leg (as well as the hand or arm). Even hiking boots offer a good measure of protection.

2. Be careful where you put your hands and feet and where you sit down, especially around rock slides and ledgy areas. Stone walls, brush piles, and rotten logs are also common hunting grounds for snakes.

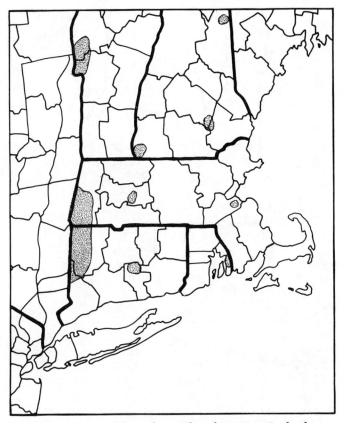

Approximate range of the timber rattlesnake in New England, 1977. Formerly found in most parts of the region, rattlesnakes now occur in a few small areas.

3. Attempting to capture a venomous snake or handling one, either dead or alive, is totally foolhardy.

SNAKEBITE

The probability that any reader thus forewarned will become the victim of snakebite is surely less than one in a million. If you are bitten by a snake, the overwhelming chances are that it will be by a harmless species. Poisonous

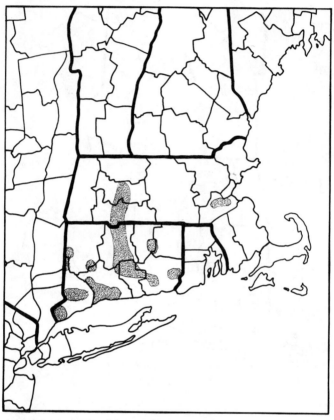

Approximate range of the northern copperhead.

snakes leave two small puncture wounds; nonpoisonous snakes usually leave a scratch or a number of tiny punctures. The first step, then, is to determine whether the bite was actually from a venomous species.

Because there is much disagreement about the treatment of snakebite, because the venom of both copperheads and rattlesnakes is relatively slow-acting, and because civilization is so close in southern New England, it would almost never be advisable to attempt to remove snake venom in the field. Instead, seek competent medical help. If possible, the victim should be carried or transported to the nearest hospital.

Dogs, cats, and other domestic animals also require medical treatment for snakebite.

Insects and Other Arthropods

Of the tens of thousands of species of insects and other arthropods such as spiders that are native to southern New England, only a tiny percentage make any kind of direct contact with man. Of these, only a small percentage could be classified as anything more than a nuisance.

WASPS

Yellow jackets or ground wasps, not poisonous snakes, are probably the most potentially dangerous animal species a person is likely to encounter in the southern New England countryside. Under normal circumstances the yellow jacket is not aggressive. Often during the summer it will appear at picnics and try to steal a bit of food. A couple of brushes with the hand will send it on its way.

The only way to bring on a wasp attack is to step on their underground nests. Wasps build their nest in dry woodlands, usually in rock crevices or abandoned field-mouse holes. The population begins with a queen who has survived the winter, and gradually increases over the summer until by September some nests are 30 centimeters (1 foot) or more in diameter and contain thousands of workers. Unlike the honeybee, wasps carry food directly to the larvae rather than storing it as honey in the cells. Their diet is variable. Although wasps do present a hazard, like other social insects they are interesting creatures to study.

In late summer and fall it is not unusual to come across wasp nests that have been dug up and destroyed by skunks, which eat the larvae. Apparently the skunks are not seriously affected by wasp stings.

You can easily spot nests by the amount of activity around them. In late summer there will be a constant stream of wasps flying in and out. If you step on a nest, leave the area as fast as possible, of course. A few wasps might follow you for a time, then turn back, though often in the confusion that follows having their nest stepped on, the wasps fly about aimlessly and never pursue their attacker. Since wasps come out of their nests singly or in pairs, the old cartoon of people being chased by clouds of these creatures is happily an exaggeration.

Even if you are chased by wasps, you have a good chance of remaining unstung. Wasps do not sting instantaneously; it takes some fraction of a second for them to land, push in their stingers, and inject their poison. They can usually be killed with a slap before they inject their poison even if they do succeed in penetrating the skin.

Bee and wasp venom is far more toxic than rattlesnake venom, though people's allergic reaction to it varies considerably. In the United States there are many more people killed by stings than by snakebite; those who die probably have a serious allergy to the venom and do not receive treatment fast enough. People who are allergic to bee and wasp venom should carry antiallergenic medicine with them, though desensitization by a series of shots is an effective means of preventing allergic reactions altogether.

BLACK FLIES

Black flies are chief among the nuisance creatures. Their appearance coincides almost exactly with the unfolding leaves and spring flowers; during May and June these flying annoyances appear on any still day, swarming around the face and flying into the eyes. Most of the species also suck blood, leaving an itchy welt. Just before the appearance of black flies in the spring, it is possible to find the tiny grayish worm-like larvae attached to rocks in swiftly moving brooks and streams.

People have varying degrees of allergy to black fly bites. Like mosquito bites, the welt is caused by an enzyme secreted to soften up the tissue prior to drawing blood. For most people, the bite produces a small welt lasting only an hour or two; though for others the bite can cause a major swelling lasting up to a day. Apparently, however, people build up an immunity to the poison, since those most seriously affected are people who have spent little time in the out-of-doors during spring. People from Europe or other parts of the world where black flies and mosquitoes are not found are especially susceptible to the bites.

The first wave of black flies is active only during the day, but later in the season other species of blood-sucking flies, far tinier than the first, with the apt colloquial name of "No-see-ums," not only bite during the day but are attracted to light and fly through screens to annoy people in their houses at night.

During black-fly season, insect repellent is second only to sturdy shoes as part of the naturalist's basic equipment. All of the newer brands offer good protection against the insect, though some have to be reapplied more often than others. These all come in small plastic containers or bottles that fit easily into a pocket.

MOSQUITOES

Mosquitoes appear about the time the black-fly season ends. Since mosquitoes remain fairly close to their birthplace, usually a body of stagnant water, they are worse in swampy areas. Although mosquitoes are not a problem in open breezy areas, unlike black flies they are particularly annoying on still evenings. Insect repellent works well also against mosquitoes.

TICKS

Ticks were formerly a problem only in the southern coastal section of the region, but in recent years they have spread inland and farther north, usually carried by vacationing dogs returning to their homes. In areas where ticks are plentiful, it is unwise to sit or lie on the ground or leave clothing there. The only danger from ticks is the slight possibility of contracting Rocky Mountain spotted fever; however, very few ticks carry this disease. Moreover, ticks may crawl around for several hours before sucking blood. The chance of any serious problem arising from ticks is therefore very small. Insect repellent also provides good protection from ticks.

SPIDERS

Spiders are a very minor potential hazard to naturalists. Though all but a few small families of spiders have poison glands, only one species native to New England produces a venom virulent enough to cause harm to man. Most species are too timid to bite even if handled roughly; the few of the larger species that might be induced to bite are said to produce a reaction less painful than a bee sting.

The northern widow spider, *Latrodectus variolus*, is the only dangerous species found in southern New England. The mature female is about 1 cm (⅜ in) long with a shiny black body. On the underside of the abdomen are one or more red spots, though occasionally the red spots are missing altogether. (The black widow spider, *L. mactans*, with a red hourglass-shaped spot on its abdomen is more common south of New England.) The spider weaves an irregular web, usually built close to the ground. The webs are found in many habitats: often under stones, logs, or holes in dirt embankments and occasionally in barns and outbuildings. Since the spider's usual position in the web is upside down, the small red spots will generally be visible.

Though its venom is quite poisonous, the northern widow spider has no instinct to attack humans; it attempts to escape even if its web is destroyed. The bite is painful and requires hospitalization but it is rarely fatal. The probability of receiving a northern widow bite in the field is of about the same order as snakebite, perhaps a million to one. Symptoms are a small whitish spot around the bite followed by pain in other parts of the body and usually difficulty in breathing.

Old Wells

Many times people traveling through the countryside will come upon old cellar holes. These old ruins are interesting to explore and perhaps to scratch about for bottles and other artifacts, but it is important to remember that all had to have a source of water, either from a spring or a dug well. Often the old well is still intact and still contains water. Needless to say, falling into an old well could put you into a serious predicament, though it is usually possible to climb out by scaling the rock-lined sides.

The early wells had wooden covers which have long since rotted away, though someone may have covered them again with boards. When pumps were installed in kitchens, the wells were often topped by a flat rock, thereby rendering them less dangerous. These old wells, then, are no great hazard if you are aware that one might be nearby and you watch your step.

Hunting Season

Deer hunting season is a time for caution, especially if you are exploring the more remote sections of the region. The vast majority of hunters are, of course, responsible, careful individuals, but with thousands of hunters in the woods, accidents do occur.

In southern New England, hunting with high-powered rifles is prohibited; shotguns, which are permitted, have a far shorter effective (and dangerous) range. Nevertheless, if you do spend time in the woods during deer hunting season probably the best precaution is to wear a knapsack, cap, or other garment of "international" or "blaze" orange, a very bright fluorescent color that shows up extremely well in the woods and cannot be confused with any natural color.

The following schedule shows the 1977 deer season in each of the three southern New England states.

Connecticut:
> Shotguns—First whole two weeks in December
> Muzzle-loading guns—Last week in November

Massachusetts:
> Shotguns—First whole week in December

Rhode Island:
> Shotguns—First whole week in December

Sunday hunting is prohibited in all three states.

Each of these states has a bow-and-arrow season before the regular firearm season, but the relatively few bow-and-arrow hunters in the region pose a less serious threat of accident.

Taking Care of the Land

THOUGH plenty of open space still remains in most of the region, there is hardly an acre that does not receive some pressure from the dense population. Most habitats absorb this pressure fairly well, but a few, like sphagnum bogs and sand dunes, are so fragile that merely walking through them can cause some damage. These fragile habitats present a particular dilemma to naturalists: on the one hand, no one wants to see them destroyed, on the other, they are often fascinating places to study.

With civilization so close by, some wear and tear on the various habitats in the region can be expected and condoned. Much harder to accept is the increasing incidence of damage done through carelessness or outright vandalism. Landowners frequently find fences broken, gates left ajar, trash scattered about, and sometimes even their property on fire, all caused by people's carelessness or willful destruction.

As a result, more and more landowners who care about their property are reluctant to allow others access to it. Though No Trespassing signs, which are on the increase, do little to deter vandals, they do restrict responsible people from access. It would be tragic indeed if, as has happened in much of Great Britain, most of the private property in the region becomes posted.

There is no simple way to stop damage done by ignoramuses or vandals, but responsible people need not inadvertently contribute to the problem. Everyone using another person's land should remember a few commonsense rules:

1. Try to obtain the owner's permission before crossing land. Most will give permission even if the land is posted.

2. Don't bend or break fences, knock stones off walls, or leave gates open.

3. Carry out all refuse or garbage.

4. Don't pick flowers.

5. Don't build fires on private property, and don't even smoke during dry periods.

6. Don't remove plants without permission.

FURTHER READING

Some Tips on Getting Started

TIME IN THE FIELD

Leopold, Aldo. *A Sand County Almanac*. New York: Oxford University Press, 1949. Regarded by many as this century's classic work on conservation. Inspiring poetic essays that articulate the present-day conservation ethic.

A LEAF FROM THOREAU'S JOURNAL

Porter, Eliot. *In Wildness is the Preservation of the World*. San Francisco: Sierra Club, 1962. Inspiring color photographs of the southern New England woodlands accompanied by quotations from Thoreau's journal.

Silber, Mark, ed. *Thoreau Country: Photographs and Text Selections from the Works of H. D. Thoreau by Herbert W. Gleason*. San Francisco: Sierra Club, 1975. Collection of superb old glass-plate photographs showing the Concord countryside at the turn of the century.

Torrey, Bradford, and Francis H. Allen, eds. *The Journal of Henry D. Thoreau*. New York: Dover, 1962. Two-thousand-page reprint of Thoreau's fourteen-volume journal. Last seven volumes are almost entirely concerned with natural history. Interesting observations on practically every page.

GROWING NATIVE PLANTS

Birdseye, Clarence, and Eleanor G. Birdseye. *Growing Woodland Plants*. New York: Dover, 1972. Reprint of one of the first native-plant gardening guides. Though written twenty-five years ago, virtually all of the information presented is still useful.

Bruce, Hal. *How to Grow Wildflowers and Wild Shrubs in Your Garden*. New York: Knopf, 1976. A superbly written and illustrated book on native plant ecology and horticulture. Centers in Bruce's home area of Delaware and Maryland, but much of the information is applicable to southern New England.

Niering, William A., and Richard H. Goodwin, eds. *Energy Conservation on the Home Grounds: The Role of Naturalistic Landscaping* (Bulletin 21). New London, Conn.: Connecticut College, 1975. A guide for homeowners on conserving energy by utilizing low-maintenance naturalistic plantings in place of large lawns.

Sperka, Marie. *Growing Wildflowers: A Gardener's Guide*. New York: Harper and Row, 1973. An excellent guide to growing 200 native plant species. Illustrations oriented to northern Wisconsin, but almost entirely applicable to New England.

Steffek, Edwin F. *Wildflowers and How to Grow Them*. New York: Crown, 1954. Practical guide to cultivating, naturalizing, and conserving native plants. Oriented toward New England plants.

Taylor, Kathryn, and Stephen F. Hamblin. *Handbook of Wildflower Cultivation*. New York: Macmillan, 1963. One of the classic works on growing native plants in the home garden. Oriented to southern New England.

Recognizing Species

Blakeslee, Albert, and Chester Jarvis. *Northeastern Trees in Winter*. New York: Dover, 1972. A reprint of the 1911 original *New England Trees in Winter*. Good photos of bark and fruit. Also includes photos of twigs and entire trees.

Brown, Lauren. *Weeds in Winter*. New York: Norton, 1976. Clearly illustrated guide to identifying the dried remains of herbaceous plants in winter.

Stokes, Donald W. *A Guide to Nature in Winter*. Boston: Little, Brown, 1976. A very useful, comprehensive field guide to winter natural history. Includes sections on winter weeds, snow crystals, trees, insect evidence, birds, abandoned nests, mushrooms, tracks, and evergreen plants.

Trelease, William. *Winter Botany: An Identification Guide to Native Trees and Shrubs*. New York: Dover, 1967. A paperback reprint of 1931 guide to the identification of woody plants in winter.

A Few Precautions

Gatty, Harold. *Nature is Your Guide*. New York: Dutton, 1958. An excellent but little-known book about finding your way in various parts of the world without map and compass.

Kingsbury, John M. *Poisonous Plants of the United States and Canada*. Englewood Cliffs, N.J.: Prentice-Hall, 1964. Standard reference work on poisonous plants. Identification, poisonous principle, toxicity.

Petersen, Richard C. *The Venomous Snakes of Connecticut*, Geological and Natural History Survey Bulletin 103. Hartford, Conn.: State Library, 1970. Balanced treatment of life history, distribution, and habitat of the rattlesnake and copperhead, New England's only poisonous species.

Taking Care of the Land

Dasmann, Raymond F. *A Different Kind of Country*. New York: Macmillan, 1968. An important book describing the need to maintain diversity in the natural and human world.

deMoll, Lane, ed. *Rainbook: Resources for an Appropriate Technology*. New York: Schocken Books, 1977. Taking care of the land is but one of the many topics covered in this splendid annotated catalog. Essential reading for all who sense the vast social and economic changes that are about to take place.

Guitar, Mary Ann. *Property Power: How to Keep the Bulldozer, the Power Line, and the Highwayman Away from Your Door*. Garden City, N.Y.: Doubleday, 1972. Explores the conflict between those who view the land as a place to live and those who treat it as a commodity. Suggests ways to protect land against encroachments.

Little, Charles E., and Robert L. Burnap. *Stewardship*. New York: Open Space Institute, 1965. Describes ways of preserving what remains of the open spaces near our metropolitan areas.

McHarg, Ian L. *Design with Nature*. Garden City, N.Y.: Natural History Press, 1969. Excellent study of rural and urban landscapes and man's relationship to the natural world. Superb illustrations.

Miller, G. Tyler, Jr. *Living in the Environment: Concepts, Problems, and Alternatives*. Belmont, Cal.: Wadsworth, 1975. A superb comprehensive treatment of the relationship of man to his surroundings.

Peskin, Sarah. *Guiding Growth and Change: A Handbook for the Massachusetts Citizen*. A resource guide for people concerned with growth and land use in Massachusetts. Much of the information is applicable to other New England states.

Swift, Ernest. *A Conservation Saga*. Washington, D.C.: National Wildlife Federation, 1967. Collection of essays, each focusing on one aspect of conservation, written by one of the most articulate and inspiring of the postwar conservationists.

PART II

Forest Geography

Forest Geography:
An Introduction

LEARNING about the landscape is learning to recognize patterns. As you travel from one part of the region to another, noting the repeating patterns of vegetation in similar habitats, you may also begin to notice changes in the patterns themselves. Sometimes these changes are so subtle and gradual as to go unnoticed. On a drive northward across Connecticut, for example, it is difficult to pick the spot where white pine becomes a major component of the woodland. Other changes may be much more dramatic: for example, the abrupt change in the character of the forest in a space of a few kilometers from the Connecticut Valley in Massachusetts westward into the Berkshires.

It is these broader vegetational patterns, the geographical rather than the ecological, that are the subject of Part II. Presenting plant geography before plant ecology may be contrary to traditional teaching about the landscape, but in this age of high-speed travel where there is a constant opportunity to observe these broader distribution patterns, an overview of plant geography will be a valuable adjunct in recognizing and interpreting the behavior of plants in the various communities and habitats discussed later in the book.

Range

The range of a particular species is that part of the world in which it is found living and reproducing naturally. A few plants native to southern New England—mostly aquatic plants, mosses, ferns, and fungi—may be found on every continent except Antarctica. Many of the common weeds, introduced into New England from Europe by the settlers, have also appeared in many other parts of the world.

Most of the native plants, however, are much more restricted in their distribution. A majority of the deciduous trees found in southern New England range across the eastern third of the country, many as far south as Florida.

A remarkable number of trees that are common in the woods of southern New England reach the northern limits of their range within a few tens of kilometers of each other, roughly along the dividing line between the areas covered by the two volumes of this series. A smaller number of northern trees reach the southern limits of their continuous range at approximately the same place. Below are listed most of the common tree species that reach the northern or southern limits of their range near this dividing line.

Common Trees Reaching the Limits of Their Ranges in Central New England

Northern Limit

Atlantic white cedar, *Chamaecyparis thyoides*
Pignut hickory, *Carya glabra*
Mockernut hickory, *Carya tomentosa*
American chestnut, *Castanea dentata*
White oak, *Quercus alba*
Swamp white oak, *Quercus bicolor*
Chestnut oak, *Quercus Prinus*
Black oak, *Quercus velutina*
Scarlet oak, *Quercus coccinea*
Sycamore, *Platanus occidentalis*
Flowering dogwood, *Cornus florida*
Poison sumac, *Rhus Vernix*

Southern Limit

Balsam fir, *Abies balsamifera*
Red pine, *Pinus resinosa*
White spruce, *Picea glauca*
*Black spruce, *Picea mariana*
*Larch, *Larix laricina*
Red spruce, *Picea rubens*
Paper birch, *Betula papyrifera*

*These persist farther south in widely separated bog habitats.

The range limits of the above species, of course, do not coincide perfectly. Some of the northern species do survive in widely separated disjunct colonies farther south, and some of the southern species do extend their ranges northward for a few scores of kilometers up the Merrimack and

Connecticut River valleys and the long valley running northward near New England's western border. Yet, in spite of these variations, the fact that so many trees, whose ranges cover most of the eastern third of the nation, all reach their northern distribution limits along such a relatively narrow band is quite remarkable.

Several other groups of trees reach the northern limits of their range in southern New England close to the coast. Many of those which occur in a few widely scattered colonies here are much more common on the Atlantic Coastal Plain from New Jersey southward. These coastal survivors include American holly, *Ilex opaca*, sweetbay magnolia, *Magnolia virginiana*, sweet gum, *Liquidambar styraciflua*, post oak, *Quercus stellata*, and persimmon, *Diospyros virginiana*. Atlantic white cedar, *Chamaecyparis thyoides*, also a common tree in wet areas along the Atlantic Coastal Plain, is found in many bogs near the coast but in only a few widely scattered inland stations.

Range Maps

Maps showing the range of plant species not only enable us to learn the natural vegetation of particular areas but also help us to understand the geography of plant species. Because of their dominance in the landscape and their economic importance, the common tree species have been mapped most systematically and carefully. The ranges of most shrubs and herbaceous plants have not been systematically mapped, but identification guides usually give at least a rough idea of their ranges.

Large-scale range maps, of course, are far more useful than small-scale ones. Most tree identification guides, if they include range maps at all, present them on such a small scale that anyone studying an area as limited as southern New England would not find them very helpful. Range maps of larger scale, compiled by the U.S. Forest Service, are included in later sections of this book.

If you know something about the climate and topography of a region, the range maps can provide some useful information about the tolerance of a particular species to climatic extremes. They can also provide an indication of the optimum conditions for its growth. The factors that limit range, however, are usually complex and interrelated. Often it is impossible, even through careful field study, to determine why a species is limited to a particular range; interpreting the behavior of a species from the range map alone is highly speculative.

As a rule, the geographic center of the range is the area of optimal conditions for that species. Climatic conditions are least favorable near the edges of its range.

The range maps of many species show scattered disjunct colonies growing at some distance beyond the limits of the continuous range. The significance of these disjunct colonies is not always clear, but when these are scattered over a wide area at some distance from each other, it is usually a sign that there has been a major contraction in the range of that species in the not too distant past. A field examination of these disjunct colonies almost always shows that the species is limited to sites with environmental conditions similar to those in its continuous range. Sometimes disjunct colonies closer to the range limit may not be relicts of larger distribution patterns but rather the advance guard of an expanding range.

Range maps, even on the scale of those in this book, however, do not present a clear picture of the actual distribution of a particular species. The range is usually shown by solid shading, the limits by a sharp line. Even near the center of its range, where climatic conditions are best, no species can populate all possible habitats. Near its range limits, where climate is less congenial, the distribution of a particular species is very sporadic, since under these conditions the plant is able to survive only on the most favored sites.

Range maps also do not show how common a tree is. Some species such as red oak are very common across a large part of their ranges, while others, like green ash and tupelo, are far less frequent, growing only in more specialized habitats.

Plant geographers compile range maps from studying herbarium specimens of pressed and dried leaves. The sheets on which these specimens are glued usually give information about the location and habitat in which the specimen was found but little information, especially on the older sheets, about the relative abundance of the particular species. The leaves and flowers on the sheet may have been collected from a single specimen growing in a town or county or it may represent a large number. The range map of white pine, *Pinus Strobus*, for example, shows the tree growing in all parts of New England, yet anyone who has looked for the tree in this region knows that it is rare in southern Connecticut, on outer Cape Cod, in the higher mountains, and in the northwestern section of Maine. In other parts of New England, however, white pine is so abundant that it becomes one of the dominant features in the forest landscape.

Yet in spite of this major drawback, these maps are among the most useful tools for learning about the vegetation of a particular area. The range limits of certain species may not be shown with total accuracy, but, in a region as extensively studied as southern New England, the chances are small of finding a particular native species growing naturally at any distance beyond its range limits.

Survival of Species
Near Their Range Limits

The range limits of a particular species are most often determined by the ability of the seedlings to survive. Most plants are particularly vulnerable to climatic extremes during the seedling stage, when their thin stems and small shallow root systems make their resistance to cold and drought precarious. As they grow larger, most plants are able to tolerate extremes in climate to a much greater degree. Experienced gardeners know that many plants, if carefully tended during their infancy, can thrive well beyond the limits of their natural range with little or no additional care. Only occasionally, however, will these introduced plants reproduce naturally in the less congenial climate beyond their range limits. Even within the natural range of a particular species, climatic and other factors will usually limit the germination of seeds and survival of the seedlings to but a tiny fraction of the total number of seeds produced.

The hardiness of plants in winter or their tolerance of summer heat is an extremely complex subject. Low temperature may be only a part of the cause of the demise of plants beyond the northern limit of their range. Duration of cold, wind chill, presence or absence of an insulating layer of snow over the roots, suddenness of and degree of a temperature drop, number of frost-free days during the growing season, and even summer climatic conditions can all play a part.

The factors that may determine the southern limits of the particular species may be even more complex. In many cases drought and high temperatures may be critical. Other species may be particularly susceptible to fungi or other pathogens that are not found in more northerly parts of their range; possibly the growth of these attacking organisms is accelerated by periods of high summer humidity. Perhaps there is simply too much competition in the greater variety of plants that occurs at lower latitudes. Most likely, the limits of range in any direction are not determined by one but by a combination of several interrelated factors.

Climate

CLIMATE exerts a huge influence on nearly every aspect of the natural environment. It is a major factor in determining the distribution of plants and animals, the properties of the soil, and, to a large degree, the surface features of the land itself. Climate may be loosely defined as the average weather at a particular place over a period of time. Its effects on the environment are a result of an extremely subtle interrelationship of temperature, light, moisture, and—under extreme conditions—the movement of air.

In this chapter we will examine the macroclimate of southern New England, that is, the broad climatic patterns, and the mesoclimate, those intermediate variations in the broader climatic pattern, such as those caused by elevation, latitude, and proximity of the ocean. Of the macroclimate, little can be said beyond the fact that it is extremely variable. On the mesoclimate there is much more substantive information—especially on those effects caused by the proximity of the ocean—that is useful to anyone studying the ecology and natural history of the region.

A chapter in Part III is devoted to the microclimate, the climate from treetop level to the ground. The relationship of plants and animals to these smaller climatic variations is even more complex and interesting. An understanding of microclimate is, in fact, crucial to understanding ecology.

Macroclimate

Data on the macroclimate of New England suggest a pleasant, equitable climate. An average annual rainfall of a little over 100 centimeters (40 inches) is evenly distributed throughout the year. Average temperatures for July center around 22° C (70° F), while the average January temperature, which is more variable from place to place, ranges from about −4° C (25° F) inland to 4° C (36° F) on the coastal islands. The pattern of weather averages out to a two-or-three-day alternation between fair and cloudy or stormy conditions.

Anyone who has lived in New England for any length of time knows how misleading such average statistics are. While it is true that New England has its share of pleasant weather, the day-to-day weather is characterized by great variability, abrupt changes, and no persistent pattern. This lack of pattern baffles meteorologists and makes planning outdoor activities difficult. In fact, it is a rare day, week, or month when the weather statistics conform to the climatic averages.

The lack of pattern in precipitation is a case in point. The mean annual precipitation figures do cluster about 106 centimeters (42 inches), but in a very wet year over 170 centimeters (65 inches) may fall while during the driest year in recent times less than 60 centimeters (23 inches) fell. Though the precipitation appears to be equally distributed throughout the year, droughts and wet spells occur during part of every year. The so-called three-day weather pattern may extend to three weeks or more of fair weather, especially in the summer and fall, and a week or more of cloudy, rainy weather, often in the early spring.

These vagaries in precipitation, especially the periods of drought, bring stress to the region's vegetation, most of which is adapted to a more or less constant supply of rainfall. Summer droughts can kill outright or retard the growth of young shallow-rooted plants and leave larger ones unpre-

FOREST GEOGRAPHY

pared for the rigors of winter. Moreover, summer showers, the form of precipitation most common to the region at that time, bring only superficial short-lived relief. The depth of soil that such a shower, even a downpour, can penetrate is usually less than an inch; most of the water from these rains is lost in runoff and evaporation. Usually several long, soaking rains are required to restore the soil moisture after it has been depleted by a drought.

Average temperature statistics, likewise, are of little use in describing the day-to-day weather. An annual temperature range from nearly $-30°$ C $(-20°$ F) to $35°$ C $(95°$ F) is not uncommon in many inland points. In a particular place, the last killing frost may occur as early as the end of March in one year and as late as the middle of May in the next. Substantial yearly variation may also be expected in average winter temperatures, number of days above $0°$ C $(32°$ F), amounts of snow, number of days below freezing, and so on. The lowest winter temperatures and the duration of cold spells, of vital interest to gardeners and horticulturists who grow less hardy ornamentals, also vary from year to year.

Mesoclimate

In the mesoclimate, the climate of the areas within the region, some discernible patterns do emerge. In the Northeast there are three major factors—latitude, elevation, and proximity to the ocean—that have a measurable effect on the climatic differences within the region. A study of the plant hardiness maps compiled by the Department of Agriculture shows in a general way the effect of each of these three factors. The zones are based on the average annual minimum temperatures but also correlate roughly with the severity and length of winter.

The zones across the eastern half of the country run generally in an east-west direction, indicating a progression from the warm winter temperatures of the South to the increasingly colder temperatures further north. In New England and in the southern Appalachians, the lower hardiness zones correspond to mountainous areas and extend southward, indicating the effect of altitude on winter climate. It can be seen on the map, also, that each hardiness

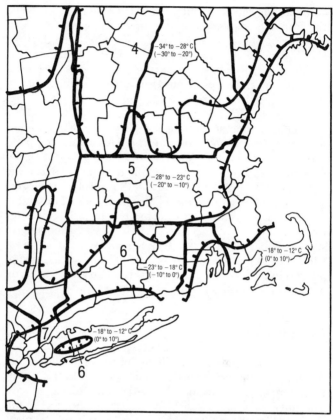

Winter hardiness zones (from U.S. Department of Agriculture map). Approximate range of annual minimum temperatures. The effects of latitude, elevation, and proximity to the ocean on the winter temperatures of southern New England can be seen on this map.

zone extends northward along the coast, reflecting the ameliorating effect of the ocean upon winter temperatures near the shore. By comparing climatic averages for various places within the region, we can get a rough idea of how each of these factors affects the mesoclimate. It is important to remember, though, that local climatic conditions also vary substantially within a small area, usually as the result of hilly terrain.

LATITUDE

The part of New England covered by this volume spans 2 degrees of latitude. If we compare climatic data for Portsmouth, New Hampshire, near the northern end, with Norwalk, Connecticut, near the southern end, we see a difference of about 3° C (4° F) in average February temperature and a two-week difference in the growing season. Both cities are on the ocean; both are only a few feet above sea level. Except for the fact that the winter seawater temperature in Long Island Sound off southern Connecticut is a bit warmer than at Portsmouth, this 3-degree difference can probably be attributed largely to difference in latitude.

ELEVATION

The effects of increasing elevation on the mesoclimate are more apparent. Climatologists have worked out an approximate equation between elevation and latitude: all other factors being equal, each 120-meter (400-foot) increase in elevation produces a climate similar to that of 160 kilometers (100 miles) farther north. On Great Blue Hill in Milton, Massachusetts, only 180 meters (600 feet) higher than Boston, for example, the July temperature averages out to be 1.1° C (2° F) cooler than Boston, a small though ecologically significant difference.

Elevation also has the effect of increasing the rainfall. Great Blue Hill receives an average of 19 centimeters (7.5 inches) or about 16 percent more rainfall than does Boston.

PROXIMITY TO THE OCEAN

In southern New England, with a north-south dimension of only 217 kilometers (136 miles) and an elevation range of about 360 meters (1,200 feet), the effects of these small differences in latitude and elevation are equally small. Often they are masked by local differences in climate.

The effects of the ocean on nearly every aspect of the region's climate, however, may be clearly perceived. Any large body of water acts as a heat storage reservoir in winter. During warmer parts of the year the water gradually heats up; as winter approaches the water gradually gives off this heat to the air around it. Land also absorbs and radiates heat, but at a much quicker rate. Coastal areas, therefore, experience several differences in climate, the most important of which for the region's ecology is probably milder winter temperatures.

Areas adjacent to the coast receive the most benefit from the relatively warmer water, although all parts of the region benefit to some extent. Nowhere is the effect of the ocean on winter temperature more apparent than on Cape Cod and the adjacent islands. The effect of the ocean may be clearly seen in the comparison between the average winter temperatures on Nantucket Island, some 60 kilometers (35 miles) off the coast, and those of an inland station such as Springfield, Massachusetts.

Average Winter Temperatures:
Nantucket Island and Springfield

	Nantucket	Springfield
December	2.3° C (36° F)	−0.3° C (31° F)
January	0.6° C (33° F)	−1.9° C (27° F)
February	−0.3° C (31° F)	−1.3° C (29° F)
March	2.8° C (37° F)	3.3° C (38° F)

As the ocean slowly cools during these months, it keeps Nantucket significantly warmer than Springfield, until March.

It is important to remember when looking at average temperatures that a difference as small as one degree is usually significant. Warming trends generally affect the whole region and skew the mean temperatures upward everywhere. As small a difference as one degree, therefore, means the occurrence of a number of much colder days at Springfield. An examination of daily temperatures at both stations would bear this out. A difference of a degree or two in mean temperatures has profound effects on the plant life.

Climatic conditions right along the coast and on the islands are less congenial than these data suggest, however. Throughout the winter the almost constant winds there make the climate in exposed areas very rigorous. In sheltered areas, though, the effect of the warmer temperature is unmistakable. Gardeners situated near the shore, but out of the strong winds, can grow plants whose cold-tenderness would cause them to succumb a kilometer or so inland.

Most of the factors that affect the survival of plants near their northern range limits are ameliorated by proximity to the ocean. It is for this reason that the Coastal Plain species of trees and shrubs mentioned in the previous chapter reach the northern limits of their range in southern New England almost within sight of the warmer waters of Long Island Sound. A number of herbaceous plants also reach the northern limits of their distribution here, though some also appear in Nova Scotia.

In addition to making the winter climate less rigorous, the ocean produces other effects on the adjacent land. Except in the Connecticut suburbs of New York City, winter seems to leave the region with reluctance. While late freezes are less common along the coast, because the ocean warms up gradually, the coming of spring is delayed rather than hastened. We can observe this lag in the spring warming if we refer to the comparative temperature data between Nantucket and Springfield. In Springfield the February average shows the temperature beginning to creep upward; on Nantucket the steadily cooling ocean causes the temperature there to continue to fall. On early spring days when there is sufficient sunlight to warm the land, a damp, cold sea breeze often keeps the immediate coast up to 11° C (20° F) cooler than the inland temperature.

Coastal fog, also a result of the cold water, cuts down the amount of sunlight reaching the land. Under certain conditions, usually in the spring, cold maritime air masses push inland, producing a phenomenon known to meteorologists as a "maritime cold front." Unlike the general west-to-east movement of nearly all other weather systems, maritime cold fronts move from east to west, often covering all of the eastern half of the region with cold and damp ocean air.

The effects of the cooler ocean on the summer climate of coastal areas are of course well known. If we look at the summer data from Nantucket and Springfield we see an even greater difference than that of winter.

Average Summer Temperatures:
Nantucket Island and Springfield

	Nantucket	Springfield
June	16° C (61° F)	21° C (69° F)
July	19° C (66° F)	23° C (74° F)
August	20° C (68° F)	22° C (72° F)
September	17° C (63° F)	18° C (64° F)

SEA BREEZES

Sea breezes are caused by heated air rising over land and being replaced with colder air blowing in from the ocean. These sea breezes are usually local in extent, affecting the climate only within a distance of 5 to 15 kilometers (3 to 9 miles) from the coast, but occasionally their cooling effect can be felt as far as 50 kilometers (30 miles) inland.

During the hot and humid spells of the summer, the wind generally comes from the west-southwest. Away from the coast these winds, which bring in moist tropical air, only serve to increase the humidity and thus offer little relief from the heat. Along south-facing coastal areas the winds tend to blow more from the southwest and are intensified by the local sea breeze effect. This constant wind keeps the adjacent land at comfortable temperatures but does increase the forest fire danger by drying out the woodlands. It is undoubtedly one of the factors that has caused so many forest fires on Cape Cod and in other parts of southeastern Massachusetts. The constant wind leaves its mark on the trees in that area: most have definitely thicker foliage and longer branches on their leeward sides, especially if the trees are growing on exposed sites.

When the region is in the grip of a real heat wave, the winds usually blow more from the west or even a little north of west—often considered a cool-weather wind direction. But these winds, which are usually light, bring in air from the interior of the continent where the ocean is too far away to have any moderating effect.

On a hot day the local sea breeze may be felt near any body of water. This breeze, which might be best considered a microclimatic effect, makes lake shores and river banks several degrees cooler than the land just tens of meters away. The shores facing the prevailing wind direction will be the coolest. These receive both the local breeze and the prevailing wind, which also cools down when passing over water. Often the body of water producing these local breezes is quite small. On hot days I have felt a strong breeze from a body of water as small as the Charles River in Cambridge, Massachusetts, though usually it doesn't reach more than a block or so from the river.

During the summer, one effect of the ocean is to cut down the amount of rainfall received by coastal areas. A large part of the region's summer rainfall comes from summer thunderstorms and other convective showers. These showers are more numerous inland, where the warm land heats up the air above it. Over the relatively cool ocean, the air is more stable and as a result high cloud buildup and local showers are less common. In fact, often during the summer you may see clear skies at sea and billowing cumulus clouds over the land. Violent summer storms, such as tornadoes and thunderstorms with large hailstones, which occasionally do occur in interior sections, are also rare along the coast. Cold fronts bringing with them worthwhile rain also diminish when they reach the cool climate of the ocean.

What the nearby ocean takes away from the southern New England climate in the spring, it gives back in the fall. Most connoisseurs of the region's climate rate fall as the finest season. The good weather is even more evident along the coast. The fogs of early summer are far less common then and the ocean, which finally reaches its warmest temperature in August, prolongs the mild weather well into the fall. This more gradual warming trend can also be seen in the chart on page 52.

Though a cold Canadian air mass may end the growing season inland as early as late September, killing frosts may not come to the coastal areas until November, during which New Englanders can almost always count on periods of pleasant weather up until Thanksgiving and sometimes beyond.

WINTER STORMS

The pattern of precipitation during the colder months of the year is quite different from that of the summer. Much of the region's rainfall during these cold months comes from the storms which gather moisture and energy over the warm waters of the Gulf of Mexico or off the Atlantic coast to the south and track northward to New England. These storms, like other low pressure areas, are characterized by a strong counterclockwise flow of air around their centers. Their approach is marked by a gradually intensifying northeast wind, from which comes their name of "northeasters."

The size, intensity, speed of movement, and track of these storms all vary, each with different consequences for New England. The most severe storms may have barometric pressures as low and winds as high as in hurricanes. The tracks of these more intense storms usually stay over the water; the resulting high tides and strong winds occasionally do considerable damage to coastal property. These coastal northeasters are perhaps less common now than they used to be.

Because of its size and intensity, a winter northeaster will draw milder air in from the Gulf Stream some distance at sea, which usually results not in snow but in rain. Most of the region's heaviest snowfall comes from coastal storms that are somewhat different.

These snowstorms usually begin farther up the coast, ordinarily from Cape Hatteras northward, in what meteorologists refer to as a "secondary low," a low pressure area that forms in conjunction with a weak inland low pressure area moving eastward across the central part of the country. These storms gather strength as they track northward up the coast and sometimes bring several inches of snow to southern New England. The storms from secondary lows rarely become as intense or as large as the true northeasters, which, as noted before, are more likely to be rainstorms.

There is a cold side and a warm side to all of these storms. The counterclockwise windflow around their centers brings mild air from the warmer ocean south of New England to those parts of the region that are east of the storm center, while the regions north or northwest of the storm center receive northeast winds. When the storm center tracks inland, coastal areas almost always receive rain; when the storm center stays at sea, the coastal areas are likely to receive snow.

FOREST GEOGRAPHY

A northwesterly shift in the wind nearly always follows the passage of one of these winter storms. Winter winds from the northwest direction bring in cold dry air from Canada; the temperatures following these storms usually plummet. The cold is further intensified if a snow cover is present, since almost all of the sun's radiation falling on white snow is reflected back into space rather than being absorbed by the darker land. As a result, air temperatures over snow-covered areas are almost always substantially colder than nearby bare ground areas. Clearing skies after a storm also mean generally cooler temperatures, since there is no cloud cover to trap some of the reflected solar radiation. Under these conditions the cold weather tends to become self-perpetuating.

In early spring, these coastal storms delay the advent of warm weather. A large, slow-moving storm may keep the weather unsettled for several days after its passage. At times the winds around the storm's center are so intense that maritime air is carried completely around it, perhaps bringing milder temperatures than otherwise, but also damp weather and cloudy skies. Once the snow cover has melted and the ground can once more absorb solar radiation, a period of cloudy weather will prevent much of this sunlight from reaching the ground. As a result, the soil remains cold and spring flowering is delayed.

ICE STORMS

When a mass of relatively warm, moisture-laden air moves over cold air at the surface, conditions may be right for a destructive ice storm. Luckily, damage from ice storms is usually local in extent, and the combination of atmospheric conditions that causes them is not common. A thick layer of cold air at the surface usually freezes the rain from the warmer layer above as it falls, turning it to relatively harmless sleet. It is when the rain falls through the atmosphere and freezes on the surface of trees and shrubs and wires that ice damage becomes severe. Severe icing is not usually associated with northeasters because the strong winds that accompany them will tend to stir up the atmosphere and lessen the chance of a thick ice layer forming on trees and wires.

The area around Wethersfield, Connecticut, experienced a severe ice storm in the winter of 1974. Damage to wires from falling limbs was so severe that parts of the town were without power for several days,

Birches, especially along the edges of a woodland, are particularly susceptible to ice damage. These flexible-trunked trees are sometimes pulled nearly to the ground by the weight of ice on their upper branches. After the ice melts, the trees remain in their bent positions. Spreading trees growing in the open can also be very badly damaged by ice. Wounds where large limbs have broken off become pathways for insects and fungus which damage the tree still further. An occasional light coating of ice, on the other hand, is actually of some benefit to forest trees by helping to break off dead lower branches so the bark can heal over the knot before decay sets in.

Forest History I:
Postglacial Migration

In the last two million years, the world has experienced perhaps the most catastrophic fluctuations in climate in its entire history. Recently uncovered evidence from several sources has indicated not four, as was previously thought, but perhaps as many as sixteen glacial periods during that time, each separated by a relatively brief period of warmer climate. During each of these cycles many of the cooler parts of the world lay buried beneath the ice for periods of 50,000 to 100,000 years. The later glacial periods, at least, were each followed by a warming of the climate that lasted between 10,000 to 20,000 years, during which the ice margin retreated northward and the glaciated areas once more became covered by vegetation.

The end of the last ice age began about 15,000 years ago. Evidence gathered from Long Island, dated at about 18,000 years before the present, has shown the ice margin to be at its most southern extent; 8,000 years later the ice margin had retreated to the Gulf of St. Lawrence.

The cause of these glacial cycles is still unknown. Evidence gathered from deep sea cores has indicated that their onset is marked by a gradual lowering of seawater temperature and their end by a sharp rise in seawater temperature. The last such rise took place between 15,000 and 10,000 years ago with an average increase in temperature of 5° to 8° C (9° to 14° F). By 10,000 years ago, New England was probably experiencing temperatures similar to today's, and between 8,000 and 5,000 years ago the climate was even warmer than at present. Since that time, a lowering of the temperature ominously suggests that the present interglacial period is coming to an end, and that soon, perhaps in a matter of a few centuries, a new ice age will begin.

Until very recently, plant geographers believed that the present-day species in the New England forests migrated northward as the ice sheet retreated from the lush forests of the southern Appalachians. Newer evidence has indicated that the climatic extremes during the glacial period were also felt in the southern Appalachians, causing a virtual elimination of the deciduous species there; although the southern Appalachians were south of the ice margins their vegetation was largely one of tundra at the higher elevations and spruce forest in the valleys.

As we shall see in this chapter, the northward migration of trees—like nearly every facet of the natural world—is proving to be far more complex than was previously thought.

Pollen Analysis

In 1916 a Swedish botanist studying peat samples taken from a bog discovered that these contained large numbers of remarkably well-preserved pollen grains apparently carried into the bog from the surrounding forest by the wind. Since each genus of trees and flowering plants produces pollen grains of a characteristic size and shape, it was possible to identify the pollen grains found in the peat by comparing them with samples taken from living plants.

Since the peat accumulates on the surface, digging down through a bog will reveal progressively older layers. Samples collected at regular intervals, then, will yield a pollen record from the surrounding forest that spans the existence of a particular bog. By counting small percentages of pollen grains taken at random from each sample and identifying these, scientists can draw some inferences about the composition of the forest in the vicinity of that particular bog over a period of time. Investigators found that pollen analysis at different depths varied substantially, suggesting that there were major changes in the composition of the forests over time.

Only the most tentative of conclusions can be reached on the basis of a few pollen profiles, of course. The process depends on several assumptions and contains variables that are impossible to measure. The very fine grains of pollen, for example, might have blown into the bog from considerable distances, perhaps from as far as a hundred kilometers or more. Furthermore, a change in the pollen content from one level to another could well be the result of changes in the local forest following a disturbance of some sort. And there are still other important potential sources of error.

But when considerable numbers of pollen profiles from widely scattered localities show a similar pattern, it is possible, in spite of these inevitable sampling errors and local variations, to interpret the changes in pollen percentages as representing widespread changes in forest geography. By the 1930s, enough data had been collected from northeastern bogs to show that indeed there had been substantial and widespread changes in the tree populations in this region.

So valuable has pollen analysis been in identifying and interpreting past forest trends that it soon developed into a separate specialized discipline known as palyonology. There are now dozens of pollen profiles from New England bogs to aid in the study of the postglacial forests.

The following pollen diagram, from a bog in southern New England, shows some of the significant trends.

The Migration of Species

The horizontal bars on the pollen diagram indicate the amounts of pollen from a particular species at a particular depth, and therefore at a particular point in time. The sudden appearance of a large amount of pollen of a certain species is generally interpreted as the point at which the

FOREST GEOGRAPHY

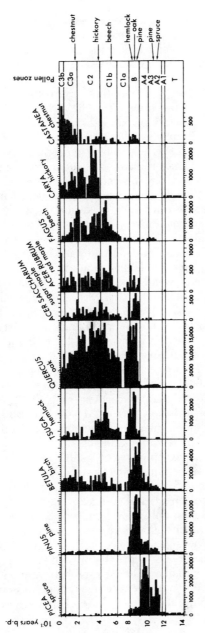

Pollen influx at Rogers Lake, Connecticut, during late glacial and postglacial time. The scale on the left is thousands of years before the present. The numbers along the bottom indicate the number of pollen grains counted in a tenth of a square centimeter sample taken from various depths in the peat.

species appeared in the area. Pollen grains are very tiny and easily carried by the wind. Small amounts of pollen in the samples below the major influx are interpreted as having been blown in from some distance. The gradual buildup in pollen amounts, before the maximum is reached, suggests that the tree species was migrating toward the particular site, moving gradually closer with time.

From the interpretation of a large number of pollen diagrams, gathered from sites all over the country, a complex pattern of reforestation is beginning to emerge. Not only did the familiar forest trees return to the region from different parts of the country, but this reforestation occurred very slowly. As the pollen diagram shows, Connecticut remained covered with treeless tundra vegetation for several thousand years after the ice sheet disappeared.

The first tree species, spruce, finally reached Connecticut about 11,500 years ago. About 1,000 years later, alder, fir, and jack pine, *Pinus Banksiana*, appeared in the spruce forest. This species weathered the glacial period on the southern Coastal Plain and probably reached New England by moving up the coast. Jack pine is now a species of the far north: it continued this northward migration almost to the Arctic Circle, leaving only a few relict colonies in the northern part of New England.

White pine, *P. Strobus*, reached New England 1,000 years later, or about 9,000 years ago. Fossil evidence from Canada has indicated that the northern range limits of pine were farther north than at present. There has also been a widespread decline in the abundance of pine in New England during the last few thousand years.

Birches and maples appeared at about the same time as pine, and shortly thereafter hemlock and oaks arrived on the scene. Hemlock apparently came northward first up the spine of the Appalachians and thence up the Coastal Plain, reaching Connecticut only a few hundred years after white pine. Hemlock was one of the fastest moving species, migrating at a rate of between 200 and 300 meters (650 to 1,000 feet) per year. By 6,000 years before the present it had reached northern Maine and, like white pine, probably grew at some distance north of its present range limits in southern Canada. Like pine also, hemlock reached its maximum abundance in New England about 5,000 years ago and has been declining in abundance since.

The oaks were also extremely fast-moving species. Their migration speed has baffled plant geographers, since the tree is both slow to reach fruiting maturity and is large-seeded. While it is true that squirrels represent an efficient seed dispersal mechanism over short distances, they probably could not account for the long yearly distance that the tree had to migrate in order to reach its present range limits.

Beech was another large-seeded but fast-moving species, migrating from its refuge in Florida to central New England in about 3,500 years, at a rate similar to that of hemlock. It may be more than coincidence that both hemlock and beech are shade-tolerant species whose seeds can germinate and grow under the closed canopy of other forest trees. It may well have been this characteristic that allowed beech and hemlock to penetrate the already existing forest.

Hickory's migration pattern is interesting. From a refuge somewhere in the South—perhaps the Boston Mountains in Arkansas—it reached lower Michigan 10,000 years ago, but did not appear in Massachusetts until 5,000 years later. Apparently, also, hickory has remained near the limits of its present range (close to the northern limit of the region) since that time. Some species, such as the shagbark hickory, are classed as moderately shade-tolerant trees, though the others native to New England are considered less so.

American chestnut was the last major species to arrive, reaching the northern limit of its former range only within the last thousand years. Though it migrated very slowly, before the blight it was a successful dominant tree in the southern New England woods.

The evidence is overwhelming, then, that following the last period of glaciation, the familiar tree species returned to New England from widely scattered parts of the country, migrating via different routes and at different speeds.

Pollen Analysis and Climate Change

From the southward contraction in range of some of the temperate climate species, from their decrease in abundance, and from the increase in abundance of such cold climate trees as spruce and fir during the last 5,000 years, it is probably safe to infer that the climate during this period has become cooler. Drawing more refined inferences about climatic change from change in pollen percentages is risky, however.

Until recently, some scientists have regarded the appearance of various trees in a region as evidence for climatic change. For example, the abundance of such dry site species as pine and oak was offered as evidence of a shift to a warmer, drier climate, while the later increase in beech and hemlock supposedly indicated a more humid climate.

The newer, admittedly incomplete evidence showing the migration patterns makes these sorts of climatic interpretations very suspect. The absence of a particular species from a particular site at a particular point in time does not necessarily mean that climatic conditions were unfavorable for its growth. It may simply have been unable to penetrate the closed forest canopy. Furthermore, an abundance and subsequent decline on a particular site may have been caused by an increase in competition from some later-arriving species or from disease. These early postglacial forest communities were without modern counterparts, and ecological relationships between species may have been totally different from those in the present-day woodlands.

FURTHER READING

Forest Geography: An Introduction

Braun, E. Lucy. *Deciduous Forests of Eastern North America*. New York: Hafner, 1974. Reprint of classic work on eastern forests. Ecological concepts out of date, but descriptive and geographical information very useful.

Gleason, Henry A., and Arthur Cronquist. *The Natural Geography of Plants*. New York: Columbia University Press, 1964. Outstanding introduction to plant geography. Superb black and white illustrations. Especially useful if you are traveling across the country.

Little, Elbert L., Jr. *Atlas of United States Trees*. Vol. 1, *Conifers and Important Hardwoods*. Forest Service Miscellaneous Publication no. 1146. Washington, D.C.: U.S. Government Printing Office, 1971. Large-scale range maps of all important tree species in the contiguous forty-eight states. Transparent overlays show relief, forest types, climatic data, extent of continental glaciation, rivers and lakes, physiographic provinces, and plant hardiness zones. Extremely useful for plant geography.

Lull, Howard W. *A Forest Atlas of the Northeast*. Washington, D.C.: U.S. Government Printing Office, 1968. Generalized maps of forest regions, soils, population density, and land use. Useful for large-scale studies of the entire Northeast, but somewhat too general for southern New England.

Thomson, Betty Flanders. *The Changing Face of New England*. New York: Macmillan, 1958. Vivid portrait of New England's geology, geography, and ecology. One of my favorites.

Climate

Brumbach, Joseph J. *The Climate of Connecticut*. Geological and Natural History Survey Bulletin 99. Hartford, Conn.: State Library, 1965. Long-term data on Connecticut's climate.

Calder, Nigel. *The Weather Machine: How Our Weather Works and Why It Is Changing*. New York: Viking, 1974. Superb layman's guide to understanding the weather and climate. Covers the human implications of the present climatic changes.

Local Climatological Data. Asheville, N.C.: National Climatic Center. Useful monthly summary of climatic data published for the following southern New England stations: Block Island, Blue Hill Observatory (Milton, Mass.), Boston, Bridgeport, Hartford, Providence, Worcester; also New York City and Albany. Single copies available.

Ludlam, David. *The Country Journal New England Weather Book*. Boston: Houghton Mifflin, 1976. Engaging collection of New England weather information. Historical weather events, climatological tables, many illustrations.

Weatherwise: The Magazine About Weather. Princeton, N.J.: Weatherwise, Inc. Excellent bimonthly magazine on all aspects of the weather. Written for amateurs.

PART III

Forest Ecology

Some Notes on the Terrain

THE GEOLOGICAL PATTERNS across most of the region are hard to perceive, especially if you are traveling on foot. Almost all of the bedrock lies buried beneath a thick layer of loose, glacially derived mantle rock; the mantle rock in turn is hidden by a green layer of plant life or its leafy debris. Nevertheless, there are some geological features that not only may be perceived by the foot traveler, but also play an important role in the distribution and ecology of the plants growing on top of them. Conversely, the plants in an area often provide significant clues to the hidden geology underfoot. The following patterns are particularly noteworthy.

Differential Weathering and Erosion

Some types of bedrock are more resistant to weathering than others. Where a marked difference in the resistance of the rocks exists, erosion attacks the softer rocks, etching out valleys and leaving the areas of harder rock behind as hills or mountains. In areas where the geology is relatively simple—in the Allegheny Mountains of Pennsylvania, for example—the long mountain ridges of resistant rock, separated by valleys underlain by softer rocks, are a classic example of this process of differential weathering and erosion. In New England, however, where the geology is far more complex, such clear examples are harder to find.

THE CONNECTICUT VALLEY LOWLAND

The Connecticut Valley Lowland presents the best example of differential weathering and erosion in the region. The lowland runs from New Haven northward to the northern border of Massachusetts, splitting southern New England more or less in half. In contrast to the hard crystalline rocks on the higher ground on either side, the rocks of the lowland are tilted beds of softer shales and sandstones. Erosion has carved out a broad valley that, near its northern end, is some 240 meters (800 feet) below the land that borders it.

The landscape within the lowland is in some ways similar

7. Connecticut Valley Lowland, looking south from Mount Holyoke. The long ridge extending into the distance is a tilted bed of hardened lava that has better resisted erosion than the softer sandstones and shales on either side.

to that of the Alleghenies. Interbedded with the sandstone and shales are three hard and resistant layers of basalt, solidified lava flows from old volcanic eruptions, that are tilted like the other rock layers and now stand above the lowland floor as sharp ridges. These basalt layers vary in thickness; those near the northern end of the lowland are only a few meters thick, but nevertheless they act as capstones on the hills and protect the softer beds beneath from eroding away.

The Connecticut Valley Lowland is of great interest to geologist and naturalist alike. Because the rocks are much younger and less altered than those on either side, the geological record is easier to interpret. Some of the strata have yielded abundant fossils, almost all of dinosaur footprints.

For the naturalist, the area exhibits a wide range of habitats, each with a distinctive community of plants. The climate in the lowland is somewhat warmer than on the higher ground on either side. As a result, there are some plants and animals normally found farther south that extend their ranges northward here. Moreover, some of the Connecticut Valley rocks contain limestone, an important ecological factor in determining what plants will grow on these sites.

Some Notes on the Terrain 67

BOSTON AND NARRAGANSETT BASINS

If you look at a map of southern New England you will see two large indentations in the coast: Narragansett Bay in Rhode Island and Boston Bay in Massachusetts. Both bays are partially inundated areas of softer rock. The Boston and Narragansett basins are two of five and possibly six sedimentary basins in southeastern Massachusetts and Rhode Island. They are underlain by soft rocks of the same age as the coal formations of Pennsylvania. In fact, some coal has been found at several places in the Narragansett basin.

Map showing areas of soft bedrock.

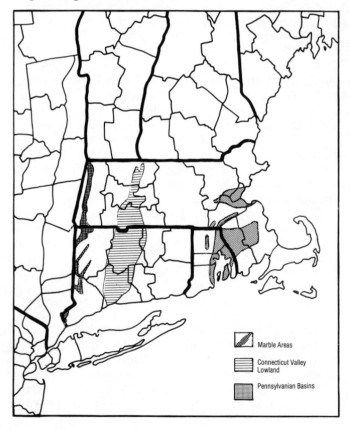

Marble Areas

Connecticut Valley Lowland

Pennsylvanian Basins

All of these basins are characterized by a topography of low relief with few outcrops and extensive areas of wetland. The glacial deposits in this part of New England are unusually thick and the character of the underlying bedrock does not, except by its absence, exert any influence on the vegetation.

MARBLE AREAS

Areas underlain by marble are also lower than their surroundings. Marble and limestone are among the least resistant types of bedrock in areas like New England that have a humid climate. Not only are these rocks soft and hence easily abraded by the ice sheets that moved across the region, but they are soluble in the weak organic acids produced by rainwater percolating through the decaying plant material in the humus layers of the soil.

In southern New England nearly all of the marble occurs in western Connecticut. Here the rock, which occurs in narrow beds, has eroded into valleys. The course of the Housatonic River from Cornwall Bridge to Gaylordsville and those of several smaller tributary streams now follow these marble valleys.

There are also a few small marble areas in eastern New England. Some of these are scattered along an area extending southwestward from Newbury, Massachusetts, into eastern Connecticut. Other marble areas occur in northeastern Rhode Island. Like those parts of the Connecticut Valley Lowland where the rocks contain limestone, areas underlain by marble also support a distinctive flora.

GRANITE AREAS

Bodies of granite and other hard rocks usually, but not always, resist erosion better than the surrounding areas. Sometimes, however, small differences in the chemical composition or physical structure in two adjacent areas of what appears to be the same rock cause them to disintegrate and erode at different rates. Sometimes, also, areas of rocks that are ordinarily resistant to weathering and erosion have been weakened by earth movements and, as a result, are more easily broken up.

8. Woodland in granite area, Milford, Massachusetts. Not all areas underlain by granite are as rocky as this.

Generally speaking, however, granite bodies in southern New England, being more resistant, are higher than their surroundings. As a rule, the more black minerals in an igneous rock, the less resistant it is to the weather. Granite and a few other closely related igneous rocks are more or less light-colored. Granite's constituent minerals—quartz, potash feldspar, and white mica—are all light-colored; these three are among the most stable and hence most resistant to chemical decomposition of any common rock-forming minerals.

Not only are these granite areas higher than their surroundings but also they form a more rugged terrain. Angular ledges, rock knobs, and large boulders strewn about are typical in areas where the bedrock is granite. Thin, stony, and strongly acidic soils are also the rule in these areas. The rough terrain produces habitats of widely varying conditions of soil moisture, from the driest of hilltops to swampy or boggy areas often close by. The vegetation in these areas is often equally diverse.

FOREST ECOLOGY

Nearly all of the granite is found east of the Connecticut Valley, most occurring in eastern Massachusetts and southern Rhode Island. In Connecticut, several bodies of granite gneiss, a metamorphic rock whose resistance approaches that of granite, give substance to a number of north-south ridges and groups of hills.

Glaciation

The passage of several huge ice sheets across southern New England left its mark, indirectly or directly, on every square meter of the terrain. The effects of these ice sheets, in turn, have been very important ecological factors in the development of the vegetation. Probably the most important of these has been the disruption of drainage; marshes and ponds are abundant in southern New England but rare in unglaciated parts of the country. Another important effect, one of special concern to naturalists, can be observed in the properties of the soils. The development of soils is a long and complex process, which will be reviewed in a later chapter. In this section we will look at the properties of the glacially derived mantle rock, the raw material from which the soil is made, as well as other less important though notable effects.

TILL

Most of the region is covered by a jumbled grayish or brownish mixture of rock particles of all sizes, from those too small to be seen with the naked eye up to boulders many meters in diameter. These rock particles are angular in shape, usually of the same type of rock as the bedrock in the area, but sometimes of types found from some distance to the north or northwest. This mixture, which geologists call till, was carried along by the moving ice and accumulated more or less in place as the ice melted. In areas underlain by softer kinds of bedrock the till contains a large percentage of clay; in areas where the bedrock is granite it is more sandy and gravelly.

Though subsequent erosion and soil creep (page 75) have thinned out this layer on hilltops and thickened it on lower

9. Drumlin in Groton, Massachusetts. The cows on the hill at the right give an indication of scale.

slopes and valleys, for the most part the till lies where the melting ice has left it. The silt- and clay-sized particles usually found in till give the soils that have developed on these sites a measure of water-holding ability that is very beneficial to the plants that grow there.

DRUMLINS

Southern New England is at or near the southern limits of the ice sheets. In many places where the bedrock was soft and shaley the amount of sticky clay-like debris became so thick that the ice rode up over it and shaped it along into streamlined oval hills called drumlins. Unlike the majority of southern New England hills with their bedrock cores, drumlins are almost always without exposure of ledges, except perhaps at their bases. These hills are relatively low, rarely exceeding 60 meters (200 feet) above the surrounding land. Their shape, like the bowl of an inverted teaspoon, makes them easy to recognize.

OUTWASH

When the ice melted, it released enormous amounts of water. Many valleys contained raging torrents of meltwater and, where the flow of water was impeded, often filled up as lakes and ponds. Where running water worked over the glacial debris, a substantially different type of mantle rock was formed. The running water held the smaller clay- and silt-sized particles in suspension and carried them away, leaving the heavier sand and gravel particles behind. The result was a porous layer of mantle—usually coarser than till—called outwash. With the smaller water-holding particles gone, rainwater sinks through outwash, so the soils derived from this material tend to dry out quickly.

The effects of outwash on the vegetation growing there should be apparent to anyone who has visited areas such as Cape Cod, where this porous mantle occurs. Although some of the same trees and other species growing on outwash do appear in more congenial habitats where the soil is derived from till, their scrubby growth form on the outwash plains bespeaks the shortage of available water. Fire, also largely the result of the dryness of the soils there, is another factor that has shaped the vegetation on these sites. The forest community that grows on outwash is described in Part VI.

In densely populated southern New England, many outwash deposits, especially those near metropolitan areas, are used for gravel. Fresh bankings in these gravel pits exhibit some of the characteristics of a water-washed deposit: layering produced when the stream flowed at different speeds, and rocks that have been rounded as they bounced or rolled along the stream beds.

10. Gravel pit in glacial outwash, Amherst, Massachusetts. The loose gravel pile at the right appears steeper than its 27°.

KETTLEHOLES

Often these outwash plains are pitted with natural depressions called kettleholes. Kettleholes form where large blocks of ice became buried by the outwash gravel and later melted. Where their depth extends below the water table, these kettleholes became ponds. Sometimes they fill in with peat and other organic material to become bogs.

ESKERS

Occasionally you may come upon long sinuous ridges of outwash, often, but not always, running through areas of swampland. These ridges, called eskers, mark the former courses of meltwater streams that flowed through cracks or tunnels in the ice. Once the confining ice walls melted away, the stream found a lower course, leaving its former channel as an elevated ridge of outwash. Often the vegetation on the porous soil of the esker contrasts sharply with that growing on the lower ground on either side.

GLACIAL LAKES

The ground on the floors of extinct glacial lakes is quite different from that of the outwash plains just described. These are places where the finer silt- and clay-sized particles carried by the meltwater came to rest. Often the soils in these lake beds are sticky and poorly drained. Usually also the ground is very flat in these sites.

STOSS AND LEE TOPOGRAPHY

One of the effects of glaciation most easily perceived by the foot traveler is the asymmetric profile of the bedrock hills: smooth and gradual on the north or northwest slopes and steep and rocky on the southern. When the moving ice encountered a bedrock knoll or hill, it ground and smoothed the bedrock as it rode up over it. Moving down the other side, however, it plucked off larger pieces, forming cliffs and steep slopes. Since the direction of glacial movement was from the north or northwest, the steep lee slopes are on the south or southeastern sides of the hill.

As one might expect, these rocky south-facing slopes with their thin soils receive the full effect of the sun's radiation and hence provide a much less congenial habitat for most plants than do the slopes facing other compass points.

A major exception to this stoss and lee pattern occurs in the basalt hills on the Connecticut Valley Lowland, where the slope of the hills has been determined by the tilted structure of the bedrock. The basalt has a tendency to break at right angles to the slope of the bedding, so that the steep side is determined by the tilt of the beds rather than by the glacier.

Slope

Practically all of the land slopes to some degree. Even the beds of the extinct glacial lakes, normally among the flattest of all geological surfaces, slope gently southward.

Most people overestimate the slopes of hills. Perpendicular cliffs, those with a slope of 90 degrees, are rare even in rugged mountainous areas. The cliff-like scarp faces on the Connecticut Valley basalt hills, for example, appear vertical, but in reality are only about 65 degrees.

ANGLE OF REPOSE

A pile of dry mixed sand and gravel, no matter how big the pile, will come to rest with a slope of about 27 degrees. This slope, known to geologists as the angle of repose, provides us with a rough means of determining slope in the field. Piles of talus, the loose rock that accumulates at the base of cliffs, are sometimes a bit steeper, as are, of course, piles of wet or sticky material. Otherwise, the angle of repose for loose dry material is surprisingly constant. The slopes on the edges of outwash plains and other sites where the bedrock exposures are not present, then, are never more than about 27 degrees.

SOIL CREEP

Even where there is no active erosion, the combination of precipitation, frost, and gravity causes soil particles on steep slopes to move gradually downward. This process, called soil creep, is more active in some soils than in others and more active on steeper slopes. Vegetation retards but does not stop it altogether. Evidence of soil creep on slopes may be seen in the curved trunks of the trees. The moving soil has a tendency to tilt trees downhill; the tree responds by attempting to right itself with upward growth. As a result, many trees on steep gravelly slopes have curving trunks with the concave side facing upslope.

Microclimate

IN southern New England, with its hilly terrain and varied cover of vegetation, substantial climatic differences often exist over short distances. This distance may be as large as between the opposite slopes of a hill or as small as between the top and bottom of a plow furrow. In general, microclimate is the climate below 2 meters, the height at which the weather instruments are usually kept. In some cases, however, microclimatic studies extend to the treetop level.

Microclimatic conditions are of vital importance in determining the habitats of plants and animals. They are especially crucial for small organisms such as insects or plants in the juvenile stage such as tree seedlings. These small climatic differences may have a beneficial or detrimental effect on farming and gardening as well.

The Climate at Ground Level

The microclimate on bare ground is so harsh that it is surprising that any small plants can survive there. Bare ground responds quickly to the sun's radiation, heating up rapidly during the day and cooling off equally fast during the night. Moreover, the temperature at the surface of bare ground may be as much as 20 degrees higher than it is a few centimeters above or below. In winter, when there is an absence of snow cover, the heat from the sun will cause the top few centimeters of the ground to thaw and refreeze repeatedly, a condition that is very damaging to small plants

FOREST ECOLOGY

whose roots are close to the surface. Often this frost action will lift small plants right out of the ground.

A covering of low vegetation such as grass alters the ground-level microclimate in several ways. Its shade lowers surface temperature and cuts down on the loss of soil moisture through evaporation. Second, a vegetation layer only a few inches high cuts down surface winds, thus further reducing evaporation from the soil and allowing the water vapor given off by the plants to remain there. As a result of the more equitable temperature and higher humidity, the ground level under a vegetation cover becomes a suitable habitat for many insects and other small invertebrates which could not survive in the harsh microclimate of bare ground.

Temperature Inversions

The plant layer in fields is a mixed blessing, however. By stopping the movement of air at ground levels, the vegetation produces local temperature inversions, which in the cold climate of New England may mean early frosts.

Temperature inversions produce all manner of vexing problems for living things. Under normal daytime conditions, the sun's radiation heats the ground much more than it heats the atmosphere. As a result, air temperatures near the ground are highest, gradually becoming lower at increasing height. The warm surface air, being less dense, rises, keeping the atmosphere in a mixed-up state. In certain places and under certain atmospheric conditions, however, a layer of warmer air aloft traps the colder air at the surface, creating the condition known as a temperature inversion. A large-scale inversion occurs when a warm front approaches. The advancing warm air mass slides up and over the cooler air, resulting in higher air temperatures at some distance above the surface of the ground.

As was mentioned in Part II, warm fronts in winter can cause ice storms, but the greatest hazard of large-scale temperature inversions in these modern times is air pollution. Under normal conditions the rising surface-air layer carries the pollutants to high levels in the atmosphere where they dissipate. When an inversion occurs, the air mass at lower levels, being colder and hence more dense, cannot rise into the warmer air above and the pollutants accumulate near the ground. Ordinarily, a brisk prevailing wind keeps the air at different levels sufficiently mixed up to prevent inversion and the resultant air pollution.

Sound carries much farther during temperature inversions. Many people attribute the fact that distant sounds are much louder on damp still days to the increased humidity in the air, but more likely it is caused by the stratification and the lack of turbulence in the air. Damp still conditions often occur when a warm front with its usual temperature inversion is approaching. Under these conditions it is possible to hear distant sounds, such as those from traffic on a highway or a train whistle, many miles farther away than one would under normal conditions when the atmosphere is more turbulent. Sounds also carry better at night, when the atmosphere is normally less turbulent and temperature inversions stronger than during the day.

Localized temperature inversions commonly occur in valleys, hollows, and sheltered spots. They are most frequent in late summer and early fall when the days are still warm but the nights are cool. On clear still evenings, cool air accumulates near the ground and flows downhill into hollows and valleys. Because there is no wind, the warm air above and the cool air below do not mix; the two air masses usually stay sharply separated. Many people have noticed this sudden temperature change when they walk or drive into a hollow. On clear evenings, smoke from a campfire burning in an area with a local temperature inversion will accumulate in a thin cloud-like layer between the two air masses. When the air is humid, dense valley fog will form at night in the cool air layer near the ground.

As fall approaches, the low air temperatures in valleys and hollows may cause frost to occur as much as several weeks before it occurs on slopes where the air is moving. It is very common in early fall to see the vegetation in such frost hollows shriveled and white with rime while nearby it remains untouched. In winter, also, the coldest temperatures occur in hollows. In central Massachusetts winter temperatures may be as much as 20 degrees colder in frost hollows than on open sloping ground. Where there is a snow cover these temperatures may be lower still.

The problems of frost pockets have important implications for agriculture. Apple orchards are almost always planted on sloping ground so that the movement of cool air along the surface of the ground will make damaging frosts less likely. Cranberry bogs, being situated in hollows, are particularly susceptible to severe frosts. Frost protection was formerly accomplished by flooding the bogs and keeping them free from grass and weeds. Now growers use large sprinklers which provide a more efficient means of protection from frost. When water freezes it gives up heat. Though the water from the sprinkler may coat the outside of the plants and the berries with ice, the berries themselves stay unfrozen and marketable. Gardeners can use the same technique on their vegetable gardens to forestall damage from occasional early frost. Keeping the weeds down both in and around the garden to improve air circulation will also lessen the danger of scattered frost.

Woodland Microclimates

Trees have a significant effect upon the microclimate beneath them. The extent of their effect depends on several factors, including the height of the stand, the thickness of the canopy, and the type of tree—whether it is deciduous or coniferous. In very thin stands the microclimate approaches that of open ground.

A deciduous woodland, the type most common in southern New England, modifies the climate beneath the canopy in several ways. The shade cast by the trees, together with the mulch of dead leaves on the ground, keeps the soil cool and retards the evaporation of moisture. In summer and to a lesser extent in winter the trees slow down the force of the wind. Calm conditions, along with moisture given off by the transpiration of the trees, increase the humidity in a woodland, though the open space beneath the canopy usually permits air drainage to occur. The insulating properties of the leaf mulch on the forest floor keeps the frost from penetrating as deeply into the ground as in open spaces and prevents the alternating freeze and thaw that often occurs in the open.

The microclimate in a coniferous woodland is somewhat different. Conifers will cut down the wind to a greater degree than deciduous trees; a half-grown stand of pines, hemlock, and spruce, for example, seems almost airless in summer. A thick stand of conifers, especially when half grown, casts such dense shade that often nothing will grow beneath them, though as the stand matures, natural thinning will gradually let in more light until some undergrowth appears.

As deciduous woodlands mature, the opposite conditions occur. The canopy gradually thickens and the light reaching the ground diminishes. The deepening shade gradually eliminates all but a relatively few shrubs and herbaceous plants whose light requirements may be met in deep shade. This increasing shade also restricts the reproduction of tree species to only those with a high degree of shade tolerance. The other growing conditions in a mature woodland, such as high humidity, equitable temperature, a thick mulch, and high humus content in the soil, are of course favorable for these shade-tolerant species. Early writers describing the then remaining tracts of old-growth forests in southern New England remarked on the luxuriant understory growth of ferns, mosses, and shade-tolerant species of flowering plants growing there. The variety of plants was small but the number of individuals was large.

Frozen Ground

As the air temperature drops below freezing, the ground freezes from the surface downward. As the freeze continues, additional ground water, which normally travels upward by capillary action, freezes onto the bottom of the already frozen layer, thereby thickening it.

Once the ground is solidly frozen, plants can absorb very little water through their roots. Deciduous species become dormant during the winter, their life processes becoming reduced almost to zero. Evergreens, on the other hand, still continue to transpire some water through their leaves; for these a deeply frozen ground layer can be damaging.

In areas of exposed wet soil, when the air temperature is below freezing but the ground temperature is not, it is often possible to see an interesting phenomenon: the formation of ice needles. These crystals grow up out of the ground, lifting leaves, stones, and small plants. On rare occasions they may grow to a height of several inches, showing a series of daily growth increments. Ice needles are often found on the edge of swamps or in the bottom of gravel pits where the water table is close to the ground level.

As is the case with many other naturally occurring phenomena, a deep frost is not totally without benefit to plant life. Deeply frozen ground will kill the larvae of many destructive insect species which spend the winter in the ground below a normal frost level. Frozen ground also prevents moles and small rodents from digging tunnels just beneath the surface. Moles themselves are somewhat beneficial since they eat insects, but mice which often occupy mole runs will feed on the roots of many herbaceous plants and young shrubs.

MUD TIME

When the frost is deep in the ground, a thaw in the surface layer leaves the soil very muddy—sometimes of almost a soupy consistency—because the frozen layer below prevents the water from sinking into the ground. These are the conditions that produce "mud time" in early spring. In areas where the frost has penetrated deeply into the ground, a deep thaw produces seemingly bottomless pits. Shoulders along the sides of dirt roads are hazardous during this time. A car venturing off the relatively better drained crown of the road can sink in mud up to its axles. People who must drive extensively on dirt roads during this time are wise to carry a cable winch to extricate their cars from the mud holes should they happen into one.

Since the water cannot penetrate into the ground beyond the frozen layer, it stays on the surface and gradually evaporates. Thus, repeated freezing and thawing tends to dry out the surface layer of the ground. During mud time this surface evaporation often leaves a deceptive layer of dry soil on top of the mud.

Snow Phenomena

Snow is a mixed blessing for plants. For small plants that spend the coldest parts of the winter buried in snow, the effect is almost entirely beneficial. Snow is excellent insulation; like other insulation, it is mostly air. A rough measure of snow density is the fact that about a foot of snow contains an inch of water; the rest is air.

Just a 5-centimeter thickness of snow is enough protection to keep the temperature inside the snow near freezing no matter how cold the air temperature above becomes. In addition, the snow protects plants from the bright sun and drying winter wind while maintaining a moist environment around them. There seem to be no cases where the snow layer becomes so deep as to smother plants, although a deep snow cover, especially if it is heavy and wet, can damage them by breaking off branches.

A cover of snow also prevents the ground from freezing deeply, thus allowing plants such as conifers and broad-leafed evergreens, which do not become dormant in the winter, to continue to draw moisture out of the soil. It further protects the plants by preventing alternate freezing and thawing. The ground under a blanket of snow gradually thaws from the earth's heat conducted upward from below. As a result, the frost is sometimes out of the ground as soon as the last of the winter snow has melted, especially if the snow cover has been constant.

For the parts of plants that protrude from the snow cover, however, climatic conditions are severe. Areas with a snow cover are almost always colder than those with bare ground because 95 percent of the sun's radiation is reflected back into space rather than warming the ground. The direct radiation from the sun plus the reflected radiation from the snow combines to give the plant a double dose of light and heat that is often as high as in summer.

This combination of direct and reflected radiation is especially strong in late winter and early spring when the sun reaches the same position in the sky as it does in September. It is during this time of year when the sun is intense and the ground is still frozen that many plants suffer winter injury, splitting bark, and, in the case of broad-leaved evergreens, the browning and drying-out of leaves. Skiers have often learned from a painful sunburn just how strong the combination of sunlight and reflection can be at this time. Other evidence of the sun's strong radiation may be observed within a few days after a snowstorm by the appearance of melt holes around every tree trunk, stem, or twig that projects from the surface of the snow, a result of heat radiating from them.

The melting process often seems to go against commonsense assumptions. The snow cover decreases, for instance, even when the temperature remains below freezing. By a process known as sublimation, the ice in snow crystals changes directly to water vapor without passing through the liquid state. Another assault on conventional wisdom is the fact that snow will melt faster on damp days than on dry days. When water vapor condenses it releases heat. The heat released by this water vapor condensing on the cold snow in turn causes the snow to melt.

Once large open spaces appear in the snow cover, melting proceeds very rapidly, since the darker, denser ground can once more absorb the sun's radiation. Though the ground still might be frozen under the snow, once it is bare the warm spring sun very quickly thaws out what little frost remains, making it possible for some wildflowers and early spring bulbs to sprout and bloom even before the snow has entirely disappeared.

SNOW AND HEAT

When snow falls on ground that is still unfrozen, as is often the case in late fall or early spring, it is possible to see a clear demonstration of the relative conductivity and insulating power of the various surfaces upon which it lands. The snow may remain on gravel roads, lawns, and on top of the forest leaf layer. Grassy or weedy fields, containing the thickest insulating layer of dead air, are most likely to be covered by snow. But usually it melts from macadam roads, sidewalks, and rocks immediately. This melting process may eventually draw enough heat from the conducting substances on which the snow has fallen to cause their temperatures to drop below freezing. At that point the wet pavements begin to freeze, and the snow that subsequently falls will remain.

Slope and Exposure

In hilly country, slope and exposure have an important effect on modifying the climate. Many people who have explored the southern New England woodlands have noticed a dramatic difference in vegetation between the north and south slopes on many of the hills. This difference in vegetation is usually the result of differences in the amount of solar radiation received by the slopes facing different directions. The differing amounts of solar radiation in turn determine in large part the effectiveness of the precipitation falling on them.

To understand the relationship between the sun's radiation and slope and exposure it is necessary to examine the changing motion of the sun from season to season. At the winter solstice about December 21, the sun rises in the southeast and sets in the southwest. At noon on that date, at the highest point of its arc, the sun is only about 25 degrees above the horizon. Northern sides of trees, buildings, and hills are totally in shadow during this period, receiving no direct solar radiation at all. Moreover, the shadows cast by such obstructions are longer; a large area behind each is in shadow for the entire day. Eastern and western exposures receive but a few hours of morning and afternoon sun while southern exposures receive direct sunlight all during the day.

Much of the strength of the sun's radiation depends on its angle to the surface of the earth. When its position is low in the sky, as it is at sunrise or sunset, or during the late fall and winter, its rays strike the surface of the earth at a low angle and it is therefore much less concentrated. At low angles, also, the sun's radiation must pass through a thicker segment of the earth's atmosphere, where dust, clouds, and various gases absorb a part of it. Another reason why it is colder in winter is, of course, that the days are shorter; the sun is in the sky for a smaller number of hours each day.

In winter, when the sun is low in the sky, a south-facing slope receiving the greatest possible amount of radiation would have to be almost a sheer cliff, about a 65-degree slope. At the same time only a very gentle north-facing slope would receive any direct solar radiation at all, and then but for a short time near the middle of the day.

At the summer solstice, about June 21, when the sun reaches its highest point in the sky, the situation is changed in several ways. The sun now rises and sets close to the northeast and northwest respectively; northern exposures such as the north-facing wall of a building or cliff receive direct sunlight in morning and afternoon. Gentle and moderate north-facing slopes receive some direct sunlight all day. Because the sun is in the sky for a longer time, both east and west slopes receive more sunlight than when the day length is shorter. Southern slopes still receive the most radiation, but now the angle of slope where radiation is most concentrated is about 25 degrees, still steep but one which will support trees and other vegetation.

The following chart summarizes this relationship between solar radiation and slope. The percentages are relative, based on 100 percent for a 20-degree south slope at noon on the summer solstice.

Relative Amount of Direct Solar Radiation Received by a 20° Slope Facing Different Directions

Slope Direction	Summer Solstice, June 21, Noon		Winter Solstice, December 21, Noon	
South	100%	As slope approaches 0°, solar radiation approaches 85%	36%	As slope steepens, solar radiation increases
North	75%	As slope steepens, solar radiation lessens	0%	As slope approaches 0°, solar radiation approaches 18%
East	85%	Radiation is strongest about noon, but slope receives some sun almost the entire day	18%	Slope receives radiation only until 2 P.M.
West	85%	Radiation is strongest in the afternoon	18%	Slope receives radiation only after 10 A.M.
Flat Ground	85%		18%	

In addition to solar radiation, two other factors affect the slope microclimate in southern New England. The southwestern slopes tend to be hotter and drier during the summer because of the stronger heating effect of the afternoon sun and because of the prevailing warm wind which blows from the southwest. Northwestern slopes are coldest in winter because they are exposed to the full force of the cold prevailing winds of winter that blow in that direction.

The relationship of slope and exposure may be clearly perceived in the pattern that the snow patches make in early spring. The locations of these snow patches are very consistent from year to year and provide a good relative measure of the amount of solar radiation received by different areas. Steep, south-facing slopes, such as those along the road cuts, lose their snow cover first, while steep north-facing grades remain snow-covered longer. For this reason, ski slopes are nearly always built facing north. East and west slopes keep their snow covers longer than the southern slopes. The difference in melting rates due to the relatively warmer afternoon sun between the east and west slopes is usually too small to see.

When considering the effects of solar radiation on the ground and organisms living there, remember that direct sunlight accounts for less than half of the total energy received from the sun. "Skyshine," the diffuse radiation from other parts of the sky, can satisfy the light requirements of many plant species even though they never receive direct sunlight. To benefit fully from this diffuse solar radiation, however, plants require large unobstructed openings to the sky.

Precipitation Effectiveness

The most important single determining factor in the distribution of vegetation in southern New England is the amount of soil moisture that is available to the plants. The mean annual precipitation varies from about 100 centimeters (39 inches) in New Bedford to about 117 centimeters (46 inches) in the hilly sections of Connecticut. This degree of difference is of but limited significance, since the amount of yearly variation from these averages is often greater than the difference between them. Yet there are places in the region, notably on Nantucket Island and the sand plains of North Haven, Connecticut, where soil conditions are so dry that trees have a difficult time becoming established. (The almost constant wind is also an important factor on Nantucket.) It would appear, then, that it is not the amount of rain that falls in a given area that affects the vegetation so much as the percentage that remains available to the plants.

The effectiveness of the precipitation depends on several factors. In the two examples just cited the dryness depends largely upon the porosity of the soils, but in other parts of the region where the water-holding ability of the soil is greater, the effect of solar radiation on the various slopes and exposures of the land becomes an important factor in determining how much moisture is available to a particular habitat.

Direct sunlight has a tendency to dry out soil. Like oil in a lamp wick, soil moisture is drawn upward by capillary action. The sun's heat at the surface quickly evaporates any moisture that reaches it, making the soil progressively drier. Where the radiation is strongest and of longest duration, then, the soil becomes driest. Where a drying wind combines with the hot sun, as for example on southwestern slopes in summer, the soil loses a still larger percentage of its moisture.

Solar radiation and porosity of the soil, however, can only partially explain the differences in precipitation effectiveness in southern New England. The glaciated topography is a third factor. The southern slopes are drier, not only because of the factors just outlined, but because the soil layer is thinner there. As was mentioned in the previous chapter, the plucking action of the glacial ice on the southern sides of the hills steepened them, hence made them more susceptible to soil creep and erosion. A thin soil layer that remains above the impervious bedrock provides a much smaller reservoir of soil moisture than does a thick layer. On steep slopes, too, more of the precipitation is lost as runoff than on gentle slopes.

Hilltops are often very dry as well. During the waning of the ice age, torrents of meltwater no doubt washed much of the accumulation of glacial debris from the hilltops, leaving a relatively thin layer of mantle to absorb and store the falling rain. A glance at the chart on page 85 shows also that the gently sloping tops of hills, like flat ground, receive up to 85 percent as much solar radiation as do steep south-facing slopes.

The proximity of the ground water table to the surface of the ground is another important factor in determining how much water is available to vegetation in an area. Normally the water table is not flat but is a subdued replica of the surface topography. Although it is higher under hilltops, it is relatively further below the surface there than on lower slopes and valley floors. When the water table reaches the surface it forms springs and merges with swamps, lakes, and streams.

Each species of tree, shrub, and herbaceous plant has a certain range of tolerance to conditions of soil moisture. The greatest variety of vegetation is found where there is an ample year-round supply of soil moisture, but where the soil is not saturated for long periods of time. The number of species that can survive at either end of the soil moisture continuum, in either very dry or very wet habitats, is smaller. Of the two extremes, however, wetlands have by far the greater variety of plant life.

In wet periods the water table rises; during drought it gradually subsides and flattens out. Habitats such as flood plains, where the water table fluctuates from near the surface in the spring to some depth later in the year, also support a characteristic community of plant species.

Soils

NEW ENGLAND SOILS clearly reflect their glacial origins. In an earlier chapter we saw that the loose mantle rock— from which the soil has developed—was the result of the grinding and abrading action of the ice as it moved across the bedrock. About 10,000 to 15,000 years ago, when the ice sheet finally stagnated and melted away, it left behind, in most places, a jumbled mixture of rock particles of all sizes.

Unlike the mantle rock in many unglaciated regions, this glacial debris was largely fresh unweathered rock. Over a period of time—a much longer time than has passed since the last ice age—the action of weather and vegetation will gradually decompose some of the minerals in this loose rock, eventually producing a soil of a substantially different composition from its parent rock. But New England soils at present are still fully charged with the minerals that they inherited from bedrock and thus reflect most of the chemical properties of this parent material.

Enough time has passed, however, for a layer of topsoil to develop. In well-drained, undisturbed sites, the topsoil layer averages between 6 and 20 centimeters (2½ to 8 inches), a depth that would make the soil suitable for agriculture if it were not for the boulders and other large-sized rocks that are usually scattered through it. Where cultivation is possible, the topsoil layer has been mixed with the upper 10 centimeters of subsoil, thus giving the appearance of a thicker topsoil layer than actually exists.

Soil Texture

Soil is generally thought of as a mixture of particles of three different sizes: sand, silt, and clay. In New England, however, we cannot overlook the particles larger than sand size, such as pebbles, stones, and cobbles. Although these larger particles do not contribute very much to the physical and chemical properties of the soil, they do play a crucial role in determining whether or not the soil is fit for agriculture, no matter how suitable it is otherwise.

When sand, silt, and clay are present in about equal amounts, the soil is known as loam. Usually, one or another predominates and the soil is then further classified as sandy loam, silt loam, or clay loam.

The preponderance of one or another of these different-sized particles determines in large part the water-holding ability of these soils; this property in turn has a strong effect in determining the particular plant species that will grow there. The richest variety of vegetation is found in soils that are neither too wet nor too dry. Loams are generally the best in this regard; the sand particles provide some drainage, thus preventing the soils from becoming waterlogged and airless; the silt and clay particles at the same time retain some moisture for the plants.

Soils that are predominantly sandy and gravelly, such as those found on outwash plains, are usually so porous and loose that rainwater sinks right on through them beyond the root zones of the plants growing there, and thus they dry out quickly. Soils that are predominantly silt and clay, such as those found on drumlins and in some lake beds, present the opposite problem; rains make these soils sticky and waterlogged. Moreover, the water stays near the surface rather than penetrating deeply. This surface water soon evaporates, leaving the soil compacted and cement-like. Enough time has passed, though, so that many of these finer-textured soils have developed sufficiently to permit some drainage through the upper layers; however, the compact and largely impervious lower layers may still retard drainage.

The depth of the water table also affects the amount of moisture available to the soils. Again, it is the midrange, where the water table is neither too deep nor too close to the surface, that provides the optimum conditions for the greatest number of plant species. Where the water table is close enough to the surface for moisture to be drawn upward to the root zone of the trees and other vegetation, yet deep enough not to drown the roots, even sandy soil can support a rich and varied forest flora. There is a splendid example of such a forest growing on sandy soil on an island in a pond near Plymouth, Massachusetts. The site receives a constant supply of moisture from the pond, and its insular location has afforded it complete protection from the forest fires that have continually laid waste the surrounding area. As a result, this island has become a rich forest oasis in the midst of the more typical pine barren vegetation of Cape Cod and vicinity (see page 239).

Even in sandy soils, however, too much water is as much a limiting factor as too little. Waterlogged sand or gravel tends to become boggy; it supports a small but distinctive group of plants adapted to living in such an environment (see page 299). Under these conditions, there is relatively little oxygen available to decay microorganisms, and gradually a thick layer of peat accumulates.

Humus

Humus, the dark-colored organic component of soil, plays a vital role in its formation and improvement. It increases both the water-holding capacity of sandy and gravelly soils and the permeability of silty and clayey soils. It also increases the heat-absorbing capacity of the soil, which in turn speeds up the chemical processes that turn the sterile parent material into soil. Lastly, it supplies most of the nutrients to the living vegetation.

Decaying plants and animals are the source of humus. Through a complex process, the action of water, air, and plant enzymes begins the decomposition of this organic debris. Earthworms and other soil animals aid in the process, but the most important agents in reducing organic matter to humus are the soil bacteria and fungi. The numbers of these tiny organisms in the soil are almost beyond belief; a single gram of rich forest soil may contain upward of ten million. Moreover, there seems to be a direct relationship between the degree of soil fertility and the numbers of bacteria and fungi that exist there.

How quickly the fresh organic matter is returned to humus also depends to a certain degree on its composition. Grasses decompose more rapidly than tree leaves. Herbaceous material decomposes more quickly than woody material. Leaves from hardwoods decompose more quickly than conifer needles. Oak leaves decay much more slowly than those of most other deciduous trees.

SOIL NUTRIENTS IN LEAF LITTER

The leaf litter of all species probably enriches the topsoil to a greater or lesser degree, but some deciduous trees play a more important role in building soil fertility than others. The chart below lists five important plant nutrients and the native tree species that supply each most abundantly.

Several interesting observations may be drawn from the soil nutrient chart. Basswood, tulip tree, hickory, and pin cherry are all important soil-improving trees. Basswood is especially valuable in this regard, ranking high in calcium, magnesium, and nitrogen, sixth in phosphorus, and ninth in potassium. Oaks, which include the most common species in

Relative Abundance of Soil Nutrients in Leaf Litter
of Southern New England Trees (by rank)

Calcium
Basswood
Bitternut hickory
Tulip tree
Pin cherry
Quaking aspen
Shagbark hickory
Sugar maple

Magnesium
Basswood
Bitternut hickory
Tulip tree
Pin cherry
Red maple

Potassium
Shagbark hickory
Tulip tree
Sugar maple
Black birch
Beech
Red oak

Phosphorus
Pin cherry
Black birch
Shagbark hickory
White ash
White oak
Basswood

Nitrogen
Hemlock
Basswood
Shagbark hickory
Quaking aspen
Black birch
White pine

southern New England, are not high on any of the lists, red oak ranking only sixth in potassium and white oak ranking fifth in phosphorus.

Another significant point is that conifers are absent from all categories except nitrogen. Analyses of soils under conifer stands show relatively low percentages of all major nutrients except nitrogen.

Soil Acidity

Acidity is another complex property of soil, which, like the development of humus and nutrient content, is of great ecological importance. The climate and forest vegetation of regions like New England tend to produce acidic soils. Soils in drier parts of the world, those of grasslands and deserts, usually exhibit the opposite property, that of alkalinity, to some degree.

Acidity or alkalinity of all substances, soils included, is measured on a scale designated by the letters pH. Neutral substances such as distilled water have been assigned a pH value of 7. Substances with a pH value below 7 are acidic; the lower the number, the greater degree of acidity. Likewise, a pH value greater than 7 indicates increasing alkalinity. An explanation of the scientific basis of the pH system can be found in any elementary chemistry text; what concerns us here is the pH value of soils from an ecological standpoint.

Each whole number decrease or increase from the neutral value of 7 represents a tenfold increase in degree of acidity or alkalinity respectively. Thus a soil with a pH of 5, for example, is 10 times more acidic than a soil with a pH of 6, or 100 times more acidic than one with a neutral pH of 7.

In recently glaciated regions, the pH of the soil, like other properties, often still reflects the pH of the parent rock. Soils in marble areas usually, but not always, tend toward a neutral pH. Slightly alkaline soils up to a pH value of 8.5 may occur in contact with the marble or in cavities or crevices in the rock. The igneous rocks of southern New England, on the other hand, tend to decompose into acidic soils. The pH of soils derived from sedimentary or metamorphic rocks varies: rocks such as sandstone, formed out of eroded particles of granite, reflect the acidity of the granite; those from ancient sea sediments often contain some lime, and therefore are less acidic.

A humid climate is favorable both for the growth of forests and the development of acidic soils. It is not surprising, therefore, that most present-day tree species, over millions of years, have evolved to tolerate a wide range of soil acidity. The seedlings of most trees grow best in soils with a pH range from about 4.5 to 6, though healthy forest stands are found on soils with pH values both somewhat above and somewhat below this range.

Below a pH value of 4, however, there is a major change in the microflora of the soil. Many of the humus-making bacteria and fungi cannot survive in such an acidic environment; at this point the decomposition of organic matter into humus becomes much slower and accumulations of organic soils such as peat and muck begin to occur.

The tree species that add a large amount of calcium and magnesium to the soil tend to render it less acidic. Where these trees grow in quantity, the pH value of soils beneath them is generally higher than in areas nearby where oaks and conifers predominate. Though oak leaves and conifer needles do contain some calcium and magnesium, they also contain various organic acids that make the leaf litter more acidic.

One conifer that is common in old fields in southern New England, eastern red cedar, *Juniperus virginiana,* usually contains more calcium in its needles than the leaves of many hardwoods. Eastern red cedar seems to grow more luxuriantly in marble areas, though investigations have shown it to be not particularly tolerant of alkaline soils.

Shrubs and herbaceous plants are more exacting in their soil acidity requirements than trees. Many will survive in soils of a fairly wide pH range but only flourish and multiply within a more narrow range. The following chart lists some southern New England woodland plants and the approximate pH of soils in which they are commonly found. Exceptions are bound to occur, but when one or more species are found growing in large quantity or where several are found in the same general area, it is safe to make some informed estimates about the soil pH.

Organic Soils

Organic soils such as peat and muck are the result of incomplete decomposition of the plant layer. These soils are usually formed in a waterlogged environment where there is little available oxygen to aid decomposition. Because decomposition is very slow under these conditions, it is not surprising to find thick-layered deposits of these materials when the environment for their formation is suitable.

Peat is almost totally composed of plant material, usually sedges, some woody plant material, and sphagnum moss. Muck is usually a mixture of both organic and inorganic material; often the organic component has undergone a greater degree of decomposition than in peat. Muck is common in marshes; peat is found in bogs.

Organic soils, especially peat, are very low in nutrients. Plants adapted to living in these soils, therefore, have relatively low nutrient requirements. Most are small and shallow-rooted and, as a result, cannot draw up whatever nutrients are available in the subsoil below. Because the

Soil pH Indicator Plants of Southern New England

The presence of one or more of these species in quantity is an indication of soils with a pH range as shown.

pH 4–4.5	pH 5–6	pH 6–8
Mountain laurel, *Kalmia latifolia*[1]	Witch hazel, *Hamamelis virginiana*	Dutchman's breeches, *Dicentra Cucullaria*[3]
Azaleas, *Rhododendron* spp.[1]	Spicebush, *Lindera Benzoin*	Herb Robert, *Geranium Robertianum*[3]
Blueberries, *Vaccinium* spp.[1]	Wild aster, *Aster* spp.	Bloodroot, *Sanguinaria canadensis*[3]
Trailing arbutus, *Epigaea repens*[1]	Marsh marigold, *Caltha palustris*	Columbine, *Aquilegia canadensis*
Wintergreen, *Gaultheria procumbens*[1]	Wild geranium, *Geranium maculatum*	Sharp-lobed hepatica, *Hepatica acutiloba*[3]
Pink lady's slipper, *Cypripedium acaule*	Blunt-lobed hepatica, *Hepatica americana*	Maidenhair fern, *Adiantum pedatum*[3]
Wood lily, *Lilium philadelphicum*	Fringed polygala, *Polygala paucifolia*	Walking fern, *Camptosorus rhizophyllus*[4]
Canada mayflower, *Maianthemum canadense*	Dogtooth violet, *Erythronium americanum*[2]	Spleenwort, *Asplenium* spp.[3,4]
Partridgeberry, *Mitchella repens*	Red trillium, *Trillium erectum*[3]	Purple cliffbrake, *Pellaea atropurpurea*[2,4]
Indian cucumber-root, *Medeola virginiana*	Interrupted fern, *Osmunda Claytoniana*	Christmas fern, *Polystichum acrostichoides*[3,5]
Climbing fern, *Lygodium palmatum*[2]	Baneberry, *Actaea* spp.	

[1] Members of the heath family (Ericaceae). No native members of this family can tolerate lime. They will grow in the marble areas only on top of a thick layer of acidic humus.

[2] Rare.

[3] Common spring flowers and ferns in the mixed mesophytic community (page 190).

[4] Walking fern, cliffbrake, and spleenworts (except ebony spleenwort) are small ferns that are nearly always found growing only on limestone or marble outcrops. Ebony spleenwort can tolerate a somewhat more acidic soil but is also common in the vicinity of limestone or marble outcrops.

[5] Christmas fern has a fairly wide tolerance of soil pH, but when found growing in great quantities usually indicates a soil that is only slightly acid.

organic remains of these plants are themselves low in nutrients, and because they do not readily decompose to the point where they release what nutrients they do contain, the percentage of nutrients in organic soils is likely to remain low. There is also very little water circulation in these deposits; most of the surface water is nutrient-free rainwater. Thus the environment is impoverished even more.

The type of decay that occurs under the airless, water-logged conditions of bogs often produces an intensely acidic soil with pH readings of 3 (10,000 times more acidic than neutral soils). Such a highly acidic environment poses a serious physiological problem to any plants not adapted to living in bogs.

A Typical Soil Profile

Although there is a large variation in the soils of the region, a hole dug in the ground where the soil has not been disturbed by cultivation, repeatedly impoverished by fire, or waterlogged by poor drainage will reveal a profile of the layers that is fairly similar across much, though not all, of the region.

Typically, such a profile will show about 6 to 20 centimeters (2½ to 8 inches) of topsoil under 6 to 8 centimeters of decomposing leaf litter. The topsoil layer may vary in color, though it is normally darkened by particles of humus carried downward from the forest floor above by rainwater. The addition of this humus has improved drainage and given the topsoil a crumbly rather than a sticky consistency.

The topsoil layer gradually grades downward into subsoil. In southern New England, the subsoil is usually a yellowish or yellowish-brown or reddish-brown color, and not as dark as the topsoil layer above. The oxidation by air and water of some of the iron minerals in the rock particles is responsible for these colors. Pebbles and stones at this depth usually show little evidence of weathering beyond discoloration of their surfaces. Below the subsoil layer is the unaltered mantle rock.

This profile is distinct from those one might observe in many other parts of the country. It is even somewhat different from those across much of northern New England, where lower temperatures prevail.

Soils, Agriculture, and Open Space

Southern New England is now about 75 percent woodland. Most of the soils are too sandy, stony, thin, or wet for

FOREST ECOLOGY

cultivation. In fact, probably less than 15 percent of the area now in woodland is potential cropland.

Except for fairly large areas in the Connecticut Valley and some relatively smaller areas in southeastern New Hampshire and elsewhere, good agricultural soils are found in isolated patches of only a few acres. Soil maps of most of southern New England resemble intricately sewn patchwork quilts, showing soils often of widely differing properties existing in close proximity. Such a condition makes modern farming almost impossible.

Fields and open pasture provide a welcome relief to the almost omnipresent woodland that covers New England. More important, open ground and woodland borders provide a rich ecological diversity. Many species of trees, shrubs, and herbaceous plants which languish in the deep shade of woods will thrive in the sunny environment along these woodland borders, and many of these plants provide food and cover for a number of birds and other animals.

As New England agriculture continues to decline, it is regrettable indeed that the ecological and scenic diversity declines with it. Yet suitable soils are a necessity for agriculture; where these do not exist, neither will farms and open spaces.

A Primer on Forest Regeneration

FOR SOME TIME following a major disturbance such as clearing for agriculture, lumbering, fire, or hurricane, the character of the recovering woodland will be quite different from that prior to the disturbance. Gradually, through a series of slow vegetational changes, and barring further disturbances or significant changes in the climate, the woodland will return to its former appearance.

In actual fact, forest regeneration is one of the most complex, least understood processes in ecology. The route taken will depend on the severity and type of disturbance, the climate, the type of former vegetation on the site, the frequency and severity of subsequent forest disturbances, and a host of other factors. These regenerational patterns following the various kinds of disturbance will be discussed in the following chapter and in Part V.

The result of a disturbance to the forest—which may range from the death of a single dominant tree to the destruction of a large forest tract—will be a gap or opening in the forest canopy. Whatever its size, the gap will change the environmental conditions below the canopy layer. The most obvious of these, and probably the most important in the subsequent process, is an increase in light. Other factors, such as changes in the amounts of moisture and available soil nutrients, also may play a role.

The opening created by a small disturbance such as the death of a single tree is often quickly closed by the growth of the surrounding trees, or it may be filled by the release of a smaller tree that was struggling to stay alive in the shady understory. Larger openings, especially in the hardwood forests of southern New England, are often closed by vigorous sprouts that grow out of the still-living stumps of the former trees, but this process takes much longer. If windthrow has exposed patches of bare ground, seeds of black birch and other small-seeded species may germinate and grow.

After severe disturbances, such as clearing for agriculture or a serious fire, the return to a mature woodland takes longer still. Under these circumstances an assemblage of trees that may be entirely different from that of the original forest appears on the site. These early trees, aptly called pioneer species, are generally small, short-lived, and sun-loving; they quickly cover the open land. The seeds of these species have either been carried to the site by the wind or animals or lain dormant in the undisturbed forest soil for many years.

Pioneer trees usually alter the environment so that they cannot reproduce themselves in the shade they have created. Other slower-growing species, which may have started with the pioneers or after them, gradually overtop the pioneer trees and shade them out. This second wave of trees, themselves possessing intermediate tolerance to shade and root competition, usually remain on the site for many years after the pioneers are gone. Subsequent minor disturbances may make it possible for these trees to live on a site for many decades before the increasingly shady condi-

FOREST ECOLOGY

tions in the understory make their reproduction and seedling growth difficult.

If the trees in a particular stand are all about the same age, we can safely assume that the land was subject to some major disturbance, usually a serious fire or clearing for agriculture. Other disturbances such as hurricane and cutting usually remove only a portion of the trees.

Unfortunately, however, whether or not the trees in a particular stand are all the same age cannot be determined by observation alone. Forest studies have shown that tree size and age do not necessarily correlate, especially after thirty years. Up to thirty years, the various hardwood trees that replace the short-lived pioneer species grow at about the same rate and hence remain the same size. After thirty years, however, the red oaks begin to outstrip the other species and by the end of sixty years are one-quarter to one-third taller with much larger trunk diameters. Though all of the trees on such a site are about the same age, a casual examination would erroneously suggest that the red oaks had been growing there for many years longer.

The only way to tell for certain whether the trees in a particular stand are all of about the same age is to sample them with an increment borer. Foresters use this drill-like tool to extract a small core of wood from the tree trunks; from this they can count the rings and thereby determine the age of the tree.

In the past, forest ecologists have theorized that if a long enough time passes without major disturbance, a third group of trees adapted to seedling germination and growth under the shadiest of conditions gradually replaces the second generation of tree species as they succumb to old age or damage. From this time onward, each subsequent generation of trees will be essentially of this same group of species: only those which are able to grow and reproduce in deep shade.

The concept of a stable, unchanging forest as an end point in forest succession is unsatisfactory on several counts. No doubt some forest tracts will reach a point where the canopy trees are replaced only by others of the same species. And some forest tracts may indeed appear to remain that way for a long time. Recent data suggest, however, that most woodlands—even those that survived the widespread cutting, burning, and clearing of the last few centuries—are in a state of slow but constant flux. Small but continuous disturbances such as windstorms keep areas even in mature woodlands open enough to permit the less shade-tolerant trees to remain in the population. Moreover, even if disturbances do not occur, small but significant climate changes that undoubtedly will continue to take place are reflected in the gradual change of the forest.

One reason why forest regeneration is so little understood is that it takes so long to observe it. No single person could live long enough to see more than part of the process; several generations of forest investigators each would be required to make careful measurements on the composition and growth of species on selected forest tracts before any long-term trends could be detected with certainty. And in the meantime, inevitable disturbances would still affect the outcome of such long-term investigations.

Moreover, it is notoriously hard to generalize from one forest tract to another on the basis of the relatively small amount of data already available. Either because of chance or because of small differences in the ecological factors that affect a particular habitat, forest regeneration proceeds not only at different rates but even in different directions. In time—probably a long time—foresters might have a clearer picture of this process in New England. The severe disturbances of the past—clearing, lumbering, fire, and destructive hurricanes—as well as the continuing disturbances of the present and a slowly changing climate, have affected and no doubt will continue to affect every acre of the region's woodland to some degree. What resulting changes might take place in the future are still largely a matter for conjecture.

Forest History II: Disturbances

IF the migration speed of trees and other plants or the effects of climate change were all forest investigators had to contend with, the postglacial history of New England's woodlands would be much simpler than in fact it is. As more is learned about the forests, the importance of continuous disturbances, large and small, in determining their character and evolution has become clear. So complete and widespread have been these disturbances that scarcely an acre of southern New England forest could be classified as untouched primeval growth. In fact investigators can only surmise what such a forest stand—one that had escaped major disturbance for several hundred years—might have looked like.

The most recent and widespread of all these major disturbances has been the clearing of the forests for cropping and pasture during the nineteenth-century agricultural boom. Close to three-quarters of southern New England became open land; most of what remained was repeatedly cut for firewood and charcoal.

Since colonial times, too, periodic fires have laid waste large forest tracts. Most of these have been accidentally started by man—sparks from early steam locomotives were a common cause of forest fires—but lightning has been responsible for some. There is also ample evidence that the Indians during precolonial times regularly set fire to the woodlands either accidentally or purposely both to manage game and to clear land for their primitive agriculture. Lightning, too, must have at least occasionally caused fires in these precolonial forests.

Enormously destructive hurricanes that ruined huge areas of the New England forest are a matter of historical record. We can assume that these hurricanes, like fires ignited by lightning, also wreaked havoc upon New England forests in prehistoric times. Disturbances, then, have probably always affected large sections of the region's forests. Today, virtually all of the woodlands are in some stage of recovery from one or more of these. During the postglacial period, however, there may have been scattered tracts of forest that escaped catastrophic disturbances for long periods of time, but the idea put forth by early writers of

New England being covered by a forest in which a squirrel could travel a hundred miles or more from one giant tree to another is probably pure fancy.

Fire

Of all the disturbances to the woodland none is so complex in its ecological effects as fire. Traditionally forest fire has been regarded as an unmitigated disaster; indeed the destruction by a severe fire of a beautiful forest tract, its wildlife, its watershed, and even the soil is a catastrophe by any standards. Yet fires of low or medium intensity, those that burn only the ground layer of a woodland, can be of great ecological benefit. In fact, in some forest regions of the country, especially in the southern pine forests, periodic fires are essential in maintaining forest productivity. Since modern firefighting techniques have greatly reduced burning, these southern forests have been hit by serious insect and fungus attacks, and undesirable changes are occurring. In fact, fire has been found to be so important in maintaining these forest types that foresters are recommending that controlled burning be a part of normal management practices.

The ecological importance of fire in the southern New England woodlands is just beginning to be explored. It is perhaps not as important here as elsewhere, but some experiments conducted at the Connecticut Arboretum in New London suggest that low-intensity ground fires may improve the forest in several ways.

It has long been known, for example, that a diversity of vegetation and habitat will support the greatest variety and number of animals. A monotonous unbroken cover of mature forest provides far less diversity than a mosaic pattern of land at every stage of succession from grassland and thickets to patches of old-growth forest. The great abundance of game in precolonial forests, as reported by the early explorers, may have resulted from such a mosaic pattern caused by Indian and naturally caused fires of varying intensity.

There are several rather obvious factors that determine the chances of a forest fire starting, the speed with which it spreads, and the amount of damage it will cause to the vegetation. A strongly blowing dry wind is probably the most important element; not only will it spread the fire rapidly once it starts, but it helps to create conditions for fire by drying out the woodland.

In parts of the region that are most fire-sensitive, such as the Cape Cod area, late summer and early fall is the most dangerous time for forest fire. The pattern of summer rainfall in New England is spotty; during this season most is received through local thundershowers of usually short duration, which offer little long-term relief to the woodlands once they have dried out. Surprisingly enough, serious forest fires also occur during early spring before the leaves come out.

Green vegetation, of course, is much less flammable than dead vegetation, one reason why fire is severe in cut-over areas, where slash of treetops, bark, limbs, and cull logs have been allowed to accumulate. Areas devastated by hurricane and—in northern New England—by insect epidemic are also very flammable for the same reason.

The properties of the soil also have a strong bearing on the flammability of the woodland and the seriousness of a fire. Sandy regions like Cape Cod have probably been swept by fire since time immemorial, partly because the loose sandy soil there dries out so quickly. Cape Cod is also particularly susceptible to fire because of the strong southwest winds that sweep across the area.

Swamp forests, where the water table is close to the surface and the soils remain damp all year, are probably at the opposite end of the scale of potential damage. A crown fire, one fanned by strong wind that races through the treetops, could wipe out even a swamp forest, but the damp humus layer is usually spared. Even so, regeneration after a fire may produce an entirely different vegetation cover (page 97).

Other sites are probably intermediate in their resistance to fire. Hilltops and ridges, being drier than lower slopes and valley bottoms, have suffered more severe fire damage, but whether repeated burning has been an important factor in modifying the vegetation on these sites in southern New England, as it seems to have been in other parts of the country, is not clear.

IDENTIFYING FOREST FIRE BURNS

The most obvious sign of forest fire damage is charcoal. A wind-whipped crown fire will reduce a forest to blackened stumps and fallen logs. Fires of intermediate severity will consume some trees and spare others. Many of these survivors, however, will show extensive fire scars that may remain visible for the life of the tree. Smaller scars will heal over in time, but, even healed, these fire scars are still visible among the growth rings on freshly cut tree stumps.

Charcoal is slow to disintegrate. Scratching about in an area suspected of having been burned will usually turn up charcoal remains from the fire. Investigators from the Harvard Forest studying a southern New Hampshire tract found broad continuous bands of charcoal just above the mineral soil, the blackened remains of trees burned in a forest fire about 1665. So well preserved were these charcoal fragments that it was still possible, 300 years later, to identify the species of trees from a microscopic examination of them.

The signs of a low-intensity ground fire are all but erased in a year or two as a new crop of fallen leaves covers the blackened layer and the small saplings burned by such a fire either decay and disappear or resprout from unburned roots.

It takes much longer for nature to heal the damage wrought by a serious fire, however. In areas where the soil has been burned or where it is naturally sandy, regeneration following a fire proceeds very slowly. There are places on Cape Cod that still bear the obvious signs of fire many years afterward.

In the oak forest region, better soils usually insure a faster regeneration. The Esterbrook Woods in Concord, Massachusetts, for example, was partially burned by a severe fire in 1910; today it is virtually impossible to see any signs of the burn without digging in the leaf litter. Within sixty-five years in that woodland, a generation of pioneer species may have grown and disappeared, and the regenerated sprout forest is indistinguishable from neighboring areas that were cut for firewood about that same time.

This stump-sprouting ability of many of the southern New England hardwoods following fire is particularly notable and may help to account for the abundance of these species in the region's forest. Oaks, hickories, and red maple, all common southern New England trees, sprout vigorously from burned stumps following fire: a number of forest biologists have speculated that continual fires during the postglacial times have been responsible for the great numbers of these species in New England woods. On the other hand, fire-sensitive tree species, such as hemlock, *Tsuga canadensis*, beech, *Fagus grandifolia*, sugar maple, *Acer saccharum*, and yellow birch, *Betula lutea*, are often eliminated from burned-over woods for many generations. Another common oak forest tree, black birch, *Betula lenta*, is also very fire-sensitive, although it will usually repopulate a burned-over area if a source of seeds is spared nearby. Mature black birches in a woodland, therefore, ordinarily indicate an absence of severe fire during the life of the trees.

Stump sprouts following cutting and fire rarely grow as single-trunked trees. Some stumps may produce as many as fifty shoots, but only a few of these grow to maturity. Nevertheless a characteristic second-growth forest following cutting or fire contains a preponderance of multiple-trunked coppice trees whose curved trunks are of little value for anything other than firewood.

In the initial stages of regeneration following fire, the sprouting stumps often produce impenetrable thickets. These sprout thickets are especially dense in areas where the previous forest itself was immature and thick following some earlier disturbance. Under such conditions, sprouting is so vigorous that competition for light and water becomes keen and tree growth is slow.

A number of shrubs are also favored by fire. Lowbush blueberry, *Vaccinium* spp., huckleberry, *Gaylussacia baccata*, sweet fern, *Comptonia peregrina*, and sheep laurel, *Kalmia angustifolia*, all quickly reappear in burned-over areas, adding further competition in the regenerating forest. In areas with a history of forest fires, these shrubs often form a continuous layer.

Among the conifers of the region, only pitch pine, *Pinus rigida*, is thoroughly adapted to periodic burning. If all its foliage is burned away, needles will grow again on the branches. If the terminal shoot is killed, a new one will develop. If the trunk is killed, a new one will sprout from the base. On some trees the cones will remain closed for several years, in many cases until the heat of a fire opens them. Trees with this characteristic have evolved in areas with the worst forest fire history.

Pin cherry, *Prunus pennsylvanica*, is another species that is favored by fire. Pin cherry is a short-lived pioneer tree that often appears in great numbers following fire. Its seeds are widely distributed by birds who eat the fleshy fruit. Many of these seeds fall to the forest floor and remain viable up to fifty years, waiting to germinate as a response to changes in the microclimate that take place following a fire or other disturbance.

In some areas quaking aspen, *Populus tremuloides*, and gray birch, *Betula populifolia*, are common pioneer trees following fire. Both have small seeds which normally require bare ground to germinate.

Gradually nature erases the signs of even a severe fire. The stumps and blackened logs disintegrate and disappear beneath the accumulating leaf mold on the forest floor. The pioneer trees give way to other more shade-tolerant species and clear-cut signs of fire become harder to find. The regenerational pattern following a forest fire may be quite different, however, and differences in the woodland may persist for a long time. If, as you walk through the woods, you come upon a sudden change in the character of the woods, especially along a line that suggests neither a naturally occurring change in the habitat, such as a break in the slope, nor a change related to former land uses, as might occur along a stone wall or fence line, you may possibly be on the edge of a forest fire burn. A search through the leaf litter may turn up bands of charcoal, which, as noted earlier, are an almost certain sign of fire.

INDIAN FIRES

Carbon 14 dating has placed Indians in Massachusetts as early as 8,000 years ago; one early estimate put the New England Indian population at the time of the first European settlement at a half million or more. There is good evidence, then, that there were large numbers of Indians in the region and that they had been here for a long time. Following the custom of aboriginal people in many parts of the world, the Indians regularly set fire to the woods both to clear it for agriculture and for primitive game management. At other times, the Indians must have unintentionally started forest fires.

Several early historical accounts mention that palls of smoke from Indian fires could be seen from some distance at sea. Other early reports describe a terrain in which the woods were so open and park-like that a man on horseback could easily pass through them. In fact, the area around what is now Boston was so denuded of trees that the early settlers had to cut their firewood from islands in the harbor.

The Indian population of New England was centered along the coast. With strong coastal winds blowing in dry weather, the incidence of forest fires was probably greatest in the eastern and southern parts of the region.

Whether or not the effects of this long history of Indian fires can still be seen in the southern New England forests today has developed into one of the liveliest controversies in New England forest ecology. One group of investigators points to the fact that the oak forest of southern New England today consists to a large extent of oaks, hickories, and red maple—all trees that sprout vigorously after fire. Such fire-sensitive trees as beech and hemlock, they note, are confined to north-facing slopes, ravines, and other moist sites that would offer some natural fire protection. The relative absence of these fire-sensitive trees from the drier upland slope forest sites, they argue, is not because these species are unable to grow in such habitats but because they were so decimated from the precolonial forests by fire that relatively few seed sources remained.

A second group of forest ecologists do not quarrel with the early descriptions of the precolonial forests or even with the importance of Indian fires in producing this open forest cover. The absence of hemlock and beech from today's forest, they suggest, is not because of Indian fires of long ago but because both of these species require cool, moist sites. The relatively warm and dry microclimate in today's immature forests may be simply beyond the limits of tolerance for these species. Secondly, the presence of these trees in ravines and on north-facing slopes is due to the fact that these slopes offer a suitable microclimate, not greater fire protection. The gradual return of the beech and hemlock to some parts of the oak forest, which does seem to be occurring, may be because the forest, as it matures, gradually produces a more shady and moist microclimate that is suitable for these species. The reappearance of these species in the woods may be part of the normal regenerational pattern of these forests. On the other hand, the reappearance of these fire-sensitive species on drier sites may be due to the effective forest fire protection that the region has been receiving for the past seventy years.

The controversy is far from being settled. Each side can muster evidence to support its case, but without any remaining undisturbed tracts of forest in southern New England with which to compare these younger forests, the whole question may never be completely resolved.

Hurricane

About once in every 150 years, large forest areas of southern New England are laid waste by a destructive hurricane. Potentially devastating hurricanes pass up the east coast each year, but the great majority of these stay far enough out to sea to do relatively little damage ashore.

The hurricanes whose paths do cross land, of course, vary in intensity. A less severe hurricane may do little more than prune dead branches from the trees and cause minor flooding, while an intense one may bring devastation beyond belief. Unusually severe hurricanes occurring in 1938, 1815, and 1635 are a matter of historical record; there is little reason to assume that such destructive windstorms did not also occur periodically through the centuries prior to this time.

The devastation wrought upon New England by the last major storm, the 1938 hurricane, provides us with some measure of the damage caused by earlier storms. The central eye of that hurricane came inland over southern Connecticut, followed a path up the Connecticut Valley, and veered northwestward across Vermont. Damage was especially severe because the hurricane was preceded by five days of heavy rain. The rainwater so saturated the ground that the

11. Windthrow from the 1938 hurricane. Hulk of a white pine that fell in the storm. Several other fallen trees all pointing northwest are nearby. Note the rocks still adhering to the old roots.

tree roots could not resist the force of wind as well as they would have had the ground been dry. Many trees that might have otherwise survived the storm were toppled.

Like other low-pressure storms, hurricane winds blow counterclockwise around the eye. The winds are strongest and hence most destructive just east of the eye. On this side of the 1938 hurricane, whole forests were leveled.

Yet even within this destructive quadrant there were substantial differences from place to place in the amount of damage the woodlands sustained. In hilly areas damages were greatest on southeastern slopes, which received the full force of the wind, while those trees growing on the northwestern slopes—in the lee of the hills—or in sheltered ravines, were often spared.

IDENTIFYING HURRICANE DAMAGE

Now, almost forty years later, it is still possible to find ample evidence of the 1938 storm's destruction. On the eastern side of the hurricane, the strongest winds blew from the southeast, toppling trees in a northwesterly direction. On the opposite side of the storm, the strongest winds blew from the northeast, toppling the trees in a southwestern direction.

Of course, not every downed tree in the woods is the result of a hurricane. Squalls with gusty winds may blow down an occasional tree. Tornadoes, which do occur in New England at rare intervals, may also cause damage that is sometimes quite severe, though generally over small areas. It is the more or less parallel orientation of many fallen logs over a wide area that indicates hurricane damage.

Overturned, sawed stumps, usually in an advanced state of decay, show where landowners salvaged downed timber after the 1938 hurricane. Smaller trees still lie where they fell, though many of these have rotted away, especially those in contact with the ground during the intervening time. Among those logs that have best resisted decay are the American chestnut, *Castanea dentata*, which had been killed earlier by the blight a decade or two before and toppled by the hurricane. If above ground, American chestnut is among the most decay-resistant of native woods; its smooth brownish-gray logs are still a common sight in much of the region.

PILLOW AND CRADLE

Windthrown trees leave evidence of their presence long after their woody parts have decayed and disappeared. When a tree is blown down, it lifts a quantity of soil and subsoil adhering to the roots. After the tree and its upturned roots have disappeared, a pillow-shaped mound of dirt that was lifted by the roots, next to the depression from which it came, remains for many years. Eventually erosion takes its toll and the pillow becomes lower and less evident, but traces may remain for as long as 500 years. Digging through the layer of leaf mold that has since accumulated on such a mound will reveal a light-colored layer of subsoil on top of a darker organic layer that marked the original ground surface. By carefully removing the leaf litter and humus from around the pillow it is often possible to find dark traces of the rotted tree trunk where it fell. In southern New England woodlands, black birch, *Betula lenta*, often seeds itself on the bare ground of these pillows; an abundance of black birch almost always is a sign of some sort of disturbance to the soil.

OTHER SIGNS OF HURRICANE DAMAGE

In addition to uprooting trees, the force of the 1938 hurricane did further damage. Many oaks and other deeply rooted trees which could resist being bowled over by the wind often lost their tops. In some woodlands it is possible to find many of the trees growing straight-trunked to perhaps 10 meters and then abruptly becoming many-branched or "stag-headed" with no main leader. Severe ice damage might also cause this form, but it often indicates that the crown was broken off by wind.

Smaller trees that managed to resist uprooting were sometimes permanently bent by the force of the wind. Subsequent growth is vertical, giving such trees a bowed trunk with the concave side facing the direction of the wind. Trees growing on a steep slope have bowed trunks as the result of soil creep (page 75), but in such cases the bow is near the base of the trunk and the concave side faces uphill. Individual trees with bent or crooked trunks due to logging damage, ice storms, or competition from neighboring trees are not, of course, oriented in any particular direction.

FOREST RECOVERY

The recovery of the forest from hurricane damage usually proceeds more rapidly than it does following fire. Larger trees bear the brunt of the wind; smaller trees growing in the understory usually survive. The holes in the canopy opened up by the loss of the larger trees encourage the growth of the smaller trees, which up to that time were suppressed by the shade of the forest. The pillows provide a seedbed for other species, especially birch, whose seeds cannot normally penetrate the thick leaf layer on the forest floor.

From an economic standpoint, hurricane damage to the forests can, of course, be severe. Especially hard-hit in the 1938 hurricane was the white pine, to that time the mainstay of New England's timber industry. Hundreds of thousands of mature pines fell. Landowners salvaged what they could and stored the logs in local ponds. In some parts of central New England so much timber was stored this way that it was possible to walk across the ponds by stepping from one log to another.

Cutting for Firewood and Timber

During the height of the agricultural boom, about 25 percent of southern New England—land that was too poor or too steep for pasture and crops—remained as woodland. At that time the coal industry had not yet become established, and wood was the primary fuel for cooking and heating. As a result, the remaining woodlands were cut over again and again for firewood, to the point that a serious wood shortage developed in much of the region. In fact, there was still a great demand for firewood even into the early part of this century, until coal-fired central heating finally replaced the parlor stove.

The early locomotives and steamboats were all woodburners. By the end of the Civil War, the railroads of Massachusetts alone were burning over 50,000 cords yearly, nearly all of it pitch pine. A century earlier, pitch pine also supported a tar and turpentine industry, located mostly in the Cape Cod region.

Prior to the use of coke, the iron-smelting industry consumed vast amounts of hardwood charcoal. Since every stick of hardwood could be reduced to charcoal, woodlands near iron smelters were clear-cut time and again. So great was the demand for charcoal in some areas that farmers are reputed to have sold their wooden fences. Remains of old circular hearths, where the wood was reduced to charcoal, are still occasionally seen, especially in western Connecticut.

Other industries also required a great deal of wood fuel.

FOREST ECOLOGY

During its heyday, the Sandwich Glass Works on Cape Cod, for example, used about thirty-five cords a day to stoke its furnaces. Since it was necessary to keep the furnaces burning seven days a week, this one company consumed an astronomical 12,000 cords per year. The early brass industry in Connecticut was also a major consumer of firewood.

The result of this huge demand for firewood was that few southern New England woodlands remained uncut long enough to produce a crop of saw timber. During this time the forests of northern New England were supplying building lumber, but it was not until the end of the nineteenth century that the farmland abandoned seven decades earlier began to yield saw timber in southern New England.

White pine was the mainstay of this revived timber industry. Between 1910 and 1920, lumbering of this old field pine reached its height and continued as an important rural industry until the 1938 hurricane. Groves of old field white pine are still common in central New England, and a small timber industry remains.

Foresters discovered, however, that the great resurgence of white pine following the agricultural boom was only temporary. Under ordinary forest conditions, white pine is at a distinct competitive disadvantage. The tree lacks the ability to sprout from stumps and its seedlings need sun for vigorous growth. Most hardwoods tolerate more shade but grow very slowly in the shadow of the pines. Once the dense pine canopy is removed, however, through either cutting or natural causes, these young hardwoods make a spurt in growth, and quickly shade out any pine seedlings that may have germinated. Thus, a great abundance of pine was only one step in forest development, a direct result of the widespread clearing and subsequent abandonment of the land a century or so earlier. Though pollen records show pine to have been abundant in New England forests at various times in the past, it apparently was not nearly as common in the early colonial times as it is now.

The hardwood forests in southern New England, on the other hand, are just reaching maturity. Red oak, *Quercus rubra*, and black oak, *Q. velutina*, are the dominant trees throughout the region. Red oak is a surprisingly fast-growing tree and one that produces strong, straight timber. Medium-sized trees respond dramatically to forest management, sometimes doubling their trunk volumes within ten to twelve years after thinning. With some management, the hardwood forests of the region could produce an impressive crop of timber by the end of the century.

The Future Landscape

ATTEMPTING to predict what the southern New England countryside will look like fifty or a hundred years from now is little short of crystal-ball-gazing. Nevertheless, there are trends that have been occurring in the last few decades that may continue at least to the end of the century, from which we can make guarded short-term predictions. Unforeseen events, of course, could radically alter the future land use of this region even in as short a time as twenty or thirty years.

There has been a continuing study of changing patterns of vegetation and land use in Massachusetts, jointly sponsored by several government agencies and the Department of Forestry and Wildlife Management at the University of Massachusetts. Middlesex County, which reaches from urban Cambridge into some still sparsely populated rural areas near the New Hampshire border, may be an excellent representative sample of the changing demographic and land-use patterns for much of the rest of southern New England. Through the study of population shifts and the changing patterns of land use in the fifties and sixties, the survey team has made predictions through the seventies and eighties.

Middlesex County, like much of the region in the densely populated northeast corridor, is now largely suburban. During the first twenty years of the survey, from 1951 to 1971, there was a substantial shift in population from high-density urban areas to low-density areas. The trend is expected to continue, but, because of increasing land prices, the rate will be slower.

Unfortunately, most of the development in the rural areas has occurred on agricultural land. During the time of the survey there was a 50 percent decline of farmland in Middlesex County, three-quarters of this going to industrial and residential development. Good farmland, level and well-drained, is the easiest on which to build. Until well into this century the marginal farmland was abandoned to woods; now the better farmland is being abandoned to houses and shopping centers. This trend is expected to continue.

The Connecticut Valley, which contains much of the farmland in southern New England, also contains some of the most flagrant examples of unrestrained urban development. Enfield, Connecticut, a small town of 10,000 in 1951, for example, is now a sprawling city of 50,000; most of this development has occurred on agricultural land.

Unless government can come up with some imaginative ways to encourage farming and preserve agricultural land, we can expect to see much of what is left lost to subdivisions and shopping malls in the next thirty years.

One hopeful sign is the interest many of the towns have in preserving the still undeveloped lands that remain to them, before it is too late. A number of towns have active conservation commissions and planning boards which are working to increase common land to insure that the inevitable development will proceed in an orderly and responsible way. The fiscal difficulties that state governments now face will probably preclude increasing the state-owned land in southern New England to any great degree, but some enlightened towns as well as private groups may be able to secure some more land. Altogether, however, the publicly acquired land in the next two decades will probably amount to but a small percentage of the total area still undeveloped.

The prospects for the woodlands may be a bit brighter. Middlesex County, as close as it is to Boston, is still just over 50 percent wooded, having lost only 4 percent of its woodlands to urban and residential development during the last twenty years. The forecast is for this trend to continue at about the same low rate, so that by the end of the century, at least, there should still be substantial tracts of forest remaining.

Moreover, the trees in the forests have been growing surprisingly fast. Hardwoods are not generally thought of as fast growers, but by 1971 the trees on most of the forest tracts in Middlesex County were at least half again as large as they were in 1951; they are expected to double their height by 1991. The actual height has increased from an average of

12. Large red oak, *Quercus rubra*, Goodwin State Forest, Connecticut. By the end of the century many southern New England woodlands will be growing trees of this size.

under 12 meters in 1951 to under 18 meters by 1971. Eighteen meters is usually considered to be a harvestable size for oaks and other hardwoods. Already at least 6 percent of the forest land is growing trees that average 18 meters high; by the turn of the century the trees in nearly 90 percent of the forests will have reached that height.

Since the energy crisis began in 1973, many people in the region are starting to realize the value of wood for supplementary heating. A good wood-burning stove can make a substantial dent in the fuel bills; the oaks and hickories of the southern New England forests are unexcelled as fuel wood. Moreover, weeding and culling out less desirable trees for firewood will greatly improve the timber trees that are left. A well-managed woodlot is reputed to be able to supply a cord of firewood per acre per year indefinitely.

The pine barrens of Cape Cod and other dry areas will probably continue to be burned by occasional fires; one hundred years from now many areas will almost surely look the same as they do today.

Hurricanes will probably continue to batter the coastal woodlands with some frequency and occasionally move across inland areas. Eventually a hurricane will again devastate the forests with the same destructive force as the 1938 hurricane; in this regard history has repeated itself all too often in southern New England. It seems almost certain, however, that other forest tracts, especially in western parts of the region, will be spared major disturbances for at least several decades.

Though New England's old-growth forests may never rival in grandeur the redwood forests and sequoia groves of California or even the rich cove forests of the Great Smoky Mountains, it is reasonable to expect that at least scattered stands of big trees will eventually make their reappearance here. There are now many forest preserves in southern New England, and though the kinds of major disturbances to the woodlands that have occurred in the past will no doubt recur in the future, it also seems quite certain that some of these forests will be spared. Walking through a magnificent stand of pines or hardwoods can be an awe-inspiring experience. Happily, it is one that should be possible for future generations of New Englanders.

FURTHER READING

Some Notes on the Terrain

Bain, G. W., and H. A. Meyerhoff. *The Flow of Time in the Connecticut Valley*. Springfield, Mass.: Connecticut Valley Historical Museum, 1963. Discusses in layman's terms the bedrock and surficial geology of New England's most interesting geological area.

Cameron, Barry, ed. *Geology of Southeastern New England*. Princeton, N.J.: Science Press, 1976. (Available from Dept. of Geology, Boston University, Boston, Mass. 02215.) Up-to-date synthesis of the very complex bedrock and surficial geology of eastern Massachusetts and eastern Rhode Island. Technical but of interest to serious students of the region's geology.

Jorgensen, Neil. *A Guide to New England's Landscape*, 2d ed. Chester, Conn.: Pequot Press, 1977. I must recommend my earlier book as an easy generalized introduction to the geology and plant geography of New England.

Moore, Fred Holmsley. *Marbles and Limestones of Connecticut*. Connecticut Geological and Natural History Survey Bulletin 56. Hartford, Conn.: State Library, 1935. Shows the marble regions of Connecticut.

Shelton, John S. *Geology Illustrated*. San Francisco: Freeman, 1966. Superbly illustrated nontechnical introduction to geology. Many aerial photographs, mostly from western United States, but much information is applicable to the Northeast.

Skehan, J. W. *Puddingstone, Drumlins, and Ancient Volcanoes*. Chestnut Hill, Mass.: Boston College, 1975. Excellent small book of geological field trips in eastern Massachusetts. Written for the layman.

Microclimate

Franklin, T. Bedford. *Climates in Miniature: A Study of Microclimate and Environment*. London: Faber and Faber, 1955. Highly readable book on practical aspects of microclimates in gardening, farming, and natural history.

Geiger, Rudolf. *The Climate Near the Ground*. Cambridge, Mass.: Harvard University Press, 1965. Definitive work in microclimates. Technical in places but very thorough. Much of the research done in Europe but applicable in large part to New England.

Plant Ecology

Coulter, Merle C., and Howard J. Dittmer. *The Story of the Plant Kingdom*, 3d ed. Chicago: University of Chicago Press, 1964. Excellent nontechnical introduction to plants.

Daubenmire, Rexford F. *Plant Communities: A Textbook of Plant Synecology*. New York: Harper and Row, 1968. A basic text of the ecology of plant communities. Examples drawn from western American forests, but concepts applicable to New England.

Daubenmire, Rexford F. *Plants and Environment: A Textbook of Plant Autecology*, 2d ed. New York: Wiley, 1959. Useful collection of information about the relationship of plants to the habitat.

Fowells, H. A. *Silvics of Forest Trees of the United States*. Agriculture Handbook no. 271. Washington, D.C.: U.S. Government Printing Office, 1965. Detailed information of life history, ecology, and range of the major American tree species. Very useful for professional and amateur.

Kormondy, Edward J. *Concepts of Ecology*. Englewood Cliffs, N.J.: Prentice-Hall, 1969. Easily understood introduction to general ecology.

Minkler, Leon S. *Woodland Ecology: Environmental Forestry for the Small Owner*. Syracuse, N.Y.: Syracuse University Press, 1975. Excellent entry point into the study of integrated and harmonious land management for timber, wildlife, recreation, and aesthetics.

Odum, Eugene. *Fundamentals of Ecology*, 3d ed. Philadelphia: Saunders, 1971. Comprehensive standard college text written for the serious student.

Oosting, Henry J. *Plant Communities*, 2d ed. San Francisco: Freeman, 1956. Excellent though somewhat dated introduction to plant ecology. Examples mainly drawn from the Southeast, though much applies to New England.

Ovington, J. D. *Woodlands*. London: English Universities Press, 1965. Forest ecology, biology, and management on a worldwide basis. Written for the layman.

Spurr, Stephen H. *Forest Ecology*. New York: Ronald Press, 1964. Comprehensive text of forest environments, communities, and geography useful for professional and layman alike. Extensive bibliography.

Watts, May T. *Reading the Landscape*, 2d ed. New York: Macmillan, 1976. Informal study of plant ecology. Emphasis on Midwest, though some coverage of New England. Useful and interesting despite somewhat chatty style.

Went, Frits. *The Plants*. New York: Time-Life, 1963. A simplified, well-illustrated introduction to the world of plants.

Wilson, B. F. *The Growing Tree*. Amherst, Mass.: University of Massachusetts Press, 1970.

PART IV

The Oak Forest

The Oak Forest:
An Introduction

IF YOU DROPPED by parachute into some randomly cho-
sen spot in southern New England, the chances are that you
would land in an oak tree. This is not hard to understand,
since the region is over two-thirds wooded and the great
majority of trees that grow in these woods are oaks. The oak
woodland, then, seems the most logical place to begin the
descriptive section of this guide.

General Appearance and Extent

Except for places where extreme conditions of soil moisture prevail—either swampland, at one end of the continuum, or dry sandy areas at the other—or on abandoned
farmland where the forest is only beginning to return, this
southern New England woodland is remarkably uniform in
appearance. The trees form a closed canopy overhead but
the understory is usually open, and the shrub layer in many
places is sparse or absent entirely. In much of Connecticut
and northward into central Massachusetts, however, mountain laurel, *Kalmia latifolia*, does form a dense, sometimes
impenetrable shrub layer. Elsewhere the woodland is so
open and park-like that off-trail travel is easy.

Though oaks of several species comprise the bulk of the
trees, they by no means include all of the species found here.
Deciduous species such as red maple, *Acer rubrum*, black
birch, *Betula lenta*, pignut hickory, *Carya glabra*, and about
a dozen others grow along with the oaks. American chestnut,
Castanea dentata, formerly was as common as the oaks and
vied with them for dominance until it was eliminated from
the forest by a fungal blight in the first half of this century.

From central Connecticut northward, conifers become an
increasingly important component in the oak forest. White
pine, *Pinus Strobus*, because of its tall stature and gray-green
foliage, gives these more northerly woodlands a distinctive
appearance. Hemlock, *Tsuga canadensis*, often limited to
north-facing slopes and other cool sites in the southern part

of the region, appears throughout the woodlands farther north.

Anyone who travels southwestward from New England along the Piedmont and Appalachians would see forests very similar in appearance to those of southern New England: many of the oaks and other familiar southern New England tree species also grow there. Because of the similarities in composition and appearance, forest investigators have grouped the forests in this large area—southern New England, eastern New York State, the northern Piedmont, and the Appalachian Mountains as far south as Georgia—into a single great forest region, one of ten that cover the eastern third of the United States and much of the adjacent parts of Canada.

Of course in an area as large as this, one extending southward for almost 1,300 kilometers (800 miles), the woodland is not completely homogeneous. In addition to the inevitable local differences due to soil moisture and other ecological factors, there are broad regional differences in composition of the forest, determined primarily by differences in climate. As a result, this large forest region is divided into smaller units called sections, of which the glaciated area of southern New England and eastern New York state is one. Yet, in spite of these sectional differences, the entire forest region shows enough similarities from one end to the other to be classified as a cohesive unit.

Unfortunately, there is now no agreement on what to call this forest region. Before its elimination by the blight, American chestnut competed successfully with the oaks in both numbers and size. Accordingly, the forest was known as the oak-chestnut forest. Since chestnut has been reduced to an insignificant forest shrub, this name is no longer applicable. Hickories or some other species may eventually take the place of American chestnut as the codominant trees in this forest region, but at present the oaks stand preeminent. Therefore merely calling this region the oak forest seems to be most satisfactory for now.

Soils

The soils beneath the oak forest show some general similarities as well. Those of southern New England, derived as they are from glacial till, are quite different in origin from those in unglaciated areas farther south that result from the slow decomposition of the bedrock, yet because of the humid climate and the generally acidic nature of underlying bedrock throughout most of this forest region, the soils are usually acidic in reaction. The leaf mold from the oaks tends to increase the soil acidity as well.

The soils underlying these oak forest sites lie between the extremes of moisture. Most contain sufficient humus and small-sized mineral particles to retain moisture; because of the generally sloping sites occupied by the oak forests, however, excess rainwater usually drains away. There is an abrupt change to different forest types where the soil becomes either very dry or very wet.

This soil acidity, coupled with the slow breakdown of the fallen oak leaves, produces a matted and compacted layer of organic material that lies on top of the mineral soil layers below and remains separated from it. This distinct humus layer, called mor humus, is sharply acidic in reaction and supports but relatively few species of shrubs and herbaceous plants that are adapted to these harsh conditions. Among the shrubs, most are ericads, members of the heath family (Ericaceae) and a couple of other closely related plant families. Ericads include such well known genera as blueberries, cranberries, rhododendrons, and azaleas. These oak woodlands usually lack the rich herbaceous flora found in other woodland communities where the soil is less acidic.

The Oak Forest Communities

Although the woodlands in these sloping, well-drained sites are remarkably similar in appearance, a discerning eye can detect some differences in the composition of trees and shrubs from one site to another. The most obvious of these differences is primarily related to how much soil moisture is available. Rocky hilltops, for example, where the soil is thinnest and drainage the greatest, are notably drier than sites farther downhill. Some experts who have studied these woodlands identify three communities, each with a somewhat different composition of trees, shrubs, and herbaceous plants, probably resulting from differences in available soil

THE OAK FOREST

moisture. The driest of these, found on hilltops and upper south-facing slopes, is the crest or hilltop community. A second, the midslope community, as its name suggests, occurs farther downhill where soil moisture is somewhat greater. Lower still is a third community, the low slope community, which occurs where there is substantially more soil moisture available to the vegetation, but where, except for a short time during the spring, the water table is still far enough below the root zone of the plants growing there that it does not saturate it.

The assemblage of plant species is different, in both distribution and frequency, in each of these three communities. But because all of the species which grow in the oak forest have some range of tolerance to varying conditions of soil moisture, there is often no neat division into one community or another; as a result, the boundaries between communities are indistinct. Moreover, some species in the hilltop community also appear in the drier sand plain community, while some plants in the low slope community also turn up in several of the wetland communities. The chart on pages 126–27 shows this overlap.

Some differences in these communities, especially in the hilltop community, are also based on geography. For example, in the cooler northern half of the region the hilltop community often resembles the midslope community of the southern half. Nevertheless, where the forest is mature, the three communities are usually distinct enough to provide you with a clear pattern.

A fourth community, the mixed mesophytic community, also appears in the oak forest but, except in marble areas in western Connecticut, it is rare in the region. This community, which seems to be based partly on the availability of ample soil moisture and partly on less acidic forest soils, supports a markedly different assemblage of plants.

Common Trees and Shrubs of the Southern New England Oak Forest by Habitat

SPECIES	COMMUNITY				
Common name *Latin name*	Sand Plain	Hill-top	Mid-slope	Low Slope	Wet-land
Chestnut oak *Quercus Prinus*		—			
Pitch pine *Pinus rigida*	—	—	- -		
Scarlet oak *Quercus coccinea*	—	—			
Black oak *Quercus velutina*	—	—		- -	
White oak *Quercus alba*	—	—		- -	
White pine *Pinus Strobus*	- -	—	—	—	- -
Pignut hickory *Carya glabra*	- -	—	—	—	
Red maple *Acer rubrum*	- -	—	—	—	—
Black birch *Betula lenta*		- -	—	—	
*Huckleberry *Gaylussacia baccata*	—	—	- -		
*Lowbush blueberry *Vaccinium* spp.*	—	—	- -		
*Sweet fern *Comptonia peregrina*	—	—	- -		
*Sheep laurel *Kalmia angustifolia*	—	—	- -	—	- -
*American chestnut *Castanea dentata*		- -	—	—	- -
Red oak *Quercus rubra*			- -	—	
Hemlock *Tsuga canadensis*			- -	—	—
American beech *Fagus grandifolia*			- -	—	—
White ash *Fraxinus americana*			- -	—	

SPECIES	COMMUNITY				
	Sand Plain	Hill-top	Mid-slope	Low Slope	Wet-land
Common name *Latin name*					
White birch *Betula papyrifera*			– – –		
Flowering dogwood *Cornus florida*			– – –		
*Mountain laurel *Kalmia latifolia*			———		
*Green-osier dogwood *Cornus alternifolia*			———	– – –	
*Maple-leaved viburnum *Viburnum acerifolium*		– – –	———		
Tulip tree *Liriodendron tulipifera*			– – –		
Shagbark hickory *Carya ovata*			– – –		
Mockernut hickory *Carya tomentosa*			———		
Hornbeam *Carpinus caroliniana*			– – –		
Hop hornbeam *Ostrya virginiana*			———		
*Pink azalea *Rhododendron nudiflorum*			– – –		
*Mountain azalea *Rhododendron roseum*			– – –		
*Witch hazel *Hamamelis virginiana*			– – – ———		– – –
*Highbush blueberry *Vaccinium* spp.			– – – ———		
Tupelo *Nyssa sylvatica*			– – – ———		– – –

*shrubs

The Hilltop Community

PRECIPITATION EFFECTIVENESS, as we saw on page 86, is an important factor in determining what vegetation a particular site will support. Hilltops and southern slopes are often notably deficient in the amount of soil moisture available to the plant community growing there. The soil layer is often thin to begin with, the ground and surface water both move downslope off the hilltops, and the water table—which may help to keep the soil moist on lower slopes—is usually at some distance beneath the surface under hills. In summer, the season when the moisture requirements of plants are the highest, these hilltops become substantially drier than sites farther downhill. Predictably, the vegetation found on hilltops and south-facing slopes is limited to those plants which can tolerate these dry summer conditions. In fact, on the driest of these sites, it is not unusual to find some of the species more commonly associated with the even drier sandy habitats of Cape Cod and elsewhere.

As one might expect, the trees growing on dry hilltops are not only smaller in stature but more widely spaced than those on more favorable sites. Root competition for moisture is intense; only the most vigorous individuals survive. Other species with higher moisture requirements may live on the hilltop community for a time, then succumb during periods of drought.

In southern parts of the region, chestnut oak, *Quercus Prinus*, is usually the major tree of the hilltop community. On many hilltop sites this species forms pure stands. In scattered hilltop stations along the Connecticut coast, post oak, *Quercus stellata*, a species normally associated with the pine barrens on the arid Coastal Plain to the south, replaces chestnut oak on the driest sites. Often chestnut oak may be found growing nearby where there is a bit more moisture in the soil. Two other oak species, both hardly more than shrubs, bear oak, *Quercus ilicifolia*, and dwarf chestnut oak, *Quercus prinoides*, also occasionally appear on dry hilltops.

Hilltop communities at the northern half of the region reflect the cooler and relatively moister summer conditions. A number of species normally found in the midslope community in the southern half of the region can survive on

THE OAK FOREST

hilltops in the northern half. Black oak, *Quercus velutina*, scarlet oak, *Q. coccinea*, white oak, *Q. alba*, red maple, *Acer rubrum*, pignut hickory, *Carya glabra*, and occasional other species often find these northerly hilltop sites within their ranges of tolerance. The distribution of chestnut oak, on the other hand, becomes more local and spotty to the north.

Both white pine, *Pinus Strobus*, and pitch pine, *P. rigida*, also appear in these hilltop communities, though usually as scattered individuals. Pitch pine is sometimes an indicator of forest fire burns; these dry hilltop sites formerly received more than their share of fires.

The shrub layer in the hilltop community is usually distinctive as well. Many of the species that grow here also appear in the sand plain community (see page 239). Often the ground is covered with a continuous layer of knee-high ericads, most commonly huckleberry, *Gaylussacia baccata*, lowbush blueberry, *Vaccinium* spp., and occasionally sheep laurel, *Kalmia angustifolia*. The blueberries and huckleberries neither bloom profusely nor set fruit in these shady habitats, however.

Herbaceous plants are few and scattered. In open rocky areas, little bluestem grass, *Andropogon scoparius*, is often found, while Pennsylvania sedge, *Carex pennsylvanica*, is an abundant woodland herb in shadier sites. Most of the other woodland herbaceous plants of the oak forest are more common in the lower communities.

Trees of the Hilltop Community

Chestnut Oak, *Quércus Prìnus,* is common on hilltops in the southern part of the region. The tree is reputed to reach a height of 18 m (60 ft) though I have never seen it on these sites taller than about 12 m (40 ft). It may be easily recognized by its characteristically shaped leaf, its heavily furrowed bark, and its dry habitat. It is more slow-growing than most other oaks, but can compete successfully on dry sites. The species is intolerant of shade, dying back to the stumps and later resprouting.

Scarlet Oak, *Quércus coccínea,* reaches 15 m (50 ft) on lower sites, but is usually much smaller on hilltops. It is most easily recognized by its deeply cut, pointed leaves. Scarlet

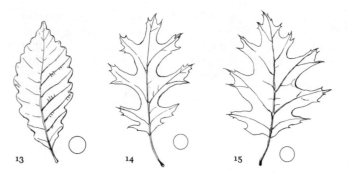

13. Chestnut oak, *Quercus Prinus*. The bark on chestnut oaks is deeply furrowed.

14. Scarlet oak, *Quercus coccinea*. The deeply cut leaves, which often turn brilliant scarlet in the fall, are characteristic.

15. Black oak, *Quercus velutina*, has leaves that are stouter than red or scarlet oak. The bark on older trees is deeply cracked and furrowed.

oak is very intolerant of shade; if not in a dominant position, it soon dies. Although the species is usually easy to recognize in the hilltop community, in some of the lower communities where it also grows it hybridizes with red oak, *Q. rubra*, producing individuals with intermediate characteristics. It also hybridizes with bear oak, *Q. ilicifolia*.

Black Oak, *Quércus velùtina*, on lower slopes may grow to 22 m (75 ft), though it rarely reaches this height on hilltops. Its leaves are pointed like the scarlet oak but stouter and not so deeply cut. Its most easily recognizable characteristic is its dark deeply furrowed bark that separates into nubbly block-like scales. The inner bark is yellowish. In the lower communities, black oak hybridizes with red oak, producing trees with intermediate characteristics.

White Oak, *Quércus álba*, is found in each of the oak forest communities, though it is common on hilltops only in the northern part of the region. It is very easy to recognize by its ash-gray flaking bark and its light green round-lobed leaves. The new leaves are almost white when they appear in the spring. It may reach 22 m (75 ft) on more favorable sites but rarely does so on hilltops.

16. White oak, *Quercus alba*. Its light gray flaking bark and light new growth are characteristic.

17. Red maple, *Acer rubrum*, the only maple commonly found in dry habitats. The light gray smooth bark on branches and young trunks is also distinctive.

Red Maple, *Àcer rùbrum*, is the most widely distributed tree in the region. It is most commonly thought of as a swamp tree, but it is also a major component of the oak forest, even on dry sites. It is relatively short-lived; its wood is subject to rot, insect attack, and ice storm damage, but, like so many of the other trees in the oak forest, it can sprout from burned or cut stumps. Young red maples have a smooth gray bark, somewhat resembling that of beech; on older trees the bark is darker gray, furrowed, and scaly. Its leaves are typical of maples but smaller than those of sugar maple, *A. saccharum*. Red maple is one of the first trees to bloom in the spring; its small red flowers give a pinkish blush to the trees. The fall leaf color is brilliant red on trees growing in strongly acidic soil, but more yellowish on soils with a higher pH.

Shrubs of the Hilltop Community

Dwarf Chestnut Oak, *Quércus prinoìdes*, appears in open hilltop sites. It is a slender shrub, 1 to 3 m (3 to 10 ft) in height. Its leaves resemble those of the chestnut oak, *Q. Prinus*, but are usually smaller with more blunted teeth.

18. Bear oak, *Quercus ilicifolia*, is usually a many-trunked shrub appearing in very dry sites.

Bear Oak, *Quércus ilicifòlia*, is most common on sand plains, but it also is often found on open sites on dry rocky hilltops. It is usually a shrub under 2.5 m (8 ft), but occasionally grows as a small tree up to 6 m (20 ft) in height. It is easily recognized by its shrub stature and its characteristic leaves.

Huckleberry, *Gaylussàcia baccàta*, is a twiggy shrub to about 1 m (3 ft), though usually lower, with small deciduous leaves that are covered with tiny brownish dots of resin. The fruit is black and sweet but seedy.

Variant forms: A form with larger blue berries and one with white berries are occasionally seen.

Lowbush Blueberry, *Vaccínium* spp., includes two species of rather similar appearance. Both are low twiggy shrubs from about 30 cm (1 ft) to about 75 cm (30 in) with small deciduous leaves without resin dots. Blueberries produce bell-shaped flowers and blue or black berries. They do not bloom profusely or set abundant fruit in the shade.

Variant form: A rare form with whitish berries has been reported.

Sheep Laurel, *Kálmia angustifòlia*, is a shrub found in many habitats including bogs, open woods, old pastures, plains, and rocky hilltops. It is a low shrub rarely growing taller than 50 cm (20 in) in shady places, though sometimes reaching about 1.7 m (5½ ft) in the open. Its evergreen leaves are oval, light green above and white beneath. The flowers are small deep magenta-purple, blooming from the leaf axils in early June. The shrub spreads by underground runners to form colonies.

Variant form: A rare form of sheep laurel with white flowers occasionally is found.

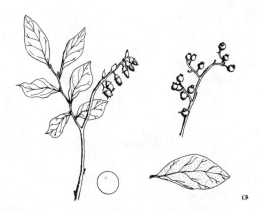

19. Lowbush blueberry, *Vaccinium* spp., leaves, flowers, and berries. Huckleberry, which also occupies dry sites, is taller and bears leaves with tiny resinous dots on the undersides (see inset).

20. Sheep laurel, *Kalmia angustifolia*, is a low shrub bearing light green leaves and flowers along the stems.

Other Hilltop Trees and Shrubs

The following trees and shrubs are sometimes found in the hilltop community, but are more common in other communities.

Black Birch, *Bétula lénta,* page 136
Pignut Hickory, *Cárya glàbra* and *C. ovalis,* page 138
Sweet Fern, *Comptònia peregrìna,* page 245
White Pine, *Pìnus Stròbus,* page 219
Pitch Pine, *Pìnus rígida,* page 241

The Midslope Community

ON MIDSLOPES there is a dramatic increase in the variety of plant life compared with the dry hilltops. Though the hilltop community may extend farther downhill on southern and southwestern exposures, on slopes facing the other points of the compass—especially on the northern slopes where the effect of the sun's radiation is smallest—the increase in soil moisture produces this greater diversity in trees and shrubs. Some herbaceous plants also begin to appear here.

Though chestnut oak, *Q. Prinus,* sometimes extends downward into the midslope community in Connecticut and Rhode Island, it is less abundant than the black, white, and scarlet oaks. Red oak, *Q. rubra,* while reaching its greatest development on the lower slopes, also appears in this community. Other midslope species include red maple, *Acer rubrum,* black birch, *Betula lenta,* white ash, *Fraxinus americana,* and several species of hickory. American chestnut, *Castanea dentata,* was formerly very common in this community; old chestnut hulks still litter the ground and stump sprouts of shrub height are common.

Near the northern edge of the region where the oak forest merges with the northern hardwood forest, as well as on cool, moist sites elsewhere, beech, *Fagus grandifolia,* hemlock, *Tsuga canadensis,* and white birch, *Betula papyrifera,* also appear, though all are more common on the still moister lower slope community.

The understory layer begins to evolve its characteristic vegetation. In the hilltop community, understory trees, if present at all, are usually smaller individuals of the same species as the dominant trees that were unable to penetrate the canopy formed by the larger ones. On midslopes such characteristic understory trees as flowering dogwood, *Cornus florida*, and hop hornbeam, *Ostrya virginiana*, can be found. Both are common in Connecticut and Rhode Island; farther north their distribution becomes spotty. Scattered white pines may also grow in the understory of the midslope community, but these can rarely penetrate through the thicker canopy at this level and eventually succumb.

It is probably the shrub layer which shows the most dramatic change. Huckleberry and lowbush blueberry also persist into the midslope community, but here they more often occur as scattered plants rather than a continuous cover. In many parts of Connecticut, and in western Rhode Island and south-central Massachusetts, mountain laurel, *Kalmia latifolia*, forms a continuous shrub layer up to 4 meters (13 feet) in height. Maple-leaved viburnum, *Viburnum acerifolium*, a low shrub whose leaves closely resemble those of the red maple, is also a common shrub in this community. Another dogwood, *Cornus alternifolia*, is also present here, especially in the northern parts. This species

21. Midslope community, Harvard, Massachusetts. Note the relative openness of the understory. The large hulk at the left is the remains of an American chestnut.

produces clusters of small flowers that are far less showy than those of the flowering dogwood.

Poison ivy also begins to appear in this community. It is more common and grows larger where there is ample moisture available to it, but it occurs often enough on the midslopes to bear watching for. The harmless Virginia creeper, *Parthenocissus quinquefolia*, whose vinelike habit resembles that of poison ivy, also occasionally grows here.

Trees of the Midslope Community

Black Birch, *Bétula lénta,* is the most common birch across much of the region. It is a medium-sized tree, reaching about 18 m (60 ft) in height. Black birch may be easily recognized by its smooth, nearly black lustrous bark on small and medium-sized trees, which becomes scaly and plated on old trees. Its twigs are very aromatic with wintergreen smell and flavor. The tree is often attacked by *Nectria* fungus, which leaves large disfiguring cankers on trunks.

Black birch requires bare ground to reproduce, since the small seeds cannot penetrate the thick leaf mulch that covers much of the oak forest. Because black birch is very fire-sensitive, its presence in a woodland usually indicates that there has been disturbance from windthrow or lumbering

22. Black birch, *Betula lenta,* may be identified by its dark bark, which is smooth on young trees and furrowed on older ones. The twigs have a wintergreen flavor.

23. White birch, *Betula papyrifera,* is easily recognized by its white bark and rounded leaves. (Compare with gray birch, page 221.)

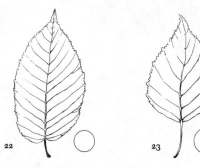

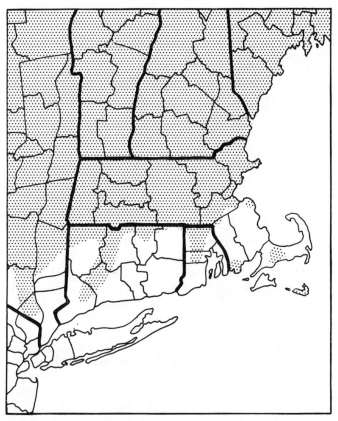

Range of the white birch, *Betula papyrifera*.

but not from fire. It is of only intermediate tolerance to shade, but there have been a sufficient number of disturbances—mostly from hurricanes—in recent years to maintain a constant reproduction. It can be found on drier sites in the northern part of the region but is most common on mid and low slope sites. I have occasionally seen it in pure stands.

Variant form: A rare form with deeply cut leaves has been found.

White Birch, *Bétula papyrífera,* becomes frequent in the oak forest in the northern part of the region. Like black

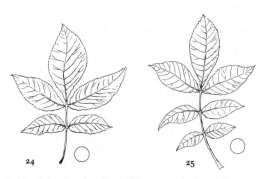

24. Shagbark hickory, *Carya ovata*, is most easily recognized by its ash-gray bark that separates into long strips. The compound leaf bearing five leaflets is also characteristic of its sister species, pignut hickory, *Carya glabra*.

25. Mockernut hickory, *Carya tomentosa*. The undersides of the leaflets are softly hairy.

birch, the presence of white birch indicates some kind of disturbance. It is easily recognized by its very white bark; the trees vary greatly in the degree to which their bark peels. Forms in which large pieces of bark peel off are more common in northern New England.

The tallest white birches reach a height of about 20 m (65 ft). White birch is a larger tree than gray birch, *Betula populifolia* (page 220), an old field pioneer. Many of the larger white-barked birches in the region exhibit characteristics intermediate between white and gray birch, suggesting hybridization between the two. White birch is common in northern New England and ranges southward to central Connecticut. It is infrequent in southeastern Massachusetts and southern Rhode Island.

Shagbark Hickory, *Cárya ovàta,* is most commonly found on mid and lower slopes. It is a medium-sized to large tree occasionally reaching heights of 22 m (72 ft). It is shade-tolerant and may become a dominant tree in the oak forest. Shagbark hickory is easily recognized by its medium-gray vertically peeling bark. Leaves are compound, usually with five leaflets. This species produces a crop of sweet nuts in September.

Pignut Hickory, *Cárya glàbra* and *Cárya ovàlis,* are two distinct species occurring in approximately the same habitats with the same colloquial name. Both grow to a height of 20 m (65 ft) on open sites. Both are intolerant of shade and do not compete well with oaks, which often overtop them and shade them out. *C. glabra* has leaves usually with five leaflets and light gray bark which becomes furrowed on older trees. *C. ovalis* has leaves usually with seven leaflets and bark about the same color as *C. glabra* but breaking into detachable plates of smaller size than those of the shagbark hickory. The nut is small but sweet. *Carya glabra* reaches the northern limit of the range almost at the northern Massachusetts border. *C. ovalis* ranges into southern New Hampshire.

Range of the pignut hickory, *Carya glabra*. The other species, *C. ovalis*, extends northward into southern New Hampshire.

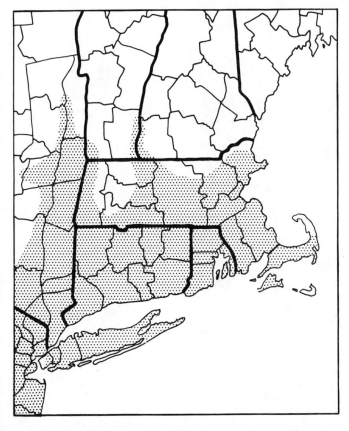

Mockernut Hickory, *Cárya tomentòsa*, is another hickory of the southern New England oak forest. It is less common than the others, especially in the northern part of the region. Mockernut hickory has compound leaves, usually with seven leaflets. The bark is deeply furrowed; the nut is large but with very little meat.

Flowering Dogwood, *Córnus flórida*, is a branching tree, reaching about 8 m (26 ft) in the oak forest understory. See full description in section following (page 150). It is easily recognized in May by its conspicuous white flower-like bracts, its rough bark, and its leaves typical of the genus. All dogwoods are easy to identify by their leaves. When a dogwood leaf is pulled apart the transparent thread-like vascular

Range of the mockernut hickory, *Carya tomentosa*.

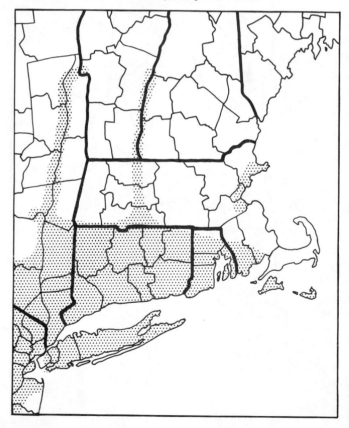

26. Dogwood leaf, showing how the vascular bundles stretch rather than break when the leaf is pulled apart.

bundles stretch rather than break. Flowering dogwood is common in Connecticut and Rhode Island and occasional in Massachusetts and southern New Hampshire.

Other Midslope Trees

In addition to the trees described in the hilltop community, the following trees also appear in the midslope community. These are more typically found in other communities, however, and are described elsewhere.

White Pine, *Pìnus Stròbus*, page 219
Hemlock, *Tsùga canadénsis*, page 316
White Ash, *Fráxinus americàna*, page 146
American Beech, *Fàgus grandifòlia*, page 316
Red Oak, *Quércus rùbra*, page 145
Sassafras, *Sássafras álbidum*, page 222
Yellow Birch, *Bétula lùtea*, page 316
Sugar Maple, *Àcer sáccharum*, page 195
Hop Hornbeam, *Óstrya virginiàna*, page 146

Shrubs of the Midslope Community

American Chestnut, *Castànea dentàta,* formerly a forest tree of the first rank, now rarely grows over 5 m (16 ft), though an occasional blight-resistant tree up to 15 m (50 ft) does occur. It is most commonly seen as a multi-trunked stump sprout. This habit plus its distinctive leaves makes it easy to recognize. A longer description of this tree begins on page 154.

Mountain Laurel, *Kálmia latifòlia,* is a handsome evergreen shrub with deep-green leathery leaves, reaching about 4 m (13 ft) in height. It produces flowers on the terminals of

27. Green-osier dogwood, *Cornus alternifolia*, bears the typical dogwood leaf on green twigs.

the branches in early June. A longer description of this plant begins on page 152.

Maple-leaved Viburnum, *Vibúrnum acerifólium*, is a small straggling shrub with leaves very similar in shape to those of the red maple, though these turn pinkish to purple in fall. Where there is sufficient sunlight, the plant produces clusters of small white flowers from which grow glossy dark-blue fruits.

Variant form: A form producing white fruit has been reported.

Green-Osier Dogwood, *Córnus alternifólia*, is an open shrub or small tree up to 8 m (26 ft) high with branches arranged in irregular platform-like whorls around the stem. Young twigs are greenish and leaves are typical of the dogwood genus (see page 140). Small white flowers occur in flattish clusters. The fruits are dark blue berries on reddish stems.

Variant form: A rare form with yellow fruits has been found.

Other Midslope Shrubs

In addition to the hilltop shrubs which persist into the midslope community, the following shrubs, each described in the low slope community section, also grow here occasionally.

Pink Azalea, *Rhododéndron nudiflórum*
Mountain Azalea, *Rhododéndron ròseum*
Witch Hazel, *Hamamèlis virginiàna*
Highbush Blueberry, *Vaccínium corymbòsum*

The Low Slope Community

THE COMMUNITY inhabiting the lower slopes of the oak forest shows an even greater diversity of vegetation than does that of the midslopes just described. Except for a few species found in the hilltop community, all of the trees and shrubs found in both of the drier oak forest habitats turn up at least occasionally in the low slope community. Other species more common in one or another of the wetland communities described in Part VII also appear here. Though the variety of subshrubs—those small creeping plants with evergreen leaves—and herbaceous plants is not great in any of these slope communities, there are far more in the low slope community than elsewhere, except, as we shall see, in the uncommon mixed mesophytic community discussed later in this section.

This variety of plants in the low slope community seems to be a direct result of the ample soil moisture present there. The community extends to where the water table lies only 10 centimeters or so beneath the surface, though this thin layer of dry land seems crucial to the survival of many of the trees and shrubs. Where the water table is closer to the surface, there is a dramatic change in the vegetation as the low slope community gives way to the less diverse wooded swamp community (page 274). Many of the trees that grow in the low slope community are adapted to a high water table; they are relatively shallow-rooted and are able to survive in a saturated soil, during short periods at least, in winter and early spring when they are not in active growth.

The ground underlying this community is often more nearly level than that under the communities farther uphill. As a result, much of the precipitation, rather than running off, sinks into the ground and thus is available for the plants that grow there. Usually, also, the soils there are thicker and the particle sizes finer than on higher sites.

It is in this community that many of the trees in the oak forest reach their greatest size. The low slope community is the preferred habitat for the largest of the native oaks, the red oak, *Quercus rubra*. During the early stages of its life, the red oak grows at about the same rate as most of the other forest trees. At a height of about 12 meters (40 feet) the

28. Low slope community, Sudbury, Massachusetts. An understory of sassafras is growing beneath a canopy of red oak and red maple. The ground is covered by a large colony of hayscented fern, *Dennstaedtia punctilobula*, a common species on these sites.

growth rates of the others begin to slow down, while the red oak continues to grow vigorously and may eventually reach a height of 27 meters (88 feet) or even taller. In the mature woodlands of Massachusetts and southern New Hampshire, red oaks tower umbrella-like above the other trees. In this community white oak sometimes grows to unusually tall heights as well.

Even taller is the tulip tree, *Liriodendron tulipifera* (see page 195), which reaches the northern limit of its range in eastern New England. Tulip tree is not as abundant as red oak in the woodlands, since its seedlings require both fertile soil and an open habitat. Red oak, on the other hand, is quite shade-tolerant and can often persist in the understory for many years until a disturbance opens up a hole in the canopy above.

It is also in this community that a well-developed understory layer appears. In the low slope community, such shade-tolerant species as flowering dogwood, *Cornus florida*, hornbeam, *Carpinus caroliniana*, and hop hornbeam, *Ostrya virginiana*, are adapted to life beneath the dominant oaks and other species of the canopy. Though both flowering dogwood and hop hornbeam also appear in the midslope community, they are usually much more abundant in the low slope community.

Other understory trees such as sassafras, *Sassafras albidum*, are not shade-tolerant, however. These only live for a few years in the shade, then gradually decline and die, only to resprout from the living roots. These suppressed sassafras trees may persist in this way for several generations until some fate befalls the canopy trees and releases them. A number of other trees, such as white ash and the hickories, though not tolerant of shade, can also persist by this means should they be suppressed by other trees above them. White pine, lacking this stump-sprouting ability, eventually dies out completely if it cannot penetrate the canopy.

The low slope community often has a well-developed shrub layer, though except where mountain laurel thickets abound the layer is not continuous enough to impede walking. Highbush blueberry, *Vaccinium corymbosum*, and either of two species of azalea, mountain azalea, *Rhododendron roseum*, in northern parts of the region, and pink azalea, *R. nudiflorum*, in the southern parts, grow in acidic soil, while witch hazel, *Hamamelis virginiana*, grows where the soil is not so strongly acidic.

Among the subshrubs and herbaceous plants, the species are, not surprisingly, ones adapted to acidic soils. These are described in the chapter beginning on page 156.

Trees of the Low Slope Community

Red Oak, *Quércus rùbra*, though growing on midslope sites, is more common in the low slope community. It is easily recognized by its tall stature, its leaf shape, which is intermediate between the stout leaves of the black oak and the lacy leaves of the scarlet oak, and its bark, which is gray with wide reddish furrows. The red, scarlet, and black oaks hybridize readily; the ensuing progeny may hybridize again. As a result, there are many southern New England oaks showing characteristics intermediate between one species and another, thus making identification uncertain. In ma-

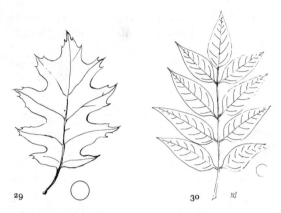

29. Red oak, *Quercus rubra*, has leaves intermediate between the stout leaves of the black oak and the lacy leaves of the scarlet oak. Tall stature and gray bark broken by wide reddish furrows are also characteristic of the species. (See also photograph on page 116.)

30. White ash, *Fraxinus americana*. Its grayish, finely furrowed bark is characteristic.

ture woodlands, however, the large size of red oak seems to be the best single criterion for recognition.

White Ash, *Fráxinus americàna*, grows in a variety of habitats but reaches its largest sizes, up to 30 m (97 ft) or more, where there is ample soil moisture. It is easily recognized by its grayish bark, which is broken into diamond-shaped furrows, its smooth gray branchlets, and its compound leaves bearing seven or nine leaflets.

Tupelo, *Nýssa sylvática*, is most common near ponds or on the edges of swamps, though it does not normally grow in permanently saturated soils. It is a medium-sized tree but occasionally reaches a height of 20 m (60 ft). It is usually quite picturesque in outline, with irregular horizontal branches and a flat top—often the result of ice damage. The leaves are very abundant, usually 5 to 8 cm (2 to 3 in) long, clustered at the ends of the shoots. They are a dark lustrous green in summer, turning a brilliant crimson in the fall.

Hop Hornbeam, *Óstrya virginiàna*, is a small understory tree growing to about 9 m (30 ft) high. It is common on moist but not boggy sites. I have found it on drier sites farther north. Hop hornbeam is easily recognized by its small sta-

31. Tupelo, *Nyssa sylvatica*, is common near ponds and the edges of swamps. It is easily recognized by its horizontally branching, twiggy habit. The fruit is a blue berry.

ture, its brownish scaly bark that shreds into small curling plates, and its finely toothed leaves; the bark is more shaggy than that of dogwood.

Hornbeam, *Carpìnus caroliniàna*, is a low, spreading tree to about 8 m (26 ft) high. It is perhaps the most common near the edges of swamps but is frequently found in the low slope community as well. It is a very shade-tolerant species and can grow in the understory. Distinguished by its smooth dark bluish-gray bark (darker than beech), it is found all through the region but is uncommon near the coast.

32. Hop hornbeam, *Ostrya virginiana*, may be recognized by its brown scaly bark, which shreds into small plates, and its small stature in the understory.

33. Hornbeam, *Carpinus caroliniana*, is distinguished by its smooth, knobby, bluish-gray bark and its small stature.

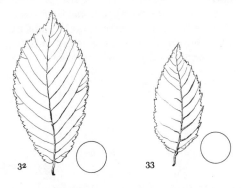

Shrubs of the Low Slope Community

Shrubs described in the midslope community may persist into the low slope community.

Witch Hazel, *Hamamèlis virginiàna,* is a large multi-trunked shrub to 5 m (16 ft) with rounded leaves from 5 to 15 cm (2 to 5 in) in length, rounded in shape and wavy-toothed along the edges. The blooms are small yellow stringy flowers that appear in late fall. Witch hazel is also common in the mixed mesophytic community. A variant form with smaller leaves from 3.5 to 10 cm (1½ to 4 in) in length, leathery in texture and covered with hairs, is occasionally seen.

Pink Azalea, *Rhododéndron nudiflòrum,* is a branching shrub up to 4 m (13 ft), with deciduous leaves clustered at the ends of branches. It is easily recognized during May by its showy pink but odorless flowers. It is more common in southern and eastern parts of the region.

Variant forms: White-flowered and purple-flowered forms have been found.

Mountain Azalea, *Rhododéndron ròseum,* is similar in appearance to pink azalea above, but its bright pink flowers have a delightful clove-like fragrance. It is found in higher sections away from the coast. (See color plate V.)

Highbush Blueberry, *Vaccínium corymbòsum,* is a coarse shrub up to 3 m (10 ft) that is easily recognizable by its several often twisting and contorted stems. Its deciduous leaves are similar in appearance to other blueberries though usually larger, from 4 to 8 cm (1½ to 3 in) in length. Its fruit is large and sweet though not so flavorful as that of lowbush blueberries. Highbush blueberry is common on the edges of swamps and in bogs.

Arrow-Wood, *Vibúrnum recógnitum,* is a deciduous shrub 1 to 3 m (3 to 10 ft) tall, having coarsely toothed rounded leaves with prominent straight veins beneath. The small white flowers bloom in clusters and the fruit is a blue-black berry-like drupe. Arrow-wood is common on the edges of swamps.

34. Witch hazel, *Hamamelis virginiana*, is a large multi-trunked shrub. Its small yellow flowers appear in late fall.

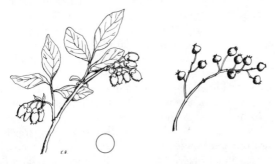

35. Highbush blueberry, *Vaccinium corymbosum*, is recognized by its often contorted woody stems bearing small leaves.

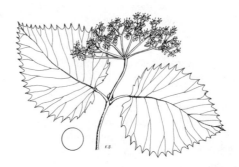

36. Arrow-wood, *Viburnum recognitum*. Sharply toothed and prominently veined leaves are characteristic of the species.

The Low Slope Community 149

Flowering Dogwood,
Mountain Laurel, American Chestnut:
Three Species of Special Interest

INTEREST, like beauty, lies in the eye of the beholder. Even the most nondescript species of plant and animal, if studied in enough depth, would almost surely yield something intriguing, though in many cases this information would be too subtle to be perceived by the casual observer. The following three species are ones that I have enjoyed looking at as I have traveled the woods. Each is common in most parts of the region; each has features that may be observed without special equipment. Two of these, the flowering dogwood and mountain laurel, produce especially handsome floral displays, while the other, the American chestnut, is interesting in that it survives at all in the face of the devastating fungal blight that has so nearly destroyed it. All three species produce unusual forms that differ from the ordinary form in one or more ways.

Elsewhere I have described two other oak forest species, the white pine and hemlock (pages 229 and 322), which also produce occasional bizarre and beautiful forms. As you become more familiar with the region's flora, you will probably take a special interest in other species which may prove to be as fascinating as I have found the three described below.

Flowering Dogwood

Flowering dogwood, *Cornus florida*, is considered by many to be the most beautiful of all native trees. In spring it produces large white blossoms; in fall its leaves turn a deep scarlet. The dogwood is an understory tree, growing well in the shade of taller trees, but like most flowering plants it will blossom more profusely in sunnier sites.

The blossoms, up to 10 centimeters (4 inches) in diameter, are so conspicuous that during its flowering period dogwood can be recognized at a glance. What we see as petals, though, are not petals but modified leaves called

37. Flowering dogwood, *Cornus florida*, may be easily recognized in May by its showy blossoms. Its fall foliage is bright red.

bracts, which cover the small buds during the winter and gradually grow to their full size in spring. When the buds first open, these bracts are yellow-green and inconspicuous; they require about two weeks to reach their full beauty.

The distribution pattern of dogwood is interesting. As is the case with so many of the eastern deciduous trees, dogwood reaches the northern limit of its range in the southern parts of Maine and New Hampshire. Farther south in Connecticut and Rhode Island, the tree is widely distributed, but in Massachusetts and northward it occurs much more sporadically.

Throughout its range dogwood apparently grows best on only slightly acidic soils. Near its northern range limits the tree is often restricted to these soils. In central Massachusetts and southern New Hampshire, I have found dogwood associated with the small fern, ebony spleenwort, *Asplenium platyneuron*, a strong indicator of soils with a pH of between 6 and 7. It would appear, then, that in these areas the more favorable soil conditions compensate for the less favorable climatic conditions. In the northern part of the Connecticut Valley Lowland, dogwood is frequently found on the basalt ridges where the rocks contain small amounts of calcium; it is much less common on the more acidic upland soils that occur on the higher ground on either side of the lowland.

The colder winters at the northern limits of its range also become a limiting factor in the distribution of dogwood. Although the tree may be hardy to −35° C (−30° F), its flowering buds are frequently killed by severe winter weather. This bud-kill of course destroys the tree's reproductive capacity for the following year.

Near the northern end of its range, individual dogwood trees with unusual bud hardiness are worth looking for. Occasionally a single individual will be found that produces flowers when its neighboring trees have been bud-killed by severe winter weather. One such tree found in Atkinson, New Hampshire, bloomed consistently even after the coldest winters. A Massachusetts nurseryman was able to propagate it and introduce it on the market. This superior clone, aptly called "New Hampshire" can now be found in many northern gardens in a climate where the ordinary dogwood would bloom sporadically if at all. Unfortunately, its discoverer is no longer living and the tree is not commercially available, but a knowledgeable horticulturist would be able to reproduce this outstanding plant from cuttings or by grafting or layering.

There are a number of other unusual and horticulturally desirable forms of dogwood that crop up from time to time. Some individuals, for example, bloom more profusely than their neighbors. The floriferousness of a particular species is most often determined by environmental conditions, especially an abundance of light during the growing season; but some trees are genetically more predisposed to bloom and often may be picked out by comparing them with others growing in the same general conditions of light and shade.

Bloom size, color, and bract number are also variable characteristics. Trees with especially large bracts are occasionally found. Pink to red forms occur, but a bud-hardy red form has probably not yet been found in New England. Occasionally a tree is found with blossoms subtended by six or eight bracts rather than the usual four.

Mountain Laurel

Mountain laurel, *Kalmia latifolia*, is probably the most beautiful of common native shrubs. Its dark-green lustrous leaves provide a pleasant contrast to the muted brown and grays of the oak woods in winter. In June, mountain laurel blooms so profusely the woodlands in many places appear covered with a layer of new-fallen snow.

38. Mountain laurel, *Kalmia latifolia*.

Like dogwood, its distribution is somewhat sporadic, especially in the north. In Connecticut, where mountain laurel is the state flower, it is very common in many parts and locally abundant elsewhere. It is local in the eastern part of Massachusetts but common in the central parts. Where the habitat is suitable, mountain laurel may form impenetrable thickets up to 4 meters (13 feet) in height. Often these are called "laurel hells" because of the hindrance they cause to foot travel.

Like other ericads, mountain laurel requires acidic soil. It is commonly found on soils derived from granite or granite gneiss and is therefore often found in areas of very rocky terrain. Most often it is found on till soils that retain some moisture but do not remain soggy. In the northern part of the region it is also found on gravelly or even sandy sites. The tiny seeds usually require a bed of moss to germinate. It is likely to appear in old pastures where a sterile acidic soil favors moss over grass.

Blooming populations of mountain laurel always bear careful scrutiny. Among variations in the flowers is a color range from deep pink to snow white. Some have larger

Three Species of Special Interest   153

individual flowers than normal. On others, the maroon dots found on most flowers sometimes coalesce into a concentric band around the flower, or are absent entirely. (See color plate V.)

Occasionally, very short, compact plants rather than the more common straggling forms can be found, but these are hard to spot in the wild since the plants sprout vigorously following cutting or pruning and are naturally compact for a time.

Across much of its range, mountain laurel is attacked by several species of leaf fungi. These pests do not usually kill the shrub but a severe attack can defoliate it, severely diminishing its value as a garden shrub. There seems to be a great deal of variability in the resistance of mountain laurel to this fungus blight. Some plants are badly hit while others nearby are untouched.

Interesting forms of mountain laurel are more difficult to collect and propagate than most other woodland species. Plants growing in the wild usually develop straggling stems that send out small masses of roots wherever they hit the ground. If plants are moved from the wild, almost invariably they need to be heavily pruned in order to survive the damage to the root system. Superior forms can be grafted, but cuttings from most plants are very difficult to root.

American Chestnut

American chestnut, *Castanea dentata*, as a forest tree was wiped out by blight that reached the southern New England woodlands over fifty years ago. The roots are disease-resistant; living stump sprouts of American chestnut are still common in the understory of many parts of the oak forest. Probably one important reason for the former abundance of this tree was this exceptional stump-sprouting ability. As many as 200 sprouts might grow from a single stump, though most of these, of course, never would have reached maturity.

These young chestnut sprouts are resistant to the blight for a few years; their smooth bark may not afford the fungus spores a proper foothold. But once the trees reach a height of about 4 or 5 meters (12 to 16 feet) and the bark begins to furrow, a patch of orange blisters, fruiting bodies of the fungus, almost invariably appears on the trunk and the young tree is doomed.

In spite of the seemingly ever-present blight fungus, occasional chestnuts do reach fruiting maturity. All of these trees may carry blight resistance to a certain degree, but they seem to fall into two distinct morphological types. The first and most common of these are vigorous young trees that grow in sunny locations and quickly reach fruiting maturity. I have seen them most frequently along the edges of woodlands and roadsides.

The others, which apparently have a stronger degree of blight resistance, grow as spindly whip-like trees. Specimens up to 15 meters (50 feet) tall with branches only on the top 2 or 3 meters are not unusual. These trees often survive a blight attack; patches of dead, loose bark are evidence of spots where the blight has occurred. But eventually they too succumb when the fungus girdles the trunk. In such cases it is common to find a ring of small branches, which sprout as the crown dies, appearing just below the infected area.

Chestnut blossoms and fruits are so distinctive that they are easy to recognize from a passing car. The flowers are cream-colored arching catkins up to 20 centimeters (8 inches) in length that blossom in late spring or summer after the trees have leafed out. The seeds occur in round, light-green, spiny fruits about the size of a golf ball, appearing in late summer and maturing in September. If you want to collect the nuts, watch the ripening process carefully in order to beat the squirrels to them.

39. American chestnut, *Castanea dentata*. The flowers and fruits are easy to recognize but not commonly seen.

Many people try planting the nuts in hopes of producing more blight-resistant chestnuts, but resistance seems to be a recessive characteristic that doesn't appear in the first generation progeny. These seedlings, even though they come from blight-resistant trees, are quickly infected.

Recently what may be the first major breakthrough in combating the blight has been discovered. Researchers at the Connecticut Agricultural Experiment Station in New Haven have produced a remission of blight symptoms by inoculating infected areas on the trees with a harmless strain of fungus. This strain somehow inactivates the pathogenic strain. Although the treatment, even if permanently successful, could probably never be used on a grand enough scale to return the American chestnut to its former status, it may be possible to preserve the tree in certain areas. More importantly, the treatment might make it possible to breed races with increased natural blight resistance. The future of this program should be of great interest to everyone who spends time in the southern New England woodlands.

Oak Forest Subshrubs
and Herbaceous Plants

THE GROUND FLORA of the three oak forest communities described earlier is often one of sparseness and wearisome uniformity. The thick slowly decaying layer of oak leaves is a natural mulch which, like garden mulches, prevents seeds from reaching the soil layer below and smothers tiny seedlings that may have managed to germinate. As a result there are often large areas in the woodlands with the ground layer completely barren of subshrubs and herbaceous plants.

Another reason for the sparseness of ground plants, I suspect, is time. Since most of the southern New England woodlands have grown up within human memory, perhaps not enough time has yet passed for the establishment of a rich ground layer. Old reports of the last remaining tracts of uncut forest in southern New England, by contrast, told of a lush carpet of these smaller plants growing beneath the giant trees. The few old-growth stands that are now beginning to appear also seem to have a larger share of subshrubs and herbaceous plants beneath the trees.

It is not surprising that the smaller plants which do manage to become established in the leafy debris of the oak forest have evolved certain reproductive strategies for survival. For example, practically all are perennial; once established they live for years. In an area such as the oak forest where seedbeds are scarce, the advantage of a perennial over an annual—whose survival depends on a new generation of plants each year—should be apparent. Annual weeds that spread explosively in plowed fields quickly disappear once this optimal seedbed is denied them.

Another reproductive advantage of a great many of these ground plants is the ability to spread by underground runners and root shoots. A whole colony of plants, each individual flowering and producing a crop of seeds, increases the chance that new plants may become established elsewhere. Because many years must pass before these ground plants form large colonies, we could expect the size of the colonies to be related in a rough way to the age of the woodland.

Though the number of species of subshrubs and herbaceous plants that do appear in these oak forest communities is small—especially in comparison with the rich flora of the mixed mesophytic community—space does not permit a description of all the plants found there. The following species, therefore, are the ones you are most likely to encounter.

Ericads

As was the case with the larger shrubs of these communities, many of the subshrubs are ericads: members of the heath family (Ericaceae) and a few other closely related plant families. Because all of these smaller ericads have evergreen leaves, a good time to study this group is in early spring and late fall, when the ground is bare of snow and the other plants are not leafed out.

Wintergreen, *Gaulthèria procúmbens,* is the most famil-

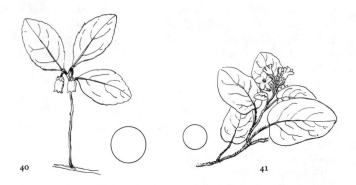

40

41

40. Wintergreen, *Gaultheria procumbens*, may be recognized by its creeping habit and dark-green leathery leaves. The fruit is a bright red berry. In winter the leaves turn a mahogany color.

41. Trailing arbutus, *Epigaea repens*, is a ground-hugging, creeping subshrub. Its leaves are about twice as big as wintergreen, and not so leathery.

iar of the low ericads. It is a creeping ground shrub never reaching more than a few centimeters in height. Its leaves are thick and leathery, oval in shape and evergreen, turning a brownish green in winter. The fruit is a bright red berry with a star-shaped design on one end.

Wintergreen may be found on all three slope communities and persists into the drier sand plain community. I have found it growing most luxuriantly in the lower slope community, where it sometimes forms mats. Its tender reddish new leaves are slightly astringent but tasty to nibble. The berries are also edible, with a delicate flavor.

Variant forms: Occasionally forms are found with berries that are larger or more abundant than average.

Trailing Arbutus, *Epigaèa rèpens*, is another creeping subshrub, much less common than wintergreen. Its leaves are about twice as big as wintergreen, light green and slightly hairy, and hugging the ground. Trailing arbutus can grow from very dry shady habitats to definitely wet boggy sites in full sun, though it grows in the latter habitat more commonly in northern New England.

Trailing arbutus, often called mayflower, is about the earliest of the native plants to bloom in the spring. Its small white to rose-colored flowers bloom half-hidden in the leaf litter in April. The flowers are very fragrant.

The species became scarce in the nineteenth century after large quantities were uprooted from the woods and sold on the streets for Christmas greens. The practice came to an abrupt end about the turn of the century when several states passed laws protecting the plants. Since that time the plant has enjoyed a modest resurgence, and is now abundant in some areas.

Variant forms: Occasionally forms with much larger leaves and flowers are found. A very rare double-flowered form has also been found. (See color plate I.)

Pipsissewa, *Chimáphila umbellàta,* is larger and more upright than wintergreen, reaching about 10 cm (4 in) in height. Like wintergreen and a number of other oak forest plants, it spreads by underground runners to form medium-sized open colonies. The long very dark-green wedge-shaped leaves up to 3.5 cm (1⅜ in) are its most outstanding characteristic. They are even thicker than those of wintergreen and are also evergreen. The flowers, which are borne on long pinkish stems, are white to pink and bloom in July. (See color plate III.)

Spotted Pipsissewa, *Chimáphila maculàta,* is also an upright-growing ground shrub, though smaller in stature than its sister species described above. It also spreads by underground runners but it usually forms small colonies of a few individual plants. The pointed oval leaves have a

42. Spotted pipsissewa, *Chimaphila maculata,* bears distinctive variegated leaves.

43. Shinleaf, *Pyrola* spp., has evergreen leaves. It blooms in summer.

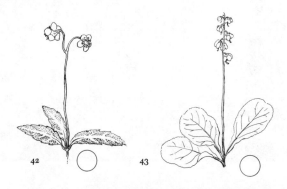

42   43

distinctive mottled appearance: greenish to pinkish variegated with white. The nodding flower is larger than pipsissewa, about 2 cm (¾ in), and very fragrant, usually blooming in August. Spotted pipsissewa is the more southerly
species of the two, reaching the northern limit of its range in
southern New Hampshire. I have seen it mostly in midslope
communities.

Shinleaf, *Pýrola* spp., are small, evergreen, but nonwoody herbs. There are three or four species found in southern New England which are difficult to tell apart. All have
distinctive broadly elliptical leaves that grow from the base
of each plant. The small whitish or greenish yellow flowers
about 1 cm (⅜ in) grow on a stalk up to 20 cm (8 in) high. They
all bloom in summer. Shinleaf is most common where there
is some moisture but does persist onto drier sites.

44. Indian pipes, *Monotropa uniflora*, whose fleshy white stems
are each topped by a single white flower. It receives nourishment
from decaying plant material, and because it requires no sunlight
may be found in dense shade.

Species of the Lily Family (Liliaceae)

This diverse and large family is another that is well represented in ground flora of the three oak forest communities just described. Species in this family range from low mat-forming ground covers to plants that sometimes reach 2 meters in height. The flowers are equally variable; a few are similar in size and shape to some of the garden lilies, while others are so small that a magnifying glass is necessary for observing their parts. In general, all have radially symmetrical flowers, usually of six parts, and leaves with parallel veins. Almost all of the temperate species die back to the ground each winter.

Wood Lily, *Lílium philadélphicum,* is the most striking member of this family to be found in oak woods. Its large bell-like flowers face upward rather than downward as several other lilies do. The flowers vary from a faded orange to a deep orange-red and are spotted purple. Usually a single bloom grows at the top of a stem about 1 m (3 ft) tall, but occasional plants are found with three or more flowers blooming in a tight group.

The wood lily seems to be a transient species that may bloom in one spot for a year or two and then appear in another spot nearby. I have found it growing in rocky habitats in the midslope community. (See color plate III.)

Variant form: A yellow form is occasionally seen.

Similar species: The Canada lily, *Lilium canadense,* is more common in our region, but only occasionally is it found in oak forest habitats, being more abundant in open or wetter habitats. It is described on page 266.

Canada Mayflower, *Maiánthemum canadénse,* is the most common member of the lily family. In appearance, however, it could hardly be more different from the wood lily just described. It is a low perennial to about 8 cm (3 in) in height, that like most of the oak forest herbs spreads by underground runners, forming extensive mats. The plant is unmistakable; its smooth light-green leaves, two on a stem, appear in late April or early May, transforming large areas of the oak forest floor into a green carpet. Its flowers are tiny, forming a yellowish or whitish clump on the terminal of the stems when they bloom in late May or June. The fruit is a small soft red berry.

45. Canada mayflower, *Maianthemum canadense*, is a common woodland herb whose light-green leafy mats cover large areas of forest floor.

The Canada mayflower is important in two ways. First, it is one of the indicator plants, along with some of the club mosses, of a strongly acidic mor humus. Second, the appearance of extensive mats of Canada mayflower in the woodlands may be useful in distinguishing between the post-agricultural community and the more mature oak forest type which we are presently examining. Because of its size, Canada mayflower probably has trouble in competing with taller shrubs and small trees that form thickets in abandoned fields; it does not usually appear in the woods until they mature somewhat. It can grow in deep shade but is almost always found in open shady areas and grows best where there is some moisture and where the leaf litter does not accumulate too deeply.

False Solomon's Seal, *Smilacìna racemòsa*, is a very common member of the oak forest herb flora. It is a large plant, single-stemmed and curving, bearing large smooth oval leaves that grow on alternate sides up the stem. When the plant is in bloom, the top of the stem is covered with a feathery mass of small greenish-white flowers that emit a strong distinctive fragrance. This plant also spreads by underground runners and forms open colonies. It is found in somewhat more open sites than some of the other oak forest plants, probably being most common on the midslope communities. It is common to find colonies of false Solomon's seal all pointing in the same direction, oriented so they can receive the most sunlight.

46. False Solomon's seal, *Smilacina racemosa*, is illustrated in fruit. The fruits are pinkish, turning red in fall. The bloom is a cluster of small feathery white flowers which appear in early June.

47. Solomon's seal, *Polygonatum pubescens*, bears blue fruit hanging from the leaf axils. The flowers are small yellow bells that grow in pairs.

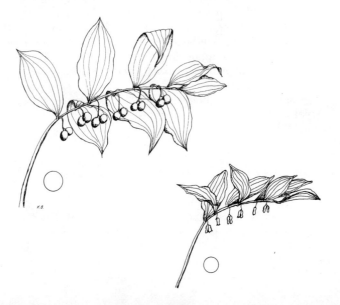

48. Wild oats, *Uvularia sessilifolia*, is smaller than false Solomon's seal and Solomon's seal. Its leaves are grayish green and its flower is pale yellow.

Solomon's Seal, *Polygonàtum pubéscens*, closely resembles false Solomon's seal in vegetative form, but its yellowish bell-shaped flowers, growing from the axils of the leaves along the stem, are very different from the feathery flowers that adorn the top of the false Solomon's seal. Solomon's seal is said to grow in the same habitats as false Solomon's seal, but I have found it more often in slightly moister sites.

Wild Oats, *Uvulària sessilifòlia*, looks somewhat like a miniature version of Solomon's seal. As its Latin name suggests, the grayish-green leaves are sessile, that is, they arise directly, without leafstalks, from the main stem of the plant. The flowers are small yellow bells. Like so many other oak forest herbs, wild oats form large mats by underground runners. It is common in midslope and lower slope communities. The plant is in no way related to what some people sow in their youth.

Similar species: Bellwort, *Uvularia perfoliata*, has a larger yellow flower and grows in moister, less acidic habitats than wild oats.

Species of the Orchid Family (Orchidaceae)

There are a number of species of orchids that grow in southern New England. Most are rather small-flowered and grow in wet habitats. The orchid species commonly growing in the drier oak forest communities are few, but these in-

THE OAK FOREST

clude the showiest and clearly the most common of native orchids, the pink lady's slipper. Orchid flowers vary greatly in color, size, and shape, ranging from the huge tropical varieties grown in greenhouses to species whose miniature flowers are only a little bigger than a pinhead. These flowers are all bilaterally symmetrical: that is, the left side looks like the right side, but the top is different from the bottom. The lower petal of each has been modified into a showy structure which botanists call a lip. In the lady's slipper, this lip is a showy, pouch-like structure; in others it is fringed or tongue-like. Though other flowers of some other plant families are also bilaterally symmetrical, with a little practice you will recognize orchids easily.

Pink Lady's Slipper, *Cypripèdium acaùle,* is well known to almost everybody who has explored the southern New England oak woods. Its solitary showy flower, situated on a bare stem approximately 20 cm (8 in) high, above two widely oval basal leaves, is impossible to confuse with any other flower. It is abundant in most parts of the region and, as more of the land returns to woods, is apparently becoming more so. Though lady's slipper seems to reproduce most vigorously in light shade and some moisture, it can be found in dry or moist habitats and all conditions of shade except the extremes of very deep shade or full sun.

There is a persistent rumor that the pink lady's slipper is becoming rare in the woods. During the agricultural boom,

49. Pink lady's slipper, *Cypripedium acaule*, the largest of the native orchids.

when the few remaining patches of woods were regularly cut and burned, the species may have indeed become scarce. In some areas now it is abundant beyond measure.

Though every gardener who works with native plants would like to grow pink lady's slipper, the species is nearly impossible to transplant or start from seed. Transplants almost invariably disappear after a year or two, and seed does poorly, even when carefully handled.

To reproduce naturally and increase its numbers, the lady's slipper has depended on the production of a tremendous number of tiny, dust-like seeds. Only an infinitesimally small percentage of these must chance upon the proper conditions for germination and subsequent growth. Furthermore, relatively few of the flowers are naturally pollinated. It is not at all unusual in early summer to find a colony of lady's slippers in which not one flower has set seeds; the long stems of these unpollinated plants end abruptly in a green leaf-like bract. The ovary, which if fertilized would have stayed attached to it and become a seed pod, falls off with the flower.

If you have a few lady's slippers in your woods and want to increase their number, you can assist nature by hand-pollinating the plants and thus increasing the likelihood that more young plants will grow nearby. Hand-pollination is a simple process. Just remove some of the yellowish sticky pollen with a wooden matchstick or small twig from one of the two receptacles on either side of the flower and rub it on the underside of the spade-like stigma between. The pollinated flower will quickly wither away and the ovary below it will begin to thicken and grow. The ovary grows into a seed pod and remains on the plant all summer, then turns brown, dries out, and splits open, releasing clouds of tiny seeds.

The seeds seem to take a long time to germinate and grow; usually several years will pass before the young plants, which superficially resemble Canada mayflower, are first noticeable. A couple of additional years must pass before these bloom. Hand-pollination of this species is a simple process, but the results are not seen for a long time.

Picking any lady's slipper flowers is usually fatal to the plant, and the reader should note that it is even illegal in some states to do so.

Variant form: Occasionally a white form of the pink lady's

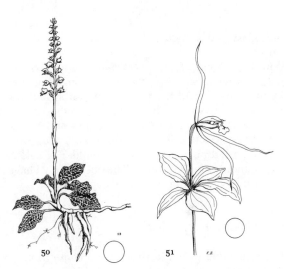

50. Rattlesnake plantain, *Goodyera pubescens*, is recognized by its bluish-green, white-veined leaves.

51. Whorled pogonia, *Isotria verticillata*, is most easily identified by its distinctive greenish-maroon flowers.

slipper will be found. These are much more common in northern New England, where they sometimes account for 50 percent of the lady's slipper population. The one white form that appeared in my woods disappeared after a dog stepped on it. (See color plate II.)

Rattlesnake Plantain, *Goodyèra pubéscens,* is the only other orchid that is common in the oak forest communities. It is a small plant which, unlike the lady's slipper, spreads by underground root stocks. The bluish-green basal leaves are covered with a network of white lines, a characteristic which makes its identification unmistakable. These leaves remain green all winter. The flowers, which are greenish white and very small, are borne on a relatively tall stem about 20 cm (8 in) tall, which appears during the summer.

Rattlesnake plantain is found in both the midslope and lower slope communities, but seems to be more common in the latter.

Similar species: There are two or three other species of rattlesnake plantain which occur in the region, though less commonly. They resemble each other so closely that a magnifying glass and a good guide are needed to distinguish them.

Whorled Pogonia, *Isótria verticillàta*, is far less common than the previous species. Its greenish-maroon flower is easily overlooked, and the plant when not in bloom grows one whorl of leaves closely resembling Indian cucumber-root, *Medeola virginiana*, which occurs in moist sites. The flowers are distinctive for their three very long petal-like sepals. Whorled pogonia is another builder of colonies by means of underground runners. The only colony I have seen was growing on a rather open midslope site.

Other Common Species

The remaining plants in this section come from various families. They are included because of their abundance, the conspicuousness of their flowers or foliage, or the known existence of interesting variant forms. There are many other herbaceous plants that appear occasionally in the oak forest, especially in areas where the soil is less acidic. These will be listed in the chapter on the mixed mesophytic community (page 190), though space does not permit descriptions. Along the transition between the oak forest and the forested wetland communities (page 274), a number of other herbaceous plants adapted to moister conditions are sometimes found.

Partridgeberry, *Mitchélla rèpens*, is one of the most familiar small plants in the oak forest. It is of low creeping habit, with rounded evergreen leaves about 1 cm (⅜ in) in

52. Partridgeberry, *Mitchella repens*, is a small creeping ground cover that is most easily identified by its small evergreen leaves, which are borne in pairs, and its bright red berries.

diameter and bright red winter berries. The berries are edible but tasteless. It bears small white trumpet-shaped flowers that are formed in pairs, blooming in July. The ovaries of each pair of flowers are united; the red berry we see has two eye-like spots where each flower was attached.

Partridgeberry is a familiar ground cover on rocky knolls, usually in midslope or low slope communities. Where there is ample soil moisture, the plant grows somewhat larger leaves. Many people grow partridgeberry in terrariums.

Variant forms: Occasionally plants are found where the pairs of flowers have grown together into a double form with ten petals instead of the usual four. A rare form producing white berries also occurs.

Fringed Polygala, *Polýgala paucifòlia,* is another short-stemmed creeping herb of the oak forest. The leaves superficially resemble wintergreen but are bluer and more pointed on the ends. Crowding of the leaves at the top of the stem also distinguishes the plant from wintergreen. Any imagined resemblance to wintergreen abruptly ends when fringed polygala blooms; each blossom, approximately 2 cm long, with its pair of wings and little fringe on the end, looks more like a butterfly than a flower. Fringed polygala is reputed to be fairly common everywhere but along the Connecticut coast. I have found it mostly in cooler northern slopes and moist shady areas of the low slope community. (See color plate II.)

Variant form: A handsome white-flowered form is sometimes seen.

Wood Anemone, *Anémone quinquefòlia,* is a low herb, about 10 cm (4 in) tall, that forms small colonies. It is easily recognized by the delicate five-parted compound leaves and the single white to pinkish-white blossom on the terminal of each little plant. Wood anemone is most common in moist, open woods or clearings. (See color plate I.)

Similar species: Rue anemone, *Anemonella thalictroides,* bears several flowers on each stem and grows in clumps. It is more common on less acidic soils.

Round-lobed Hepatica, *Hepática americàna,* is a low perennial herb usually growing as single widely separated plants. It is easily identified by its evergreen three-lobed rounded leaves and its small bluish or lavender blooms, about 1 cm in diameter, which are borne on hairy stems and appear in April before the plant produces new leaves.

The round-lobed hepatica is found occasionally throughout the area. I have never found it in what appears to be a strongly acidic habitat. (See color plate I.)

Variant forms: Forms with white, deep purple, clear pink, or blue flowers are occasionally found. A very rare double-flowered form has been seen two or three times.

Similar species: The pointed-lobed hepatica, *Hepatica acutiloba,* is definitely a plant of neutral or only slightly acidic soils. Natural hybridization between the two species must occur, because forms with characteristics that are intermediate between the two species are often found.

White Baneberry, *Actaèa pachypòda,* is a taller plant, reaching 60 cm (2 ft). Its compound leaves are toothed and deeply cut. The small white flowers, which appear in late May, are borne in feathery clusters on the terminal of the stems. The fruits; clusters of conspicuous white berries each with a small black dot on the end, borne on thick red stalks, make this plant easy to recognize. These white berries, which are mildly poisonous, have given rise to the plant's colloquial name of "Doll's-eyes." White baneberry is most common in shady midslope and lower slope communities. It may be less sensitive to soil acidity than many plants since it also is found in neutral soil areas. I don't remember ever seeing it on strongly acidic sites in close association with the ericad shrubs.

53. White baneberry, *Actaea pachypoda,* is most easily recognized in summer by its distinctive white fruit. Red baneberry, *Actaea rubra,* is similar in appearance, except that its fruits are bright red.

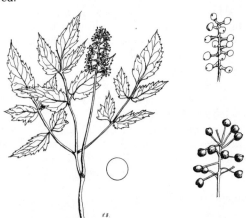

K.B.

A (left). Round-lobed hepatica, *Hepatica americana*, low slope community

B (right). Marsh marigold, *Caltha palustris*, wetland and watercourse communities

C (left). Trailing arbutus, *Epigaea repens*, rare double form, oak forest and sand plain communities

D (right). Wood anemone, *Anemone quinquefolia*, low slope community

Early Spring Wildflowers

(April to early May)

PLATE I

A (left). Lady's slipper, *Cypripedium acaule*, pink and uncommon white forms, oak forest communities

B (right). Arethusa, *Arethusa bulbosa*, acidic wetlands

C (left). Fringed polygala, *Polygala paucifolia*, low slope community

D (right). Wild geranium, *Geranium maculatum*, rare white form, low slope community

May Wildflowers

PLATE II

A (left). Wood lily, *Lilium philadelphicum,* oak forest communities

B (right). Pipsissewa, *Chimaphila umbellata,* oak forest communities

C (left). Plymouth County gentian, *Sabatia Kennedyana,* rare, coastal wetland communities

D (right). Prickly-pear cactus, *Opuntia humifusa,* coastal sand plain community

Late Spring and Early Summer Wildflowers
(June and July)

PLATE III

A (left). Turk's cap lily, *Lilium superbum*, south coastal wetland communities

B (right). Cardinal flower, *Lobelia cardinalis*, with sweet pepperbush, *Clethra alnifolia*, in background, wetland and watercourse communities

C (left). Fringed gentian, *Gentiana crinita*, wet meadow community

D (right). Turtlehead, *Chelone glabra*, wetland and watercourse communities

Late Summer Wildflowers

(July and August)

PLATE IV

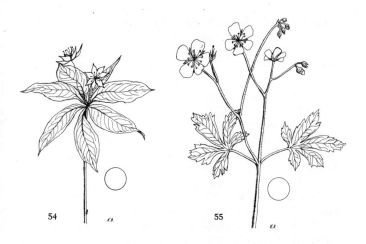

54. Star flower, *Trientalis borealis*, is recognized by its whorl of unequal-sized leaves and its two seven-petaled flowers.

55. Wild geranium, *Geranium maculatum*, is a tall plant with distinctively shaped leaves and rosy-purple flowers.

Variant forms: Occasionally a plant bearing light-red berries is seen.

Similar species: Red baneberry, *Actaea rubra*, is very similar in appearance except that the fruits are cherry-red and borne on slender stalks.

Star Flower, *Trientàlis boreàlis*, is a small (approximately 15 cm) erect perennial with a whorl of somewhat unequal pointed leaves at the terminal of the stem. One or two white star-like flowers appear on long thread-like stalks above the leaves. The star flower is definitely an acid-soil plant, occurring on midslope or low slope communities and extending into wetter habitats. It is usually found in shade.

Wild Geranium, *Gerànium maculàtum*, is a larger woodland plant up to 50 cm (20 in) tall. Its leaves are round in general shape but deeply cut into five parts. The rosy-purple five-petaled flowers, 2 to 3 cm in diameter, are borne in sparse, open clusters on the terminal. The wild geranium is quite common in the oak forest, growing on all but the driest sites. It is occasionally found in fields as well. I have seen it commonly associated with false Solomon's seal in shady sites. It is only distantly related to the house plant called geranium, which actually belongs to a different genus.

Variant forms: These handsome plants do not seem to receive the attention they deserve from naturalists and horticulturists. In any large population it is possible to find plants with larger or more abundant flowers and slightly different color forms. A rare white-flowered form occurs. (See color plate II.)

Wood Aster, *Áster* spp., comprises a group of fall-flowering herbaceous plants. These vary in leaf shape and flower size, but most of the woodland species bear numerous white daisy-like flowers.

Wild Sarsaparilla, *Aràlia nudicaùlis,* is a familiar perennial herb of the oak forest that reaches about 30 cm (1 ft) in height. It bears one large compound leaf, made up of finely toothed leaflets, which forks from the stem at ground level or just above. The small flowers are borne on the smooth stem in spherical arrangements called umbels, which are usually below the large leaf. There may be several of these umbels

56. Wood aster, *Aster divaricatus,* a common fall flower in dry woodlands.

57. Wild sarsaparilla, *Aralia nudicaulis,* is recognized by its one compound leaf and its spherical clusters of small white flowers.

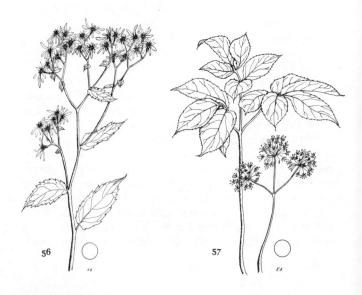

56   57

on one plant. The fruit is a dark blue berry. Aralia is common throughout the southern New England oak woods. It is usually more common on the lower slope community but persists onto the drier sites. It spreads by underground runners to form open colonies.

Similar species: Two similar species, the bristly sarsaparilla, *Aralia hispia*, and the spikenard, *Aralia racemosa*, both bear flowers that resemble those of the wild sarsaparilla, though both show important differences in habit and habitat. The first bears smaller leaves and occurs in dry habitats while the latter is substantially taller, occurring in more neutral soil areas.

Ferns and Clubmosses of the Oak Forest

IN NEW ENGLAND and other regions that receive ample rainfall, the ferns and clubmosses are an integral part of the woodland ground vegetation. In many parts of the Midwest where yearly rainfall amounts are lower, ferns and clubmosses are notably absent from the woodlands. Indeed, naturalists in these areas must often travel many miles to view the same number of ferns that we might find in a single acre here.

The ferns and clubmosses are the two most abundant and varied groups of nonflowering vascular plants. Both groups depend on the production and dissemination of tiny dustlike spores, rather than flowers and seeds, for their reproduction. But, like the more familiar flowering plants, both groups contain vascular tissue, that is, the supporting and conducting tissue that enables these plants to attain height and receive moisture and nourishment from the roots. Three other groups of nonflowering plants—the quillworts, the horsetails, and the spikemosses—also contain vascular tissue, while the algae, fungi, lichens, and liverworts do not, and as a result must remain close to the ground. The mosses do contain primitive vascular tissue and thus act as an evolutionary link between these two important divisions of the plant kingdom.

The ferns and clubmosses enjoy a largely undeserved reputation of being difficult to identify. While it is true that many of the illustrations in the fern identification guides look distressingly similar and that a few of the common species lack distinctive and easily recognizable features, there are only about eighteen species that occur in the oak forest with any abundance, a number that any serious naturalist would find manageable. If we add to this the few species that grow in the region's wetlands, the number is still well within the ability of most people to know. It is only in neutral soil areas, where a dozen additional species—mostly of ferns—appear, that a beginning naturalist might feel overwhelmed; but, in comparison to the hundreds of native flowering plants, the variety is still quite small.

Ferns

In spite of this relatively small variety, the ferns are a fascinating group of plants to study. A number of species cross with one another; hybrids with characteristics inter-mediate between the parent plants will reward a diligent search. Other species produce interesting variant forms, both as geographical varieties and as mutations. In fact, there are probably more variant forms of the ferns than any other comparable group of native plants. In addition, a number of species native to the region are rare or very local in their distribution. And several species have such exacting ecological requirements that their presence or absence in an area are useful indicators of soil and climatic conditions.

GROWTH REQUIREMENTS

A continuous source of soil moisture seems to be the major ecological requirement for most, but not all, ferns. Not surprisingly, the variety and abundance of ferns is greater in the moist low slope community than elsewhere in the oak forest. Though most ferns prefer the shade of a woodland habitat, some thrive in full sun if their roots are supplied with continuous and ample moisture. Indeed, some wetland ferns actually seem to prefer a sunny habitat.

Two very common oak forest species, the bracken, *Pteridium aquilinum*, and the hayscented fern, *Dennstaedtia punctilobula*, will grow in habitats that by late summer may become quite dry. In fact, the bracken seems to prefer dry, sterile habitats. The Christmas fern, *Polystichum acrostichoides*, and the marginal woodfern, *Dryopteris marginalis*, though normally woodland plants, will survive in drier and at least partially sunny habitats. Perhaps the leathery evergreen leaves of both species are an adaptation to survival in drier conditions.

The mixed mesophytic community, with its moist conditions and less acidic soils, supports a far greater variety of ferns than do the more acidic soils of the low slope community. Most of the common ferns found in the low slope community grow equally well in the mixed mesophytic community, but in addition there are a number of ferns which demand a neutral or near-neutral soil. I have found that a large number of Christmas ferns growing in an area is an almost certain sign of less acidic soil; in these sites maidenhair fern, *Adiantum pedatum*, and other neutral soil species will usually turn up. Because neutral soil areas are uncommon in southern New England, these species that require neutral soils are also uncommon.

At the other end of the pH continuum there are a few ferns that seem to prefer a strongly acidic habitat. The Virginia chain fern, *Woodwardia virginica*, is rarely found outside the intensely acidic habitat of sphagnum bogs. Its close relative, the net-veined chain fern, *W. areolata*, also grows only in acidic environments, usually in swamps near the coast. The rare climbing fern, *Lygodium palmatum* (page 13), is another species of strongly acidic soils.

FERN LIFE CYCLE

Though the ferns depend on the production of tiny airborne spores for their dispersal into new habitats, they also have a sexual stage in their life cycle. Occasionally during the summer, you may come across an area of moist bare ground on which are growing some fern prothalli, tiny green plants each consisting of a single heart-shaped leaf-like membrane sometimes reaching 5 millimeters in diameter. These plants contain both the male and female reproductive organs of the fern. Fertilization takes place on the outside of the prothallus with the aid of moisture from the air, and from this tiny prothallus the more familiar spore-bearing leaves begin to grow. During the prothallus stage, if two different species are growing in close proximity, hybridization may occur. Once the spore-bearing plant is established, many species then increase their numbers by underground runners.

Though unquestionably successful for many millions of years, chance dispersal of spores is a highly inefficient means of reproduction. Bare spots where the spores can germinate and grow are not common in woodland habitats; the tiny prothalli and the developing ferns require a constant supply of moisture for survival. Because of these exigencies, ferns must produce a vast number of spores. One botanist has estimated that a single mature marginal woodfern leaf produces upward of 50 million spores. A little arithmetic would show that if only one spore from each woodfern leaf germinated each year, marginal woodferns would soon fill every available habitat.

Ferns are fairly easy to grow from spores, but the process is a slow one, often requiring two or three years to complete the life cycle. Directions are available in several of the references at the end of Part IV.

IDENTIFYING FERNS

For serious study of ferns you will need an identification guide. If you are a beginner, however, your first encounter with such a guide may seem discouraging. Recognition is largely based on characteristics of the leaves, which on many of the species seem to be identical. Three key considerations will help you identify ferns: you should know whether the illustrated species is normally small, medium, or large; whether it is common, occasionally found, rare, or absent altogether from southern New England; and whether it occurs in the normally acidic soils of the oak forest, only in the mixed mesophytic community, or only in wetlands. If you note size, relative abundance, and ecological preference in the margins of your identification guide, you should have little difficulty learning the ferns.

The chart on pages 178–79 includes information for the

ferns of the oak forest and mixed mesophytic communities. Wetland ferns are described in the chapter beginning on page 330.

VARIANT FORMS, RACES, AND HYBRIDS

There is more variation in the ferns than in probably any other comparable group of plants. The lady fern, *Athyrium Filix-femina,* and the spinulose woodfern, *Dryopteris spinulosa,* both produce a number of geographical varieties that differ from one another in clearly recognizable ways. In fact, some taxonomists award the status of separate species to some of these.

Species of the woodfern genus also hybridize with one another. Though the hybrids are not common, in a large population containing two or more woodfern species it is often possible to find individuals exhibiting characteristics intermediate between the parent plants. Often these hybrids are taller than either of the parents, but rarely do they produce fertile spores.

Scott's spleenwort, *Asplenosorus ebenoides,* is a very rare intergeneric hybrid between the walking fern, *Camptosorus rhizophyllus,* and the ebony spleenwort, *Asplenium platyneuron.* The fern occasionally appears in neutral soil areas where the two species grow in close proximity.

It is probably the mutant forms, however, that are of most interest to naturalists. Some of these are so bizarre that their identification is difficult, while others so closely resemble the normal form that only an expert can tell them apart. The most easily recognizable variant form, one that occurs in a number of different species, is the crested form, in which the tips of the leaflets (the entire frond of a fern is considered to be a leaf) are forked. These forms are never common but are occasionally seen.

Crested forms have been reported for the following species that are common in the oak wood communities: hayscented fern, lady fern, Christmas fern, fragile fern, *Cystopteris fragilis,* and broad beech fern, *Dryopteris hexagonoptera,* and several other native species of other habitats.

Some fern species are more variable than others. These produce many other interesting and easily recognizable

Ferns of the Oak Forest and Mixed Mesophytic Communities

SPECIES (Common name / Latin name)	Size	Abundance	COMMUNITY: Sand Plain	Hilltop	Midslope	Low Slope	Mixed Mesophytic	Wetland
Bracken / *Pteridium aquilinum*	M–L	C	──	──	─ ─	─ ─		
Rusty woodsia / *Woodsia ilvensis*	S	R		──				
Marginal woodfern / *Dryopteris marginalis*	M	C		─ ─	─ ─			
Hayscented fern / *Dennstaedtia punctilobula*	M	C		─ ─	─ ─			
Common polypody / *Polypodium virginianum*	S	C		─ ─	─ ─			
Lady fern / *Athyrium Filix-femina*	M–L	C			─ ─	──	──	─ ─
Christmas fern / *Polystichum acrostichoides*	M	C			─ ─	──	──	
Fragile fern / *Cystopteris fragilis*	S	O			─ ─	──	──	─ ─
New York fern / *Dryopteris noveboracensis*	M–S	C			─ ─	──	──	
Spinulose woodfern / *Dryopteris spinulosa*	M	C				──	──	
Broad beech fern / *Dryopteris hexagonoptera*	M	O				─ ─	──	
Long beech fern / *Dryopteris Phegopteris*	M	O				─ ─	──	
Oak fern / *Dryopteris disjuncta*	S	R				─ ─	─ ─	

Common name / *Scientific name*	Size	Abundance
Ebony spleenwort / *Asplenium platyneuron*	S	O
Grape ferns / *Botrychium* spp.	S–M	C
Maidenhair fern / *Adiantum pedatum*	M	O
Silvery spleenwort / *Athyrium thelypteroides*	M–L	O
Bulblet fern / *Cystopteris bulbifera*	M	O
Blunt-lobed woodsia / *Woodsia obtusa*	S	O
Ostrich fern / *Pteretis pennsylvanica*	L	O
Glade fern / *Athyrium pycnocarpon*	M–L	R
Goldie's fern / *Dryopteris Goldiana*	L	R
Maidenhair spleenwort / *Asplenium Trichomanes*	S	R
Walking fern / *Camptosorus rhizophyllus*	S	R
Interrupted fern / *Osmunda Claytoniana*	L	C
Cinnamon fern / *Osmunda cinnamomea*	L	C
Royal fern / *Osmunda regalis*	L	C

Size
L — Usually over 60 cm (2 ft)
M — Usually 30 to 60 cm (1 to 2 ft)
S — Usually under 30 cm (1 ft)

Abundance
C — Common
O — Occasionally found
R — Rare

Distribution
—— Frequently found
- - - Less frequently found

forms. Christmas fern, lady fern, and polypody, *Polypodium virginianum*, are always worth examining for noticeably different forms.

Damage to ferns, especially when the fronds are just unrolling in the spring, often results in forms that deceive you into thinking that you have discovered something unusual. In such cases the next year's growth will be normal.

Clubmosses

Of the several other groups of nonflowering vascular plants, the so-called "fern allies," clubmosses, are best known. Clubmosses are small evergreen creeping or trailing plants with flattened or needle-like leaves that resemble conifer needles. This superficial resemblance of the clubmosses to the conifers has given rise to such common names for them as "running pine" and "ground cedar." It should be clear to anyone who examines them in any detail, however, that these clubmosses are very different from coniferous trees.

Clubmosses most commonly increase in number by their creeping rootstocks, which grow along the surface of the ground or just under it. A few, such as shining clubmoss, *Lycopodium lucidulum*, found in the low slope community, also increase by tiny bulblets which fall off the plant and root.

Like ferns, all clubmosses also reproduce from spores. These are produced in enormous quantities on cone-like projections called stroboli that grow on the tops of plants or project above them. Those spores ripen in September; walking through a patch of fruiting clubmoss at this time will stir up clouds of yellowish dust-like spores that will coat shoes and pant-legs. The clubmosses also have a sexual generation, but in most species it is hidden beneath the ground. Often many years must pass before the spore-bearing plants appear at the surface.

The relatively small number of clubmoss species found in the region, as well as the distinctive ecology and growth habit of each, makes them easier to identify than ferns.

Common Ferns of the Oak Forest

Fern nomenclature is in the process of revision. The new Latin names of a few are given in parentheses.

Bracken, *Pterídium aquilínum*, is a large coarse triangular fern commonly to about 1 m (40 in) tall. Bracken is the most common of the ferns, growing in dry woods, old pastures, railroad embankments, and burned-over areas. Its presence usually indicates poor soil. Unlike most other ferns, it is not often found in rich soil or moist habitats. Bracken is the only fern that is common on sand plains.

Marginal Woodfern, *Dryópteris marginàlis*, has leathery evergreen leaves, bluish-green above and light green below, which usually reach about 50 cm (20 in) in height and grow as a clump. The marginal woodfern receives its name from the position of the rounded fruit dots along the margins of the leaflets. Like several other members of the woodfern genus, the leaf stalks are covered with golden brown chaff-like scales. It may be found in all of the oak forest communities, but it is particularly common on shaded rocky slopes.

Hayscented Fern, *Dennstaèdtia punctilóbula*, is another very common oak forest fern that is found in a variety of habitats. It is a medium-sized lacy fern whose deeply cut yellowish-green leaves are approximately 40 cm (15 in) tall and are sweetly scented when crushed. The leaves grow singly but the fern spreads by underground rootstocks to form large colonies. (See photograph, page 144.)

Variant forms: A crested form, a dwarf form with the leaflets crowded together, and several other variants have been reported.

Common Polypody, *Polypòdium virginiànum*, a small mat-forming fern almost always found growing around boulders and rock outcrops. Its leathery evergreen leaves rarely exceed 20 cm (8 in) in length.

Variant forms: A number of interesting variants including ones with deeply cleft or crested leaflets have been reported.

Lady Fern, *Athýrium Fìlix-fémina*, a common medium- to large-sized fern, is variable in height though often reaching about 75 cm (30 in). It is a delicate lacy fern whose leaves grow in a roughly circular cluster. It usually grows in rather moist habitats. Its variability in form makes it a dif-

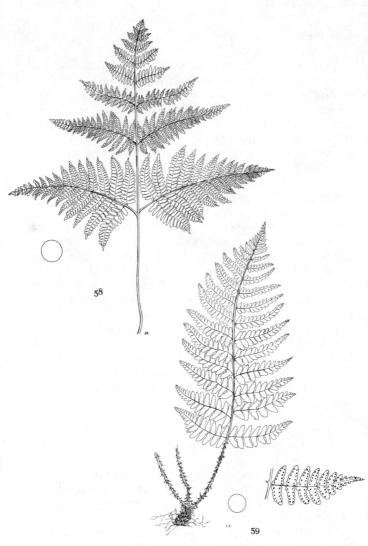

58. Bracken, *Pteridium aquilinum*, is a large coarse fern common in dry sterile soil.

59. Marginal woodfern, *Dryopteris marginalis*, forms neat clumps on dry rocky sites. Its blue-green leaves with the fruit dots near the leaf margins are distinctive. It is one of the few ferns to remain green all winter.

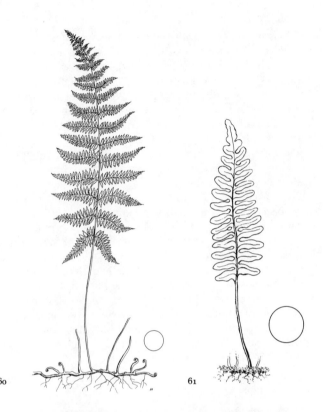

60   61

60. Hayscented fern, *Dennstaedtia punctilobula*, often forms large colonies, spreading by underground runners. (See also photograph on page 144.)

61. Common polypody, *Polypodium virginianum*, is a small mat-forming fern that usually grows on rocks. It is evergreen.

ficult fern to identify, but perhaps its most distinctive characteristics are the presence of a few scales on the leaf stalk and a chevron-like arrangement of fruit dots on the undersides of the fertile fronds. The woodferns and Christmas ferns all have leaf stalks thickly covered in scales.

Variant forms: The lady fern is one of the most variable of the ferns, consisting of many geographic varieties and innumerable vegetative forms, including ones with crested leaves. A form with wine-red leaf stalks is fairly common.

Christmas Fern, *Polýstichum acrostichoìdes,* is easily recognized by its shiny leathery evergreen leaves which grow in clusters from a single rootstock. Christmas fern is a medium-sized fern occasionally reaching a height of 60 cm (2 ft). It is usually found in groups of two or three clumps, but occasionally it forms large colonies, especially in areas of limy soil. Each leaflet has a small ear at its base which gives it some resemblance to a Christmas stocking.

Variant forms: A number of interesting variant forms, including ones with forked, twisted, or deeply toothed leaflets have been reported.

New York Fern, *Dryópteris noveboracénsis (Thelýpteris noveboracénsis),* is a small to medium-sized delicate fern usually between 20 and 45 cm (8 to 18 in), spreading by underground rootstocks but forming clusters of two or three leaves. New York fern is the only fern of this size whose leaves taper toward both their tops and their bases. The double taper suggests that the fern was named after the New Yorkers, who are reputed to burn their candles at both ends.

Spinulose Woodfern, *Dryópteris spinulòsa,* is a deeply cut lacy fern, quite variable in height but often about 75 cm (30 in) on moist sites. Like the marginal woodfern described

62. Lady fern, *Athyrium Filix-femina,* is a large lacy fern growing in loose clumps.

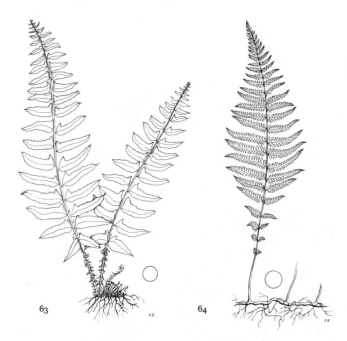

63. Christmas fern, *Polystichum acrostichoides*, bears coarse leathery leaves that remain green through the winter.

64. New York fern, *Dryopteris noveboracensis*, is the only medium-sized fern with a double taper to the leaves.

above, it grows in bouquet-like clumps and its leaflets are very scaly at the base, though its delicate lacy foliage is quite different.

Variant forms: Authorities recognize a number of geographic varieties which intergrade from one to another. A form with forked leaflets has also been found.

Long Beech Fern, *Dryópteris Phegópteris (Thelýpteris Phegópteris),* is a small to medium-sized fern reaching about 30 cm (12 in) on favored sites. It is easily recognized by its narrow triangular shape and the downward-pointing direction of the lower two leaflets, which are separated from the others. The long beech fern is very common in northern New England; in southern New England it is restricted to cool shady sites, usually on acidic soil.

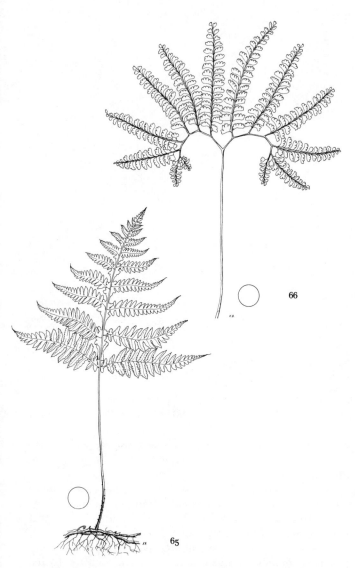

65. Broad beech fern, *Dryopteris hexagonoptera*, may be identified by its broadly triangular leaf. The long beech fern is narrower and grows in cooler areas.

66. Maidenhair fern, *Adiantum pedatum*, has a distinctive unfernlike leaf shape.

THE OAK FOREST

Broad Beech Fern, *Dryópteris hexagonóptera (Thelýpteris hexagonóptera)*, is similar in size and general form to the long beech fern, except that it is more broadly triangular, and the two lower leaflets, which are attached by wings to the upper leaflets, do not point down. The broad beech fern is more commonly found in rich, less acidic soils. It is uncommon in sharply acidic soils.

Variant forms: A form with forked leaflets has been reported.

Fragile Fern, *Cystópteris frágilis,* is a small bright-green fern of damp rocky ledges. It is one of the first species of fern to appear in the spring and often disappears during summer dry spells. It may be recognized by its small size, rarely over 25 cm (10 in), its smooth leaves and stems, and its habitat preference.

Variant forms: Among the several variant forms are ones with toothed and forked leaflets.

Maidenhair Fern, *Adiántum pedàtum,* has a distinctive growth form that makes recognition unmistakable. Its fronds are shaped like horseshoes, borne on wiry dark-brown stalks and reaching a height of about 50 cm (20 in) on favorable sites. Maidenhair fern, along with large colonies of Christmas fern, is almost always an indicator of a more neutral soil. In these habitats the two species are often found growing in close proximity. Because neutral soil areas are scarce in this region, maidenhair ferns are also scarce.

Interrupted Fern, *Osmúnda Claytoniàna,* is one of the largest ferns of the oak forest, reaching heights of 1 m (40 in). The fern derives its common name from the appearance of the fertile leaves; four or more pairs of brownish spore-bearing leaflets interrupt the line of green sterile leaflets. The fern grows in moist, though not wet, sites. It is one of the most common and prominent ferns in the region.

Similar species: The interrupted fern is very similar in appearance to the cinnamon fern, *O. cinnamomea* (page 333), which normally grows in wetter sites. The spores on the cinnamon fern are borne on a single fertile stalk which turns cinnamon-brown before withering away.

Grape Ferns, *Botrýchium* spp., are a group of often overlooked oak forest ferns. All but one species, the rattlesnake fern, *B. virginianum*, are quite small, usually no taller than 8 cm (3 in) and consisting of a single fleshy leaf and a

67. Interrupted fern, *Osmunda Claytoniana*, may be easily recognized in the spring by the location of the dark spore-bearing leaflets on the fertile leaves.

single spore-bearing stalk. Most appear in late spring or early summer after the other ferns have emerged. The grape ferns belong to a different, more primitive family that is not closely related to the other ferns. The rattlesnake fern is common in neutral soil areas.

Common Clubmosses of the Oak Forest

Ground Cedar Clubmoss, *Lycopòdium complanàtum,* is probably the most abundant of the clubmosses. It is common in both moist and dry shaded areas, often forming large colonies. Its small scaly leaves, irregular straggly growth habit, and candelabra of one to four spore-bearing cones should aid in its recognition.

Similar species: L. tristachyum, also called ground cedar, grows in sandy woods and may be distinguished by its blue-green color, its more erect growth habit, and its spore-bearing candelabra, usually of four cones.

Staghorn Clubmoss, *Lycopòdium clavàtum*, is more common in the northern part of the region. It is an upright-growing, branched plant thickly covered with small ever-green leaves and spreading by runners along the surface of the ground. Unlike ground cedar, it does not form dense colonies, but rather spreads along the ground more or less in a line.

Tree Clubmoss, *Lycopòdium obscùrum*, has thin almost needle-like leaves and a branching tree-like habit, as its

68. Ground cedar clubmoss, *Lycopodium complanatum*, often forms tangled mats in shady woodland areas.

69. Tree clubmoss, *Lycopodium obscurum*, is the tallest of the native clubmoss species.

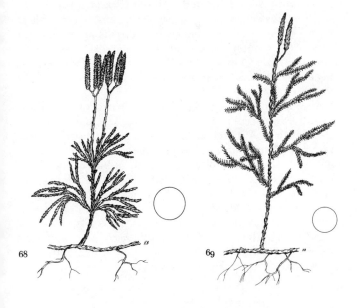

common name suggests. It is usually a bit taller than the other clubmoss species, sometimes reaching 30 cm (12 in) in height.

Shining Clubmoss, *Lycopòdium lucídulum*, is easily recognized by its dark-green shining leaves about 15 cm (6 in) high and its usually unbranched (or sometimes once-branched) growth habit. It is common in rich acidic soil with an ample supply of moisture, where it forms open clumps.

Similar species: Stiff clubmoss, *L. annotinum,* resembles shining clubmoss in general growth habit though it is smaller in stature and its leaves are a dull light green. It is occasionally found in the northern part of the region.

The Mixed Mesophytic Community

IN southwestern Connecticut there are some woodlands of a quite different appearance from the oak forest communities just described. Oaks and hickories may still be present but they are not necessarily the most abundant species. Other trees such as sugar maple, *Acer saccharum,* tulip tree, *Liriodendron tulipifera,* yellow birch, *Betula lutea,* white ash, *Fraxinus americana,* butternut, *Juglans cinerea,* black cherry, *Prunus serotina,* and basswood, *Tilia americana,* all trees less commonly found in the other oak forest communities, may comprise a major part of the forest. The last species, basswood, is an especially useful indicator species for this community.

Absent from these woodlands is the cover of ericad shrubs and other plants that indicate a strongly acidic soil; their absence is a significant clue to the ecology and distribution of this forest community. In the place of these acid-soil plants a rich herbaceous flora often grows, including many of the showy woodland wildflowers that New Englanders more often see in books than encounter in nature. These include such species as wild ginger, *Asarum canadense,* bloodroot, *Sanguinaria canadensis,* Dutchman's breeches, *Dicentra Cucullaria,* herb Robert, *Geranium Robertianum,* as well as species occasionally found in the low slope community such as red trillium, *Trillium erectum,* and dogtooth violet,

Erythronium americanum. All are plants most commonly found where the soils are only slightly acidic.

The understory and shrub layers are also well developed. Flowering dogwood thrives in the sweet soil underlying these sites as do witch hazel, spicebush, *Lindera Benzoin,* hornbeam, and hop hornbeam. Bladdernut, *Staphylea trifolia,* and leatherwood, *Dirca palustris,* also occasionally appear in this community, though rarely elsewhere. The mixed mesophytic community also supports a distinctive and unusual fern flora. Such species as Christmas fern, *Polystichum acrostichoides,* maidenhair fern, *Adiantum pedatum,* broad beech fern, *Dryopteris hexagonoptera,* and rattlesnake fern, *Botrychium virginianum,* all grow abundantly here. Except for the first, all are uncommon on other sites. In rocky areas it is also worthwhile to look for such small ferns as walking fern, *Camptosorus rhizophyllus,* and maidenhair spleenwort, *Asplenium Trichomanes,* which grow in crevices in moist ledges. Ebony spleenwort, *Asplenium platyneuron,* is found on slightly drier sites. Other rare ferns such as Goldie's fern, *Dryopteris Goldiana,* and glade fern, *Athyrium pycnocarpon,* occur in southern New England only in this community.

Not surprisingly, the mixed mesophytic community appears in areas where the bedrock is of marble or some other calcareous rock. If a map showing the marble areas of the region is superimposed on one showing the mixed mesophytic communities, the two would coincide in many cases. Sites in the Connecticut Valley Lowland and the few scattered areas in eastern New England where the forest shows at least some of the characteristics of the mixed mesophytic community also are places where the bedrock contains some calcium and, as a result, the soil is sweeter. These mixed mesophytic communities bear a striking resemblance to the great mixed mesophytic forest that covers much of the Appalachian Plateau and Ohio Valley, an area in which many of the rocks contain abundant lime.

The soils of the mixed mesophytic community differ from those of the other oak forest communities not only in pH but in appearance as well. In place of the mor humus, with its thick organic layer sharply delimited from the sterile mineral soil below, we find a type of humus that blends into the soil to some depth, thus increasing its fertility and mois-

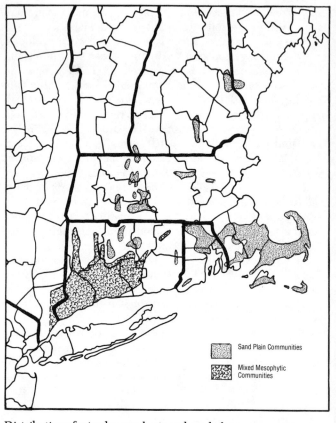

Distribution of mixed mesophytic and sand plain communities.

ture-holding ability. Mull humus, as this type of humus is
called, occurs under tree species whose leaves decompose
rapidly and where the underlying soil is not excessively
acidic. Since bedrock containing abundant marble or other
calcium minerals tends to break down more quickly in
humid climates such as that of southern New England, these
mixed mesophytic communities are usually lower and hence
moister than the surrounding woodlands. In a sense, then,
the mixed mesophytic community could be described as a
low slope community on only slightly acidic soil.

There are many sites, especially in southwestern Con-

THE OAK FOREST

necticut, that seem to be intermediate between the mixed mesophytic and low slope communities. While moisture conditions are usually, though not always, similar, I believe that the important variable is soil acidity. Hence, species like beech and hemlock, which are normally found growing on acidic soils, are often absent from true mixed mesophytic communities, though there are a few places where both beech and more typical mixed mesophytic species like basswood grow side by side.

The role of chestnut oak, *Quercus Prinus*, in these communities is also interesting. In this region the tree is usually seen growing as rather stunted individuals on hilltops; in the mixed mesophytic community it sometimes reaches magnificent proportions, though it is not common in other sites. Occasionally, also, yellow oak, *Q. Muehlenbergii*, a species very similar in appearance to chestnut oak, appears in these western Connecticut mixed mesophytic woodlands, thereby confusing the picture even more.

Like bogs, rock ravines, and other uncommon plant habitats, these mixed mesophytic communities make a contribution to the diversity, richness, and ecological interest of the southern New England landscape that is of far greater proportion than their small sizes and scattered numbers would suggest. Local and regional conservation groups should consider them important targets for preservation.

Trees of the Mixed Mesophytic Community

Basswood, *Tília americàna*, is one of the best indicator trees of the mixed mesophytic community. Though the tree does occasionally grow elsewhere—along fence rows, woodland verges, and bottomlands, it has always been present in

70. Basswood, *Tilia americana*, may be recognized by its heart-shaped leaves and strap-like seed-bearing bracts.

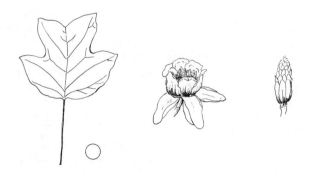

71. Tulip tree, *Liriodendron tulipifera*, bears unique four-lobed leaves and showy spring flowers.

Range of the tulip tree, *Liriodendron tulipifera*.

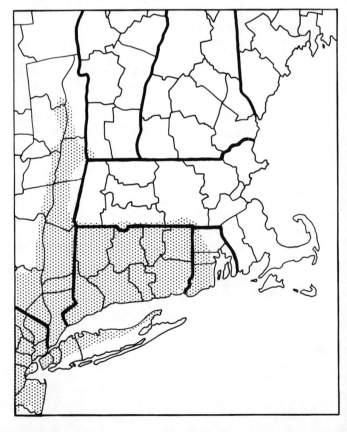

the southern New England mixed mesophytic communities that I have observed. The tree is very easy to recognize by its toothed oval to heart-shaped leaves, which average about 11 cm (4 ½ in) in diameter, and its hard pea-like seeds growing on pale strap-like bracts. It is shade-tolerant and one of the most prolific stump-sprouters of any American species.

Tulip Tree, *Liriodéndron tulipífera,* is the giant of southern New England deciduous trees. Like the basswood, it is restricted to sites with a midrange of soil moisture, but unlike this other species, it is very intolerant of shade and, though long-lived, must be regarded as a pioneer tree. The tulip tree is easy to recognize by its bright green four-lobed leaves about 10 cm (4 in) long, by its conspicuous orange and green flowers, and, in mature woodlands, by its large size. The wood is rather brittle, and, as a result, the tree often suffers wind damage on exposed sites. The tulip tree grows in Connecticut and Rhode Island. The northern limits of its range are close to the Massachusetts state line.

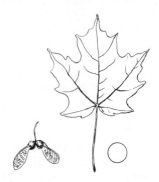

72. Sugar maple, *Acer saccharum,* is much less common in southern New England than farther north. Its leaves are larger than those of the red maple and bear two extra lobes at the bottom.

Sugar Maple, Àcer sáccharum, is occasional in the slope communities of the oak forest near its northern border, but in most of southern New England it is more commonly found on sites where the soil is less acidic. Not surprisingly, it is a common tree in the mixed mesophytic community. Sugar maple is a large tree, occasionally reaching 27 m (90 ft). In open sites it is short-trunked and spreading, while in the

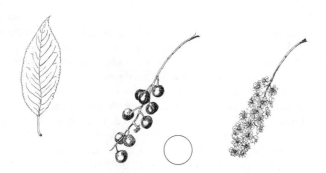

73. Black cherry, *Prunus serotina*, has a dark bark that sometimes resembles that of black birch. Its leaves are also similar, but more coarsely veined.

forest it grows straight and tall. It is recognized by its deeply and irregularly furrowed grayish-brown bark and its large five-lobed leaves. Unlike red maple, *A. rubrum*, sugar maple is very tolerant of shade and therefore tends to replace other less tolerant species where it grows.

Black Cherry, *Prùnus seròtina*, grows in a number of sites but reaches its best development in the mixed mesophytic community. It is a medium-sized tree, rarely taller than 15 m (50 ft) in New England but occasionally topping 36 m (120 ft) in the Allegheny Mountains. Its bark resembles that of the black birch, dark brown and lustrous when young, black and scaly when old. On young trees the horizontal scars are coarser than those of black birch, however, and on old trees the bark scales are smaller and more regular in size and shape. The leaves are also similar in size and shape to those of black birch, but are more prominently veined. Its small white flowers, typical of plants in the rose family, appear in clusters about a week after those of choke cherry, *P. virginiana*. Its small reddish-black fruits are sweet and juicy.

Butternut, *Júglans cinèrea*, is a minor tree in the mixed mesophytic community, and is found along roadsides and stream banks as well. The combined characteristics of deeply furrowed, narrow-ridged bark, long compound leaves bearing nine to seventeen leaflets, and greenish sticky fruit that ripens in October should help make it distinguishable from other species. Butternut is intolerant of shade and competition. Though on some southern Appalachian sites it may reach 30 m (100 ft) it rarely grows taller than about 13 m (43 ft). Butternut is susceptible to a debilitating fungus disease that progressively kills the branches and eventually weakens the tree until it dies. It is estimated that nearly all these trees are diseased to some extent. Like its sister species, walnut, *J. nigra*, butternut secretes a substance from its roots which is toxic to many other plants.

Other Mixed Mesophytic Trees

Any one of the oak forest species may turn up in the mixed mesophytic community. Other trees include the following:
Hemlock, *Tsùga canadénsis*, page 316
American Beech, *Fàgus grandifòlia*, page 316
White Ash, *Fráxinus americàna*, page 146
Yellow Birch, *Bétula lùtea*, page 316

Shrubs of the Mixed Mesophytic Community

Bladdernut, *Staphylèa trifòlia*, is a deciduous shrub up to about 5 m (16 ft). For people who have trained their eyes to perceive poison ivy, the three-leaved foliage of the bladdernut should be easy to spot. Its upright, loosely branching habit and greenish striped branches should clearly distinguish it from poison ivy. The papery bag-like fruits, in which the seeds rattle when ripe, are also distinctive.

74. Bladdernut, *Staphylea trifolia*, is a medium-sized shrub whose compound leaves with three leaflets superficially resemble those of poison ivy. Its fruits, encased in a papery bag-like covering, are also distinctive.

Leatherwood, *Dírca palústris,* is a small single-trunked shrub, usually under 3 m (10 ft) in height and of nondescript appearance. Its many branches are soft and brittle but the bark is pliable and strong. The leaves are oval and smooth, its flowers small and yellow, and its fruit green turning red. The plant superficially resembles spicebush, *Lindera Benzoin,* though the bark on the twigs is light gray and leathery-smooth.

Other Mixed Mesophytic Shrubs

Except for the ericads, any shrub from other oak forest communities may also appear in the mixed mesophytic community. The following shrubs commonly appear here:

Spicebush, *Líndera Benzòin,* page 327
Witch Hazel, *Hamamèlis virginiàna,* page 148
Green-Osier Dogwood, *Córnus alternifòlia,* page 142

Galls

IF YOU ARE in the oak forest in late spring or early summer and examine a number of oak and hickory leaves, you are almost sure to find a variety of unusual growths of different sizes and shapes on them. The largest and most notable of these is the oak apple, a spherical fruit-like growth up to 3 centimeters in diameter, green and fleshy in summer and turning brown and papery in fall.

These growths are galls. They show one of the most intricate relationships between plant and animal in all of nature. If you cut an oak apple in half, the function of these curious growths will be apparent. Inside the gall, surrounded by a mass of radiating fibers, is a harder knot-like structure. Inside this central mass is a tiny chamber in which lives an even tinier worm-like larva. Other creatures—mostly insect larvae—live inside other types of galls. Most galls, then, are nurseries that provide the developing insect with food and shelter.

Oaks and hickories, two of the most common oak forest tree genera, are hosts to the greatest variety of gall-makers. Nearly 800 different kinds of galls grow on oaks alone, though not all of these are found in southern New England. Each of these galls is of a characteristic size and shape; each is found on a certain part of the tree. Galls also grow on roots, flowers, and twigs. Each kind is produced by a different species of insect, usually the larva of a small wasp.

Hickory galls contain larvae of a different group of insects, usually midges or aphids. Those of the aphids look like flat blisters or small spheres, while those of the midges are either spherical or elongated—one of the most common varieties is shaped like a tiny dunce cap. The aphid galls appear in late spring, the midge galls later in the summer.

Another common gall, one found in old fields, is the goldenrod spindle gall. This gall, produced by a small moth, is an elongated swelling on the stems of goldenrod. The adult lays its eggs on the stems of old goldenrods in fall. The eggs hatch the following spring and the tiny caterpillars burrow into the stem of the new goldenrod plants, where they live until adulthood. A small fly produces the spherical galls on goldenrod.

How these insects manage to cause their plant hosts to grow these intricate structures is not clear. Apparently either the adult or the larva secretes a chemical that some-

75. Oak apple galls on the twigs of a young oak tree. The galls, which are light green in spring and summer, turn light brown and become papery in fall.

how changes the nucleic acid in the plant cells nearby. These respond by growing the abnormal structures that provide food and shelter for the larva.

The ecology of these galls is often very complex. Other insect species parasitize the larvae; still others use the gall merely for shelter. Later on, yet other insect species may occupy the abandoned gall.

Fungi, nematode worms, mites, viruses, and in a few instances mechanical irritation also produce galls on plants. The grotesque gelatinous growths on the eastern red cedar, *Juniperus virginiana*, are one stage of the cedar-apple rust that affects apple trees nearby. The huge disfiguring lumps that sometimes appear on tree trunks are galls caused by a virus.

FURTHER READING

General Floras

Eaton, R. J. *A Flora of Concord: From Thoreau's Time to the Present Day*. Cambridge, Mass.: Harvard University Museum of Comparative Zoology, 1974. Annotated catalog of plants found in Concord, Massachusetts, by one of New England's great amateur botanists. Valuable historical and ecological information about southern New England's most carefully studied botanical area.

Fernald, M. L. *Gray's Manual of Botany, Eighth Edition: A Handbook of the Flowering Plants and Ferns of the Central and Northeastern United States and Adjacent Canada*. New York: American Book Co., 1950. Standard catalog of northeastern plants. Technical, requiring mastery of extensive vocabulary.

Gleason, H. A. *New Britton and Brown Illustrated Flora of the Northeastern United States and Adjacent Canada*. New York: Hafner, 1963. Standard botanical reference that includes large line drawings for every species. Technical, but drawings make it more useful for the amateur than *Gray's Manual*.

Graves, C. B., et al. *Catalogue of the Flowering Plants and Ferns of Connecticut*. Connecticut Geological and Natural History Survey Bulletin 14. Hartford, Conn.: State Library, 1910. Long out of print, long out of date, but still a useful catalog of Connecticut plants.

Harger, C. B., et al. *Additions to the Flora of Connecticut* (Supplement to Bulletin 14). Connecticut Geological and Natural History Survey Bulletin 48. Hartford, Conn.: State Library, 1930. Includes additional Connecticut plants found after the publication of Bulletin 14.

Harris, Stuart K. *A Flora of Essex County, Massachusetts*. Salem, Mass.: Peabody Museum, 1975. Plant species by town in this northeastern Massachusetts county.

Seymour, Frank. *The Flora of New England*. Rutland, Vt.: Tuttle, 1969. Comprehensive technical key to New England's flowering plants. Information on frequency of occurrence, habitat, and flowering dates. Lists localities where species have been recorded.

Tree and Shrub Identification Books

Angelo, Ray. *Concord Area Trees*. Cambridge, Mass.: Concord Field Station, Harvard University, 1976. An excellent little illustrated guide to trees of the Concord, Massachusetts, area. Covers most of the common southern New England trees.

Brockman, C. Frank, and Rebecca Merrilees. *Trees of North America*. New York: Golden Press, 1968. Portable guide to North American trees. Range maps, illustrations of leaves and tree habit. Nontechnical.

Dame, Lorin, and Henry Brooks. *Handbook of the Trees of New England*. New York: Dover, 1972. A reprint of an excellent turn-of-the-century tree guide. Fine illustrations. Useful information on ranges. Some of the Latin nomenclature is out of date.

Harlow, William. *Trees of the Eastern and Central United States*. New York: Dover, 1942. Excellent little guide to eastern trees. Photographic illustrations of leaves, bark, seeds, etc. Information about habitat and uses of the wood.

Peattie, Donald Culross. *A Natural History of Trees of Eastern and Central North America*. Boston: Houghton Mifflin, 1966. Beautifully written description of the eastern trees. Contains information on ecology, distribution, and economic importance of the various species.

Symonds, George W. D. *The Shrub Identification Book*. New York: Morrow, 1963. Useful companion volume to *The Tree Identification Book*, below. Visual key based on photographs.

Symonds, George W. D. *The Tree Identification Book*. New York: Morrow, 1958. Large identification guide based on photographs of leaves, bark, twigs, seeds, and flowers. One of the best for beginners.

Viertel, Arthur T. *Trees, Shrubs, and Vines*. Syracuse, N.Y.: Syracuse University Press, 1972. Excellent but little-known illustrated guide to woody plants.

Vegetation Surveys

Egler, Frank E., and William A. Niering. *The Vegetation of Connecticut Natural Areas, No. 1: Yale Natural Preserve, New Haven*. Niering, William, and Frank E. Egler. *The Vegetation of Connecticut Natural Areas, No. 2: Audubon Center of Greenwich, Greenwich*. Egler, Frank E., and William A. Niering. *The Vegetation of Connecticut Natural Areas, No. 3: The Natural Areas of the McLean Game Refuge, Granby*. Connecticut Geological and Natural History Survey. Hartford, Conn.: State Library, 1965, 1966, and 1967. Three informative booklets describing the distribution of plants in various preserved natural areas.

Mountain Laurel

Jaynes, Richard A. *The Laurel Book*. New York: Hafner, 1975. Describes the ecology, distribution, genetics, and horticulture of these beautiful American shrubs. Handsome color illustrations of variant forms.

Oak Forest Subshrubs and Herbaceous Plants

Dwelley, Marilyn. *Spring Wildflowers of New England*. Camden, Me.: Downeast Enterprise, 1973. Fine nontechnical pocket guide to native spring flowers. Organized according to flower color. Colored drawings.

Dwelley, Marilyn. *Summer and Fall Wildflowers of New England*. Camden, Me.: Downeast Enterprise, 1977. Companion volume to *Spring Flowers of New England*, above.

Newcomb, Lawrence. *Newcomb's Wildflower Guide*. Boston: Little, Brown, 1977. Excellent new guide to wildflower identification. Easy-to-use key. Fine illustrations.

Peterson, Roger Tory, and Margaret McKenny. *A Field Guide to Wildflowers of Northeastern and North-Central North America*. Boston: Houghton Mifflin, 1968. Nontechnical guide to wildflowers arranged according to flower color. Excellent illustrations.

Rickett, Harold W. *Wildflowers of the United States*. Vol. 1, *The Northeastern States*. New York: McGraw-Hill, 1967. A large and expensive two-volume book of colored photographs covering most of the northeastern flowers. Nontechnical. Beautiful illustrations.

Ferns and Clubmosses of the Oak Forest

Cobb, Boughton. *A Field Guide to the Ferns*. Boston: Houghton Mifflin, 1956. Probably the easiest introduction to this confusing group of plants. Laura Louise Foster's illustrations alone are worth the price of the book.

Roberts, Edith A., and Julia R. Lawrence. *American Ferns: How to Know, Grow and Use Them*. New York: Macmillan, 1935. Long out-of-print but still useful book on fern ecology, identification, and horticulture.

Wherry, Edgar T. *The Fern Guide*. Garden City, N.Y.: Doubleday, 1961. Comprehensive guide to the northeastern ferns. Slightly more advanced than Cobb's *Field Guide to the Ferns*.

Galls

Hutchins, Ross E. *Galls and Gall Insects*. New York: Dodd, Mead, 1969. An interesting and well-illustrated introduction to this intricate plant-animal relationship. Though written for younger readers, the book should appeal to naturalists of all ages.

PART V

Postagricultural Land

Postagricultural Land:
An Introduction

IN THE COOLNESS and shade of a maturing woodland, it is difficult to picture the land as anything but forested. Yet, for any particular tract, the chances are better than even that the land was once cleared for pasture or crops. The clues are everywhere.

How long ago were these southern New England farmlands abandoned? Statistics from Worcester County in central Massachusetts probably follow the downward trend of open land throughout the region. In 1840, about 76 percent of the land in the county was cleared for agriculture and livestock raising. By 1880 abandonment had begun and the percentage was down to 71 percent. After 1880 the rate of abandonment increased: by 1920 only 52 percent remained open, and by 1975 the percentage was down to only 13 percent.

In sandy regions like Cape Cod, of course, the percentage of open land was never so high. On the other hand, in the Connecticut Valley much of the farmland, where it has not been abandoned to housing subdivisions, is still under cultivation.

Perhaps 70 percent of the entire woodland area of southern New England was once farmland. Indeed, much of today's woodlands has grown up within human memory. For the purpose of this discussion, I have arbitrarily marked the end of the postagricultural or old field community with the virtual disappearance of such short-lived, sun-loving species as gray birch, *Betula populifolia*, and eastern red cedar, *Juniperus virginiana*. By this definition, perhaps one-quarter to one-third of the present woodlands in southern New England could still be classified as postagricultural communities.

Clues to Former Land Use

WITH SO MUCH recently abandoned farmland in the area, it would be surprising indeed if there were not many signs of this former land use still visible. If you live in a town, your local historical society will almost certainly have a collection of old photographs showing the land as it once was, but even without such evidence there are many extant clues to help you make some informed guesses about the use and appearance of a particular tract of land a hundred or more years ago.

Stone Walls

Stone walls are always a sign of formerly cleared land. All of these old walls, many running through deep woods, were once boundaries for open pasture and crop lands.

These stone walls vary in height and durability. Many were low walls topped with split rails of chestnut or, after the 1870s, a strand or two of barbed wire. Still others are nothing more than elongated stone piles where rocks uncovered by plowing were dumped along a vanished fence line. In parts of western Connecticut, zigzag piles of rocks sometimes mark the line of old snake-rail fences.

Building the immense network of stone walls was a prodigious task. They were built not so much because Yankee ingenuity had found a way of using the ever-present and unwanted rocks in the fields as because wood had become so scarce. In those days, also, there was no adequate way of preserving fence posts from rot. Unless a farmer was fortunate enough to get rot-resistant locust wood for fence posts, he would have to replace a fence perhaps every twenty or thirty years—an enormous task when one had only hand tools to work with, and one requiring also an inordinate amount of wood.

It is important to remember that not all cleared land was necessarily enclosed by stone walls. In gravelly areas, the rocks are either too small or too rounded to be used in wall-building. Here farmers had to rely on wooden fences.

A strand of barbed wire along a wall or fence line would indicate that the enclosure was still being used for pasture during the 1870s or later. The presence of barbed wire does not necessarily indicate that the land was still clear at that time, however. As agriculture declined in the region, many farmers were still pasturing small herds in land grown to brush or woods.

Often the woodlands on either side of a wall are markedly different in their tree composition. For example, you may occasionally find small enclosures of almost pure stands of black birch in the midst of a mixed deciduous woodland. Or on one side of a stone wall the woodland may contain a great many white pine and hemlock, while on the other side there may be none. The explanation for these differences is probably more than mere coincidence. Knowing something of the seed bed requirements of the various species, their desirability as livestock browse, or even whether the land on one side of a wall was abandoned before the other may help you to make informed guesses by way of explanation.

Wolf Trees

Wolf trees offer us a particularly interesting glimpse into the past landscape. In the forester's terminology, a wolf tree is a large spreading tree that usurps more than its share of

76. Wolf trees along an abandoned road in central Massachusetts. Compare the large spreading maples on the right with the straight-trunked younger trees on the left, which grew as the land returned to woods.

canopy space and restricts the growth of smaller trees around it. A short-trunked spreading habit is typical of trees that grow in the open. Forest-grown trees, on the other hand, are typically long-trunked and tall, in response to competition from other trees nearby.

When you encounter one of these great spreading trees in the midst of a young woodland, you are probably looking at a tree that reached maturity when that land was still field or pasture. Sometimes a row of these large trees follows a stone wall or marks an old fence line. Perhaps these grew from seeds buried by a squirrel along the edge of a field and survived to maturity because they were too close to the wall or fence to be reached by the mower. Larger trees growing along country roadsides similarly may have escaped the mowing machine and browsing by livestock.

Plow Furrows and Rock Piles

Long after a cultivated field is abandoned, the traces of plow furrows may still be seen. The last furrow on the edge of a plowed field, where the plow left a sharp banking, remains longer. These old furrow marks sometimes show up better in late winter when a long patch of snow remains in the depression. Also, during the winter when the trees are bare, shadows from the slanting rays of the sun make them easier to detect.

Since virtually all of the upland soils in the region contain stones, rock piles along the edges of the old fields are also a sign of plowing or at least of the planting of orchard trees. Sometimes farmers dumped the rocks over a banking into a gulley. Other times they left the rocks piled on areas of ledge that outcropped in the fields.

Fruit Trees and Garden Plants

If you explore the woodlands in May, you are very likely to come across blossoming apple or pear trees. A single tree, especially if it is found near a road, may very well have grown from a discarded core or perhaps from a seed dropped by a bird. Large old trees, particularly if there are several growing in the vicinity, are more likely to be the remnants of an abandoned orchard.

Neither apples nor pears are native American trees. Like so many other agricultural plants, they arrived in America with the early European settlers. Although both trees have become naturalized—that is, they can germinate and grow in the wild without man's help—neither competes well with the taller-growing native trees.

Apples are still an important crop in southern New England. However, the area now in working orchard is probably only a fraction of what it was one hundred or so years ago, though in the days of the family farm the individual orchards were smaller than those still in production today.

Garden shrubs and flowers found growing in the woodland or along a country road are a sure sign of an abandoned farmstead. Most of the old garden flowers are sun-loving and hence quickly disappear after abandonment, though some, like lilac, phlox, and day lilies, persist on a site for many years. Myrtle, *Vinca minor*, the dark-green vine-like ground cover found in many gardens of today, thrives in shade and remains for an indefinite period after a garden is abandoned. When you find these plants you will almost certainly find a cellar hole nearby. Remember our note of caution about exploring abandoned cellar holes: keep a close lookout for the well, which may no longer be covered, and for the poison ivy that so often grows on these sites.

Red Cedar

Although several species of trees are likely to invade abandoned farmland, most of these will also appear in woodlands following fire or other disturbance. An exception is eastern red cedar, *Juniperus virginiana* (page 219). Since red cedar seeds almost always germinate only in turf, its presence is a sign that the land on which it is growing was once a grassy field. Like most pioneer trees, however, red cedar cannot compete with taller-growing oaks and hickories and eventually disappears from postagricultural woodlands.

Seed Survivors

When forested land is lumbered or otherwise disturbed, there is often a sudden explosion of certain shrubs and herbaceous plants that seemingly come from nowhere. In many cases the species are ones that are not found growing close enough for their seeds to have been dispersed into the site by any normal means such as wind or animals. In fact, many of these species bear seeds for which there is no known means of dispersal.

After a number of tests conducted over many years, biologists have concluded that many of these species that spring up following disturbances are not invaders from other sites in the vicinity but survivors whose presence in a particular area had been maintained by buried seeds which remained viable for an exceptionally long time.

Mullein, *Verbascum Thapsus*, whose light-green woolly leaves and dense, cylindrical spike of small yellow flowers is a common summer sight along roadsides and other waste places, is the Methuselah of viable seeded plants. In Denmark—the species is a European import that has become naturalized in America—mullein plants sprouted from dirt gathered from beneath the foundation of a medieval church after being buried there for at least 650 years.

While no other species can match that of mullein for long seed viability, a number of common weeds that may have originally become established in fields and pastures over a century or more ago still appear when a disturbance opens up the woods or stirs up the soil.

Smartweed	*Polygonum* spp.
Dock	*Rumex* spp.
Goosefoot	*Chenopodium* spp.
Pigweed	*Amaranthus* spp.
Pokeweed	*Phytolacca americana*
Cinquefoil	*Potentilla* spp.
White clover	*Trifolium repens*
Bramble	*Rubus* spp.
Evening primrose	*Oenothera biennis*
Black nightshade	*Solanum nigrum*
Indian tobacco	*Lobelia inflata*
Fireweed	*Erechtites* spp.

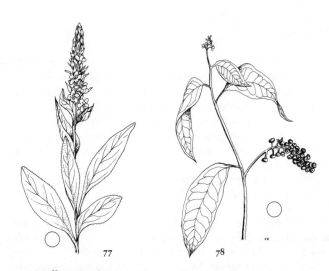

77. Mullein, *Verbascum Thapsus*, is a common plant of roadsides, old fields, and waste ground. It is easily recognized by its light gray-green leaves and dense spike of yellow flowers.

78. Pokeweed, *Phytolacca americana*, is a common weed of disturbed ground. It is easily recognized in late summer by the clusters of maroon berries. All parts of the plant are poisonous, although the young shoots, if boiled in two changes of water, are excellent spring greens.

Among shrubs, sweet fern, *Comptonia peregrina*, smooth sumac, *Rhus glabra*, and staghorn sumac, *Rhus typhina*, all produce seeds that retain their viability for an exceptionally long time. Pin cherry, *Prunus pennsylvanica*, and black locust, *Robinia pseudoacacia*, are tree species that produce seeds with a long period of viability. There is some evidence that the seeds of the tulip tree, *Liriodendron tulipifera*, and those of some of the birches may also share this property. Significantly, all of the above species in all three categories—trees, shrubs, and herbaceous plants—are considered to be old field pioneers.

The herbaceous species include some of the most unattractive, noisome weeds in our flora. Many have been the bane of gardeners both here and in Europe for centuries. And yet, these species springing up in a woodland clearing after having lain dormant for generations do provide us with

POSTAGRICULTURAL LAND

a fleeting glimpse into a vanished era in New England's history, a time before woodland replaced a landscape of pasture and field.

The Development of Postagricultural Forests

PEOPLE who try to generalize about old field succession may immediately find themselves on shaky ground. Often successional trends carefully worked out for a certain abandoned field are of little value in predicting what is likely to occur nearby. The main reason for this uncertainty is the important role that chance plays during the initial stages. A good seed year for a particular species of tree growing nearby, for example, might determine the composition of the rising forest for the next seventy years. Likewise, a summer dry spell could favor the seedlings of one species over others and have the same long-term effect. A number of other random events, such as hurricane and fire, could also affect the ensuing forest development.

Though we can never predict with certainty what the successional pattern for a particular old field will be, two factors, recruitment and former land use, do exert an important influence on the initial composition of the postagricultural forest and, to some extent, on the subsequent generation of trees.

Recruitment

Recruitment refers to the availability and supply of seeds that can fall into an area and germinate. A heavy rain of seeds from trees near a particular abandoned field greatly increases the chances of those species appearing in the field. Although a large tree can produce thousands or sometimes millions of seeds, only a tiny fraction of these germinate and survive even under the best of conditions. Of course, those species with tolerance during their seedling stage to the dry sunny conditions of the field, as well as those adapted to germinating in an old field seedbed, whether it is bare ground or grassy turf, would have a distinct competitive advantage.

However, even those species not well adapted to these conditions might find suitable spots for germination and growth here and there if enough seeds fell into the site. Though some species are clearly more adapted to growth in the old fields than others, I know of no upland forest tree that could not at least occasionally germinate and grow in this habitat. Even beech and hemlock, species not normally considered to be able to tolerate the dry sunny conditions of an old field, do occasionally appear along its shady north-facing edge if there is a seed tree nearby.

The more seeds that fall onto a site, the greater are the chances that germination and subsequent survival of the seedlings will occur. A large tree growing along the edge of a field—one that may later appear in the young forest as a wolf tree—can determine the subsequent composition of the forest in the vicinity for many years to come. The dispersal of large-seeded species such as oaks and hickories will, of course, not be as far as species such as ash and white pine, whose smaller winged seeds the wind can scatter over a much greater area. The paper-thin seeds from a large white pine, for example, may be carried a kilometer or more by a brisk wind. A number of species such as sumac, *Rhus* spp., gray dogwood, *Cornus racemosa*, sassafras, *Sassafras albidum*, and poplar, *Populus* spp., if established along the edges of an abandoned field, will also spread into the field by root sprouts.

Former Land Use

Whether the formerly cleared land was cultivated, pastured, or hayed may also have an important bearing on the forest that subsequently grows there. The following patterns of development often, but not invariably, occur.

CULTIVATED LAND

The bare ground that results from cultivation is a perfect

seedbed for a host of annual weeds that are adapted to this kind of disturbance. The first year or so after initial cultivation, the field may remain relatively free of weeds, but after that there is a gradual yearly increase in their number and variety. Regular cultivation merely gives farm crops a competitive edge; each time the soil is stirred up, more weed seeds are mixed in with the soil. One study of a plowed field in North Carolina turned up an average of 7,000 weed seeds in each square foot of soil to plow depth. A number of these weed species also reproduce prolifically from cut stems or roots.

The species of grass that form turf in pasture and hayfields are totally eliminated by about two years of plowing and harrowing. When cultivation ceases, these grasses rarely reappear naturally. Instead there is usually an explosion of the annual weeds. By the end of the first summer after abandonment, there is hardly a square centimeter of bare soil showing anywhere in the field.

A listing of these annual weeds reads like the rogues' gallery of gardening. A few of the most common are such familiar pests as crabgrass, *Digitaria* spp., ragweed, *Ambrosia* spp., and pigweed, *Amaranthus* spp., but a whole host of others may also be found. Some, such as the South American *Galinsoga*, are so recently introduced that they have no common names.

These weeds share a number of characteristics. They require light, they withstand dryness, they possess a deep root system, and they are highly adaptable to a variety of soils. Since land generally does not remain open and sunny for very long, their existence on a particular site is relatively short and their survival depends on the production of a large quantity of either highly mobile or very long-lived seeds. These annual weeds are known as fugitive species; like fugitives they remain constantly on the move from one suitable site to another.

Not surprisingly, these weeds of disturbed ground are mostly Old World species, having spread across Eurasia during the thousands of years that farming has gone on there. Nearly all arrived during the colonial period in crop seed, wool waste, and straw packing. By contrast, prior to the coming of the European settlers, there was little farming in America and, as a consequence, few suitable habitats that would favor the evolution and spread of native American annual weeds with similar requirements.

If the field continues to remain fallow, coarse perennial herbs, sometimes called forbs, soon replace these annual species in abandoned cultivated fields. These include such familiar species as goldenrod, *Solidago* spp., wild aster, *Aster* spp., milkweed, *Asclepias* spp., pokeweed, *Phytolacca americana*, smartweed, *Polygonum* spp., brambles, *Rubus* spp., and many others. Because of the thick cover of annual weeds, these perennials usually appear, at least initially, as scattered individuals, many of which then increase by creeping rhizomes to form clumps.

On bottomlands and other moist sites, such rampant trailing vines as wild grape, *Vitis* spp., poison ivy, *Rhus radicans*, wild morning glory, *Ipomoea* spp., bindweed, *Convolvulus* spp., bittersweet, *Celastrus scandens*, and black bindweed, *Polygonum convolvulus*, often form continuous cover over large areas and thus slow down reforestation. These vines spread across any young trees that might have become established and pull them down, shade them out, or actually strangle them by twining tightly around their small trunks. Purple loosestrife, *Lythrum Salicaria*, and other rank-growing herbs also discourage reforestation on wetter sites.

Where vines have taken hold, the vegetation often assumes a mosaic pattern that persists for many decades. Scattered trees that do manage to grow to maturity may remain and be separated from each other by a tangle of vines and other low vegetation. Some species of vines, such as poison ivy, may also discourage competition by secreting compounds toxic to other plants. Even when the woodland canopy finally becomes more or less closed, scattered open glades of vines may still persist.

PASTURE LAND

Light grazing encourages the development of turf grasses, those species which form a continuous cover by spreading underground rhizomes. Overgrazing, of course, harms the turf and usually results in an increase of unpalatable species. Though most of the pasture grasses can stand grazing, if the leaves are kept constantly clipped back the plant will decline in vigor and may eventually die. This is understandable since the leaves of the grass, like those of other green plants, are the main organs of photosynthesis, the process that utilizes the sun's energy to produce carbohydrates for growth. Since grasses are heavy users of soil nutrients, constant cropping will also eventually result in a decline of soil fertility.

A thick layer of turf inhibits the establishment of other plants, but as the top growth is removed, there is a corresponding decline in root growth and eventually holes appear in the turf. Red cedar and pine can become established where the turf is thin and such small-seeded species as gray birch and many of the perennial weeds will germinate in bare spots.

When young, many of the weedy herbs such as goldenrod and plantain, *Plantago* spp., are palatable to livestock and are therefore kept under control by grazing, but others such as thistle, *Cirsium* spp., and hawkweed, *Hieracium* spp., are rejected and thus may increase in number. Cattle and sheep also reject the sour, spiny conifer seedlings such as pine, red cedar, and ground juniper, *Juniperus communis*, and will not usually browse on gray birch. As a result, these trees may appear in a pasture prior to its abandonment and, as a result, gain a head start over other species.

Common juniper is an especially interesting old field shrub. In areas of poor, rocky soil, especially where overgrazed, juniper often becomes the dominant shrub, sometimes forming a continuous, impenetrable cover. Juniper will shade out grass, but apparently the bare ground beneath the shrub provides a suitable seedbed for quaking aspen and gray birch. In addition, squirrels enter the juniper thickets to bury acorns and other nuts. In old pastures, white pine can compete with juniper if both are recruited at approximately the same time, though the taller-growing pine eventually shades out the juniper.

On particularly dry pasture land, such as that underlain by sandy and gravelly soils, reforestation proceeds very slowly. Scattered eastern red cedar may appear on the site before abandonment or shortly after, but it may be several decades before a closed canopy of trees will develop. On these sites there is often an intermediate stage of several decades where a sod-forming species of native grass, little

79. Pioneer trees growing in an abandoned apple orchard, Little-
ton, Massachusetts. A young forest of gray birch and aspen has
overtopped the apple tree in the background. Poison ivy, goldenrod, and several species of grasses still persist beneath the trees.

bluestem, *Andropogon scoparius*, may grow to form a continuous cover that eliminates other herbaceous species. Little bluestem, also aptly called poverty grass because of the
poor sites on which it grows, is a very common species, easily
recognized by its silky stems that are blue-green in summer
and a distinctive silvery brownish-orange in fall and winter.

Clumps of little bluestem develop extensive root systems—sometimes over two meters deep—which capture
most of the available moisture. Only such large-seeded
species as oaks and hickories, which produce a deep initial
taproot, can compete. But it is usually not until the cedar is
well established that squirrels and other rodents will venture into the abandoned pasture to disperse these seeds. As a
result, perhaps six decades must pass on such a dry site
before a deciduous forest becomes established.

HAYFIELDS

Most hayfields were mowed twice a summer. Mowing
eliminates conifer seedlings which cannot resprout from the

cut stems, but many deciduous species, once established, will continue to resprout when cut. Shrubs are especially adept at resprouting from cut stems. When a hayfield is abandoned, the open conditions will encourage vigorous growth of shrubs, sometimes producing a thick enough cover to slow down reforestation.

If the turf remains thick, fine-seeded species such as gray birch and most of the perennial weeds cannot take hold. Annual weeds, which are common on formerly cultivated fields during the initial stage of succession, similarly are unadapted for germination in turf. The seeds of white pine and red cedar, however, will germinate in turf, so that the woodland that subsequently appears on old hayfields may eventually be indistinguishable from that growing on abandoned pasture.

Trees of the Postagricultural Forest

Under certain conditions almost any tree species of the oak forest could invade old fields. Often among the pioneer species described below, you will find oaks, hickories, red maple, and other species not normally considered to be old field pioneers.

White Pine, *Pìnus Stròbus,* in the northern part of the region is one of the most common and easily recognized trees. It may be found in nearly every dry land community, though it reaches its best development on old fields. White pine's dense irregular habit, distinctive gray-green foliage, and large size make the tree recognizable up to a kilometer away. There is a longer discussion of white pine on page 229.

Eastern Red Cedar, *Juníperus virginiàna,* is the most common old field conifer in southern and coastal sections. In New England, it usually ranges between 3 and 12 m (10 to 40 ft) and is a dark green color. Its needles are of two different kinds: some are sharply pointed while others, particularly on older trees, are flattened and overlapping. The fruit is a deep blue berry covered with a whitish bloom. Sometimes red cedars are found with bizarre gelatinous masses growing on them; these are galls of the cedar-apple rust. There are two varieties of eastern red cedar, one spreading and broadly pyramidal, which is common in marble areas, and another,

80. Eastern red cedar, *Juniperus virginiana*, is a dark-green columnar evergreen found in many old pastures in southern New England. The older needles are scaly; the young needles are thin and pointed.

narrow and columnar in shape, more common along the seaboard. The two varieties intergrade especially in central Connecticut.

Variant forms: There are over thirty named variant forms. Varieties with very narrow, pendulous, rounded, or vase-shaped growth habits or interesting needle colors may be seen at arboretums and nurseries.

Gray Birch, *Bétula populifòlia*, is another very common old field tree in the region. When growing in the open, gray birch is a slender well-shaped tree rarely exceeding 10 m (35 ft). It is easily distinguished from white birch by its distinctly triangular leaves, by the dark horizontal lines and black branch scars that give the bark a grayish appearance, and by its short stature. In northern sections, gray birch crosses with white birch, *B. papyrifera*. The resulting hybrids are taller and more shade-tolerant than the gray birch.

Quaking Aspen, *Pópulus tremuloìdes*, is a small to medium-sized tree ordinarily reaching about 12 m (about 40 ft) though sometimes growing taller. Quaking aspen is easily recognized by its bark, a smooth light greenish-gray becoming dark with age, and by its small grayish-green rounded leaves that flutter in the slightest breeze. Quaking aspen grows on nearly every site except swampland. It is commonly found on sterile mineral soil along highways and in burned-over areas, though on both of these sites its growth is usually slow.

Big-toothed Aspen, *Pópulus grandidentàta*, is very similar to quaking aspen in habit, habitat, and bark color. Its

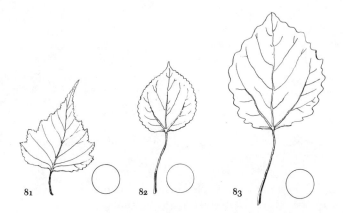

81. Gray birch, *Betula populifolia*, is a common old field tree. Its distinctly triangular leaves, small stature, and grayish-white bark make it easy to identify.

82. Quaking aspen, *Populus tremuloides*, is recognized by its small rounded leaves that move with the slightest breeze, and its distinctive greenish-gray bark.

83. Big-toothed aspen, *Populus grandidentata*, closely resembles quaking aspen except for its larger and very coarsely toothed leaves.

leaves are larger and coarsely toothed. In the spring, the two species may be distinguished by the color of the unfolding leaves: those of the big-toothed aspen appear cottony white while those of the quaking aspen are yellowish green. Big-toothed aspen cannot endure as much soil moisture as quaking aspen, but on drier sites the two species are often found growing together and occasionally hybridize.

Choke Cherry, *Prùnus virginiàna*, is a small tree of old fields, low ground, and roadsides, whose clusters of small black fruit in late summer look inviting but taste bitter and astringent. Choke cherry ranges in size from a shrub to a small tree up to 7 m (23 ft) high. Its leaves are oval or oblong in shape and are finely toothed. Numerous elongated spikes of small white flowers appear in May. Choke cherry is common in the northern parts of the region, becoming rare near the southern Connecticut coast and in southeastern Massachusetts.

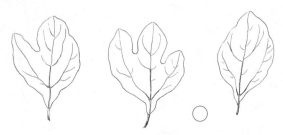

84. Sassafras, *Sassafras albidum*, has leaves of three different shapes on the same tree.

Variant forms: Both choke cherry and pin cherry (below) are occasionally found with yellow fruit.

Pin Cherry, *Prùnus pennsylvánica*, is a small tree similar to the choke cherry in habit and occupying many of the same sites. It is readily distinguished from choke cherry by its fruits and flowers, which occur in small open clusters rather than in elongated spikes. Another common name for pin cherry is fire cherry, because of its tendency to invade burned-over lands. Pin cherry is more common in northern New England. It is frequently found in Massachusetts and occasionally in Connecticut and Rhode Island.

Sassafras, *Sássafras álbidum*, is a small tree that often invades abandoned fields from its edges by root sprouts. Though occasional large trees are seen, in southern New England, close to the northern limit of its range, sassafras rarely tops 15 m (50 ft) and is usually much shorter. Sassafras may be easily identified by its sweetly aromatic leaves of three different shapes: most commonly oval, less commonly divided into three lobes, and occasionally two-lobed or mitten-shaped. On older trees the bark is orange-brown and deeply ridged and the new shoots bright yellowish green. Sassafras leaves color brilliantly in the fall, ranging from yellow through orange to salmon-pink. Its fruit is a small deep-blue berry.

Black Locust, *Robínia pseudoacàcia*, an introduced tree, was brought into the Northeast from its original range in the southern and central Appalachians during colonial times, and has since become thoroughly naturalized in many places. Open-grown trees may be distinguished at a distance by their crooked and forked habit and at close range by dark and deeply furrowed bark. The leaves are compound with up

85. Black locust, *Robinia pseudoacacia*, may be recognized by its compound leaves of a dull grayish-green color, its deeply furrowed bark, and its usually picturesque shape. The pea-like flowers are often high on the tree.

to nineteen oval leaflets alternately arranged on the long leaf stem. The color, a dull grayish-green, further aids recognition at a distance.

Black locust is a legume. Like clover and other legumes, it has the ability to enrich the soil by fixing nitrogen. Its leaf litter is rich in nutrients such as potassium, calcium, and magnesium, which not only enrich the soil but also decrease soil acidity. In Cape Cod, where locust was extensively planted, presumably to enrich the soil and—because of decay resistance—for fence posts, there is often a luxuriant growth of grass under the trees, especially notable in comparison with the scrubby grass and ericad cover more commonly associated with this region. The species reproduces readily by sprouts from the roots. Groves of locust trees are thus more common than single specimens.

Variant form: The shipmast locust, *R. pseudoacacia* var. *rectissima*, is straighter trunked and more narrow in habit. The original trees may have come to New England from West Virginia via Long Island. This form does not set seed and hence must be propagated from root sprouts.

Hawthorn, *Crataègus* spp., is a large and complex genus of small trees and shrubs. About 150 different species have been identified but these cross and recross to the point that only expert taxonomists can identify individual trees with any certainty. Hawthorns belong to the rose family; their flowers and fruit resemble those of the apple, though they are much smaller. Probably the most distinctive characteristic of the genus, however, is the long sharp spines that grow on the branches of many species. Occasionally hawthorns form thickets in old pastures.

Other Postagricultural Trees
Black Cherry, *Prùnus seròtina*, page 196
White Ash, *Fráxinus americàna*, page 146

Shrubs of Postagricultural Land

The number of shrub species in old fields is even larger than that of the trees. On moister sites many of the typical wetland species will colonize the open land while on upland sites practically any of the shrubs described in various slope communities (pages 128–49) may appear. The shrubs described below are ones that require sunny conditions to grow; like the pioneer tree species, they decline and disappear once they become shaded.

Common Juniper, *Juníperus commùnis*, is a common shrub of dry, rocky pastures. Like other conifers it is unpalatable to livestock and therefore is usually established before the land is abandoned. Common juniper is easy to recognize by its low spreading habit, its bluish or grayish green color, and its sharply pointed needles. Its fruit is about the size of a small pea. In some abandoned pastures it forms impenetrable waist-high thickets, but these are more common in northern New England than in this region. Large

86. Common juniper, *Juniperus communis*, is easily recognized by its shrubby stature and its prickly bluish-green foliage.

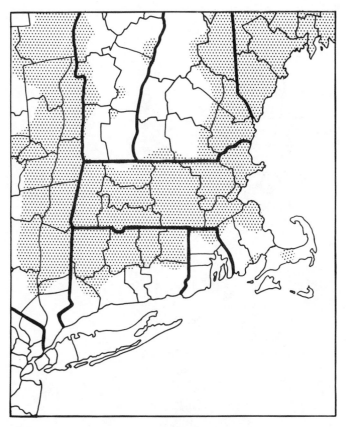

Range of the common juniper, *Juniperus communis*.

plants disappear quickly in shade though scattered small seedlings may persist in the woodland understory for many years.

Variant forms: Occasionally common juniper grows in an upright habit as a small tree. A trailing short-needled form is also sometimes found. A form of juniper with berries up to 13 mm (½ in) has been reported from other parts of its natural range.

Smooth Sumac, *Rhùs glàbra,* is a common invader of dry pastures and other disturbed places. It should not be confused with its sister species, poison sumac, *R. Vernix,* found

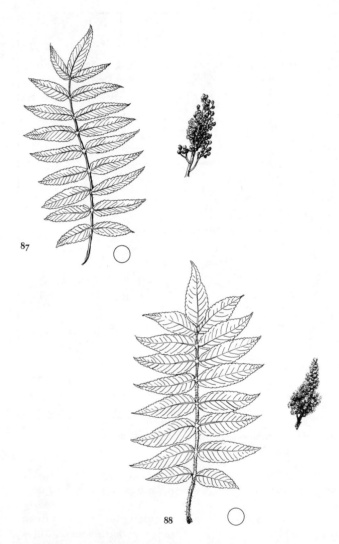

87. Smooth sumac, *Rhus glabra*, is a large coarse shrub with smooth-surfaced compound leaves.

88. Staghorn sumac, *Rhus typhina*, is similar in appearance to smooth sumac except that its leaves, branches, and fruit are densely covered with soft hairs.

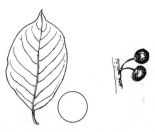

89. Alder buckthorn, *Rhamnus Frangula*, is recognized by its shining leaves and speckled bark. Its fruit is a black berry.

in bogs and other wet places, though a few people are also allergic to smooth sumac and the staghorn sumac (below) as well. Sumac (properly pronounced *shoomac*) is a very common and easily recognizable species. It is a medium-sized shrub, about .5 to 3 m (about 20 in to 10 ft) tall, usually spreading by underground runners to form extensive clumps. It bears compound leaves up to 50 cm (20 in) long with 11 to 31 leaflets sharply toothed and whitened beneath. The leaves appear fairly late in the spring and become deep brilliant red in the fall. The flowers are greenish yellow, blooming in tight clusters on the terminals. The red fruit persists after the leaves drop off in the fall.

Variant form: A form with more deeply cut leaves is occasionally seen.

Staghorn Sumac, *Rhùs typhìna*, is very similar in appearance and habitat to the above except that the branches and leaf stalks are densely covered with soft hairs, which give them a velvety appearance. It is a taller shrub, sometimes reaching 10 m (35 ft) in height. It is often hybridized with the smooth sumac (above), producing a form with intermediate characteristics. It is perhaps a bit less common in this region than smooth sumac.

Similar species: Dwarf sumac, *R. copallina*, resembles the two sumacs above in appearance and habitat. It can be distinguished by its shorter leaves with conspicuous wings between the leaflets.

Alder Buckthorn, *Rhámnus Frángula*, is a European introduction first reported in New England in 1915. Spreading rapidly since then, it is now common in eastern areas and likely to become invasive. It is a shrub up to 7 m (23 ft) tall with prominently veined smooth-edged shining leaves between 3 and 7 cm (1¼ to 2¾ in) long. The flowers are small and solitary, growing from the leaf axils, and the fruit is a small red berry, turning black in late summer. The bark is brown speckled with white. It is among the last shrubs to lose their leaves in fall.

Gray-stemmed Dogwood, *Córnus racemòsa,* is a shrub of medium height, rarely exceeding about 2 m (6½ ft) and usually forming dense thickets. It may be recognized by the grayish stems on the new growth and the flat clusters of roundish fruits, which are about 5 to 7 mm (³/₁₆ in) in diameter, at first lead-gray in color, then becoming white. Like those other members of the dogwood genus, the leaves when carefully pulled apart yield clear filaments (page 140).

Wild Grape, *Vìtis* spp., is a common plant of abandoned agricultural land. Technically, it is not a shrub but a vine, though its woody stems persist like shrubs through the winter. The most common grape species in the region is fox grape, *V. Labrusca,* source of most of the native cultivated strains and parent of many more. Another common strain, river grape, *V. riparia,* as its name suggests, is more common on flood plains and river banks. The species are hard to distinguish; all have rounded three-lobed leaves that are similar in shape. Often grapevines persist in woodlands long after the trees have matured, apparently having been carried upward with the trees as they grow. Though grapevines have no thorns they often grow in such dense tangles, especially along flood plains, that they are difficult to penetrate.

Brambles, *Rùbus* spp., is another large and complicated genus of the rose family. Brambles are technically not shrubs but biennials, producing stalks called canes from perennial roots. During the first year, these canes, then known as primocanes, reach their full size but remain unbranched and do not flower. During the second year, the stalks, now known as floricanes, branch and flower on the terminals. Often the leaves are simple on the primocane and compound on the floricane. Like other members of the rose family, the small flowers resemble apple blossoms in shape.

Blackberry, *R. allegheniensis,* is the most common member of the genus. Like many other members of this genus, most blackberries have very sharp and imposing prickles that can draw blood and easily penetrate all but the heaviest clothing. The fruits of these species vary in size and quality, some producing excellent berries.

Raspberry, *R. idaeus*, is also common in old fields. The cultivated raspberries came from a European strain of the species; the native strain has smaller berries. Raspberries may be distinguished from blackberries by the way the berry separates from the flower base or receptacle: raspberries are readily detached while blackberries are not.

The White Pine

THOUGH white pine, *Pinus Strobus*, may turn up in nearly every conceivable dry land habitat—and some of the wetland habitats as well—it grows best in old fields. It is, however, unlike the typical old field pioneer trees in many ways. While pine is a sun-loving species, as are the other trees that first populate abandoned farmland, unlike other small and short-lived pioneers it is among the tallest of eastern trees and may live 400 years or more. In size, the reputed record-holder for this species was a 60-meter (200-foot) giant cut down in Pennsylvania at the end of the last century. Trees of 45 meters apparently were not unusual in colonial New England, but such large trees are rarely encountered today.

White pine does grow naturally in all southern New England counties, but it is common south of an irregular line crossing central Connecticut and Rhode Island and rare on outer Cape Cod. In the northern part of the region, however, it is one of the most common trees, perhaps seeming even more so because of its distinctive foliage and often large size.

The need of white pine for an open sunny habitat should be clear to anyone who looks at small pines growing in the shady understory of a woodland. If these small trees cannot penetrate the canopy above—as is usually the case—they eventually waste away and die. Pines show each yearly increment of growth by a whorl of branches; on many of these shaded pines the whorls are only a few centimeters apart. By contrast, young pines on open, fertile sites may

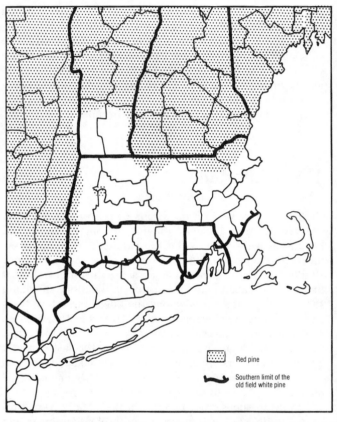

Distribution of pines in southern New England. The dotted over-
lay shows the range of the red pine, *Pinus resinosa*. The hachured
line designates the southern limit of the old field white pine stands
(though some pines do occur naturally farther south). The third
native species, the pitch pine, *Pinus rigida*, ranges throughout the
area.

add 50 centimeters a year to their height, though the rate
slows down as the trees get older.

Moreover, young pines practically never grow in the
deep shade under a parent tree. In mature pine groves there
will often be a suppressed but surviving generation of
hardwoods in the understory. When the old trees are lum-

bered or blown down, these understory trees make a rapid spurt in growth. The fast-growing hardwoods will greatly reduce chances that any slower-growing pine seedlings that might be in the opening will be able to reach the canopy before the larger hardwood saplings close it in. Thus, once a stand of old field pine falls, there is only a small chance that it will replace itself. On sandy loams in northern New England, however, if the pine is cut after a good seed fall and the soil is scarified, pines may be induced to repopulate the site.

White pine makes up for this lack of shade-tolerance in other ways. As was mentioned earlier in this section, recruitment is an extremely important factor in old field succession. In a good seed year—usually every three to five years—dominant pine stands may produce as much as 100 kilograms of seed per hectare (about 90 pounds per acre) with perhaps as many as 100,000 of the tiny, winged seeds per kilogram.

Pine appears commonly in old pastures where, because of its distastefulness to livestock, it gains a competitive advantage over grasses and most hardwood seedlings. Near a pine grove, however, the seed fall may be so copious that seedlings appear in old hayfields, orchards, or abandoned

90. The three native southern New England pines growing on the same site in central Massachusetts. On the left is pitch pine, *Pinus rigida*, with its characteristic irregular shape, in the middle is white pine, *P. Strobus;* on the right is red pine, *P. resinosa*, with its long needles growing in tufts.

cultivated land, especially if they are covered with short grasses.

Like most other native trees, white pine is not without its enemies. Probably the most serious of these is the white pine blister rust, a fungus disease that attacks the cambium layer, especially of young trees, usually girdling and killing them. The disease was first discovered in North America in 1906 on pine seedlings imported from Europe to fill a heavy demand for planting stock at that time, and it has since spread across the natural range of pine. Gooseberries and currant, *Ribes* spp., are the alternative hosts for this fungus; if every one of these shrubs is rooted out and destroyed within a radius of 300 meters (about 1,000 feet) of the pines, adequate control is usually achieved. In very windy conditions, however, the rust spores have been known to travel over 1,600 meters. Though the disease will probably never be eradicated, control is thus possible.

Another common enemy is the white pine weevil. In summer, many young pines may be found with dead terminal shoots, killed where the weevil bored through the thin stems. Though one of the lateral branches usually becomes the new leader, continuous weevil damage often results in a spreading forked-trunked tree that is worthless for timber. However, these old spreading pines are ideal nesting sites for many species of wildlife.

Witches-Brooms

A number of unusual forms of white pine have been found. These include trees with a prostrate growth habit, pendulous branches, or downward-pointing needles which grow in radiating tufts. By far the most common of these variant forms, however, is one that is spherical or flat-topped in shape and dwarfed in stature. These dwarf forms grow from seeds that are produced by a witches-broom. Witches-brooms are abnormal growths on pines and some other trees caused by a parasite fungus or perhaps some other organism. As the name suggests, they look very much like the twig brooms of colonial times, though in the case of pines they are densely covered with needles. They are more commonly found in mature pines, though occasionally they appear on

91. Witches-broom in a white pine. Where witches-brooms occur in trees near a field, as is the case here, a population of globular dwarf pine seedlings is almost certain to be found.

smaller trees as well. Witches-brooms may grow on the very top of the tree (where they are easily seen) or on a lateral branch.

The pathogen that causes this abnormal growth apparently enters a single cell on the growing tip and alters its genetic code. Subsequent cellular divisions result in the characteristic tightly constricted growth. Like some kinds of tumors, these growths often appear more vigorous and healthy than the rest of the tree; witches-broom trees themselves sometimes appear to be in declining health.

This unusual growth habit is passed on via the seeds from cones on the witches-broom. About 50 percent of the seedlings grown from these are dwarf forms while the other half grow to normal trees.

The distribution of these white pine witches-brooms raises several questions. Though they could hardly be called common, their occurrence is frequent enough that people who remember to look for them will almost certainly locate one or more. In rural parts of central Massachusetts they seem to occur with a frequency of about two per town. Though I have looked carefully for several years now, I have never found one north of Portland, Maine. One competent horticulturist who is interested in these forms has located an inordinate number in old cemeteries; most of those I have seen occur along highways or near cultivated or otherwise disturbed land. Perhaps the fungus or other causative agent is soil-borne and carried into the tree by the wind. It is difficult to make any general statements, however, on the basis of such a small number of samples.

When you find a pine with a witches-broom growing on it, it is always worthwhile to search the land around for the dwarf progeny. If there is open land nearby you will very often find some. In dense woodlands, where the chance of germination and subsequent survival of the seedlings is slim, these dwarf pines are much less common.

As with any natural population, the dwarf trees vary in their characteristics. They thrive in full sun to light shade on any well-drained soil. Needless to say, if left in their wild habitat on the shady forest floor or among the rising thicket in an abandoned field, their chances of survival are small. However, the parent tree will continue to produce them as long as it continues to set seed and a suitable seedbed remains available.

Witches-brooms occur on other species as well. Pitch pine, jack pine, *P. Banksiana*, and hemlock witches-broom also are occasionally the source of unusual seedling forms, though I have never found any. In northern New England, black spruce grow witches-brooms, usually as a result of infection by dwarf mistletoe *(Arceuthobium pusillanum)*. This pathogen does not produce unusual seedling forms. Among deciduous species, highbush blueberry, *Vaccinium corymbosum*, and hackberry, *Celtis occidentalis*, also grow witches-brooms.

Other Pine Species

Red Pine, *P. resinòsa,* whose southern range limits barely reach the northern border of the region, is occasionally seen as reforestation plantings on sandy areas in cooler sections. It is easily distinguished from white pine by its reddish-brown scaly bark and its longer needles borne in twos, instead of the usual five of white pine, growing at the ends of the branches in tuft-like groupings.

Scots Pine, *P. sylvéstris,* is an introduced European pine that has become naturalized in some places. It has shorter needles than the white pine and a bright orange peeling bark on the upper part of the trunk and branches.

FURTHER READING

Postagricultural Land: An Introduction

Russell, Howard S. *A Long, Deep Furrow: Three Centuries of Farming in New England.* Hanover, N.H.: University Press of New England, 1977. A big, scholarly, well-written history of New England agriculture.

PART VI

The Sand Plain Community

92. Typical sand plain community on Cape Cod. Pitch pine, bear oak, and bearberry, three of the most common sand plain species, may be seen in the photograph.

The Sand Plain Community

CAPE COD and other sandy or gravelly areas in southern New England support a landscape far different from that of the typical oak forest communities described previously. Oaks are still the most common trees—indeed, many of the oak forest species also appear here—but in place of an assemblage of the tall, widely spaced trees of the more typical southern New England woodland, vast areas are covered by a sorry collection of small, shrubby, and crowded trees.

Scattered through this woodland—one could hardly call it a forest—and usually taller than the oaks are pitch pine, *Pinus rigida*, a species so often found in this community and so easily recognizable that it can be considered an indicator of this plant community.

The sand plain community is distinctive more for its soils and its botanical characteristics than for its topography. The hilly land on parts of Cape Cod, where some of the most striking examples of this woodland community may be seen, could hardly be considered a plain. But elsewhere on Cape Cod and in other parts of southern New England the community is commonly found on sandy outwash plains. These may be elevated above the surrounding countryside and here and there pitted with kettleholes, but otherwise the surface of the land is fairly flat.

Like the other woodland communities of southern New England, the sand plain community has affinities with woodland areas in other parts of the country. A similar woodland covers much of eastern Long Island; the famous Pine Barrens of southern New Jersey are also similar in both general appearance and floristic composition. In fact, some botanists refer to the Cape Cod woodlands as "pine barrens."

Forest investigators have included this woodland in another of the great forest associations of eastern America, the oak-pine forest. Farther south, on the Atlantic Coastal Plain and in sandy areas in the Piedmont, areas where this forest association most commonly occurs, other species of pine and oak join those found in New England. But like the southern parts of the oak forest, the oak-pine forest to the south still bears a strong resemblance to that of southern New England.

Dryness is the most salient characteristic of the sand plain community. Most of the soil is porous, made so when glacial meltwater carried away the silt- and clay-sized particles that otherwise would help to retain rainwater. In most cases, the rainwater sinks right through the upper layers of the soil until it is beyond the root zones, and hence out of reach of the vegetation.

Though rainfall is ample all through the region, some of these sand plain communities remain virtual deserts. For example, the North Haven sand plain, now largely vanished beneath the expanding urban sprawl, was such a dry and inhospitable environment that not even poverty grass, *Andropogon scoparius,* would grow on some parts. On other parts, a grassland community of sorts remained more or less indefinitely, the habitat being too inhospitable for the growth of those tree and shrub species normally adapted to these dry sites. There is even a species of cactus, prickly pear, *Opuntia humifusa,* that grows in dry and sandy sites near the coast, but it has not been reported from the North Haven sand plain.

The Role of Fire

During rainless periods, especially in summer, these woodlands become tinder dry. Not surprisingly, most have had a long history of fire. Indeed, the sand plain community on Cape Cod is the only part of southern New England where serious forest fires still occur. As we saw in the chapter on climate, the strong southwestern winds that blow across the area in summer not only make Cape Cod more dry than it might otherwise be, but also fan any fires that might get started. These fires often consume the water-holding humus layer in the soil, thus making the sand plain community drier still.

All of the species inhabiting the sand plain community are ones that can survive forest fires. The oaks and pitch pine sprout vigorously from burned stumps, but such fire-sensitive species as beech, *Fagus grandiflora,* hemlock, *Tsuga canadensis,* and white pine, *Pinus Strobus,* normally found on sandy soils (though usually on lower sites where there is more soil moisture available), are found only in protected places, such as islands in some of the larger ponds, that have escaped the ravages of fire. In fact, east of the Cape Cod Canal, hemlock grows naturally in only one place, a point of land in Wakeby Pond in Mashpee that has escaped fire for perhaps 200 years. An island in Halfway Pond near Plymouth supports a rich community of beech, hemlock, white pine, yellow birch, *Betula lutea*, and a number of other fire-sensitive species that stand as an oasis in the scrubby burnt-over woods surrounding the pond.

The oak species inhabiting sand plains are mostly the same ones found in the oak forest hilltop community, another community that in the past has often received more than its share of forest fires. Much of the area is covered by bear oak, *Quercus ilicifolia*, though black oak, *Q. velutina*, scarlet oak, *Q. coccinea*, and white oak, *Q. alba*, also grow here. However, chestnut oak, *Q. Prinus*, and dwarf chestnut oak, *Q. prinoides*, both species of dry, rocky habitats, are less common in the sand plain community.

The distribution of the oaks reflects in general the incidence of fire. Though all of these species can sprout vigorously from burned stumps, repeated severe fires gradually eliminate first the white oak and then the black and scarlet oaks. Scrub oak can produce acorns at a younger age, and hence is favored by repeated fire.

Trees of the Sand Plain Community

Of the following species, post oak and American holly are found only in southeastern Massachusetts and other coastal areas.

Pitch Pine, *Pinus rígida*, is so common on these habitats that it may be considered an indicator plant for the sand plain community. It is a low to medium-sized tree, usually less than 15 m (50 ft) though occasionally reaching 20 m (66 ft). The branches are arranged in regular whorls on young trees but become very irregular as the tree reaches maturity. The irregular arrangement of the branches, plus a curving, often gnarled trunk and deeply furrowed scaly bark, makes this pine recognizable at a glance. The foliage is a distinctive yellowish green. There is a longer discussion of the pitch pine in the chapter following.

93. Post oak, *Quercus stellata*, has a distinctive leaf shape. Note also the limited range of this species.

Range of the post oak, *Quercus stellata*.

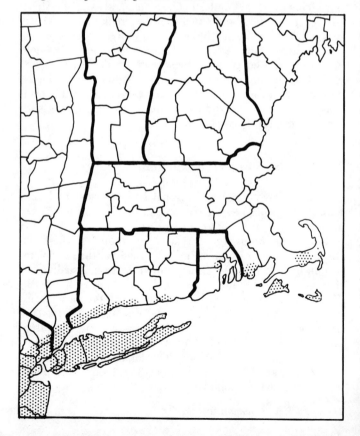

Variant form: A rounded dwarf form similar to those growing from white pine witches-broom seeds is occasionally found. These may also originate from witches-brooms.

Similar species: White pine, *Pinus Strobus*, appears on more congenial sites in the sand plain community.

Bear Oak, *Quércus ilicifòlia*, is a shrub or small tree usually under 2.5 m (8 ft). The leaves are variable in shape though usually with short triangular lobes. It is probably the most common oak species across much of Cape Cod, sometimes forming solid thickets of many acres and preventing other more desirable species from growing. It occasionally crosses with the red oak and the black oak, producing hybrids with characteristics intermediate between the two. (See photograph, page 238.)

Post Oak, *Quércus stellàta*, occurs only along the coast. It reaches its northern range limits on Cape Cod from Falmouth to Brewster, and also is found in Rhode Island near Wickford and a few places along the Connecticut coast. Though post oak grows to be a huge tree farther south, near its northern limit in Massachusetts it rarely grows taller than 10 m (35 ft). It is best recognized by its characteristic leaves as well as its localized distribution.

American Holly, *Ìlex opàca*, while not precisely a tree of the sand plain community, is closely associated with it. Holly reaches the northern limit of its range in Quincy, Massachu-

94. American holly, *Ilex opaca*, has leathery evergreen leaves. Female trees bear bright red berries. Note the limited range of this species.

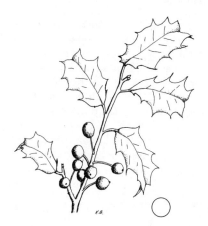

243

Range of the American holly, *Ilex opaca.*

setts, becoming frequent in southeastern Massachusetts, in southern Rhode Island, and occasional in southern Connecticut. Like several other species found in this section, American holly is a Coastal Plain species that occupies sandy habitats similar to those found farther south, but ones that are more moist than the typical sand plain. It is easily recognized by its smooth gray bark, spiny evergreen leaves, and red berries. It is usually an understory tree, reaching a height of 10 m (35 ft), though larger specimens may occur.

Variant forms: Because of its splendid horticultural qualities, many excellent forms of American holly have been sought after and found. Some of these trees are exceptionally well shaped, large-berried, and very fruitful. Among the unusual forms are trees bearing leaves without spines and ones with orange and yellow berries.

Other Sand Plain Trees
  Dwarf Chestnut Oak, *Quércus prinoìdes*, page 131
  Chestnut Oak, *Quércus Prìnus* (not found in the Cape Cod region), page 129
  Black Oak, *Quércus velùtina*, page 130
  Scarlet Oak, *Quércus coccínea*, page 129
  White Oak, *Quércus álba*, page 130

Shrubs of the Sand Plain Community

All of the ericads described under the hilltop community also appear in the sand plain community. They include:
  Huckleberry, *Gaylussàcia baccàta*, page 132
  Lowbush Blueberry, *Vaccínium* spp., page 132
  Sheep Laurel, *Kálmia angustifòlia*, page 132
In addition, ericad subshrubs—wintergreen, *Gaultheria procumbens*, and trailing arbutus, *Epigaea repens*—are common here. Other shrubs include the following (asterisks indicate those found only in Cape Cod and other coastal sections):

Bearberry, *Arctostáphylos Ùva-úrsi*, is a very common subshrub on Cape Cod, occasionally found in other sandy coastal regions though infrequent on inland sand plains. It is a trailing shrub, with leathery leaves about 1 to 3 cm (⅜ to 1¼ in) forming mats. It is common on roadsides and other sunny sites. Its small pale-pink or white bell-shaped flowers appear in late May or early June.

Variant form: A form with an additional blooming period in the fall is also found on Cape Cod and Nantucket. The autumn flowers are red or purple, while those in the spring are the typical white or pink.

Sweet Fern, *Comptònia peregrìna*, is a straggling twiggy shrub about .3 to 1.5 m (11 in to 5 ft) occupying dry roadsides and woodland clearings. It is easily recognized by its thin fern-like leaves and the fragrant aroma of its leaves and twigs. Sweet fern thrives in sunny sites but soon disappears in shade.

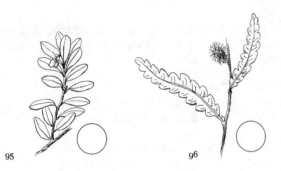

95   96

95. Bearberry, *Arctostaphylos Uva-ursi*, is a trailing subshrub easily recognized by its lustrous dark evergreen leaves and its mat-forming tendencies.

96. Sweet fern, *Comptonia peregrina*, is a low shrub that is recognized by its grayish-green distinctively shaped leaves, which are very aromatic when crushed.

97   *K.B.*   98

97. Inkberry, *Ilex glabra*, is usually a straggling evergreen shrub with black berry-like fruits.

98. Broom crowberry, *Corema Conradii*, is a tiny subshrub that can be recognized by its linear leaves and clusters of purplish flowers, which appear in early May.

*Inkberry, *Ilex glàbra*, like its relative American holly, *I. opaca*, is a Coastal Plain species that grows in low though usually sandy sites. It is variable in height, occasionally reaching 3 m (10 ft), but it is usually about half that size. Inkberry can be identified by its leathery evergreen leaves and its black solitary berry-like fruit that grows in the leaf axils.

*   **Prickly-Pear Cactus,** *Opúntia humifùsa,* is the only cactus species found in the East. It is another Coastal Plain species that is found in southern New England only in dry sunny habitats near the coast. Prickly pear is unmistakable in appearance. Its flattish bristly cactus-like stems creep along the ground, sometimes forming sizable clumps. Its bloom is a handsome yellow flower appearing in late June. (See color plate III.)

*   **Broom Crowberry,** *Corèma Conrádii,* is a many-branched low shrub common in the region only on dry habitats on outer Cape Cod. It is easily recognized by its narrow heath-like leaves arranged around the stems in whorls. The male flowers are purple tufts without petals; the female flowers are insignificant.

The Pitch Pine

OF ALL THE TREE SPECIES that grow in the sand plain community, pitch pine, *Pinus rigida,* seems to be uniquely adapted to life in this inhospitable environment. Though the tree is normally considered one peculiar to very dry sites, it will grow much more vigorously and reach a taller size where there is ample soil moisture, although its lack of shade tolerance usually prevents it from becoming established on more favorable sites. On dry sites with their history of repeated fires, however, this intolerance to shade is not an ecological disadvantage, since forest regeneration in these fire-ravaged woodlands rarely reaches a point where pitch pines are shaded out or are replaced by a generation of other more shade-tolerant trees.

After a fire, pitch pines, even of seedling size, usually sprout energetically from dormant buds at the base of their trunks. Older trees retain this stump-sprouting ability for many years, though their thick bark also offers a good measure of protection from fires of medium intensity. Repeated burning will eventually produce twisted and slow-growing trees. In fact, the deformed and picturesque shape of pitch pine is usually the result of fire damage.

Pitch pine, like bear oak, reaches fruiting maturity much earlier than other species. The cones open erratically, so that the probability of at least a few seeds finding enough moisture for germination and growth is enhanced. The cones of some pitch pines growing in areas where fires have been particularly severe remain closed until a subsequent fire has singed them (and the probability of an open seedbed following fire exists). Pitch pine is one of the few tree species that germinate readily on sterile mineral soil with no humus at all.

Like other trees on dry sites, pitch pines produce a very deep root system which not only helps them extract every bit of moisture from the soil but also provides them with protection from windthrow during hurricanes—another forest disturbance that has regularly visited the southern New England coastal areas where these trees often grow.

PART VII

Wetland and Watercourse Communities

Wetlands: An Introduction

A GLANCE at nearly any southern New England topographic map will reveal an abundance of those blue, grassy symbols that denote swamps, bogs, and marshes. Indeed, in some low-lying areas, such as parts of southeastern Massachusetts, wetland accounts for over half of the land surface. Like lakes and ponds, wetlands are found mostly in glaciated areas, where the great ice sheets scraped out hollows in the bedrock or clogged pre-existing valleys with the piles of rocky debris left behind when they melted.

These wetlands, lakes, and ponds are among the most ephemeral of geologic features. Already in the relatively short time since the ice disappeared from southern New England, many ponds and wetlands have filled up or drained away. One reason, perhaps, for the greater abundance of lakes and wetlands in parts of northern New England is that this region has more recently emerged from beneath the glacial ice.

The vast acreage of wetlands that still remains, along with the rocky soil, is another insurmountable obstacle to widespread agriculture in southern New England, and thus has played an important part in the region's shifting economic fortunes. On the other hand, in heavily populated and industrialized areas, now typical of so much of the region, these wetland areas make several vital contributions to maintaining the quality of the environment, including flood control, water table recharge, pollution filtration, oxygen production, and reduction of harmful nitrogen compounds. Wetlands also provide a great measure of scenic and biologic diversity.

Wetland and Watercourse Communities

The most useful classification of freshwater wetlands has been made on the basis of the plant community growing in each. In the following chapters these wetland communities are described, from the wettest habitats to the driest.

The marsh community occupies the wettest sites. Marshes are characterized by shallow standing water the year round and by floating or emergent vegetation such as reeds and cattails. A drier community closely related to the marsh community, but whose vegetation is chiefly grasses, is the wet meadow community.

Somewhat drier habitats, where trees and woody shrubs can gain a foothold, become swamps. Most swamps are initially populated by shrubs and hence become a shrub swamp community. Gradually these change to a wooded swamp community as trees, usually stands of red maple, *Acer rubrum*, shade out and replace the shrubs.

Another wetland community occurs on low ground along rivers or large streams that may be flooded during late winter and spring but remain mostly dry for the rest of the year. This intermittent flooding creates a plant community different from either swamps or marshes. The flood plain community consists of species that can survive periods of both immersion and dryness.

A much rarer wetland community in southern New England is the bog community. Bogs are characterized by knee-high evergreen shrubs, sedges, and sphagnum moss that have grown to form a floating mat that begins around the edges of a pond and in time may grow across it. If this occurs, trees may be able to gain a foothold and the bog community will slowly change to a swamp. In most of the region the typical wooded swamp of red maple has probably been the next successional stage, but occasionally along the coast and more rarely inland a pure stand of Atlantic white cedar, *Chamaecyparis thyoides*, replaces the bog vegetation. This conifer swamp community is different from the wooded swamps.

The last two wetland communities described in this part of the book, the rock ravine and stream bank communities, may technically lie outside the wetland category, since many of the plants most commonly found in each prefer a more well-drained soil. However, a cool, moist environment, in part supplied by running water, probably is the most important ecological factor of both of these communities, hence their inclusion in the section. Under the rock ravine community, I have included a number of northern species that are not restricted to this habitat but also grow in other cool sites such as the steep north-facing slopes.

Composite and Transitional Wetlands

Nature is never as simple as ecology books suggest. Although it is possible to find more or less pure exemplars of each of the wetland communities in our region, more often wetlands are composites of one or more of these. A particular wetland, for example, may contain areas of shallow water supporting typical marsh vegetation as well as areas of wooded or shrub swamp. Sometimes bog vegetation will be found on the shady north-facing side of a pond while marsh plants such as cattails grow where there is more sun.

As is the case wherever a mosaic pattern of different types of vegetation is found, these composite wetlands support a great abundance and variety of wildlife. All other factors being equal, the total length of the boundaries between the different communities, known to wildlife biologists as edges, is roughly proportional to the productivity of a particular composite wetland. Wetlands where the communities exist in concentric rings or bands are therefore less productive.

A study of wetlands is further complicated by the fact that these communities change over both time and space. Many swamps, for example, are in the process of changing from a community of shrubs to one of trees. In the uneven terrain of the region, stream courses often pass through a whole series of different habitats, from rock ravines to swamps, one gradually blending into the next, each with a corresponding gradual change in the plant community. Such transitional communities also defy neat categorization.

The Marsh Community

MARSHES are the wettest of the various wetland communities. They are generally characterized by areas of shallow standing water and an abundance of herbaceous plants, both floating and emergent. Experts recognize two distinct freshwater marsh types: deep marshes, where the depth of water ranges between 10 centimeters and 1 meter (4 inches to 40 inches), and shallow marshes, where the depth of water is less than 10 centimeters. Each of these two types supports

99. Marsh community, Concord, Massachusetts. The emergent plants are mainly arrowhead, *Sagittaria* spp. The tiny floating plant, duckweed, *Lemna* spp., covers the surface of the water.

a somewhat different plant community, but for the purposes of this book the distinction is not too important.

Marshes can usually be identified on topographic maps by the wetland symbol and an absence of the green overprint that indicates woods. Every marsh over approximately 2 hectares (about 5 acres) that I have looked at has a substantial inflow and outflow. The indication on the map of a brook or stream flowing through a particular wetland is another clue that it is probably a marsh.

The soil underlying marshes is usually a soft dark muck, made highly organic by the decaying remains of earlier generations of plants. Since marsh vegetation is herbaceous, hence dying back each winter, a large portion of the plant nutrients are recycled and thus become available for the next year's growth. Because water in marshes is relatively shallow, there is also a high ratio between surface area and volume. As a result, there is a relatively high amount of dissolved oxygen available both to the water plants that live there and to the decay bacteria submerged in the muck layer below. This abundance of oxygen tends to hasten decay of the organic remains and helps to prevent the intensely acid conditions found in bogs from evolving. If the stream feeding the marsh is unpolluted, it may also supply additional dissolved oxygen. Because decay is relatively rapid in most marshes, the muck layer is thin, though thick enough to make most marshes difficult if not impossible to cross on foot.

Marsh Succession

As is the case with other wetlands, marshes smaller than 2 hectares tend to be very short-lived unless they border on a large body of open water. Though marshes are not characterized by the thick layer of organic material found in bogs, organic material and silt eventually accumulate to the point that woody shrubs can take hold, and the marsh is then on the way to becoming a shrub swamp. In small acidic marshes, the tussock sedge, *Carex stricta*, seems to play an important role in succession. This sedge species eventually grows into hummocks which remain above the water. Because of its dense growth habit other plants have difficulty in gaining a foothold, but eventually an alder or maple seed may germinate and grow on these sedge tussocks, and the marsh may begin its slow change to swampland.

Buttonbush, *Cephalanthus occidentalis*, plays an interesting role in marsh succession. It is one of the few woody plants which can survive with its roots submerged for long periods of time; sometimes a solid cover of buttonbush will be found growing (or at least surviving) in areas covered by shallow water for most of the year. This suggests that there may be a direct successional line from open water to a shrub swamp without an intervening marsh stage. Buttonbush seems to grow more vigorously, however, in slightly drier sites where its roots are wet but not totally submerged.

Large marshes are long-lived. Many occur in the beds of

extinct glacial lakes. The fact that areas of relatively shallow open water have managed to remain for the several thousand years since the disappearance of the ice from the region gives some testimony to their longevity. Because of climatic changes that are believed to have occurred in the region since the ice age, however, the successional histories of these large marshes may be more complex. Perhaps, for example, during the cooler, wetter periods some of these marshes may have supported bog vegetation, as indeed many in interior areas still do. Corings taken from these might reveal a thick layer of sphagnum or sedge peat buried beneath the top layer of muck derived from the present-day marsh vegetation.

Likewise, the future successional pattern of a particular marsh can only be conjectured. Small climatic changes could have a profound effect on the vegetational changes that take place. A drier, warmer climate, for example, might dry up the marsh and accelerate the growth of trees and shrubs, while a cooler, moister climate might slow down succession or encourage a bog community to form.

Herbaceous Plants of the Marsh Community

Grasses, reeds, sedges, and rushes make up a large percentage of marsh vegetation. Most species in each of these groups produce small, inconspicuous flowers, making specific identification difficult. I have therefore described only general features that should enable you to decide to which group a particular plant belongs. Anyone seriously interested in these plants may refer to one of the identification guides listed on page 337.

Cattail, *Typha* spp., is one of the most common and easily identifiable marsh plants. A robust emergent, whose linear leaves sometimes top 2 m in height. It is easily distinguished by the inflorescence: dark-brown sausage-shaped spikes in summer, buff-colored and fuzzy in winter. The root stalks, lower leaf stems, young shoots, and flower heads are all edible, tasty, and highly nutritious.

The most common cattail species in the region is *Typha latifolia*, the broad-leaved cattail. A second species, the

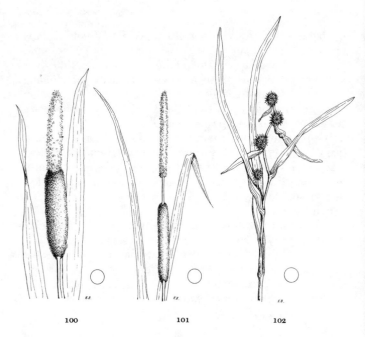

100   101   102

100. Broad-leaved cattail, *Typha latifolia*, bears leaves that are between 1 and 2 centimeters wide.

101. Narrow-leaved cattail, *Typha angustifolia*, bears leaves between 4 and 8 millimeters wide and is less common than the broad-leaved cattail.

102. Bur reed, *Sparganium* spp., is easily recognized by its spherical bur-like fruit.

narrow-leaved cattail, *T. angustifolia*, is easily distinguished from the broad-leaved species by the width of its leaves, usually under 7 mm (¼ in). The narrow-leaved cattail prefers alkaline or basic habitats; in most southern New England marshes its presence indicates pollution from sewage, which is alkaline in character.

Bur Reed, *Spargànium* spp., is an emergent plant usually found growing in shallow water or on muddy shores. The flattened linear leaves may reach a height of 1 m (about 3 ft). Bur reeds are easily distinguished by their fruits arranged in one to five spherical, bur-like heads.

Arrowhead, *Sagittària* spp., is a low emergent plant with distinctive arrow-shaped leaves and white three-petaled flowers.

Pickerelweed, *Pontedèria cordàta,* is a stout emergent plant growing in shallow water or muddy banks. The fleshy leaves are quite variable, though commonly they are an elongated heart-shape. The species is easily recognized by the dense spike of violet-blue flowers.

Sedge (Bulrush), *Cypèrus, Scírpus,* and *Càrex* spp., are three common genera in a large and variable family of grass-like herbs. In the northeastern United States this family, the Cyperaceae, is represented by about 450 different species; a large percentage of these may be found in wetlands and other sites in southern New England. Many, but by no means all, sedges may be distinguished from grasses by a stem that is triangular in cross section and by the way the grass-like leaves clasp the stem when one tries to peel them off. (Grass stems are easy to peel since the lower part of the grass leaves are not solidly around the stem.)

Tussock sedge, *Carex stricta,* is among the most important and easily recognizable marsh sedges. A large species, its very thin leaves may reach 60 cm (2 ft) in length. As mentioned earlier, one of the chief characteristics of this

103. Arrowhead, *Sagittaria* spp., bears distinctive arrow-shaped leaves and white three-petaled flowers.

104. Pickerelweed, *Pontederia cordata,* is most easily recognized in spring by the dense spike of violet-blue flowers.

103   104

sedge is to form elevated tussocks that may in time provide a dry foothold for shrubs and trees. It is common in wet meadows, marshes, and swamps. A very competent field botanist once told me that the presence of tussock sedge in wetland areas nearly always meant an absence of orchids and other interesting small wetland plants.

Several other sedge species form tussocks, but none are as common as *C. stricta*. The soft rush, *Juncus effusus*, is also a tussock-forming species in wet meadows and pastures. Unlike their close relatives, the grasses, these sedges offer little nourishment to livestock and are often unpalatable to them. In wet pastures, then, grazing may favor the growth of sedges by keeping competing plants in check.

Reed, *Phragmites commùnis*, is a conspicuous true grass that grows in fresh and salt marshes, especially around civilization. It is easily identified by its tall size (up to 4 m), its habit of forming dense stands, and its whitish plume-like inflorescence. Its normal ecological requirement of a neutral soil suggests that its presence, like that of the narrow-leaved cattail, may be a sign of pollution from sewage.

Purple Loosestrife, *Lỳthrum Salicària*, is a large, aggressive perennial herb, originally imported as a garden flower from Europe. First reported in the wild in the early 1900s, purple loosestrife now covers huge expanses of marsh and wet meadows. It is easily identified by its showy spike of magenta flowers. So rank-growing is purple loosestrife that it usually crowds out the native vegetation. The plant has no value as food for wildlife except for honeybees.

Variant form: A rare white form occurs.

Duckweed, *Lémna* spp., is a group of tiny light-green floating plants that sometimes covers large areas of open water in marshes. Botanists report that it is the smallest flowering plant known. At least one authority attributes the aggressive behavior of duckweed in some wetlands to an increase of nutrients from sewage pollution.

Sweet Flag, *Ácorus Cálamus*, is identified by its light-green sword-like leaves and a spadix of tightly packed florets (similar to the inside of the flower of the jack-in-the-pulpit) that juts at an angle from the flat blade-like stem. When crushed, the plant yields a pleasant aromatic odor. Along the Concord River in Massachusetts, sweet flag used to be a

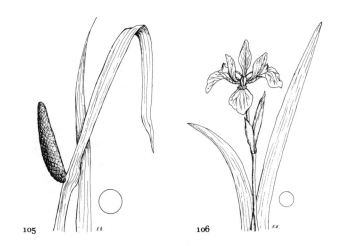

105. Sweet flag, *Acorus Calamus*, bears light-green sword-like leaves that emit a pleasant aromatic odor when crushed.

106. Blue flag, *Iris versicolor*, is easily recognized by its showy blue flower, which appears in June.

common plant. In recent years it has become scarce, perhaps as a result of pollution.

Blue Flag, *Iris versicolor*, is the most common native iris in the region. It has the slender sword-like leaves typical of this genus and showy blue-violet flowers which appear in mid-June.

Variant form: A rare white-flowered form occurs.

Similar species: Slender blue flag, *I. prismatica*, occurs in brackish and fresh marshes near the coast. It may be distinguished from *I. versicolor* by its thin, almost grass-like foliage.

Yellow Iris, *Iris Pseudácorus*, is an introduced species that has become thoroughly naturalized in many southern New England wetlands. Its handsome yellow flower, which blooms in June, makes yellow iris easy to identify. Its distribution is sporadic, abundant in some wetlands and absent from others.

Joe-Pye Weed, *Eupatòrium* spp., is a genus of tall plants up to 2 m high growing on marsh edges and wet meadows.

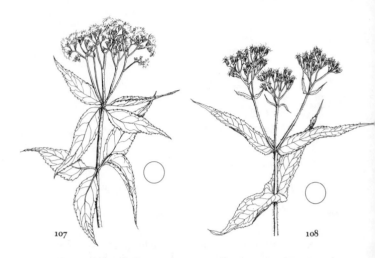

107. Joe-pye weed, *Eupatorium* spp., is a common late summer plant that is recognized by its pale pinkish-purple fuzzy flowers.

108. Boneset, *Eupatorium perfoliatum*, bears white flowers and light green leaves that unite at the bases and encircle the stem.

Flowers of all species are a dull pale pinkish-purple, borne in fuzzy massive clusters on the tops of the plants. All species bloom in late summer.

Boneset, *Eupatòrium perfoliàtum*, belonging to the same genus as joe-pye weed, also grows in marshes and wet meadows. Boneset is a tall plant characterized by numerous fuzzy white flowers borne in clusters at the top of the plant. The species is easily identified by pairs of light-green wrinkled leaves that unite at their bases and encircle the stem.

Similar species: There are a number of other species of *Eupatorium* that are difficult to distinguish. A number live in marshes, especially those near the coast, as well as in other wet sites. The leaves on these different species are sometimes distinctive, but at other times they exhibit confusing variations. The species also hybridize freely.

Yellow Pond Lily, *Nùphar ádvena*, is a floating plant of open water, identified by its oblong-oval leaf blades and its yellow cup-like bloom.

Similar species: Water lily, *Nymphaea odorata*, is distinguished by its rounded leaves and its showy white many-petaled flowers.

Marsh Pink, *Sabàtia* spp., is a genus containing several species growing up to just under a meter in height. All are characterized by showy pink flowers, each with a yellow eye bordered by red. Most are found in fresh sandy marshes and lake shores near the coast. (See color plate III.)

Jewelweed, *Impàtiens capénsis,* a large plant sometimes exceeding 2 m (6 ft) in height. Its soft foliage is grayish-green and exudes a clear juice when broken. Probably the most easily recognizable characteristic is its crimson-orange, spotted, irregularly-shaped flowers, up to 3 cm (1¼ in) long, which are borne singly on drooping stems. These appear over most of the summer. The elongated seedpod pops open at a touch, scattering the seeds some distance. The juice from the foliage is reputed to relieve the effects of poison ivy and stinging nettles.

Variant forms: Numerous flower variations, including plants with lemon yellow, deep orange, white, cream-colored, and unspotted blossoms, occur. Occasionally very heavily flowering plants are seen.

Similar species: Pale jewelweed, *I. pallida,* closely resembles *I. capensis* except that its flowers are pale yellow and shorter. It is more common in wet places on calcareous soil.

109. Jewelweed, *Impatiens capensis,* is recognized by its light grayish-green foliage and its distinctive spotted orange flowers.

K.B.

The Wet Meadow Community

SOME EXPERTS recognize a drier type of marshland which they call a wet meadow. Though the water table—especially in summer—may be slightly below the level of the ground, the soil on these sites receives a continuous supply of moisture. Grasses, not sedges, are usually the dominant vegetation in wet meadows, though sedges and other marsh plants grow in sloughs and mudholes where the grassy turf may have been lifted by frost during the winter and stripped away by the spring freshets.

The ecology of these wet meadows is complex. In a heavily forested region such as southern New England, where all areas but salt marshes or sand dunes support some tree species, we would expect that wet meadows would be a rather short successional phase between marshland and swamp or moist woods. While it is true that many wet meadows would soon grow to shrubs or trees if not kept artificially open either through mowing or grazing, others tend to remain open for long periods of time with no help from man. Early records indicate that natural open meadows were present along both the Connecticut and Concord rivers in precolonial times; the early European settlers used them as a source of hay for livestock.

Periodic Indian fires may have been a factor in keeping these meadows open, though in Concord, where the meadows have been neither burned nor mowed for over fifty years, many show little natural reforestation. Why some of these meadows have remained open while others have become quickly reforested is a question for which there is no satisfactory answer. Perhaps late summer flooding, the result of occasional tropical storms, has helped to keep the growth of trees in check. Many swamp trees can endure flooding during the winter but a layer of warm standing water over their roots during the growing season will kill them. In wet meadows bordering the Concord River, where flooding from late summer tropical storms has been occurring at least once every thirty years, observers have noted that after the floods there is an abundance of dead maple saplings in these sites.

On balance, however, as more and more farmland is

abandoned, wet meadows—especially the smaller ones—are returning to woodland. As a result, a number of plants that were formerly found in the wet meadow habitat are now becoming scarce. Some of these are described below.

As is the case with nearly every other community, variable factors such as soil moisture and acidity have an important bearing on the variety of plants. Where these sites are strongly acidic—as indicated by patches of sphagnum and haircap moss, blueberries, and other acid-loving plants—several different species of orchid may occur. Some of these are found in quite wet environments, others in much drier parts.

Herbaceous Plants of the Wet Meadow Community

Arethusa, *Arethùsa bulbòsa,* is a small orchid of bogs and wet meadows. It was probably never common in the region, even when there was a great deal more cleared land; now it is rare and probably becoming more so. One characteristic that may be contributing to its disappearance is its small size. Though it is reported to reach a height of 35 cm (14 in), the few that I have found seemed closer to 12 cm (5 in). These smaller plants would probably have difficulty competing with the grasses and other taller plants found in these sites. The single flower borne on the top of the stem is large for the size of the plant, occasionally reaching 5 cm (2 in) in length. It is usually magenta pink with a prominent spotted yellow and purple lip. The three sepals typical of orchids are erect and of the same magenta color as the petals. In this region the plant blooms around the first of June. (See color plate II.)

Variant forms: Forms with bluish-lilac or white flowers have been reported. Needless to say they are not commonly seen.

Rose Pogonia, *Pogònia ophioglossòides,* is more common than arethusa in acidic wet meadows and bogs. It is a taller plant, occasionally reaching a height of about 50 cm (20 in) though usually smaller. The single deep to pale pink fragrant flower is usually smaller than that of the arethusa, reaching

110. Rose pogonia, *Pogonia ophioglossoides*, is taller and more common than arethusa. It bears rose-pink petals.

only 3 cm (1¼ in) in length. Its distinctive floral characteristic is the lip, which is veined with red and fringed with yellowish hairs. It blooms in June.

Variant forms: A white-flowered form sometimes is seen. *Gray's Manual of Botany* reports unusual forms with two or three lips on the blossoms.

Grass Pink, *Calopògon pulchéllus*, is another orchid of bogs and wet meadows that is becoming scarce in the region. Grass pink blooms are loose clusters of two to ten concave magenta to rose-pink or lilac flowers. The flowers are about the same size as the two species described above, ranging from 2.5 to 4.5 cm (1 to 1¾ in). The lip on the grass pink flowers is above the other parts, giving the flowers an upside-down appearance in comparison with other species. Grass pink is a summer-blooming orchid with flowers usually appearing in July.

Variant forms: Larger more abundantly blossoming plants are sometimes found. A rare white-flowered form has also been reported.

Common Ladies'-Tresses, *Spiránthes cérnua,* is a small plant of wet meadows as well as drier sites. In late summer it sends up a spiraling spike of small white or cream-colored flowers that may reach 15 cm (6 in) in height.

Similar species: There are a number of other species of ladies'-tresses in the region. Some occupy wet sites, others dry. All are characterized by the spiral arrangement of the flower.

Fringed Gentian, *Gentiàna crinìta,* is another casualty of the disappearing wet meadow habitat. Its blue tube-like flowers are 3.5 to 6 cm (1⅜ to 2½ in) in length, each with four delicately fringed petals on top, blooming in September. Fringed gentian is a biennial whose survivàl in an area is tied to the chance dispersal of its seeds. Young plants require full sunlight and have difficulty growing in tall grass; thus the plant was more common in regularly mowed wet meadows and is now gradually disappearing in the region. (See color plate IV.)

Variant forms: Though deep blue is the usual color of fringed gentians, light-blue to white forms are occasionally seen. In fact, the two stations of fringed gentian that I have

111. Grass pink, *Calopogon pulchellus*, bears several flowers on a single stem.

112. Common ladies'-tresses, *Spiranthes cernua*, is a late summer orchid that is recognized by its spike of small white flowers.

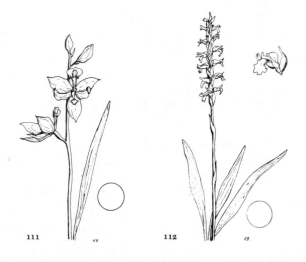

111   112

113. Canada lily, *Lilium canadense*, is a tall plant bearing distinctive yellow or orange spotted flowers that appear in summer.

seen in the wild both had white-flowered forms growing with the more common blue-flowered plants.

Canada Lily, *Lilium canadénse*, is a tall plant sometimes reaching 2 m (6½ ft) in height. Its leaves are borne in whorls around the stem. From 1 to 22 showy spotted yellow or orange flowers bloom from branches at the top. The flowers are six-petaled and bell-shaped.

Variant form: A beautiful red-flowered form is occasionally seen.

Similar species: Turk's cap lily, *Lilium superbum*, resembles the Canada lily in plant habit. Its spotted flowers are usually a deeper orange and the petals recurved (see color plate IV). The tiger lily, *Lilium tigrinum*, is an old garden lily from eastern Asia that occasionally escapes and becomes naturalized in the region. Although its flowers resemble those of the Turk's cap lily, it is easily distinguished by the shiny black bulbils that form at the leaf axils.

Other Wet Meadow Species

Like other wetlands, the wet meadow community grades into others. The following species, described under other communities, may also appear in the wet meadow community.

Fringed Orchid, *Habenària* spp., page 308
Cardinal Flower, *Lobèlia cardinàlis*, page 328
Marsh Fern, *Dryópteris Thelýpteris*, page 334
Sensitive Fern, *Onoclèa sensíbilis*, page 334
Steeplebush, *Spiraèa tomentòsa*, page 272

The Shrub Swamp Communities

IF WOODY PLANTS do gain a foothold in the marsh or wet meadow, a different wetland community, the shrub swamp, may gradually evolve. In most cases the shrub swamp is probably a relatively short transitional stage between open wetland and a wooded swamp, since many wetland trees can survive under the same conditions of moisture as the shrubs. These trees will gradually shade out the lower plants. One exception, as we noted on page 254, is buttonbush, which sometimes forms pure extensive thickets on very wet sites.

There is some evidence from a site in Connecticut that suggests, however, that a thick shrub layer may resist the subsequent invasion of trees for several decades. The dense shade cast by the shrub layer as well as other competitive factors may effectively prevent the germination of tree seedlings.

Two Shrub Swamp Communities

Two fairly distinct shrub swamp communities occur in the region: the alder-willow thicket and the sweet gale–ericad swamp. As with nearly all other ecological classifications, the categories are not absolute; species from one do occur in the other. Yet the two types seem sufficiently distinct to warrant separate discussion.

The alder-willow thicket is more common on postagricultural land in low meadows and along brooks. This community also often appears in wetlands that have been disturbed.

114. Shrub swamp community, Hampton, Connecticut. Sweet pepperbush, *Clethra alnifolia*, and leatherleaf form a continuous shrub cover. The dead tree at the right suggests a recent rise in the water level.

The shrubs are taller but do not form as thick a cover as do the dense shrubs found in sweet gale–ericad swamps. As a result, elms, red maples, and other wetland trees can easily gain a foothold, and this shrub swamp community then becomes a wooded swamp. Sometimes, however, rabbit browse on the hardwood seedlings keeps them suppressed, and the alder-willow thicket remains relatively stable for a long time. Often large areas of sensitive fern, *Onoclea sensibilis*, and such herbaceous flowering plants as jewelweed, *Impatiens capensis*, are also found on these sites.

The sweet gale–ericad swamp, on the other hand, contains many of the species found in bogs, though the sphagnum mat characteristic of bogs is not present. I suspect that the soil in this community is substantially more acidic than that of the alder-willow thicket. Furthermore, these swamps are more common in cooler parts of the region and may represent a transitional stage between marshes and bogs; bogs are far more common in cooler northern New England. This type of swamp is also more likely to be found in wet areas that are underlain by sand and gravel. Unlike bogs, though, which form over deeper water, the open water and muck of the sweet gale–ericad swamp is usually only a meter or so deep.

Sweet gale, *Myrica Gale*, shadbush, *Amelanchier canadensis*, and ericads such as leatherleaf, *Chamaedaphne calyculata*, sheep laurel, *Kalmia angustifolia*, highbush blueberry, *Vaccinium corymbosum*—all common in bogs—as well as several species of dogwood and viburnum grow in these more acidic swamps or along their margins. Sweet pepperbush, *Clethra alnifolia*, may also be found here, though it is seen more often in shadier sites. Poison sumac, *Rhus Vernix*, is also all too common in these acidic swamps. Everyone exploring shrub swamps should learn to recognize this shrub. A description can be found on page 23.

Shrubs of the Shrub Swamp Communities

It should be noted that many of the herbaceous plants of the open marshlands, especially such robust emergents as

115. Buttonbush, *Cephalanthus occidentalis*, is a common shrub often growing in very wet places. Its spherical head of white flowers makes it easy to identify when in blossom.

116. Alder, *Alnus* spp., is a tall straggling shrub. Its fruit, which resembles tiny pine cones, is distinctive.

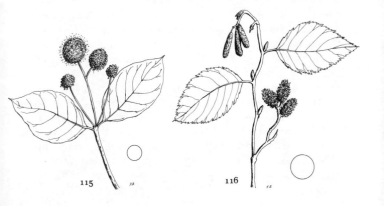

115   116

cattails, persist into the ericad swamps, though in the taller alder-willow thickets they are shaded out.

Buttonbush, *Cephalánthus occidentàlis,* is a nondescript swamp shrub which may reach about 3 m (10 ft) in height, through usually it is far shorter. Its most distinctive characteristics are its bloom, a dense spherical head, about 3 cm (1 in) in diameter, of tightly crowded white flowers, and its shiny dark-green leaves. Buttonbush is one of the few woody shrubs that can survive shallow flooding for long periods of time during the growing season. In some swamps it forms solid thickets.

Alder, *Álnus* spp., is a genus containing two very similar species which grow side by side in much of their range and frequently hybridize. Both are open shrubs reaching up to 5 m (16 ft) in height. One has smooth bark, the other speckled bark. Alders are easily identified by their persistent dark-brown cone-like fruits about 1 cm long.

Willow, *Sàlix* spp., is a large and complex genus of shrubs and trees. All possess one distinct characteristic, a single scale covering the winter buds. All other New England shrubs have buds covered by two or more scales. Most willows also have narrow gray-green leaves. A common and easily identifiable species growing in shrub swamps and other wet places is pussy willow, *S. discolor,* whose fuzzy buds appear in late February. Several other less easily distinguishable species are also common in shrub swamps. The larger black willow, *S. nigra,* is included in the flood plain community descriptions, on page 295.

Dogwood, *Córnus* spp., is a genus containing several swamp shrubs as well as the familiar flowering dogwood, *C. florida,* of the oak forest communities. These other dogwoods lack the showy bracted blossoms of the flowering dogwood, though all bear clusters of small white flowers. Dogwood leaves have a distinctive pattern of curved veins; when a leaf is carefully pulled apart these veins stretch out as small transparent hair-like filaments. The most common swamp dogwood in the region is probably the silky dogwood, *C. Amomum,* whose red stems make winter identification easy. The less common red-osier dogwood, *C. stolonifera,* also has red stems and twigs; however, the fruit of this species is white while that of the silky dogwood is dark blue.

Viburnum, *Vibúrnum* spp., is a genus including about a

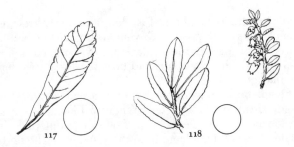

117. Sweet gale, *Myrica Gale*, has grayish-green aromatic leaves and a small cone-like fruit.

118. Leatherleaf, *Chamaedaphne calyculata*, bears distinctive brownish-green leaves and small bell-like flowers. It is very common in acidic swamps and bogs.

dozen species native to the northeastern United States. The species that grow in southern New England swamps superficially resemble the dogwoods in flower and fruit. Unlike the dogwoods, their leaves lack the pattern of circular veination and have serrated edges.

Black-berried Elder, *Sambùcus canadénsis*, is a common swamp shrub up to 3 m (10 ft) tall. It is easily recognized by its toothed compound leaves and its fragrant flat-topped clusters, up to 15 cm (6 in) in diameter, of small white flowers that bloom in middle to late June. The new growth on the elder is soft and nonwoody. The fruits are small, purple-black, edible berries. It is found in wooded sites but is more common and blooms more freely in open marshes and meadows.

Similar species: A red-berried elder, *S. pubens,* with ill-scented white flowers, is more common in wet woodland sites.

Sweet Gale, *Myrìca Gàle*, is a deciduous shrub up to 1.5 m (5 ft) tall with grayish-green aromatic leaves. The flowers are insignificant and are borne in small (1 cm) catkins. The fruit is a small cone-like nutlet about 1 cm long. Though it is not generally regarded as an acid-soil shrub, sweet gale is often associated with leatherleaf and other bog plants.

Leatherleaf, *Chamaedáphne calyculàta,* is a common bog shrub that, like sweet gale, also appears in some acidic shrub swamps. It is a small shrub, rarely reaching over a meter in height. Leatherleaf is identified by its brownish-green leathery evergreen leaves and its small white bell-like flowers, which are borne at the leaf axils at the ends of the branches. In shrub swamps and bogs it often forms dense low thickets.

Steeplebush, *Spiraèa tomentòsa,* is a sparsely branching twiggy shrub up to 1 m tall. When in bloom it is easily recognized by the steeple-shaped cluster of tiny pink five-petaled flowers that bloom from the top down. The under-sides of the leaves are woolly and brownish. Steeplebush is common in old pastures and in dry sterile habitats as well as in wet meadows and on the edges of shrub swamps.

Similar species: Meadowsweet, *S. latifolia,* is taller, with a broader head of light-pink to white flowers. It occupies the same habitat.

Winterberry, *Ìlex verticillàta,* is common in semishady habitats. It is a medium-sized deciduous shrub up to about 4 m (13 ft), quite variable in growth habit and leaf characteris-tics. As in other members of the holly family, the flowers are nondescript, but the bright red fruits, about 6 mm, remain-ing along the stems of the plant during the late fall and winter make identification of the plant easy at this time of year. (See color plate V.)

Variant forms: A rare yellow-fruited form has been re-ported. Probably orange-fruited forms exist. Although the amount of fruit the plant sets varies from year to year and is also dependent on, among other factors, the amount of sunlight it receives, occasionally a very heavily fruiting plant is found.

Similar species: Smooth winterberry, *I. laevigata,* is simi-lar in appearance to *I. verticillata.* Its fruit is a bit larger, about 8 mm in diameter, and is an orange-red. It is com-monly found in white cedar swamps near the coast.

Shadbush, *Amelánchier* spp., is a large, complex genus of shrubs and small trees. *A. canadensis* is probably the most common species in southern New England, being found in acidic shrub swamps and other wetland sites. It is easily identified in May by the clusters of drooping whitish flowers which appear before the grayish-green foliage.

Purple Chokeberry, *Pỳrus floribúnda,* is a small spread-ing shrub up to about 1 m (40 in) in height, bearing clusters of white appleblossom-like flowers at the tops of the stems in

119. Winterberry, *Ilex verticillata*, is most easily recognized in fall and winter by its bright red berries. Its leaves are deciduous. (See also color plate V.)

120. Shadbush, *Amelanchier canadensis*, bears drooping white flowers in May, which appear before the grayish-green foliage.

121. Purple chokeberry, *Pyrus floribunda*, bears small white flowers in terminal clusters and a dark purple fruit.

late June and dark purple fruit up to 1 cm in diameter in early fall. It is occasionally found on drier sites.

Similar species: Red chokeberry, *P. arbutifolia*, is similar in appearance to *P. floribunda*, though much rarer. Occasionally found in southwestern Connecticut and in coastal Massachusetts to Essex County, it is distinguished by its red fruit and fuzzy new growth.

Other Shrub Swamp Species

The following species also appear in shrub swamps, though they are probably more common in other habitats and therefore are described elsewhere.

White Swamp Azalea, *Rhododéndron viscòsum*, page 282
Highbush Blueberry, *Vaccínium corymbòsum*, page 148

Spicebush, *Líndera Benzòin*, page 327
Sweet Pepperbush, *Cléthra alnifòlia*, page 282
Poison Sumac, *Rhùs Vérnix*, page 23

The Wooded Swamp Community

BY FAR the most common wetland community in the region, the wooded swamp should be familiar to anyone who
has spent time in the southern New England countryside.
Red maple, *Acer rubrum*, a common tree in almost all of the
other woodland communities, becomes especially abundant
in wooded swamps, often forming pure stands. Near the
coast and occasionally inland, Atlantic white cedar, *Chamaecyparis thyoides*—also often growing in pure stands—is
a common swamp tree. Because of their specialized geographic distribution and what is thought to be a different
successional history, a description of these white cedar
swamps (page 310) is included in the chapter on another
community, the conifer swamp community.

Travel in Swamps

Wooded swamps are shown on topographic maps by a
combination of the blue wetland symbol and the green overprint designating woodlands. It is impossible to tell from the
map alone, however, whether foot travel is possible through
them. Many mature red maple swamps are so shady as to be
practically free of a shrub layer. In summer and early fall,
when the water table drops, these swamps are often as
passable as an open oak forest. Where a shrub layer persists
or where greenbrier thickets have developed, however, foot
travel may be very difficult or impossible.

Stream courses in wooded swamps also may present problems to the walker. Because drainage is often very sluggish,
even small brooks that normally would be easy to step across
on sloping ground become wide quagmires that are impossible to cross without sinking knee-high into mud.

Travel through a wetland that is changing from a shrub

swamp to a wooded swamp is often especially difficult and hazardous. Under these conditions, the shrubs have reached their greatest development and have not yet been shaded out by the trees. The shrubs often grow so thickly as to make them well-nigh impenetrable. The hazardous part of traveling through these high shrub swamps is not quicksand or bottomless mires, but the all too common poison sumac, *Rhus Vernix*, described on page 23.

Characteristics of Wooded Swamps

The boundary between the low slope community and the wooded swamp community is usually dramatic and sharp. Where the sloping land reaches to within a few centimeters of the water table, the rich variety of the low slope community abruptly gives way to a rather monotonous cover of red maple. Other trees, such as tupelo, *Nyssa sylvatica*, black ash, *Fraxinus nigra*, and swamp white oak, *Quercus bicolor*, normally considered to be swamp trees, are more often

122. Wooded swamp, Harvard, Massachusetts. The trees are predominantly red maples. Note the poison ivy growing on several trees. Sensitive fern, *Onoclea sensibilis*, growing at the left, and tussock sedge, *Carex stricta*, at the right, are both common herbaceous plants in wooded swamps.

found on the slightly higher ground along the margins of the swamps.

Though red maple can endure this very soggy habitat, it too will die if its roots are totally submerged for any length of time. In every maple swamp where pools of standing water or muddy spots persist through the summer, the red maple and the few other species that occasionally are found there are growing on slightly elevated mounds or hummocks. Perhaps the tree seedlings germinated on a sedge tussock during an earlier successional stage or on the stump of an earlier tree, but by the time the tree is mature, these raised mounds seem to consist of little more than the tree's own root structure.

Yellow birch, *Betula lutea*, a species that sometimes appears in swamps near the northern end of the region as well as in other cool sites, sometimes presents an even more bizarre type of elevated root system called stilt rooting. The tiny birch seeds often germinate on a rotted log or stump and the roots grow downward into the ground below. When the log or stump beneath it rots away, the tree stands elevated on its own root system. Some red maples may begin the same way but their fibrous root systems tend to fill in the open spaces, so the result is not so noticeable.

Hemlock, *Tsuga canadensis*, and, surprisingly enough, white pine, *Pinus Strobus*, also grow on hummocks in wooded swamps. Hemlock is adapted to moist conditions, but white pine is normally regarded as a tree of drier upland sites, yet both trees seem to survive on mounds that are not much larger than those beneath the red maples.

The variety and abundance of shrubs that grow in the maple swamps is far less than that of the shrub swamp or the adjacent low slope community. In some swamps the combination of sogginess and deep shade has completely eliminated the shrub layer. In other slightly drier sites, such acidic-soil shrubs as highbush blueberry, *Vaccinium corymbosum*, and white swamp azalea, *Rhododendron viscosum*, grow well in wooded swamps though neither may set many flowers in deep shade. In maple swamps and other moist woodlands within 50 kilometers (30 miles) of the coast, sweet pepperbush, *Clethra alnifolia*, is another common shrub. Poison sumac, *Rhus Vernix*, declines in the deepening shade of the wooded swamps, but may persist as stump sprouts for many years. Its relative, poison ivy, *Rhus radicans*, may grow luxuriantly on these sites, though in some swamps it is totally absent.

The herbaceous flora is also variable in quantity and variety, but because of the deep shade, flowering species are generally uncommon. The aptly named skunk cabbage, *Symplocarpus foetidus*, a species that seems to prefer shade and saturated soil, is one of the few plants that we can almost count upon finding in wooded swamps. In fact, so often is skunk cabbage associated with wooded swamps that it is a good indicator plant for this wetland type. Conversely, the Canada mayflower, *Maianthemum canadense*, which often forms its characteristic light-green carpet in low woodlands, abruptly ends at the swamp margins, suggesting that the absence of this species is also a reliable indicator of swampland.

Mosses and Liverworts

Though light levels are too low for most flowering plants, nonflowering plants such as ferns, mosses, and liverworts are usually abundant. Like flowering plants, however, the different species have varying requirements; not all can survive in the acidic soil of swamps. Those that are adapted to a swampy habitat, though, do grow abundantly there.

Unlike ferns and the flowering plants, mosses and liverworts lack well-developed vascular systems, roots, and leaves. With no means to transport water upward from the ground, these plants have had to remain small and close to the ground where they can absorb water directly into their cells. Because they have no roots that can draw water from some depth below the surface, most of these plants are restricted to perennially damp environments, though a few of the mosses have evolved adaptive mechanisms to allow them to survive in drier sites.

Not only is specific identification of mosses and liverworts difficult, but sometimes it is even hard to distinguish to which of these two groups a particular specimen belongs. A rough and by no means perfect distinction between the mosses and liverworts is that liverworts are usually a flat ribbonlike plant while mosses are stemmed, with tiny leaf-like structures called thalli growing from the stems. One group of liverworts also grows stems, but on those plants the thalli are arranged in two rows while mosses characteristically grow the thalli on all sides of the stem. Both mosses and liverworts are anchored to the ground by tiny hair-like filaments. The spore capsules on mosses are persistent while those on the liverwort last only a short time.

Succession in Wooded Swamps

In southern New England, it is possible within the distance of a few kilometers to encounter wetlands in every stage of development, from sedge marshes in which the maple saplings are just beginning to appear to mature stands of red maple with trunk diameters of 40 centimeters or more. The question may be asked, however, whether these mature red maple swamps are the end point in wetland succession. Will yet a different community of trees in time replace the red maples?

Indeed, in some cases the familiar red maple swamp may be only a temporary successional stage eventually giving way to a low slope community of sorts. Few swamps in southern New England have clearly shown this trend as yet, although there is some evidence that, if enough time passes in which a particular swamp remains free of disturbance, these changes may occur.

The major reason for expecting some replacement of the red maple is to be found in the red maple itself. In swampland the species is quite intolerant of shade; it is virtually impossible to find young red maple saplings in the deep shade cast by the mature trees. As one by one the old maple trees die, we might expect them to be replaced by more shade-tolerant species such as hemlock, various oaks, and ash, which might have germinated on the mounds and survived for a time, at least, in the understory.

If this further step does in fact occur, it will take a long time to happen. Many of the mature red maple swamps are notably free of tree saplings and seedlings of any kind. The hummocks, formed almost entirely of maple roots, are probably the only places dry enough for tree seedlings to germinate but seem to be inhospitable places for the germination and growth of even those tree species that could tolerate the shady environment.

Moreover, other studies of succession in the various eastern forest communities point up the role of continuously occurring natural disturbances in retarding the development of a stable forest community. Though fire, cutting, clearing for pasture, or flooding by beaver may no longer be significant disturbances in southern New England swamps, wind damage and flooding from an occasional hurricane is almost certain to occur again. Holes in the canopy caused by scattered windthrown trees may encourage the growth of more tolerant species, though widespread blowdowns or drowning would tend to result in another generation of red maples.

Small climatic changes, too, could have a profound effect on succession in the red maple swamps. Though the long-term tendency for swamps is to become progressively drier, a shift to a slightly moister climate could raise the water table in some swamps just enough to kill off the trees. It is even possible to envision some of these swamps returning to marshland, thus beginning the successional cycle again.

In time, many of the familiar southern New England red maple swamps may indeed evolve into a somewhat different forest community, but because of the slowness of the process and the vicissitudes of the New England climate it is safe to assume that the red maple swamp will remain an integral part of the landscape for a long time to come.

Trees of the Wooded Swamp Community

Red Maple, *Àcer rùbrum*, forms pure stands in many southern New England swamps. Its characteristics are described on page 131.

Similar species: Silver maple, *A. saccharinum*, the only other maple found in wetlands, can be easily distinguished from red maple by its more deeply cut, grayish leaves, its short-trunked stature, and its habitat: flood plains rather than swamps. (See also page 288.)

Black Ash, *Fráxinus nìgra*, is the most common ash species found in swamps. It is a slender tree, rarely exceed-

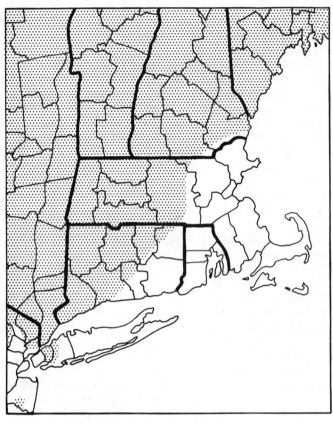

Range of the black ash, *Fraxinus nigra*.

ing 50 cm (20 in) in diameter. Like other species of ash, the black ash has compound leaves, usually with nine leaflets. Except for the terminal leaflet, which has a short stem, the other leaflets are attached directly to the leaf stalk. Black ash is most commonly found along the margins of swamps rather than in the wettest parts. It is more common away from the coast.

Similar species: Red ash, *Fraxinus pennsylvanica*, is more commonly found on river bottoms and swamps near the coast. It is distinguished from black ash by its slightly smaller leaves, though the distinction is usually difficult to make in the field. (See also page 296.)

123. Black ash, *Fraxinus nigra*, bears compound leaves with leaflets that arise directly from the stem.

124. Sweet gum, *Liquidambar styraciflua*, though often used for landscape plantings, grows naturally only in extreme southwestern Connecticut.

Sweet Gum, *Liquidámbar styraciflua*, is a southern tree that reaches the northern limit of its range in the southwestern corner of Connecticut. It grows in swamps near Long Island Sound about as far east as Norwalk. Although in the south sweet gum may attain a height of 45 m (150 ft), in New England it rarely reaches a height of 18 m (60 ft). Sweet gum is easily identified by its glossy, five-to-seven-pointed, star-shaped leaves and its prickly seed balls, approximately 2.5 cm in diameter, which turn dark brown in winter.

The Wooded Swamp Community

Other Swamp Trees

Hemlock, *Tsùga canadénsis*, page 316
White Pine, *Pìnus Stròbus*, page 219
Tupelo, *Nýssa sylvática*, page 146
Yellow Birch, *Bétula lùtea*, page 316
American Elm, *Úlmus americàna*, page 290
Swamp Cottonwood, *Pópulus heterophýlla* (southern Connecticut only), page 295
Swamp White Oak, *Quércus bícolor*, page 294
Pin Oak, *Quércus palústris* (Connecticut River Valley and southwestern Connecticut only), page 294
Atlantic White Cedar, *Chamaecýparis thyoìdes*, page 310

Shrubs of the Wooded Swamp Community

Species more common to the open habitat of the shrub swamp may persist in the increasingly shady understory of the developing wooded swamp. Also, shrubs of the low slope community may be found close to swamp margins.

Sweet Pepperbush, *Cléthra alnifòlia*, is a very common understory shrub in low woods, swamps, and lakeshores within 50 km (30 miles) of the coast and is occasionally found farther inland. Like members of the Ericaceae, to which it is closely related, sweet pepperbush requires acidic soil. It is a medium-sized shrub up to about 3 m (10 ft) high with deciduous dark-green leaves 3.5 to 7 cm long. It is readily identified in mid to late summer by its small white blossoms borne in slender clusters, and at other times by the spherical seed clusters that look somewhat like peppercorns. The flowers are sweetly (for some, sickeningly) scented. Sweet pepperbush is one of the few shrubs that reproduce by underground runners. In some areas it forms a continuous understory. (See color plate IV.)

Variant forms: Plants with pink flowers are occasionally found.

White Swamp Azalea, *Rhododéndron viscòsum*, is a late-flowering azalea commonly found in swamps and other wet places. It is a branching shrub up to 3 m tall, with dark-green slightly hairy leaves about 2 to 6 cm long, borne in rosettes. It is a summer-flowering shrub, blooming several weeks after the other native azaleas. Its white flowers

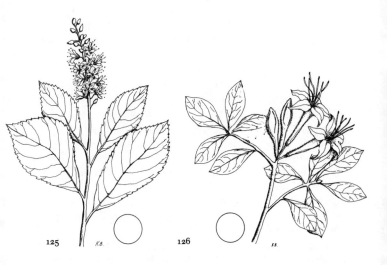

125. Sweet pepperbush, *Clethra alnifolia*, is a common swamp shrub within 50 kilometers of the coast. Its flowers, which appear in summer, are strongly scented.

126. White swamp azalea, *Rhododendron viscosum*, bears fragrant white flowers in summer.

are strongly fragrant and covered with sticky hairs.

Variant forms: Plants with pink, rose-purple, or carmine-red flowers are occasionally seen. More floriferous or larger-flowered forms also occur, as does a form with grayish leaves.

Rosebay Rhododendron, *Rhododéndron máximum,* is one of the rarest and one of the showiest shrubs in the region. It is very abundant in the woodlands of the central and southern Appalachians, but in southern New England it is found only in a few widely scattered colonies. The largest of the native species of the *Rhododendron* genus, it occasionally reaches a height of 5 m (16 ft). Its large evergreen leaves are two to three times the size of those of mountain laurel. The rounded trusses of pinkish flowers up to 20 cm (8 in) in diameter are unmistakable. It is a late-blooming species, the flowers not usually appearing until early July. Rosebay rhododendron is often planted in shady gardens.

Herbaceous Plants
of the Wooded Swamp Community

Skunk Cabbage, *Symplocárpus foètidus*, is a familiar plant to anyone exploring wetlands. Its purplish, mottled, hooded blossom is among the first to appear in the spring, followed by bright green leaves from 30 to 60 cm (1 to 2 ft) long. When bruised or stepped upon the plant emits a skunk-like odor. Skunk cabbage is most commonly found in shady wet habitats, but it also occasionally grows in full sun on the edges of marshes. (See cover photograph.)

Similar species: Skunk cabbage is often confused with Indian poke, *Vèratrum viride* (page 328). The unfolding leaves superficially resemble each other, but the two species are quite different when fully grown.

Jack-in-the-Pulpit, *Arisaèma* spp., is a common plant of swamps and other moist shady habitats. It is a genus of four native species, three of which have the familiar flowers that resemble a preacher in a covered pulpit. These vary in color from light green to deep purple; some are longitudinally striped. The fruit is a cluster of bright red berries. The leaves are compound, divided into three stemless leaflets, and vary in size, reaching 50 cm (20 in).

Similar species: The three-leaved habit of the jack-in-the-pulpit resembles that of the trillium; seen from above, however, the leaves of the former are arranged like a T, while those of the trillium form a Y.

127. Skunk cabbage, *Symplocarpus foetidus*, bears distinctive flowers in early spring. Its cabbage-like leaves emit a disagreeable odor when crushed.

The Flood Plain Community

FLOOD PLAINS, bottomlands, or, more colloquially, inter-
vales are terms used to describe yet another wetland community. A fluctuating water table—usually at least two or
three meters between high and low water—is the defining
characteristic of the flood plain habitat. Plants that grow here
must have the ability to survive flooding, sometimes for
several weeks during the spring, yet endure fairly dry conditions during summer and fall when the water level recedes.
In this way the flood plain habitat differs from the lower wet
meadow habitat, described on page 262, where flooding
often occurs during the spring but the water table remains
close to the surface throughout the summer.

The soils on flood plains are often relatively fertile, usually consisting of silt and other fine-grained alluvial deposits
left by the river during its flood stages. The drier conditions
of the summer and fall make it possible to grow crops here;
indeed the generally rock-free soil of the flood plains accounts for the only agricultural land in many parts of the
region.

Because of a fairly substantial difference between the
height of high and low water, true flood plains are more
commonly found in flat areas along some of the larger rivers
and streams. Sometimes, however, flood plains will occur
where a fairly small brook cuts a deep channel in the floor of a
small extinct glacial lake, though this type of occurrence is
more common in mountainous areas farther north.

This is not to suggest, however, that the habitat along
flood plains is by any means uniform. Low swales and gulleys
marking the former courses of the stream often cut through
it. At various places beaches and backwaters, each with
distinctive flora adapted to these conditions, occur. And of
course the flood plain habitat will grade into the wet meadow
where the yearly fluctuations of the water table are not so
great. Nevertheless, the vegetation along the river banks
and flood plains, where they have not been cleared for
agriculture, is quite distinctive.

Natural Levees

Flood plains often illustrate a number of interesting geological features. Probably the most common of these is the natural levee, a low ridge that forms along the river bank. Natural levees have a distinctive cross section; they are highest closest to the river and slope gently away across the flood plain.

These natural levees are built up by flood waters. A short explanation of stream transport, the process by which rivers and streams move sediments, should make the formation of these features easy to understand. The capacity of running water to move sediments is directly related to how fast it moves. Anyone who has observed a river during periods of high water has noticed how much faster the water moves. Specifically, if the velocity of the stream doubles, its capacity to carry rock fragments of a given size increases by the power of 5. In other words, if the velocity of a stream doubles it can carry about 32 times as much sand, silt, and other material than before. Under flood conditions, some rivers have been known to increase their velocity as much as ten times; a little arithmetic will show what an awesome force a river in flood can be.

When flood waters leave the deep river channel, however, and spill out across the flat flood plains, there is a sudden drop in their velocity. This is why flooded areas look more like large lakes than very wide rivers. As soon as the velocity of the stream slows down, the waters drop their load of sediment, the largest amount and coarsest particles piling up along the stream banks while the smaller particles come to rest farther away. This accounts for the sloping asymmetric cross sections of these natural levees.

Oxbow Lakes

Oxbow lakes are another feature common on flood plains. A small obstruction along one shore of the river may divert the current enough to start it cutting away at the opposite bank. Since the current of the river is strongest on the outer edge of· a curve, it tends to cut away—especially during times of high water—at this banking, gradually enlarging the curve and changing the river from a straight to a meandering course. As time goes by, this meander curve becomes more pronounced, first semicircular then tear-shaped, until eventually the river cuts through the narrow neck and once more forms a straight channel. The former meander remains as a curving lake that eventually becomes separated from the main channel of the river by a new natural levee.

Though they do fill up with silt rather quickly and disappear, oxbow lakes are common features on flood plains. Probably the most famous oxbow lake in southern New England occurs along the west side of the Connecticut River just south of Northampton, Massachusetts. This lake came into existence in 1830 when floodwaters finally cut through the narrow neck of a three-mile-long meander. Today the old course of the Connecticut is plainly visible as a long curving lake.

Though oxbow lakes are short-lived, the former sites can often be seen as elongated, curving swamps from the air or from topographic maps. The site of a still older oxbow may sometimes be seen as an area of light-colored soil in the flood plain, forming a ghostly outline of the river's former course.

Flood Plain Soils

In addition to the fluctuating water table, the nature of the soil also plays a part in determining the community of plants that will thrive on flood plains. River alluvium is mostly silt and sand. In some flood plains which were the sites of glacial lakes, these coarser soils are underlain by beds of clay-sized particles which gradually settled out after a time. These clay beds tend to produce a wet, poorly drained soil, though the alluvial soils deposited above them are better drained.

When these alluvial soils form a thick layer they may become quite dry by late summer, especially if the sand content in them is high. The plants growing on such flood plains, then, cannot be assured of a constant supply of soil moisture late in the season, but on the other hand they must be able to survive an excess of moisture during flood stages. There are a surprising number of trees which not only can survive in this habitat but seem to prefer it.

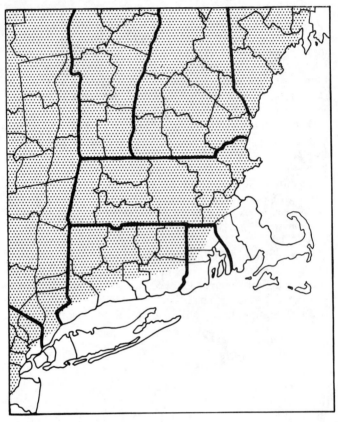

Range of the silver maple, *Acer saccharinum*.

Trees of the Flood Plain Community

Silver Maple, *Àcer saccharìnum,* is probably the most common tree of this community. It may be distinguished from red maple, which also grows on these sites, by its more deeply cut, lacy leaves that are silvery white beneath. Mature trees have short stout trunks and pendulous branches. Silver maples were formerly planted in great numbers as shade trees and are still commonly seen around older houses.

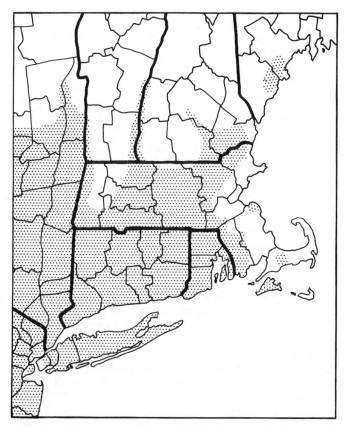

Range of the American sycamore, *Platanus occidentalis*.

Variant forms: A number of different forms have been reported, one with very deeply cut leaves, another with leaves divided almost to the base, others with weeping branches, with unfolding leaves of a yellowish bronze color, or with a narrow pyramidal shape.

American Sycamore, *Plátanus occidentàlis,* is another common river-bottom tree that was formerly planted as an ornamental. Its mottled peeling bark, maple-like leaves, and spherical seed balls make its identification unmistakable. Unfortunately, sycamore foliage is attacked by *Anthracnose*

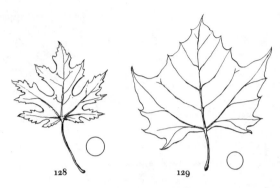

128. Silver maple, *Acer saccharinum*, is usually a short-trunked and branching tree. Its leaves are gray-green and more lacy than other maples.

129. American sycamore, *Platanus occidentalis*, is easily recognized by its mottled gray and white bark.

fungus that causes the leaves to turn black and drop off, an affliction that seems to be more severe in cool wet summers. The American sycamore grows to a larger diameter than any other American hardwood. A tree in Sunderland, Massachusetts, has a trunk over 6 m (20 ft) in circumference. The tree may be found growing wild in all parts of the region except in southeastern Massachusetts. It is, however, rarely found near the coast north of Boston.

American Elm, *Úlmus americàna*, was also widely planted as a shade tree. Flood plains are its preferred habitat

130. American elm, *Ulmus americana*, bears asymmetrical leaves that have a rough texture.

131. Swamp white oak, *Quercus bicolor*, has shaggy bark and a twiggy appearance.

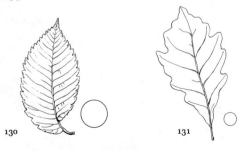

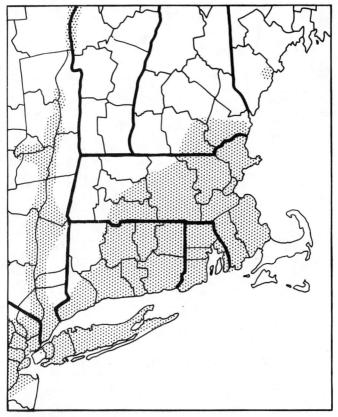

Range of the swamp white oak, *Quercus bicolor*.

though in recent years the Dutch elm disease has practically wiped it out in some areas. The bleached hulks of dead elms are now a common sight in many flood plains. Elm reproduces prolifically and young trees are still fairly common. Although flood plains where the water table drops about 2 meters during the summer are its preferred habitat, it can grow in definitely wetter sites with a water table as close as only 60 centimeters beneath the surface, and it often appears in wet pastures. Mature elms can be easily recognized at a distance by their vase-like shape. Their rough brownish-gray bark and coarsely toothed asymmetric leaves are also distinctive.

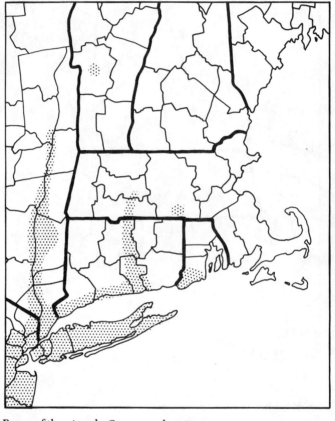

Range of the pin oak, *Quercus palustris*.

132. Pin oak, *Quercus palustris*, bears leaves that are smaller than the other native oaks and lighter green in color.

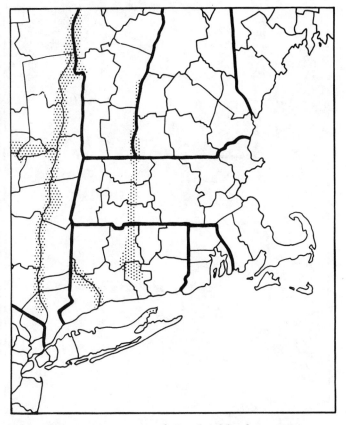

Range of the eastern cottonwood, *Populus deltoides*.

133. Eastern cottonwood, *Populus deltoides*, is easily recognized in spring by the masses of fluffy white cotton that aid in the dispersal of its seeds.

Range of the swamp cottonwood, *Populus heterophylla*.

Similar species: Slippery elm, *U. rubra*, is a small tree, lacking the graceful shape of the American elm. It is occasionally found throughout the region except in eastern Massachusetts, where it is rare.

Swamp White Oak, *Quércus bícolor*, occasionally appears in swamps and wet woods but is more common on flood plains. Young trees may be recognized by their very twiggy appearance and flaking bark; older trees have deeply furrowed bark and clear trunks. The leaves are light green with about ten irregularly rounded lobes.

Pin Oak, *Quércus palústris*, reaches the northern limit of its distribution in the Connecticut Valley north of Springfield. It is much more common in the southern parts of Connecticut and Rhode Island near Long Island Sound. Pin oak is a symmetrically shaped handsome tree often used in ornamental plantings. Its deeply cut, pointed leaves resemble those of the scarlet oak though they are smaller in size. They are a lighter shade of green than the other oaks of the region and turn a brilliant red in fall.

Eastern Cottonwood, *Pópulus deltoìdes,* is a large river-bottom tree that is frequent in the Connecticut, Farmington (Conn.), and Housatonic valleys but rare elsewhere. It is most easily identified in spring by the masses of fluffy white cotton attached to the seeds as a dispersal mechanism. Eastern cottonwood is a short-trunked tree with massive branches that become somewhat pendulous at the extremities. Its leaves are triangular and coarsely toothed.

Similar species: Swamp cottonwood, *P. heterophylla,* is found in wetter sites than normally support eastern cottonwood. It is found only in southern Connecticut but may be frequent in some places there. It is smaller than the eastern cottonwood and has leaves that are less deeply toothed. Several other members of this genus grow in the region but these are found as pioneers on postagricultural or waste ground.

Black Willow, *Sàlix nìgra,* is probably the most notable of several willow species found on river banks and flood plains. It is a large shrub to medium-sized tree reaching about 12 m (40 ft) in height. It is easily distinguished from other willows by small leaf-like appendages called stipules growing where the linear grayish-green leaves are attached to the stem.

134. Black willow, *Salix nigra,* is distinguished from other willows by the leaf-like stipule at the base of the leaf.

Variant form: A form with extremely narrow leaves has been found.

Similar species: There are several other native willows in the region. All of these are smaller shrubs and lack the stipules at the base of the leaf stems. The other large willows—white willow, *S. alba*, crack willow, *S. fragilis*, and weeping willow, *S. babylonica*—are all larger than the native black willow. These were introduced from Europe during colonial times for, as one authority reports, "ornament, sentiment, shade, and gunpowder charcoal."

Red Ash, *Fráxinus pennsylvánica,* is a medium-sized tree occasionally found along river courses. It is notably resistant to flooding and remains healthy when flooded up to 40 percent of its growing season. It resembles white ash, *F. americana,* though the latter is seldom found in wetlands except for the stream bank and rock ravine communities. Both species have compound leaves, normally with seven leaflets; on the red ash the leaflet stems are shorter (though not absent like those of the black ash, *F. nigra,* page 279) and are covered, along with the branchlets, in dense fuzz. It is sparingly distributed through the region.

Variant form: Green ash, *F. p. lanceolata,* has no fuzz on the leaf, stems, or branches.

River Birch, *Bétula nìgra,* only occurs in the northeastern and southwestern ends of the region, abundantly in and around the Merrimack Valley of Massachusetts and southern New Hampshire, and sparingly, perhaps as an introduction, in the lower Housatonic Valley near Bridgeport, Connecticut. The frayed and peeling reddish-brown bark is so distinctive that the tree may be identified at a glance from a passing car. River birch is a medium-sized tree, rarely growing taller than 15 m (50 ft) in this region. Except for its bark, river birch resembles yellow birch, *B. lutea* (page 316).

Box Elder, *Àcer negúndo,* is a small tree that is probably native in the region only in the Housatonic Valley. Once commonly planted as an ornamental, it has escaped from cultivation and become naturalized in many other parts of southern New England. The compound leaves, usually bearing three leaflets, more closely resemble those of poison ivy than other maples. The fruit is typical of the maple genus, however.

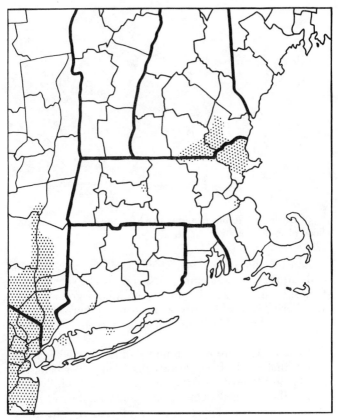

Range of the river birch, *Betula nigra*.

Other Flood Plain Plants

Probably because of continuous spring flooding, there is no distinctive shrub flora in bottomlands, nor are shrubs usually found in great quantity. Black-berried elder, *Sambucus canadensis* (page 271), and silky dogwood, *Cornus Amomum* (page 270), are about the only species frequently found on flood plains, though others do occur sporadically.

One type of vegetation commonly found on river banks and flood plains is vines. Sometimes such rank-growing species as Virginia creeper, *Parthenocissus quinquefolia*,

135. Dewberry, *Rubus hispidus*, is a common creeping vine on flood plains and other moist sites.

poison ivy, *Rhus radicans*, clematis, *Clematis virginiana*, and various species of grape, *Vitis* spp., can be seen growing high into the trees or forming a continuous ground cover. Dewberry, *Rubus hispidus*, a low-growing thorny vine with small blackberry-like fruit, sometimes covers large open areas.

In addition there are a number of rank-growing annual weeds that reach their greatest size along river banks and flood plains. Nettles, *Urtica* spp., are often painfully abundant in these habitats. One brush against the stinging hairs is all that is necessary for a positive identification of this genus. Another annual weed, the giant ragweed, *Ambrosia trifida*, grows up to 5 meters tall on some western Connecticut flood plains.

Many other species of annual weeds are likely to occur on these sites. Some, of course, are related to the agriculture that has gone on in many of these valleys since colonial times, their seeds having been inadvertently introduced along with crop seed imported from Europe. A smaller number are native species which find the habitat suitable.

A (left). Spicebush, *Lindera Benzoin,* low slope and watercourse communities (April)

B (right). Mountain azalea, *Rhododendron roseum,* mid and low slope communities (May)

C (left). Mountain laurel, *Kalmia latifolia,* rare banded form, mid and low slope communities (June)

D (right). Winterberry, *Ilex verticillata,* wetland communities (fall fruiting)

Native Shrubs

(bloom time in parentheses)

PLATE V

A (left). Hickory, *Carya* spp., oak forest community
B (right). Tupelo, *Nyssa sylvatica*, low slope and wetland communities

C (left). Sumac, *Rhus* spp., postagricultural community
D (right). Red oak, *Quercus rubra*, oak forest community

Fall Foliage

PLATE VI

A (left). Spotted salamander
B (right). Two-lined salamander

C (left). American toad
D (right). Pickerel frog

E (left). Wood frog
F (right). Green frog

Amphibians of Southern New England

PLATE VII

A (left). Wood turtle
B (right). Painted turtle

C (left). Box turtle
D (right). Northern water snake

E (left). Milk snake
F (right). Northern copperhead

Reptiles of Southern New England

PLATE VIII

The Bog Community

THE BOG COMMUNITY is probably the least common of all the wetland communities in the region, yet it is one that holds more fascination for naturalists than perhaps any other. Bogs represent a successional pattern that is quite different from the marsh to shrub-swamp succession described earlier. Their chief component is a mat of leatherleaf, *Chamaedaphne calyculata*, along with other ericaceous shrubs, sphagnum moss, various species of sedges, and occasional small trees, floating on the surface of a pond.

Although bogs are perhaps the most common successional route in parts of northern New England and Canada, in southern New England, where climatic conditions favoring this type of succession are at best marginal, well-developed bogs are both few and widely separated.

Unlike marshes, with their variety and teeming abundance of animal life, bogs are practically destitute. An average city vacant lot will contain a far larger assortment of plants. Why then are bogs of such great interest? Part of the answer undoubtedly lies in the fact that this wetland type is so uncommon in the region; naturalists are always interested in rare occurrences. Other and probably more compelling reasons are the number of unusual plant species that are endemic only to bogs, the specialized nature of these plants, and the interesting successional patterns that may sometimes occur in this community.

In this chapter we will touch only upon the mode of formation and succession; a more extended discussion of bogs will be found in the companion volume on northern New England.

Physical Appearance

Many people aptly if redundantly refer to bogs as "quaking bogs." When walked upon, the flexible surface of the bog does quake and undulate like a giant waterbed. The mat may be flexible but in most places it is so interlaced with roots that it is difficult to penetrate even with a sharp spade. If you stand too long in one place, however, the mat will sink gently

136. Small quaking bog, Townsend, Massachusetts. Both white and pitch pines are growing on the mat.

beneath your feet until you are soon in ankle-deep water. This phenomenon should suggest the appropriate footwear for bog exploration.

Holes in the mat do occur; it is possible to fall into the water and peat mixture beneath. These holes, which usually appear as wet spots, are easily avoided if you exercise some care and walk gingerly. If you do have the misfortune to fall through the mat and cannot easily extricate yourself, remain calm and wait for someone to pull you out. It may be possible through violent struggling to become more deeply mired, but the possibility—advanced by horror story writers—of being slowly sucked down by quicksand simply does not exist.

Textbooks often depict bog vegetation as occurring in concentric, roughly circular zones around an area of open water in the middle, the inner zone being the floating mat of low shrubs, the next of tall shrubs and small conifers, grading into an outer zone mostly of larger conifers. In northern New England this indeed is the usual pattern; in southern New England it is rarely so.

Rather than completely encircling the pond, the bog mat here more commonly occurs as a relatively narrow crescent on the southern side of the pond. Here the shade from trees in the adjacent woodland may help to provide a sufficiently cool microclimate for bog vegetation to develop. In this region the encroaching swamp forest may be red maple rather than conifers. More common in this region are semibog habitats, where marsh and bog plants grow together and where a well-developed bog mat is lacking.

On many sites in southern New England, furthermore, succession has passed beyond the bog stage. Trees now grow where an open mat may once have been; thus the former bog has been totally converted to a wooded swamp. In eastern and southern parts of the region, dense stands of Atlantic white cedar, *Chamaecyparis thyoides*, often mark the sites of former bogs. Many of the familiar red maple swamps were once bogs; often corings will reveal a thick layer of peat beneath them.

Bog Development

As is true of all plant communities, climate is the most important single factor in controlling the geographical distribution and development of bogs. Bogs are among the most common wetland types in areas of the world where a cool, moist summer climate prevails; where summers are hot and dry, bogs are usually, though not always, absent.

The present summer climate across much of southern New England is marginal for bog development. Not surprisingly, active bogs, the kind described in textbooks, rarely occur except in the highest and therefore coolest inland areas, and in coastal sections where a cool maritime summer climate prevails.

Other factors such as composition of the underlying mantle rock and the amount of dissolved materials in water may also determine whether a particular body of water will evolve into a bog or some other wetland type. In northern Maine and other cold areas these ancillary factors tend to be overshadowed in importance by climate, but in the southern New England region a favorable combination of them is necessary for bogs to develop.

One of these factors, the availability of oxygen and plant nutrients dissolved in the water, is a case in point. Deep spring-fed ponds with little surface water inflow are more likely to become bogs than are ponds where nutrient and oxygen-rich tributary streams flow into them.

This shortage of nutrients is also governed by the composition of the mantle rock underlying a pond. Sand and gravel, which is usually derived from granitic bedrock, is usually very deficient in a number of important plant nutrients. It is not surprising, then, that southern New England bogs are rarely found outside of sandy or gravelly areas.

The types of plants that become established in this environment are those adapted to acidic conditions; leatherleaf, sphagnum moss, and several species of sedge begin growing along the shore. The lack of oxygen in the water retards the decay of this plant material, which in turn keeps the few available nutrients locked up in plant tissue rather than recycled for later generations of plants. This lack of dissolved oxygen coupled with the slow decay process increases the soil acidity to an even greater degree. A soil with a pH of 3, usual in bog habitats, is 10,000 times more acidic than neutral soil areas such as those of western Connecticut underlain by calcareous bedrock. Needless to say, such a strongly acidic environment is well beyond the ecologic amplitude of most plants.

A layer of undecayed organic material begins to accumulate along the shore, and the bog plants begin to form a floating mat which may gradually grow inward across the pond. The drowned but undecayed roots of leatherleaf form a framework for this floating mat while sphagnum moss and sedge gradually accumulate under the mat and the pond begins to fill in. If a cool climate prevails, the mat may eventually become thick enough to support larger shrubs and trees, and the bog may in time convert to a low woodland.

In southern New England, since the end of the ice age, many bogs have already completed this process. In others the floating bog mat seems to remain static, with little or no inward growth.

Shrubs of the Bog Community

Among the most common species in the bog community are some which regularly occur in shrub swamps and wooded swamps, both far more common habitats in the region than bogs. People familiarizing themselves with the bog flora should begin with the following species:

Leatherleaf, *Chamaedáphne calyculàta*, page 271
Sheep Laurel, *Kálmia angustifòlia*, page 132
Sweet Gale, *Myrìca Gàle*, page 271
Poison Sumac, *Rhùs Vérnix*, page 23
Highbush Blueberry, *Vaccínium corymbòsum*, page 148
White Swamp Azalea, *Rhododéndron viscòsum*, page 282

Water Willow, *Décodon verticillàtus*, is a shrubby plant usually found at the very edge of the bog mat. Its arching branches root at their tips, gradually forming a tangled low thicket at the water's edge. The deciduous leaves are borne in twos or whorls of three with clusters of small magenta flowers at their bases. Water willow is very common along the shores of ponds and in bogs in this region.

Bog Laurel, *Kálmia polifòlia*, is the third and least common species of the laurel genus in our area. It is a small straggling shrub reaching about 60 cm (2 ft) in height. Its leaves are lustrous green on the upper sides and whitish beneath, borne in pairs on the stem, usually with the edges rolled under. The flowers are magenta, about the size of mountain laurel, *K. latifolia*, though occurring much more sparsely. Unlike sheep laurel, *K. angustifolia*, they bloom at the tips of the stems rather than along the leaf axils.

Bog Rosemary, *Andrómeda glaucophýlla*, is a low shrub, usually well under 50 cm (20 in). Its leaves are blue-gray above and whitish beneath. Like bog laurel, the leaves are inrolled. The flowers are small pink bells arranged on the stems in drooping clusters. Bog rosemary has a spotty distribution in southern New England bogs, being common in some and absent in others.

Labrador Tea, *Lèdum groenlándicum*, is a northern bog shrub that barely reaches this region. It is absent from most of Connecticut and Rhode Island, but is occasionally found in bogs in Massachusetts, becoming more common northward. The leaves of Labrador tea are distinctive: dark green, aromatic, and leathery on the upper sides, covered with

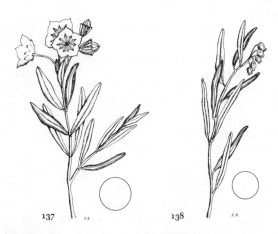

137. Bog laurel, *Kalmia polifolia*, is distinguished by its leaves, which are green with white undersides. The flower is typical of the genus.

138. Bog rosemary, *Andromeda glaucophylla*, is a small shrub with blue-gray leaves and pink bell-shaped flowers.

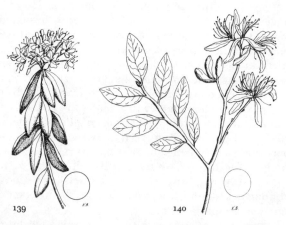

139. Labrador tea, *Ledum groenlandicum*, bears leaves that are covered with brownish fuzz on the undersides. The flowers are white.

140. Rhodora, *Rhododendron canadense*, bears grayish-green leaves. The magenta-pink flowers bloom in May.

thick brownish fuzz on the undersides. Its small flowers are white, borne in clusters. It is said that the leaves of Labrador tea were brewed as a substitute for tea during colonial times.

Cranberry, *Vaccínium* spp., consists of two species of creeping vine-like habit, both bearing small white flowers with rolled-back petals. The larger species, *V. macrocarpon*, may be distinguished by leaves over 6 mm (¼ in) in length and a fruit that is over 1 cm in diameter. Both leaves and fruit on the other species, *V. Oxycoccos*, are smaller.

Rhodora, *Rhododéndron canadénse*, is a small shrub growing to 1 m, with grayish-green deciduous leaves. Its showy, three-lobed, azalea-like magenta flowers bloom in May before the leaves appear.

Variant form: A rare white-flowered form occurs.

Insectivorous Plants

Nearly everyone knows that there are plants that capture and digest insects. The most famous insectivorous species, the Venus flytrap, *Dionaea muscipula*, is for sale in flower shops, supermarkets, and mail order houses (and as a result, practically extinct in its native habitat). Perhaps fewer people know that there are several species of these insectivorous plants growing right here in southern New England.

Though the relationship between these species and their insect prey is among the most bizarre of the entire plant kingdom, it is incorrect to think of insectivorous plants as "vegetable anteaters," gorging themselves with numbers of insects to meet their energy requirements. These are all green plants; like other green plants, they all grow and function by converting sunlight into chemical energy. The captured insects supply these plants with important nutrients such as nitrogen, phosphorous, potassium, and a few other elements that they require in small amounts but are unable to obtain from the sterile habitat of bogs in which they grow. These captured insects are, in other words, merely a source of fertilizer that the plants absorb through their leaves rather than their roots; yet the adaptations that the insectivorous plants have evolved to accomplish this are truly marvelous.

Pitcher Plant, *Sarracènia purpùrea*, is the most notable of the group. There are about ten species of pitcher plant in the United States, most of which are native to the southeastern states. *S. purpurea*, our indigenous species, is so common in bogs that it might be considered an indicator plant for this habitat.

Pitcher plants are unmistakable in appearance. The large tubular leaves, sometimes reaching 20 cm (8 in) in length, grow in a rosette from the base of the plant. When mature, these leaves fill with water and become traps for unwary insects. The leaves have evolved other characteristics that aid them in this function. Their smooth interiors provide no foothold for the victims; the top of the leaf is covered with downward-pointing hairs that encourage an insect to travel downward into the pool below, but hinder its movement upward out of the trap. Even its color, often a reddish purple with reddish vein-like lines on the lip, attracts insects by the suggestion of carrion.

Once an insect drowns in the water-filled pitcher, enzymes secreted by the leaf digest the soft parts. If you cut open a mature leaf you will probably find a mass of the undigestible chitinous parts of the insect carcasses at the bottom.

As if this evolutionary turn of events were not fantastic enough, at least one species of small mosquito, *Wyeomia smithii*, has managed to go one step further. This insect actually lays its eggs inside the leaves and the larvae develop

141. Pitcher plant, *Sarracenia purpurea*. The pitcher-like water-filled leaves and the flower are distinctive.

in the enzyme-rich water of the pitcher, apparently without adverse effects to the larvae or the insect. As is so often the case when organisms evolve into such a specialized niche, the larvae of this particular species are found nowhere else; the tiny wrigglers can be seen in most of the leaves you examine.

There are several small flies that also fly into the leaves when the water level is low, feeding on the disintegrating mass of insect carcasses at the bottom of the leaf. Apparently they also are unaffected by the plant's digestive secretions.

Sundew, *Drósera* spp., is even more common than the pitcher plant in the wet acidic environment of bogs, though because of its small size it is more often overlooked. The entire plant, whose leaves form a basal rosette, is rarely over 5 cm (2 in) across. It is also found in wet sandy habitats such as the shores of ponds.

There are about 100 species of sundew worldwide, of which three grow in southern New England. The most common of these is the round-leaved sundew, *D. rotundifolia.* Like the pitcher plants, the leaves of this plant have evolved to capture insects. In the sundew, however, the mechanism is a sticky dew-like secretion on leaf hairs. Once an insect becomes stuck, the leaf gradually folds over the insect and absorbs the nutrients. The leaves of the round-leaved sundew are circular pads only a centimeter across; the insects it can capture are therefore very small. Often it is possible to see sundew leaves with the carcasses of these small insects still adhering to them.

Less common sundew species include *D. intermedia* with oval leaves and the very rare thread-leaved sundew, *D. filiformis,* which is found only in a few coastal bogs.

Bladderwort, *Utriculària* spp., is the genus which includes the other insectivorous plants in southern New England. Of the 300 worldwide species, about 10 are found here. The species are quite difficult to tell apart; some are aquatic and some are amphibious, the latter growing in the sphagnum mat of bogs. Like the sundew, bladderwort is small and easily overlooked, though the aquatic species sometimes grow long stems. Small bright-yellow snapdragon-like flowers and thin many-branched filament-like leaves are the identifiable characteristics of bladderwort. Scattered along the leaves are tiny hollow bladders about the size of a pinhead. These are equipped with trap doors that snap shut when the prey enters. Water fleas and other tiny crustaceans are about the largest animal that a bladderwort can trap.

Bog Orchids

Orchids are another group of plants well represented in the bog flora. As mentioned earlier, the flowers of the northern orchids, except for the lady's slippers, are relatively small, usually under a centimeter or two in diameter. But because most bloom in a spike of many flowers, the overall effect is more showy than the small size of the individual flowers might suggest.

As a group these bog orchids are among the rarest plants in the region. They are rare here because their requirements are so exacting that they can survive in very few habitats. Attempting to transplant these orchids to the uncongenial environment of a backyard garden means almost certain death for them. Even in their preferred habitat they are often scarce. When you explore bogs and other places where these orchids grow, be careful where you step, since the loss of only a few plants may tip the balance toward extinction in a particular site.

Fringed Orchid, *Habenària* spp., is the most common genus of bog orchids in southern New England. All have small flowers that bloom in spikes on the plants. All habenarias have a long spur corresponding to the pouch of the lady's slipper; most, but not all, have a fringed lip or lower petal. The habenarias are wetland species; they grow in marshes, swamps, wet woods, and bogs. They vary in size from tiny plants only a few centimeters tall to species that may reach a height of one meter. The flowers of the various species bloom in several colors: white, pink, magenta, yellow, orange, and green. Most bloom in summer.

Other Bog Orchids

Rose Pogonia, *Pogònia ophioglossòides*, page 263
Arethusa, *Arethùsa bulbòsa*, page 263
Grass Pink, *Calopògon pulchéllus*, page 264

The Conifer Swamp Community

IF AND WHEN succession toward woodland conditions occurs, the number of tree species that could tolerate the soggy, sterile, intensely acidic bog environment is, of course, small. Except for the ubiquitous red maple that appears in many southern New England bogs, the trees that can normally tolerate this condition are all conifers. In this region, especially in eastern and coastal sections, Atlantic white cedar, *Chamaecyparis thyoides*, is an aggressive invader of old bogs. In high inland areas and occasionally elsewhere, black spruce, *Picea mariana*, and larch, *Larix laricina*, may appear in bogs, though there are probably none in the region where they form such a solid stand as does the white cedar.

142. Interior of Atlantic white cedar swamp, Cape Cod National Seashore. So closely spaced are the trees that few flowering plants can grow in the dense shade.

Small white pine trees are surprisingly common in many bogs. They grow very poorly in this habitat, but when one considers that their preferred habitat is dry old fields, it is astonishing that they survive at all. On white pines the whorl of branches up the trunk represents a year's growth. By counting the whorls and measuring the distance between them it is possible to get a rough measure of the age and yearly growth rate of a particular tree. Quite evidently, many of these pines growing on the bog mat are near their limit of tolerance. The trees are usually older and stunted, the distances between their whorls being often but a few centimeters. Moreover, their shorter-than-normal needles, often colored a sickly yellow, are another indication of the poor growing conditions that these plants are enduring.

Trees of the Conifer Swamp Community

Atlantic White Cedar, *Chamaecyparis thyoides*, is a tree of the Atlantic Coastal Plain that reaches the northern limit of its distribution close to the northern end of the region covered by this volume. Under suitable conditions, Atlantic white cedar forms pure stands which are reputed to be the densest of any North American trees. Though there is some natural thinning-out in older stands, a half-grown stand of white cedar is often impenetrable.

In southern New England, white cedar swamps are most common in the low sandy parts of southeastern Massachusetts, Rhode Island, and eastern Connecticut. The largest of these, the Acushnet Cedar Swamp near New Bedford, is

143. Atlantic white cedar, *Chamaecyparis thyoides*, is more grayish-green in color than the eastern red cedar. Its wetland habitat is also distinctive.

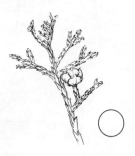

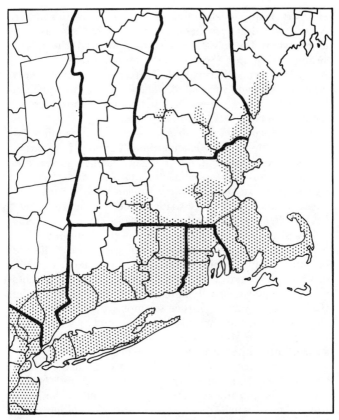

Range of the Atlantic white cedar, *Chamaecyparis thyoides*.

regarded by some ecologists as the last bit of wilderness remaining in southern New England. Because of the density of the cedar trees, the only way into the many parts of the seven-square-kilometer swamp is by following the frozen outlet streams in winter.

Like other wetland habitats, the white cedar swamp may not be the ultimate stage in the successional route. A study of cedar swamps in the deep South has suggested that in that region, at least, their establishment is a temporary stage following fire. In the southern swamps, white cedar gradually gives way to deciduous species. Whether fire has played any part in the development of cedar swamps in southern New England has not been established, but in coastal regions, where there is a long history of fire and where cedar swamps are found, the possibility indeed exists.

Variant forms: Forms with light gray to nearly silvery-white needles and variegated, yellow, or reddish branchlets have* been found. Trees of much more compact growth habit, either tall or shrub-like, also occur.

Black Spruce, *Picea mariàna*, is the most common bog tree in northern New England and Canada. It is rare in southern New England, occurring occasionally in scattered inland stations in Massachusetts and a handful of sites in Connecticut. In southern New England, black spruce is a small slender irregularly-shaped tree, rarely reaching a height of 9 m (30 ft). The dark or bluish-green needles (often yellowish in bogs) are about 1 cm long and curving.

In northern New England, black spruce often invades bogland, forming dense, sometimes pure stands. In southern New England, where spruce swamps are far less common, the species usually appears as scattered trees rather than in dense stands. Spruce swamps are uncommon near the coast; these sites are usually preempted by white cedar. In fact, in one eastern Connecticut swamp where both black spruce and white cedar were growing, the spruce disappeared, apparently from competitive pressure of the cedars.

For many years botanists regarded the scattered stands of black spruce and other northern species as relict colonies left from a time when the local climate was colder. Some botanists now take the opposite view that these species are the advance guard of the northern flora, which is moving southward in response to slightly cooler long-term climate.

Variant forms: Occasionally a dense columnar form of spruce is seen. A slow-growing form with very slender branchlets and thin needles of lighter bluish-green also occurs.

Similar species: Red spruce, *P. rubens*, white spruce, *P. glauca*, and balsam fir, *Abies balsamifera*, are northern conifers that may just reach the extreme northern edge of the region. They are almost entirely absent from the rest of southern New England.

Larch, *Lárix larícina*, is seen in southern New England swamps a bit more frequently than black spruce. As one

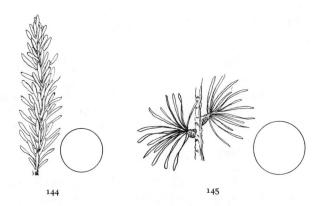

144. Black spruce, *Picea mariana*, is rare in southern New England bogs, but common in the north. Its foliage is dark green.

145. Larch, *Larix laricina*, has light-green soft needles that turn yellow and drop in the fall. It is rare in southern New England.

might expect, it is more abundant in the cooler northern and inland parts of the region, especially along its northern border. It is occasionally found in northern Connecticut, reaching as far south as Danbury in the western part of the state.

Larch is most commonly found in bogs, though farther north it is a component of a drier, low woodland community; at the northern border of the region larch is occasionally found in these other sites. In bogs it remains a small tree rarely growing over 12 m (40 ft) though on more favorable sites it may reach 30 m (100 ft) or more.

Larch is the only New England conifer that sheds its needles in winter. In summer the tree is easy to identify at a distance by its light gray-green foliage (much lighter than pine) and feathery appearance. Its needles, which grow in tufts up to 2.5 cm (1 in) long, are gray-green, but in less favorable sites, such as on the inner bog mat, they are much shorter and a yellowish green. Before they drop in the fall, the needles turn a bright orange-yellow.

The Rock Ravine Community

WEBSTER defines a ravine as "a depression worn out by running water, larger than a gully and smaller than a valley." New England's most famous "ravines," the great glacial cirques in the flanks of Mount Washington and other White Mountain peaks, are technically not ravines at all, since they were not worn out by running water nor, probably, are they within the defined size range.

Rock ravines are steep-sided: on topographical maps they are represented as small valleys with closely spaced contour lines on either side. Nearly always there is water—usually running as a brook or stream but occasionally standing as swampland—in the bottom of the ravines.

In southern New England, where a landscape of low relief has been slowly evolving over millions of years and where irregularities in the surface have been further modified by the glaciers, it seems surprising that any such narrow, steep-sided valleys even exist. Probably nearly all occur in areas where a narrow band of normally less resistant bedrock has eroded. This weakness may be physical, as for example along an old fault zone where the movement of two great rock masses has caused a band of bedrock to become shattered and hence more easily eroded. Others may occur in areas where a vertically tilted bedrock may have contained a narrow stratum of a chemically less resistant rock, such as marble or some other calcareous rock. Though the vegetation in most ravines I have visited suggests a typically acidic soil, the absence of ericads and other acid-soil indicator plants in the bottoms of a few—notably ones that follow the strike of a deeply dipping layered bedrock—suggests that the soil acidity in these is not as great as would normally be expected in such a cool, damp site, perhaps indicating a calcareous bedrock below.

A cool, moist microclimate is typical in these sites. Usually ravines are shady, at least on one side; during the summer their sheltered position allows the cooler and more humid air to accumulate there. Often rock ravines exhibit temperature inversions (page 77); on still evenings they may be several degrees cooler than the land around. In winter, these steep-sided valleys may accumulate cold air to

146. Rock ravine, Pepperell, Massachusetts. Yellow birch, beech, and hemlock are common in these sites. The shrub at the right is hobblebush viburnum, *Viburnum alnifolium*.

become frost pockets. Average temperatures in these depressions may be substantially lower than on the higher ground on either side. If there is sufficient air drainage along the sloping bottom of the ravine, however, this phenomenon may not occur.

The cool, moist microclimate is the ecological factor that makes rock ravines botanically interesting. Often the plant community found in these sites contains species common in the cooler climate of northern New England, which rarely, if ever, appear in the warmer or drier sites more typical of southern New England.

The rock ravine community, like so many others in the region, blends into other communities, particularly the low slope and stream bank communities. Also, the vegetation on steep and rocky north-facing slopes, a habitat that is uncommon in much of southern New England (page 74), will be similar to that of the rock ravine community. Gravel ravines, on their shady sides, sometimes support many of the same plants as the rock ravine community, though their drier, more porous soils are usually better suited to other oak forest species.

Ravines, both rock and gravel, often contain some of the largest trees one is likely to encounter. The moist microclimate may have protected these sites from forest fire; their sheltered position has protected them from hurricanes; and their inaccessibility and the steep ravine sides have protected them from lumbering, especially from the non-mechanized operations of the last century.

Because of both the large trees and the northern vegetation that are likely to be encountered in these sites, as well as the wild (by southern New England standards) and steep terrain, I would rate rock ravines after bogs as the most interesting of all the various wetland communities in the region.

Trees of the Rock Ravine Community

Canadian Hemlock, *Tsùga canadénsis*, though it grows on other sites, is almost always present in rock ravines. It is a large tree, often reaching heights of 25 m (80 ft). Smaller trees are irregular in shape, becoming conical as they mature. The dark-green needles about 1 cm in length, borne on drooping branches, make this species easy to recognize. A longer discussion of the hemlock will be found in the next chapter.

American Beech, *Fàgus grandifòlia*, like hemlock, also appears in other oak forest communities, but is nearly always found in rock ravines. It is easily recognized by its smooth light-gray bark and its coarsely toothed light-green leaves that turn yellow and then rust color in fall. Because of the similarity of its ecological requirements to those of hemlock, the two trees are discussed together in the next chapter.

Yellow Birch, *Bétula lùtea*, is another tree of cool moist habitats that commonly appears in the rock ravine community. Yellow birch is easily identified by the color and texture of its bark, silvery gray or yellowish, detaching into thin filmy layers. On older trees, the bark is dark and lusterless.

Yellow birch is the most shade-tolerant of the birches. It can grow on both well-drained and poorly drained sites, though on the former it may give way to hemlock, beech, and sugar maple, *Acer saccharum*, which are even more shade-tolerant. As is the case with most trees of the rock ravine community, yellow birch is very sensitive to fire; the bark is highly flammable. Rot will often kill trees that have survived fire damage, and ice damage also may provide entry for decay organisms.

Variant form: A brown-barked form that closely resembles black birch, *B. lenta*, is occasionally found.

Striped Maple, *Àcer pennsylvánicum*, is a very common understory tree in ravines and other cool sites. Like the other vegetation usually found in these habitats, striped maple is common in many parts of northern New England, but in parts of southern New England it exists only in scattered enclaves of northern vegetation. The species reaches southward to Cheshire, Connecticut, but is absent from coastal areas. Striped maple is a small tree, rarely exceeding 7 m (23 ft) in height. Its distinguishing characteristic is its smooth greenish bark covered with thin pale to dark stripes. Its usually large three-lobed leaves only remotely resemble those of the more common species, though the green winged fruit borne in long drooping clusters is typical of the maple genus.

147. Striped maple, *Acer pennsylvanicum*, is a small tree with smooth green bark covered with dark stripes.

Variant form: A form with bright red branches in winter has been found.

Similar species: Mountain maple, *Acer spicatum*, is similar in size to striped maple but it is not as common. It is found in cool moist habitats in inland parts of the region, usually at an elevation of above 150 m (about 500 ft). Its reddish brown bark is not striped and its leaves are less prominently lobed.

Other Rock Ravine Trees

Red Maple, *Àcer rùbum*, page 131
Sugar Maple, *Àcer sáccharum*, page 195
White Ash, *Fráxinus americàna*, page 146
Black Ash, *Fráxinus nìgra*, page 279
Basswood, *Tília americàna*, page 193
Black Birch, *Bétula lénta*, page 136
White Birch, *Bétula papyrìfera*, page 137
Red Oak, *Quércus rùbra*, page 145
Hornbeam, *Carpìnus caroliniàna*, page 147
Hop Hornbeam, *Óstrya virginiàna*, page 146

Shrubs of the Rock Ravine Community

The variety and number of shrubs in rock ravine habitats are quite variable, depending among other factors on the availability of light, soil pH, and terrain. Shrubs of the low slope, stream bank, and swamp communities may also appear in rock ravines. Spicebush, witch hazel, and mountain laurel are very common in some. There are only a few shrubs that are found chiefly in this habitat.

Hobblebush Viburnum, *Vibúrnum alnifòlium*, is rarely if ever found in this region outside rock ravines. It too is far more common in parts of northern New England. It is a low straggling shrub up to 3 m (10 ft) high, though most commonly remaining close to the ground. It is easily identified by its large rounded to slightly pointed leaves, usually 10 to 18 cm (4 to 7 in) in diameter, and its flat-topped white clusters of flowers that appear in June. The flower cluster is made up of two different kinds of flowers; the inner fertile flowers are small and nondescript while the showy, sterile flowers on the margins are five-petaled, 2 to 3.5 cm in diameter. The fruit is a red berry borne in clusters; both

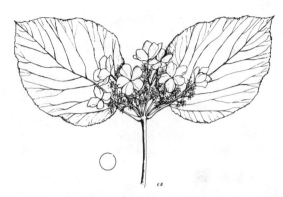

148. Hobblebush viburnum, *Viburnum alnifolium*, is a straggling shrub with large heart-shaped leaves. (See also photograph on page 315.)

flowering and fruiting are less common in shady sites.

Variant form: A pink-flowered form of this species is sometimes seen.

Canadian Yew, *Táxus canadénsis,* a creeping shrub whose needled branches somewhat resemble those of hemlock. The low straggling habit, rarely reaching over a meter in height, makes yew easy to distinguish, however. As with other members of this genus, the fruit is a red berry about 5 mm in diameter, open at the top and enclosing a hard, very poisonous brown seed.

Yew is only found in cool, very shady woods that usually contain an abundance of conifers. Its occurrence in this region is largely restricted to rock ravines.

Variant forms: Among the interesting forms reported is one with short flattened needles, one with white tips on the young shoots, an upright pyramidal form, a dwarf conical form, and a weeping form.

Mountain Holly, *Nemopánthus mucronàtus,* is one of the more difficult shrubs to identify. The flowers are small, less than 5 mm in diameter; the leaves are elliptical, between 2 and 5 cm (about ¾ to 2 in) long, with smooth or minutely serrated edges. Mountain holly has red fruit borne on stems about 3 cm (1¼ in) long. Most often found in cool damp woodlands in this region, it is uncommon in the southern parts but becomes occasional to frequent in these habitats farther north. It is also occasionally found in bogs and swamps.

Variant form: A rare yellow-fruited form has been reported.

Fly Honeysuckle, *Lonícera canadénsis,* is another northern species that may grow in rock ravines of this region. It is a straggling shrub with variably shaped and sized leaves 3 to 12 cm (about 1 to 4½ in). Its trumpet-shaped flower is pale yellow, between 12 and 22 mm (from a half-inch to nearly an inch) long, appearing in May or June. Its fruit is a red berry.

Other Rock Ravine Shrubs

Witch Hazel, *Hamamèlis virginiàna,* page 148

Mountain Laurel, *Kálmia latifòlia,* page 141

Maple-leaved Viburnum, *Vibúrnum acerifòlium,* page 142

Spicebush, *Líndera Benzòin,* page 327

Herbaceous Plants of the Rock Ravine Community

The community of herbaceous plants found on these sites is even more variable than that of the shrubs. A wide variety may be found in rock ravines, especially if the two sloping sides receive differing amounts of sunlight, as is usually the case where the ravine runs in an east-west direction. On the sunny south-facing slope may be found nearly any herb of the oak forest community; it is the shady north-facing slope and the bottom of the ravine that are more likely to support a distinctive northern herb flora.

Wood Sorrel, *Óxalis montána,* is a creeping herb with shamrock-shaped leaves up to 3 cm (1¼ in) in diameter, with single white flowers, veined with pink. It is one of the few herbaceous plants that will bloom in deep shade.

Variant forms: Purple or rose-colored flowers are occasionally seen.

Twisted Stalk, *Streptòpus ròseus,* is an erect herb 25 to 60 cm (10 to 24 in) high. It is distinguished by its zigzag stem, its alternate sessile leaves, and pink or rose-purple bell-shaped flowers hanging from the leaf axils.

Goldthread, *Cóptis groenlándica,* is another northern

149. Goldthread, *Coptis groenlandica*, bears leathery evergreen leaves and gold roots. The flower is white.

herb, though it is not restricted to rock ravines, being found also along the margins of swamps, in cool woods, and in other mossy habitats. It is a small creeping herb easily recognized by its shiny, three-lobed, coarsely toothed evergreen leaves up to about 4 cm (1½ in) in diameter, and its bright yellow roots.

White Violet, *Viola blánda*, is one of several violet species that appear in rock ravines and other moist shady habitats. It is a small creeping species with heart-shaped leaves and white irregularly shaped flowers. There are several other white, blue, and occasionally yellow violets that appear in these moist cool sites. As a group, the genus is large and the individual species are difficult to identify.

Bluebead Lily, *Clintònia boreàlis*, is another northern plant that is sometimes found in rock ravines and cool shady habitats. Its most easily recognizable characteristic is its light green, oval, leathery leaves, sometimes reaching 30 cm (1 ft) in length. In the spring it produces a loose clump of greenish-yellow star-shaped flowers about 2 cm (¾ in) long at the end of a tall stalk. The fruit, which ripens in the summer, is a bright blue berry. Bluebead lily is rare in southern Connecticut, becoming occasional to frequent in the cooler northern parts of the region.

Variant form: A white-berried form is occasionally found.

Painted Trillium, *Tríllium undulàtum*, is regarded by many as the most beautiful of all the trilliums. Like other trilliums the plant is in three parts: three petals, three

150. Painted trillium, *Trillium undulatum*, is easily recognized by its three-petaled white flower with a line of red across each petal.

sepals, and three leaves. The flower is white, the petals narrow with a distinct red stripe near the base. The fruit is a single scarlet berry, oval in shape, up to 2 cm (¾ in) long. Painted trillium is only found in very cool shady sites. Like many others of these northern plants, it is rare in southern Connecticut but occasionally seen in the higher elevations farther north.

Wood Nettle, *Lapórtea canadénsis*, is a woody plant with a single stem, alternate toothed heart-shaped leaves, and inconspicuous flowers in loose clusters at the terminals. The foliage is covered with stinging hairs which cause mild discomfort (in comparison to the more virulent stinging nettle, *Urtica*, of river bottomland and waste places).

Similar species: False nettle, *Boehmeria cylindrica*, sometimes found in rock ravines, closely resembles the wood nettle. Its leaves are opposite and lack the stinging hairs. Its minute flowers grow in tight greenish clusters from the leaf axils.

Hemlock and Beech:
Two Species of Cool Habitats

ALTHOUGH of two widely separated families, American beech, *Fagus grandifolia*, and Canadian hemlock, *Tsuga canadensis*, are trees whose ecological preferences are so similar that they can be discussed together. In southern New England, where one grows, the other is almost sure to be found.

Hemlock and beech are among the most shade-tolerant of American trees. Both grow luxuriantly, holding their lower branches for many years, in the understory of woodlands that are too shady for most other species. Not only do hemlock and beech grow well in the shade, they reproduce well in the shade, hemlock by seeds and beech generally by root sprouts. In fact, in this area, root-sprouting by beech is probably its most common means of reproduction; medium-sized trees are commonly found with a number of smaller trees growing around them.

Both species do well on acidic soils. Beech, especially, seems intolerant of calcareous soils; its nut-like seeds germinate better and more seedlings survive in the acidic mor humus than on the normally more hospitable mull humus. Hemlock needles are strongly acidic and decay slowly, thus imparting an even greater degree of acidity to the soils on which it grows. In fact, the combination of deep shade, sharply acidic soils, and surface-feeding roots, characteristic of both species, usually renders the ground beneath the trees totally barren of plant life.

Both species are also fire-sensitive. Unlike the oaks and other deep-rooted trees, neither tree will sprout from burned stumps. Repeated fires eliminate both species from the woodlands, a fact that some forest investigators believe is the reason why in southern New England beech and hemlock are more commonly found in cooler and moister habitats that may have offered some protection from the many fires that apparently burned the region's woodlands during precolonial times and later. Now that the incidence of major forest fires has been greatly reduced by improved fire-fighting techniques, both species may be beginning to enjoy a modest resurgence on drier sites, though neither tree thrives in hot and dry habitats. The presence of both species in the upland oak forest communities is more common toward the northern end of the region.

When variant forms are considered, however, the comparison between the two species ends. Most of the beech variants, such as the copper, cutleaf, and weeping forms, that one sees advertised in nursery catalogs are from the

European beech, *F. sylvatica*. A single specimen of American beech with a roughened bark was discovered in Mississippi, but aside from that and an occasional form with fuzz on the undersides of the leaves, beech trees show a high degree of genetic uniformity.

The hemlock, on the other hand, has produced more interesting variant forms than any other native tree. Growers and horticulturists have named perhaps 100 of these, many more interesting forms remain unnamed, and probably scores of other outstanding forms remain as yet undiscovered. One of the earliest of these variant hemlock forms to be described, the Sargent weeping hemlock, was discovered about a century ago on a mountain top near West Point, New York. It is a dense, multi-trunked shrub whose arching branches fall like fountains to the ground. Cuttings of this superb form root with comparative ease, and the form is still available from nurseries.

Since the discovery of the Sargent weeping hemlock, other variant forms of nearly every conceivable size and shape have come to light. These range from tiny pincushions that grow less than a centimeter a year, through ones shaped like globes or birdnests, to horizontal growers that hug the ground and thin columnar forms. These hemlock variants also show an equally wide range in the color, shape, and size of the needles. Most remain dwarf and many make handsome garden shrubs. The seeds of many of these forms will also produce a second generation of interesting variants.

As you travel through woodlands where hemlocks grow you should constantly be alert for these unusual forms. They are more prevalent than you might expect. Sometimes a whole population of such variants may be found, as is the case in the town of Harvard, Massachusetts, where in a certain tract of woodland about one-third of the hemlocks grow in a curious open form, with long, horizontal branches and needles that are shorter than normal and tightly packed together.

The Stream Bank Community

IF YOU FOLLOW a stream—any stream—far enough toward its source you will eventually reach a point where the gradient is steep enough to move the water along quite rapidly, and the banks on either side are high enough to allow soil drainage. Because floodwaters are of such erosive force in these fast-moving streams, usually the stream has long since adjusted its channel to carry occasional large volumes of water. As a result the ground on either side is rarely if ever flooded, except perhaps as a result of a severe tropical storm. The volume of water, however, may fluctuate wildly as a result of heavy rains and snow melt. In mountainous watersheds where runoff may be rapid, highly destructive flooding in small streams sometimes occurs, but in the subdued terrain of southern New England this is less likely to happen.

151. Stream bank community in eastern Massachusetts. Indian poke, *Veratrum viride*, a typical stream bank herbaceous plant, grows on the left. Skunk cabbage grows at the lower right.

Though the soil along stream banks may remain saturated during early spring when the streams are high with snow melt, the water level usually drops sufficiently before the start of the growing season to provide the plants with a moist though not soggy root zone. Ample moisture for plants remains available throughout the summer, even though the water level may drop considerably.

Generally speaking, where the water runs the fastest, the soil is less acidic; the moving water helps to supply oxygen to the layers of soil, which in turn prevents the more acidic conditions of, say, a stagnant red maple swamp or bog from developing. Where a stream flows through a sandy or gravelly area, however, the greater assemblage of acid-loving plants usually found on these sites may indicate stronger soil acidity.

Streams also tend to flow more slowly in sandy or gravelly areas, having already deepened their channels through this soft material until they have reached a shallow gradient. A number of streams flowing through ancient lake deltas in the Connecticut Valley clearly illustrate this process.

The stream bank habitat with its midrange of soil moisture and usually of soil acidity provides conditions that fall within the ecological requirements of more woodland species than any other. Because the conditions along stream banks are similar to those of the low slope or mixed mesophytic communities, the plants found in these other sites also appear along stream banks. Only a few plants specifically prefer stream banks over other habitats.

This moist habitat is also ideal for a large variety of ferns. Areas with less strongly acidic soil will support the greatest numbers, though even in strongly acidic habitats there is usually luxuriant growth of the fewer species that can tolerate these conditions.

The abundance and variety of flowering herbaceous plants is more variable, however. With many, the availability of light becomes as important an ecological factor as soil moisture and acidity.

Though the stream bank community itself cannot be easily defined by vegetation growing there, it is, in one sense, a middle ground which may grade into three other communities, each with more extreme ecological conditions and a commensurately more restricted and characteristic vegetation. Specifically, if the stream valley becomes deeper and more steep-sided, hemlock and other trees of the rock ravine community will undoubtedly be found. If the stream slows down and its banks become low and muddy, the stream bank community will grade into that of the swamp. Less common, but occasionally found, is the transition from stream bank to flood plain communities.

Stream banks are interesting places to explore. Usually there is great variety and abundance of vegetation, the terrain is varied but generally easy to walk, and the changing scenery—where not spoiled by civilization—is often very beautiful.

Shrubs of the Stream Bank Community

With the possible exception of the white ash, *Fraxinus americana*, which also requires a sunny habitat to reach maturity, there are no species of trees that could be considered indicator species for this community. Of the many shrubs that grow along stream banks, only the following species seems to prefer the stream bank community over others.

Spicebush, *Líndera Benzòin*, is easily identified in early spring by the dense clusters of small yellow flowers along the stems. Its dull green leaves are about 6 to 12 cm (2½ to 5 in) long, and strongly aromatic when crushed. The crushed leaves, when rubbed on the skin, are reputed to be an insect repellent, but in my experience they have never seemed to work. The fruit is an oval drupe, turning red in late summer. Spicebush is not commonly associated with the ericads, a fact which suggests that it may prefer a less acidic soil. (See color plate V.)

Variant form: As is the case with many red-fruited shrubs, forms bearing yellow fruit are occasionally seen.

Other Stream Bank Shrubs

Of the many possible species likely to be encountered in this habitat, I have found the following to be most common. (Although alders are more common on open sites they may persist in wooded sites for a time.)

Witch Hazel, *Hamamèlis virginiàna*, page 148

Highbush Blueberry, *Vaccínium corymbòsum*, page 148
Arrow-Wood, *Vibúrnum recógnitum*, page 148
Alder, *Álnus* spp., page 270

Herbaceous Plants of the Stream Bank Community

All of the herbaceous plants found in the low slope community and the mixed mesophytic community will grow along the banks of streams as long as there are a few centimeters of soil above the water table. Along open streams, marsh plants are sometimes found. In low muddy spots along streams, such swamp plants as blue flag, *Iris versicolor* (page 259) and skunk cabbage, *Symplocarpus foetidus* (page 284) may grow. The following species seem to prefer the stream bank habitat, however.

Cardinal Flower, *Lobèlia cardinàlis,* is a stream bank plant whose brilliant red flowers, appearing in mid to late summer, make identification unmistakable. Because it is a biennial, cardinal flower is transitory, sometimes growing abundantly in a site one year and disappearing completely in another. Probably indiscriminate picking has made the flower rare near civilization, but it is frequently found in more remote areas. (See color plate IV.)

Variant forms: Several forms with unusual flower colors, including rose, pink, white, and orange, have been reported.

Marsh Marigold, *Cáltha palústris,* is another herbaceous plant whose preferred habitat is muddy shores and shallow, slowly moving streams, though I have also occasionally found it in swamps. It is easily recognized by its yellow buttercup-like flowers (up to 4 cm or 1¾ in in diameter), which appear very early in the spring, and its rounded glossy leaves. (See color plate I.)

Variant forms: A double-flowered and a white-flowered form have been reported (though *Gray's Manual of Botany* lists neither).

Indian Poke, *Veràtrum víride,* is a large conspicuous plant, sometimes reaching a height of about 2 m (6½ ft) but more commonly about 1 m (40 in) tall. Its leaves are large, heavily ribbed, and clasp the stem. The flowers are greenish

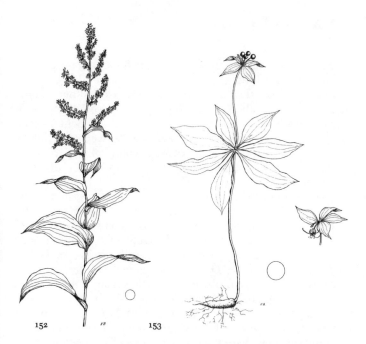

152. Indian poke, *Veratrum viride*, may be recognized by its light-green clasping leaves. It disappears in summer.

153. Indian cucumber-root, *Medeola virginiana*, bears two whorls of leaves. Its white root is edible.

and borne in large clusters at the top of the plant. The plant usually disappears in June shortly after blooming. Indian poke is reputed to be quite poisonous if eaten.

Indian Cucumber-Root, *Medèola virginiàna*, is a single-stemmed herb from 20 to 90 cm (8 to 36 in) tall. It is easily recognized by the whorls of five to nine narrow leaves near the middle of the stem and a whorl of three or four smaller leaves at the top. The flowers, which appear at the top of the stem, are small and greenish yellow; they are followed by a blue berry-like fruit. The whitish tuber-like roots are edible, having the texture of a radish and the flavor of a cucumber. Indian cucumber-root is most commonly found near running water, but it also grows in the low slope community of the oak forest.

Wetland Ferns

FERNS are a major part of the wetland flora. In some of these habitats ferns form a continuous layer of ground vegetation, but in others they grow interspersed with other plants. Despite their abundance, the variety of wetland ferns in southern New England is rather small. Only about a dozen species are commonly found in the various wetland habitats; several of these have such exacting ecological requirements that they are limited to only one or two of the different communities.

Like other green plants, the ferns help to maintain the oxygen–carbon dioxide ratio so vital to most terrestrial life. But, beyond this, ferns play a curiously small ecological role. Although a few caterpillars occasionally roll the young fronds into cocoons and one or two species of birds use the fuzz of the· cinnamon fern, *Osmunda cinnamomea*, to line their nests, there is practically no interaction of any kind between ferns and animals. Except for the ostrich fern, *Pteretis pennsylvanica*, whose unrolling fiddleheads are a spring favorite of human wild food gourmets, there are no other animal species that I know of which regularly feed on ferns. And, as we saw in the section on oak forest ferns, these plants rely only on wind and water for their reproduction and dissemination.

Though of limited ecological importance, then, the ferns of both woodland and wetland habitats make an outstanding contribution to the beauty of the region. Many people would consider the form and texture of their leaves most beautiful among all the plants. But their very abundance in the region may diminish their impact: perhaps it takes a journey to drier parts of the country where ferns do not normally grow for their aesthetic importance to become evident.

Moisture is, of course, the major ecological requirement of ferns. A number of species normally found in shade will thrive in full sun if their roots are supplied with continuous moisture. Others, like the marsh fern, *Dryopteris Thelypteris*, require sunlight and do not grow well in shade. As might be expected, most of the wetland species grow in soils of varying degrees of acidity, but only Virginia chain fern, *Woodwardia virginica*, thrives in the intensely acidic sub-

Ferns of the Wetland Communities

SPECIES — Common name / *Latin name*	Size	Abundance	Marsh	Wet Meadow	Shrub Swamp	Wooded Swamp	Bog	Flood Plain
Royal fern / *Osmunda regalis*	L	C					- -	
Cinnamon fern / *Osmunda cinnamomea*	L	C				—	- -	
Marsh fern / *Dryopteris Thelypteris*	S–M	C	- -		- -	- -		
Sensitive fern / *Onoclea sensibilis*	M	C	- -		- -	—		—
Crested woodfern / *Dryopteris cristata*	M–L	C	- -		- -	—		—
Lady fern / *Athyrium Filix-femina*	M–L	C	- -					—
Climbing fern / *Lygodium palmatum*	M	R			- -	—		
Spinulose woodfern / *Dryopteris spinulosa*	M	C			- -	—		
Massachusetts fern / *Dryopteris simulata*	M	O			- -	—		
Net-veined chain fern / *Woodwardia areolata*	M	R				- -	- -	
Virginia chain fern / *Woodwardia virginica*	L	O				- -	—	
Ostrich fern / *Pteretis pennsylvanica*	L	O					- -	—

Size
L — Usually over 60 cm (2 ft)
M — Usually 30 to 60 cm (1 to 2 ft)
S — Usually under 30 cm (1 ft)

Abundance
C — Common
O — Occasionally found
R — Rare

Distribution
— Frequently found
- - Less frequently found

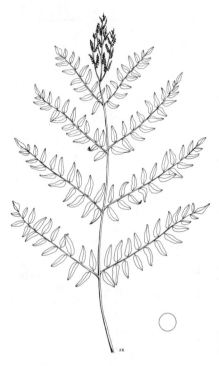

154. Royal fern, *Osmunda regalis*, is a large coarse fern of wet habitats.

strate of sphagnum bogs. The ostrich fern, on the other hand, prefers a more neutral soil.

Most of these wetland fern species will grow in saturated soil, but only the royal fern, *Osmunda regalis*, and the Virginia chain fern can grow in shallow standing water. Others, like the marsh fern, will not appear until the water level where they are growing has dropped below the surface of the ground.

The chart on page 331 shows the distribution of the wetland ferns by habitat. It is important to remember that these species may appear in almost any of the wetland habitats with the possible exception of bogs; likewise, a number of the oak forest fern species, described earlier, may appear in the relatively drier rock ravine and stream bank communities and along wetland borders.

Common Ferns of the Wetland Communities

Royal Fern, *Osmúnda regàlis,* is a large coarse fern lacking the typical fern-like foliage that one associates with this group of plants. The spores are borne in hundreds of tiny light-brown capsules on the tops of the leaves. Royal fern is common near the edges of acidic marshes as well as in wooded swamps.

Cinnamon Fern, *Osmúnda cinnamòmea,* is a large wetland fern usually reaching at least 1 m (40 in) in height. It is common in both shady and sunny wetland habitats, growing well wherever there is a constant supply of moisture. It is easily recognized in the spring by its narrow club-like fertile

155. Cinnamon fern, *Osmunda cinnamomea,* is a large fern, most easily recognized in spring by its cinnamon-brown fertile frond.

156. Marsh fern, *Dryopteris Thelypteris,* bears light green leaves on dark wiry stems. It is a small to medium-sized fern.

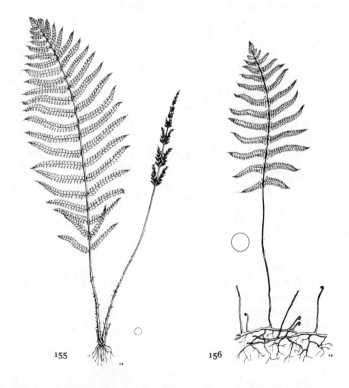

155   156

frond that comes up green but turns a bright cinnamon-brown. This fertile frond soon wilts but may be seen lying on the ground throughout the summer. Another spring recognition feature is a dense covering of cinnamon-brown wool that covers the unrolling fronds.

Similar species: The interrupted fern, *O. Claytoniana* (page 187), closely resembles the cinnamon fern but lacks the spike-like cinnamon-brown fertile frond and is generally found in somewhat drier habitats.

Marsh Fern, *Dryópteris Thelýpteris (Thelýpteris palústris)*, as its common name suggests, is most often found in sunny moist habitats such as marshes and wet meadows. It is easily recognized by its relatively small size, 15 to 45 cm (6 to 18 in) in height, light green color, long leaf, and dark wiry stem. It grows luxuriantly in less acidic soils.

Sensitive Fern, *Onoclèa sensibilis*, is a coarse spreading fern, about 40 cm (16 in) tall, though sometimes reaching 60 cm (2 ft). The fertile frond appearing in early autumn looks like a series of small beads attached to a long stick; it turns dark brown in winter. The sensitive fern derives its name from the tendency of its sterile leaves to succumb with the first frosts. The sensitive fern occurs along the edges of marshes and in shady and muddy places. It is not usually found in highly acidic habitats. (See photograph, page 275.)

Similar species: The net-veined chain fern, *Woodwardia areolata*, superficially resembles the sensitive fern. Its more spiky fertile frond, smaller size, and a distribution that is mostly limited to acidic coastal swamps should make the two easy to tell apart.

Crested Woodfern, *Dryópteris cristàta*, is the member of the woodfern genus that occupies the wettest habitat. It is a medium-sized to large fern, usually reaching 75 cm (30 in). The ferns grow in clumps of a few very narrow leaves with widely spaced and horizontally tilted leaflets.

Similar species: Clinton's woodfern, *D. c.* var. *Clintoniana*, regarded by some as a separate species, grows in the same habitat as the crested fern but is larger and not as narrow. Boott's fern, *Dryopteris* × *Boottii*, is a fairly common hybrid between crested fern and the spinulose woodfern, *D. spinulosa*.

Massachusetts Fern, *Dryópteris simulàta (Thelýpteris simulàta)*, closely resembles the marsh fern in size and form.

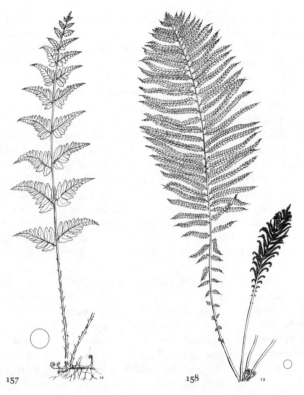

157. Crested woodfern, *Dryopteris cristata*, may be recognized by its leathery, rather narrow leaves.

158. Ostrich fern, *Pteretis pennsylvanica*, is a large fern recognizable by its distinctive shape. The dark-brown fertile frond remains erect through the winter.

Unlike the marsh fern it is usually found in very shady acidic habitats and is far less common. The only clearly identifiable difference—requiring the aid of a hand lens—is in the veination of the leaflets: those on the marsh fern are forked, those on the Massachusetts fern are not.

Virginia Chain Fern, *Woodwárdia virgínica*, is a large coarsely toothed fern whose leaves resemble the cinnamon fern in size and shape. Unlike the cinnamon fern, which grows in clumps from individual crowns, the Virginia chain fern grows as single often closely spaced leaves from a creeping rootstock. A dark purple-brown leaf stalk is another recognizable characteristic. The Virginia chain fern is one of the few species commonly found in bogs, though it does grow in some wooded swamps as well.

Ostrich Fern, *Pterètis pennsylvánica (Matteùccia Struthiópteris),* is the largest fern growing in the region. Specimens with fronds up to 1.7 m (70 in) are occasionally encountered. Ostrich fern leaves are shaped like an ostrich plume, rounded at the top and gradually tapering to the stem at the bottom. The inside of the stem is deeply grooved. Perhaps the best recognition feature of this species is the fertile fronds, similar in shape to the sterile fronds but much smaller (up to about 30 cm), coarser, and turning a dark brown in fall. These fertile fronds remain erect through the winter. Ostrich ferns are often found growing in large colonies on flood plains, river banks, and neutral soil areas.

Ostrich fern fiddleheads are one of the very few kinds that are edible and delicious. Many people regard them as among the tastiest of the wild foods. They may be prepared in any way one prepares asparagus. The fiddleheads, which appear between mid-April and early May, must be picked when they are just beginning to unroll. Since these ferns, like other green plants, need their leaves to grow, you should pick no more than half the unrolling fiddleheads from each plant. Ostrich ferns spread by underground runners; a light pruning such as this seems to stimulate the colony to increase its size.

Other Wetland Ferns

Lady Fern, *Athýrium Fìlix-fémina,* page 181
Spinulose Woodfern, *Dryópteris spinulòsa,* page 184

FURTHER READING

Wetlands: An Introduction

Leopold, Luna B. *Water: A Primer*. San Francisco: Freeman, 1974. A small, clearly written text describing the water cycle and geologic processes related to water.

Niering, William A. *The Life of a Marsh*. New York: McGraw-Hill, 1966. A splendid introduction to the marsh habitat by one of New England's expert ecologists. Many excellent color photos.

Niering, William A., and Richard H. Goodwin. *Inland Wetland Plants of Connecticut*. New London, Conn.: Connecticut College, 1973. Excellent introduction to the southern New England inland wetland communities and illustrations of the plants found in each. Discussion of the ecological role of wetlands.

Reid, George K. *Ecology of Inland Waters and Estuaries*. New York: Reinhold, 1961. One of the standard texts in the field. Somewhat dated but still useful.

Thomson, Betty F., ed. *Preserving Our Freshwater Wetlands* (Bulletin 17). New London, Conn.: Connecticut College, 1970. A collection of essays on the ecological value of wetlands and steps that may be taken to save them.

PART VIII

Animals of
Southern New England

Mammals
of Southern New England

DESPITE THE INROADS of civilization, southern New England still is host to a large variety of mammals. In fact, the varied terrain of thickets, woods, and abandoned fields existing in much of the region provides an ideal habitat for a large number of mammal species. Even deer, regarded by most people as an animal of the deep woods, are far more common in this type of habitat than in heavily forested areas. Other animals such as the gray squirrel, cottontail rabbit, raccoon, and chipmunk have become thoroughly acclimated to civilization and are commonly found within city limits.

Winter Tracking

Learning much about small mammals from direct observation in their native habitats is very difficult. Except for squirrels, chipmunks, and a few other diurnal species, most are abroad only during twilight or nighttime. Many others spend much of their lives concealed in the grass or underground in burrows and are rarely visible.

When snow conditions are ideal, however, the tracks and signs that these small mammals leave provide a wealth of information about their behavior and ecology. And since it is possible to follow tracks across a greater area than you could cover from a concealed blind, tracking will often reward you with even more information than you could gather remaining in one place.

It should be made clear at the outset, however, that identifying mammal species with certainty from their tracks alone is often difficult and sometimes impossible. Even when snow conditions are perfect, the tracks may not appear to be identical with illustrations in the field guides. Tracks in soft mud are better defined but are usually impossible to follow for great distances. As in identifying the local flora, it helps to narrow down the possibilities by knowing what animals are *likely* to have made a particular set of tracks. Also, having some information about the behavior of the species will make it easier to identify tracks. In the following pages I have included descriptions of many of the small mammals whose tracks are likely to be found, even several which are almost never casually seen during the daytime.

Ideal conditions for snow tracking do not occur very often. The clearest tracks are seen when there is a fresh dusting of new snow on top of a hard base. Many animals do not move as much if the snow cover is deep. Old snow, if frozen, is too hard to register tracks and, if melted and refrozen, too granular for sharp imprints. A few hours of thawing temperatures obliterate all but the deepest tracks from the snow.

A base solid enough to support you is a great help in tracking; otherwise you must wear snowshoes or be prepared for hard going. Serious tracking is difficult on cross-country skis, since many of the small mammals live in a brushy habitat.

HABITAT

The number and variety of winter tracks offers a clear indication of the type of habitat preferred by these small animals. Tracks are always more plentiful in areas where several different habitats exist within a short distance of one another. A mixed terrain—open fields and orchards, thickets along fence rows and along the edges of woodlands, cut-over areas with their characteristic vegetation of brambles and stump sprouts, interspersed with patches of mature forest with large pines and den trees—offers a habitat that will support a rich variety and large numbers of wildlife. In these places you may find so many tracks that it becomes difficult to follow a single set.

The reasons this mosaic pattern provides such an excellent habitat for wildlife are not hard to understand. Probably most important is that each of the habitats within it produces its own distinctive vegetation, and together they provide a variety of food and cover that is suitable for many different species. Furthermore, most food plants needed for wildlife grow better and set more seeds and fruit where there is abundant light. Open land also grows thick vegetation cover; these thickets provide protection, especially from such winged predators as hawks and owls.

DENS, NESTS, AND TRAILS

Snow tracking is a good way to find animal dens. Although many small mammals go to great lengths to conceal their dens, the large number of tracks in the snow leading in and out of them often reveal their location. In addition to tracks, sometimes an animal will leave bits of hair adhering to the entrances when it squeezes in and out. This hair of course can provide an excellent clue to the identity of the inhabitant. Often the entrance to a den seems too small for a particular animal to be able to squeeze in, but in many cases a thick winter coat makes an animal appear larger than it is. Piles of brush, rocks, or stumps along the edges of newly cleared land are particularly rich den sites.

Large isolated pines in a deciduous woodland are also excellent places to look for wildlife. These trees provide more wind protection than do the bare deciduous trees; a careful look high into the tree very often will reveal a large nest of some kind, or at least the remains of one. Tracks and other signs around the bases of these big trees may provide other clues to the identity of their inhabitants. Old chestnut hulks which still stand in some woodlands are also likely spots to look for dens.

FOOD

Snow tracking can also lead you to a particular animal's food supply. Mammals that do not hibernate must spend the largest part of their waking hours in a relentless search for food. Small animals must consume a large amount of food to maintain their body temperature. The smallest of the native mammals, the shrew, for example, must consume close to half its body weight of food each day to avoid starvation.

Most of the small mammals are plant eaters. Tracks of these species often lead to dead weeds, where scatterings of seeds on the snow show where the animals have been feeding. Squirrels dig through the snow to reach buried caches of acorns; these holes are common sights wherever squirrels are found. Other small mammals such as field mice make tunnels in the snow where they feed on grass, seeds, and bark. When the snow melts, these tunnels become visible just above ground. In new orchards, if owners did not take such countermeasures as surrounding the young trunks with wire mesh sleeves, these field mice would tunnel to the base of the young trees, gnaw the bark from around their bases, and kill them.

Snow tracks also may reveal signs of predation. Sometimes a set of tracks will be joined by a larger set, and signs of a small scuffle and perhaps a drop or two of blood will show where a predator was successful. Some predators such as shrews and weasels may follow their prey into burrows or tunnels and do their killing underground, but signs of a small mammal's demise are still occasionally seen on the surface.

Flying predators, especially owls, capture a tremendous number of small animals. Owls have an extremely sensitive sense of hearing and steal up on small nocturnal mammals so quietly that they catch them unaware, and they are such efficient predators that little evidence of their kill can be seen. An abrupt ending to a set of tracks and a set of wing prints in the snow could mean that an owl or other aerial predator has struck. Hawks hunt during the day, making squirrels and chipmunks likely victims.

PELLETS

After hawks and owls digest their prey, instead of allowing the sharp bones, fur, and other indigestible material to pass through their intestines, they regurgitate it in elongated masses called pellets. These pellets may superficially resemble the droppings of foxes or some other carnivore, but being totally free of any digestive residue they are completely clean, dry, and odorless. Pellets, usually from owls, are easy to spot on the snow. They are commonly found under a large pine or dead tree where the bird stopped to digest a meal and roost. In spring, when owls are nesting, the ground under their nests is littered with these pellets; it is always worthwhile to check the ground under a likely looking nesting site for pellets.

These pellets often contain the clean skulls of the small mammals which were captured and eaten. By a careful study of the teeth, it is sometimes possible to identify the victim from its skull. Several mammal identification guides contain the dental formulas of the various species, but identification from the skulls alone requires practice.

The following southern New England mammals are likely to leave winter tracks:

Gray squirrel, *Sciurus carolinensis*
Red squirrel, *Tamiasciurus hudsonicus*
 (less common than gray squirrel)
Porcupine, *Erethizon dorsatum*
White-tailed deer, *Odocoileus virginianus*
Cottontail rabbit, *Sylvilagus* spp.
Opossum, *Didelphis marsupialis*
 (tracks uncommon in woodlands)
Red fox, *Vulpes fulva*
Gray fox, *Urocyon cinereoargenteus*
Weasel, *Mustela* spp.
Bobcat, *Lynx rufus*
*Striped skunk, *Mephitis mephitis*
*Raccoon, *Procyon lotor*
*Eastern chipmunk, *Tamias striatus*

*Seen only in early or late winter and occasionally during winter warm spells.

A Note about Keeping Small Mammals

Despite the existence of several books giving instructions for keeping small mammals in captivity, the practice is only rarely satisfactory. Certain mammals such as flying squirrels and chipmunks respond well to captivity if taken when very young. People also do tame such naturally placid animals as skunk and porcupine when they are young and manage to keep them for many years. However, rearing wild animals in captivity leaves them totally unprepared for life in the wild and most will quickly succumb when released. If you plan to keep a "wild pet" you should plan to keep it for its entire life, perhaps a commitment of several years. Many of these animals often require special diets, usually eat a great deal of food, and excrete an equally large amount of waste, thus requiring constant attention to feeding them and keeping their cages clean.

Adult animals captured from the wild seldom adapt well to captivity. They remain wild and resist any attempts at taming. When not trying to escape, they do their best to remain hidden from view.

Healthy animals are difficult to catch. Any wild animal acting tame or deviating from its normal behavior pattern should be regarded with great suspicion; such unusual behavior may be a symptom of rabies or some other disease.

Rabies is not a serious threat in southern New England, though it is known to occur. Bats are normally the only mammals in the region that carry the disease, although two rabid foxes were taken in Connecticut in 1976. In 1973 a study of bats collected in Massachusetts showed about 4 percent to be rabid. Bats rarely bite another animal, but, since an untreated bite from a rabid animal is usually fatal, it is very important to leave bats strictly alone. It is also wise to refrain from handling any small mammal, especially if it is acting strangely.

Some Selected Mammals

A detailed description of all the mammals that are found in southern New England would be of little use to the reader of this book, since many of the animals are seldom encountered during the day or are found only in the most remote parts of the region. Some of the latter are included in the companion volume on northern New England.

Among the species described below are the diurnal mammals and most of the larger nocturnal species. Mice and other small species that usually remain concealed during the day are omitted.

Gray Squirrel, *Sciurus carolinensis*, is the most familiar of all the mammals native to southern New England. It has adapted well to civilization, since man's terrestrial habitat and the squirrel's arboreal habitat do not conflict to any great degree. Aside from occasionally taking up an uninvited residence in an attic or raiding bird feeders, squirrels do not impinge on man's activities. Around civilization squirrels easily become accustomed to people, but those in more remote areas remain shy.

It is surprising that the oak forests of southern New England do not support even more squirrels than they presently do. Squirrels may reach a population of forty per hectare,

159. Gray squirrel and its track (scale in meters). These tree-dwelling mammals coexist well with humans in both urban and rural areas.

but away from civilization in the deep woods the population is rarely more than four per hectare, if that.

The apparent scarcity of squirrels in mature woods is probably related to their diet. Contrary to popular belief, acorns make up only a part of what they eat. Gray squirrels also eat fungi, seeds, berries, an occasional small bird, even carrion along the sides of highways. Their special fondness for sunflower seeds makes winter bird-feeders a constant target.

Acorns do make up an important part of the squirrels' winter diet, however. They collect the ripened acorns in the fall and bury them in shallow depressions in the ground. Though the squirrels manage to locate many of these caches under the snow, probably by an acute sense of smell, apparently they do not retrieve all of them. When warm weather returns, many of these missed acorns germinate and grow. For this reason, a number of biologists believe that the gray squirrel has been an important factor in the northward migration of the oak forest following the ice age.

Gray squirrels either den in hollow trees or build aerial nests on the branches. In both cases they prefer a high site, usually at least 10 meters above the ground. Their nests, built of twigs and leaves, appear to be so ramshackle and flimsy that they would hardly survive a fresh breeze, but in reality they are well constructed and may last for years with occasional repairs. After they are abandoned by the squirrels other mammals and birds sometimes occupy them.

Variant forms: Occasionally squirrels with very dark or very light fur are seen.

Red Squirrel, *Tamiasciurus hudsonicus*, is the other diurnal tree squirrel one is likely to encounter in the region. Although the range of the red squirrel overlaps with that of the gray squirrel in a part of the eastern United States, the red squirrel is clearly the more northerly species. Its range extends to the Arctic Circle and includes much of the great Canadian spruce forest.

One reason the red squirrel is able to exist in the relatively impoverished habitat of the northern spruce forest is that conifer seeds are one of the mainstays of its diet. In the southern region, then, it is not surprising that red squirrels are more common in woodlands where pine and other conifers grow, although they are also found in deciduous woodlands.

To reach the small seeds, the squirrel opens the cones by shucking off the scales. Large piles of pine and spruce scales under a favorite branch, fallen log, or stump is a sure sign of red squirrel activity. Sometimes these piles, called "squirrel middens," may contain over a bushel of scales.

Like most other small mammals, the red squirrel has a varied diet. In addition to pine seeds, red squirrels will also eat other seeds, nuts, and fruits. They will eat a wide variety of mushrooms, including such poisonous species as the fly amanita, to which they seem to be immune. Drying mushrooms laid out on a limb or wedged in a crotch of a tree is another sign of red squirrel activity in an area.

Unfortunately, the diet of the red squirrel does not stop with vegetation. One authority has claimed that the red squirrel may rival the house cat when it comes to killing birds. The figure he quotes—200 birds killed by a single squirrel in a year—does seem far-fetched, though, when one considers the relatively small home range of an individual squirrel, a radius of about 100 meters. Predatory birds, especially hawks, also take their toll of red squirrels.

In the deciduous forest the red squirrel will den in hollow tree trunks and cavities where limbs have rotted away. In the coniferous forest, where hollow trees are rare, it builds spherical nests out of twigs and grass. Occasionally a red squirrel will also nest underground.

Red squirrels may also move into attics or unoccupied dwellings, where they can become a serious nuisance. They gnaw on furniture and fabrics, tip over dishes, lamps, and utensils, and litter the floor with pine scales and other debris.

Since the red squirrel spends more of its time in trees than the gray squirrel, the likelihood of finding tracks is not as great. Its tracks resemble those of the gray squirrel except that they are smaller and do not toe out.

The red squirrel is an aggressive, noisy little animal that strongly defends its territory against other red squirrels. It will attack and invariably drive away the larger but more placid gray squirrel.

Eastern Chipmunk, *Tamias striatus,* is probably the second most commonly seen diurnal mammal in the region, after the gray squirrel. Chipmunks are classified as ground squirrels, living in subterranean burrows. During the fall, however, it is not unusual to find them high in oak trees gathering acorns for the winter.

The many stone walls in southern New England seem to play an important role in the chipmunk's habitat. The little animals use them quite literally as highways and lookouts from which they can spot predators. The crevices in the rocks also provide them with instant shelter should danger approach.

Chipmunks, like the other small rodents, subsist on a varied diet. In addition to acorns, they eat seeds and nuts, fruits, eggs, meat, and insects. In fact, a recent study has shown that insects may comprise as much as 20 percent of the chipmunk's summer diet.

Chipmunks spend the winter denned up in their burrows. They probably sleep a good deal of the time but awaken periodically to eat. During winter warm spells chipmunks may venture above ground, but return to their burrows until early spring. Chipmunks also have a period of

160. Eastern chipmunk. Chipmunks are probably the region's most frequently seen wild mammal species.

161. The woodchuck can often be found during the day sitting outside its burrow.

decreased activity during the heat of the summer.

Since their metabolic processes continue at a fairly high level during the winter, it is necessary for them to store enough food to carry them through this time. Investigators have found that a single chipmunk will store up to a bushel of food in the several storage chambers of its burrow.

Chipmunks are solitary animals. They are strongly territorial, aggressively defending their home grounds from others of their species. During the breeding season, which is in spring and again in late summer, the males sometimes have fierce fights over a female, and during the season there is much chasing as one animal tries to displace another in its territory. Their call, a whistling chatter, may be heard during mating seasons in spring and early fall.

Like the gray squirrels, chipmunks coexist well with human beings. They occasionally dig up small seedlings in the garden during dry periods, eat bulbs, and burrow where they are not wanted; but, on balance, their attractive appearance and interesting behavior far outweigh these shortcomings.

House cats, hawks, and weasels are probably the three most important enemies of the chipmunk, but other predators such as skunks, red squirrels, and foxes also kill some

Woodchuck, *Marmota monax,* also known as groundhog, is a common animal on the edges of fields and roadsides. It digs extensive burrows which can be easily spotted by the dirt piles around the main entrance. There are also one or more concealed emergency exits to the burrows as well.

Woodchucks have a varied diet, including all kinds of succulent plants as well as insects and an occasional small rodent such as a mouse or vole. Their penchant for plants makes them a serious nuisance if they are living near vegetable gardens.

Before hibernation they double their weight, and then barricade themselves in their dens until February or March. The woodchuck's state of hibernation is so deep that the animal appears dead. Groundhog Day comes in midwinter. Needless to say, the chances of a woodchuck rousing out of a deep hibernation and looking for its shadow are slim indeed. Since woodchucks do hibernate, their tracks in snow are almost never seen.

NOCTURNAL MAMMALS

The following mammals are more active at night or during twilight. They are only occasionally seen during the day.

Flying Squirrel, *Glaucomys* spp., is reputed to be the most abundant squirrel in southern New England. It is a pity that these handsome and interesting little creatures are nocturnal and therefore only rarely observed. Flying squirrels do not actually fly; they glide, sometimes up to 50 meters, with great control and accuracy, by spreading a thin furry membrane which grows between the front and hind legs. By controlling this membrane they are able to steer around obstacles and brake to a soft landing.

Flying squirrels most commonly take up residence in old woodpecker holes, hollow trees, and occasionally attics. I have found several old chestnut hulks containing flying squirrels. Unlike the other squirrel species, flying squirrels are gregarious; sometimes as many as twenty will den together during the winter.

If you suspect that a hollow tree may contain a flying

squirrel den, sometimes a sharp rap on the trunk with a stick or other hard object will make them appear briefly at the den entrance. Also you can detect the presence of flying squirrels at night by their high-pitched twittering noise. Since their undersides are white, they sometimes may be seen gliding from tree to tree in the late dusk or by the light shining through a window. Their eyeshine is reddish orange.

Another clue to the presence of flying squirrels is the characteristic way in which they open hickory nuts. Flying squirrels make one smooth circular or elliptical opening through which they are able to extract the nut meat. Other squirrels and chipmunks cut the nut into many pieces, while deer mice, another species that feeds on hickory nuts, open the nut from two sides.

It is surprising that flying squirrels can apparently coexist with the larger gray and red squirrels. Probably their nocturnal habits and gliding ability, as well as their small size, are important factors.

Porcupine, *Erethizon dorsatum,* is unmistakable in appearance. It is a medium-sized to large rodent, ranging in weight from about 5 to 12 kg (10 to 28 lbs), dark gray to black in color, and covered with thousands of yellowish quills.

Porcupine quills are very sharp, and barbed like fish hooks. Once they become attached, they will gradually work their way in deeper if not removed. When alarmed, the porcupine will raise the quills on its back and lash about with its tail. Contrary to legend, though, it does not have the power to shoot its quills.

With such a strong defense mechanism, the porcupine needs little else for protection. Consequently it has evolved into a sluggish, slow-moving creature which in southern New England has few natural enemies, with the exception of man. Dogs or other animals that try to attack porcupines learn a painful lesson.

Winter is the best time to look for porcupines. Sometimes they stay in the same tree—usually a big white pine or hemlock—for days, littering the ground beneath with pine twigs and droppings. When you find these signs around a tree, there is a good chance that the animal is perched asleep on the upper branches.

Porcupines are considered a nuisance by country people. Their diet of the inner bark of trees makes them destructive

162. Porcupine, and its track in snow. Porcupines appear most often in trees, where they feed on buds, inner bark, and small twigs. (Track after O. J. Murie.)

to timber. Also, they crave salt, and in remote areas will gnaw axe handles, canoe paddles, or any other wood that people have touched. They have a taste for sweet corn, too, and can seriously damage a cornfield.

Although porcupines may spend a great deal of time feeding in trees, females, at least, den up in hollow logs or in piles of loose rocks. These dens are slovenly things, easily recognized by the piles of droppings and an occasional loose quill found near the opening. In winter you can often find porcupine trails leading from their dens to the feeding trees.

Muskrat, *Ondatra zibethica,* is the most nearly aquatic member of the rodent family. It is most frequently found in marshes and ponds, where it feeds on cattails and other aquatic vegetation as well as clams, frogs, and fish. Muskrats often go ashore in the evening to feed on land vegetation as well. Muskrats are far more common in southern New England than beaver, although the two often occupy the same pond.

The most prominent signs of muskrats are their roundish or conical houses built of matted vegetation and mud, either just on the shore or in shallow water. Muskrats also live in burrows in the banks.

The muskrat is well adapted to its aquatic life. Its fur is so thick that the animal never gets wet to the skin; its vertically flattened tail serves as both a rudder and cooling organ if the animal must move quickly. It can stay submerged up to twelve minutes, which allows it to root out aquatic vegetation and feed under the ice.

In early winter, muskrats build hollow piles of vegetation that may be entered by a hole in the ice. When covered by a layer of snow, these plunge holes usually remain open, thus allowing the animals to reach their food supply without venturing into the open.

Muskrats are preyed upon by many animals, not the least of which is man. Muskrat pelts provide more fur for commercial use than all other native fur-bearing species combined. About 20 million are trapped in America each year. Yet the animal is so prolific that its numbers are in no way threatened.

Among its other predators are raccoon, fox, weasels, snapping turtles, snakes, large fish, hawks, and owls. The young muskrats are shoved out of the nest when they are still quite small, and at this stage are particularly vulnerable to predators.

Beaver, *Castor canadensis,* is much more common in less populous northern New England, but occasionally is found in more remote parts of the southern region. Here, beavers tend to become a nuisance, damming up culverts and flooding low areas. Their presence is easily recognized by the gnawed trees and by their complex and beautifully engineered dams.

Beavers are among the few truly nocturnal mammals and hence are rarely seen except very early on summer mornings.

White-tailed Deer, *Odocoileus virginianus,* is the only big game mammal that one is likely to encounter in southern New England. Despite the inroads of civilization in the region, the deer population is surprisingly high. This is probably due to a number of factors: a potentially high reproductive rate, good state management programs, an absence of natural predators, and the brushy terrain that is still present in recently abandoned farmland. Dogs, hunting either singly or in packs, put pressure on deer populations, but the seriousness of this problem has not been clearly assessed.

Deer are classified as browsers, feeding on twigs, shrubs, bark, apples, and acorns. They will also eat grass and herbaceous plants and occasionally garden vegetables. Deer also do considerable damage to young orchards. In some places deer are such a problem that apple growers are forced to put high fences around the orchards to keep the deer out.

The home range of deer is surprisingly small, usually less than two kilometers across. They are usually seen on the edges of woodlands in the morning and evening twilight. Deer become attached to the area in which they were raised and will not move even when threatened with starvation. As a consequence, local overpopulation can occur.

Deer are active all winter but during the cold weather they often retire to swamps or south-facing slopes, where the sun warms more efficiently. Southern New England swamps where greenbrier thickets make passage difficult are often winter habitats for deer. Herds of up to twenty sometimes congregate in these places.

Deer tracks are distinctive and very easy to recognize. I have seen innumerable tracks during my life but have encountered the animals only rarely. When you sight a deer during the winter, you can track the animal for quick glimpses, since they run for only short distances, then stop to rest.

Cottontail Rabbit, *Sylvilagus* spp., seems to have declined slightly in numbers as a result of the changing habitat. An animal of fields and thickets, the cottontail is probably less well adapted to life in maturing woodlands.

Predators take a heavy toll of young rabbits; a high birth rate seems to be one of their main means of survival. The female rabbit gives birth to her young in open nest-like depressions in the grass that give the defenseless nestlings little protection from either predators or the elements. Not only are they easy prey to virtually all of the carnivores, but a late freeze or downpour can also destroy them.

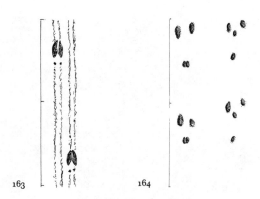

163   164

163. Walking track of white-tailed deer in snow.

164. Two track patterns of cottontail rabbit in snow. (Scale for both is in meters.)

    The female rabbit gives birth to a litter of young about three or four times during the warmer part of the year. The young of the first litter, usually born in April, stand the best chance of survival since they have the longest time to mature before the cold weather. Apparently these early litters also receive less pressure from predators than do the later ones.

    As gardeners and farmers know all too well, the cottontail consumes a great quantity and variety of vegetable food. In fact, the vegetable diet of the rabbit is more varied than that of any other North American mammal. In winter, bark and twigs are the most common food.

    There are two distinct species of cottontail rabbit living in southern New England. The two so closely resemble each other that they are almost impossible to distinguish in the field. The eastern cottontail, *S. floridanus,* reaches the northern limit of its range approximately along the dividing line between southern and northern New England. It is the species more commonly found in open habitats.

    The other species, usually known as the New England cottontail, *S. transitionalis,* was until about 1900 the only native New England rabbit species. Since that time, however, the eastern cottontail has been moving northward and displacing it. Though both species are still found in southern New England, the New England cottontail is less abundant.

165. Opossum. The white face with black ears and the prehensile rat-like tail are characteristic of this species.

The New England cottontail is more likely to be seen in denser woodlands and swamps.

Opossum, *Didelphis marsupialis,* is another recent newcomer to the region. Although the animal is only poorly adapted for cold weather—many New England opossums lose parts of their paper-thin ears and bare tails to frostbite—it seems to be increasing in numbers here. Perhaps the reason for its success is a high reproductive rate and omnivorous diet.

Although opossums may turn up in various kinds of habitats, they are most commonly found near civilization, living under sheds and barns.

CARNIVORES

Under normal conditions, whenever and wherever a population of plant-eating animals develops, a population of predators soon follows. The largely defenseless plant-eating mammals therefore must depend upon a high birth rate for their survival as a species. The muskrat, for example, may produce as many as eighteen offspring in a single year, while some of the smaller animals such as mice and voles have even higher birth rates (one meadow vole in captivity produced seventeen litters in a single year).

Yet it is simplistic to think that a population of predators is necessary to keep these small mammals from overrunning the region, or for that matter, outbreeding the food supply or living space. Overpopulation in certain animal species does temporarily occur; but in natural populations, provided that the environment remains fairly stable, there seems to be a built-in mechanism for population control. This is usually seen as a lower reproductive rate in response to disease, crowding, and food shortages. While populations of animals sometimes do fluctuate wildly as the result of many different factors, the specter of hordes of small rodents taking over the world can be laid to rest.

The predators, like the prey, are most active in the twilight or at night. None are commonly seen during the day, yet their tracks in the snow will almost always be found wherever a large number of herbivore tracks are found.

Red Fox, *Vulpes fulva*, is probably the more common of the two fox species native to New England. The red fox prefers a habitat of open fields, thickets, and woods, the type of habitat shared by so many small animals.

Foxes are members of the dog family and therefore are classified as carnivores. Though it is true that their diet is most commonly meat, foxes will also eat fruit, nuts, and berries.

Fox tracks are easy to identify. They resemble those of a small to medium-sized dog, but, unlike the usual erratic pattern of dog tracks that seem to meander with no definite direction, fox tracks generally follow straight lines. By midwinter most foxes have paired up prior to mating; often at this time fox trails will show two sets of tracks proceeding in the same direction.

When foxes live in the vicinity, they may occasionally be heard barking on late winter nights. Foxes have a repertoire of several different sounds; the times that I have heard them they have made a rather high-pitched strangling sound.

Like other members of the dog family, foxes occasionally carry rabies. Any fox that comes into civilized areas and acts tame should be regarded with great suspicion.

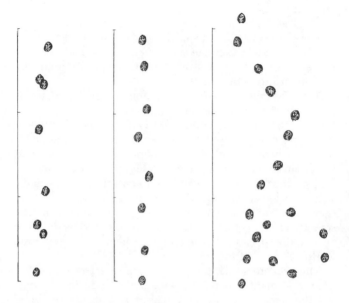

166. Two track patterns of red fox. At left is a loping gait, in the center a walking gait. At right is the typical meandering pattern of a small dog. (Scale is in meters.)

167. Gray fox. Its salt-and-pepper-colored coat and black-tipped tail are distinctive features.

Gray Fox, *Urocyon cinereoargenteus,* the other native New England fox species, has gradually extended its range into New England from farther south. Apparently its migration was assisted by sportsmen who introduced the gray fox into the north after mange had decimated the population of the red fox.

The gray fox differs in appearance from the red fox in several ways. As its name suggests, its grayish fur makes it easily distinguishable from the reddish brown of the red fox. In addition, the gray fox has a black tip on its tail while the red fox has a white tip. The gray fox is also smaller and shorter-muzzled than the red.

Its preferred habitat is different as well. The gray fox generally inhabits deeper woods, often close to marshes, where it can hunt for ducks and muskrat. There is enough overlap in the two habitats, however, to make identification on this basis alone very uncertain. Gray foxes climb trees, especially those with slanting trunks, both for protection and for food.

Weasel, *Mustela* spp. The weasels, of which there are at least three different species in southern New England, are wide-ranging animals, turning up almost anywhere other small mammals may be found. All are most active at night, although I have seen one in the day.

168. Young weasel. Its kitten-like appearance belies a fierce and aggressive nature.

The weasels are efficient killers, usually dispatching their victims with a bite through the skull or backbone. The short-tailed weasel, *M. erminea*, with an adult weight of only 400 gm (1 lb), can kill a rabbit nearly five times as large. The larger, semi-aquatic mink, *M. vison*, regularly preys on adult muskrats, which are even larger.

The smaller species often take over mouse burrows, lining them with the fur of their victims. Weasels often den under farm buildings, from which they occasionally launch an attack on poultry.

The tracks of weasels in winter vary with the species, snow conditions, and speed of travel, but the usual gait through the snow is a bouncing run in which the hind feet land in the tracks made by the front feet. As a result, weasel tracks often, but not always, appear as á line of only two prints, usually with one a little ahead of another.

Striped Skunk, *Mephitis mephitis*, is to the weasel family what the porcupine is to the rodents: it has such a strong defense mechanism that it is relatively safe from predators. All weasels have scent glands in their anus, but in skunks they are so well developed and the scent so powerful that the presence of a skunk is almost always first detected by the smell. This means of protection—skunk spray—is not only odorous but will cause temporary blindness if aimed at the eyes.

Unlike other members of the weasel clan, the skunk is a sedentary creature that eats insects, grubs, carrion, garbage, berries, and an occasional mouse. Skunks often live quite close to civilization and sometimes learn to open garbage cans. They can present a problem if surprised while they are in a garbage can feeding.

Skunks stay denned up during snowy weather, but, like the raccoon and chipmunk, may appear in warm spells during winter. They spend their winters in rock crevices, in hollow logs, under buildings, or in ground burrows. Often a den can be detected by the faint skunk smell and traces of black and white hair around the entrance.

Although they can hardly be called shy animals, they will use their spray only if violently startled or as a last line of defense. Given an open escape route, they will scurry away with surprising speed, in view of their usual slow, waddling gait.

Dogs will usually attack a skunk but once. The malodorous results of such an encounter will linger for weeks and reappear for a long time thereafter on wet days. A bath with tomato juice helps to get rid of the odor. The great horned owl is the only predator which will normally attack a skunk; their dens often reek of skunk spray. This owl species has been known to knock down a person who was out at night wearing a light-colored hat—which in all likelihood was mistaken for a skunk.

Raccoon, *Procyon lotor*, is another native mammal that has been able to coexist well with humans. Although raccoons are more common in rural areas, a surprising number can be found in built-up areas as well. The secret of its success in civilization is probably its fearlessness of dogs and its adaptable diet. The raccoon will eat practically anything, from small birds and small mammals to fruit, nuts, garden vegetables—especially sweet corn—and garbage.

The raccoon is more gregarious than most mammals. The male is solitary but the young will stay with the female for the summer and may often be seen with her during the night. During the daytime it is sometimes possible to find a raccoon family asleep high in an old pine.

169. Raccoon. The mask and ringed tail make this mammal easy to recognize. Raccoons are chiefly nocturnal.

The most common den for raccoons is a hollow tree; old chestnut hulks are often used in this region. They also den up in hollow logs, rock crevices, or ground burrows.

Raccoons are supposed to make a tremulous owl-like call, but the only sound I have ever heard was a squawking wail made by a young raccoon who became caught in a hollow tree, and a series of sharp barking snarls while I was freeing him.

The raccoon stays denned up for most of the winter, so its tracks are not generally seen in the snow. During the spring and summer its tracks are often found on sand bars near rivers. The tracks are very easy to recognize. The front paw produces a hand-like imprint while the rear paw leaves a track like a long-toed flat foot.

Amphibians
of Southern New England

ALTHOUGH the variety of amphibians native to southern New England numbers only twenty-one different species, they are among the most abundant vertebrates in the region. Yet despite this abundance, probably less is known about this group of animals than any other. Even among some of the most common species many unanswered questions about their physiology, life history, taxonomy, and ranges still remain.

The amphibians have been grouped and studied with the reptiles under the study of herpetology, but the two vertebrate classes are very different and only distantly related. Amphibians are clearly the more primitive of the two, being the first major group to leave a totally aquatic environment. While some species are better adapted to terrestrial life than others, none have been able to forsake the water entirely, despite the passage of many hundreds of millions of years. Most species still return to the water to breed; most still pass through an aquatic larval stage; all require a cool, moist environment in order to survive.

There are two major orders of amphibians that have sur-

170. Bullfrog, *Rana catesbeiana*, with its short body and highly developed legs, represents a major evolutionary departure from the amphibian norm.

vived this immense passage of time: the salamanders and the frogs. The salamanders, with their streamlined bodies and undulating way of swimming, bespeak their ancestral relation to the fish. The frogs, on the other hand, with their tailless bodies and tremendously developed hind legs, represent a major evolutionary development that has made them radically different from their aquatic ancestors.

Probably the most distinctive trait of the amphibians is the larval stage through which the young pass. During this stage both the anatomy and the physiology of the young amphibian is not at all like that of the adult. Frog larvae, the tadpoles, are well known to most people; larval salamanders, characterized by feathery external gills on either side of the gills, are generally smaller and not so often seen. Most species are aquatic during this time. A few salamander species have evolved a completely terrestrial lifestyle, though the larvae develop in very moist environments.

The most easily recognizable field characteristic of amphibians is their moist and scaleless skin. Although most amphibians possess lungs (in a few species of salamanders the lungs have atrophied as a later evolutionary development), all species also absorb water and oxygen through their skins. For this process to occur, the skin must remain moist. Many species maintain a moist exterior by secreting a mucous-like substance. This covering, which also makes them more difficult to capture, may contain antibiotic compounds to help them resist infection. Most species, however, will desiccate and die in a relatively short time if trapped in a hot and dry environment. Even such highly adapted terrestrial species as the toads require some moisture in their environment. It is not surprising that during summer dry spells the terrestrial amphibians are difficult to find; during these times they burrow deeply into the ground and aestivate.

Because amphibians are cold-blooded they must also regulate their body temperatures by moving to warmer or cooler surroundings. In addition, some can regulate their rate of heat absorption to some degree by darkening and lightening their skins. During cold weather most of the species bury themselves below the frost line and hibernate. Many also lower the water content of their bodies, which helps them resist being frozen solid.

Despite the fact that they are cold-blooded, a number of native species emerge from hibernation early in the spring when the water temperatures of their breeding pools are only a little above freezing.

The wood frog, a very common New England species, seems especially well adapted for a colder climate. In this region it is the last of the frogs to hibernate, usually not before the end of September. It is also the first to emerge, usually breeding before the spring peepers begin to call. The wood frog can also respond to temperature changes by lightening or darkening its skin color to a greater degree than other species. With these adaptations to the cold it is not surprising that the wood frog is one of the few amphibians that can live in the far north.

Though the tadpoles of most frogs are vegetarians, the diet of all the rest of the amphibians is wholly carnivorous. The salamanders and most of the aquatic frogs merely grab their prey with their mouths, but the terrestrial frogs, much of whose diets consists of flying insects, have evolved long tongues that are attached to the front of their mouths. The tongues of some species such as the common toad are at least half as long as their bodies. When an insect or other small prey comes within range, the tongue flips out with lightning-like speed and the prey is swallowed whole.

Many amphibians do fairly well in captivity. Terrestrial salamanders will live in a woodland terrarium, though usually they spend virtually all of their time hidden from view. A small toad will do well in a large terrarium, but most of the other terrestrial frogs are too active to be kept in such a confined place. Tadpoles and aquatic salamanders may be kept quite easily in an aquarium, but the adult aquatic frogs, such as the green frog and bullfrog, require a daily change of water and, except for very small specimens, usually require more space than it is possible to provide indoors.

As is often the case with carnivorous animals, a diet of live food is a necessity. If an amphibian is to be kept through the winter the requirement for a continuing and varied supply of live food becomes a very important consideration. Many amphibian species are very interesting creatures to study, but several have specialized requirements that must be met if the animal is to survive. Before attempting to keep any species you should refer to one of the books in the bibliography for specific directions.

Common Salamanders

Red-spotted Newt, *Notophthalmus viridescens,* is probably the species of native salamander most often casually seen, though it is only locally abundant. Newts are exceedingly variable in appearance, but all have red spots within black circles. The adults, which are normally aquatic, are most often a yellowish or olive-green up to about 10 cm (4 in) in length.

In cooler habitats the newt often goes through a terrestrial stage in its life. Soon after the larvae become transformed to the adult stage, the young newt leaves the water and may live up to three years on land. During this time, its skin changes to a brick-red or orange and the newt goes by the common name of red eft. In warmer habitats the red eft stage may be bypassed and the newt remains aquatic for its entire life. It is not known why newts are abundant in some ponds and absent from others.

Spotted Salamander, *Ambystoma maculatum*, is a terrestrial salamander that spends most of the time underground, and hence is not often casually seen. A large salamander, the adult may range in length from 15 to 20 cm (6 to 8 in). It is easily recognized by its coloration: round yellow or orange spots arranged in an irregular row on a slate-gray or black background. Large numbers are often seen in ponds during the breeding season in spring, but despite its abundance, in other times of the year it is only occasionally found, and then usually during wet weather under logs or stones. In drier periods it may burrow more deeply underground. (See color plate VII.)

Similar species: The marbled salamander, *Ambystoma opacum*, is smaller in size than the spotted salamander, with a body covered with bands of white or light gray on a background of black or dark gray. It is more common in drier sandy or gravelly habitats near the coast.

Red-backed Salamander, *Plethodon cinereus*, is the most abundant terrestrial species in the region. In most woods it is often found under nearly every log or stone. The red-backed salamander is a small slender salamander, rarely exceeding 9 cm (3½ in). It occurs in two distinct colorations: the red-backed form has a brownish or reddish stripe down its back, and dark gray sides; the lead-backed form is uniformly dark gray. In some areas the two forms are equally abundant; in others one or the other might predominate. The red-backed salamander belongs to a small group of salamanders which have no lungs but breathe through their skin and the linings of their mouths. They are one of the few groups of amphibians that are wholly terrestrial, laying their eggs in damp places, usually under rotting logs.

Similar species: The two-lined salamander, *Eurycea bislineata*, is primarily a brook-dweller. It is about the same size as the red-backed salamander but is yellowish or tan in color with a dark band down either side. (See color plate VII.)

Common Frogs and Toads

American Toad, *Bufo americanus,* is such an abundant denizen of the southern New England woodlands that most people are already familiar with it. There is considerable variation in its color, ranging from a dull brick-red through numerous shades of brown to yellow. Some are uniform in color but others, especially females, have a patterned or spotted appearance. (See color plate VII.)

The skin of a toad is dry and covered with warts; these cannot be transmitted to human beings. Toads, like many other amphibians, however, do secrete a rather strong poison. This is produced in the two large glands behind their eyes, known as the parotoid glands. If pressed or injured, they will secrete a compound that is poisonous when swallowed and very irritating to the mucous membranes. Though I have handled toads many times without ill effects, it is recommended that people wash their hands after handling toads.

Not surprisingly, toads have few natural enemies. Skunks will eat them, but only after they have rolled them over and over on the ground to drain out the venomous secretions.

Toads eat earthworms and a great variety of insects. At night, they are attracted to light, where they feast on the insects that are also attracted to it. Toads make excellent terrarium pets, but, like all amphibians, if they are to be kept through the winter provision must be made for a constant supply of live food. Unlike most frogs, several toads will live together amicably in the same terrarium.

Toads breed in shallow water, even puddles and temporary pools. The female lays as many as 20,000 eggs in long strings of jelly. The eggs hatch in about four days and the tadpoles change into the adult form in about a month. Because of this haphazard choice of breeding pools, probably the majority of toad eggs and tadpoles dry up and die before reaching maturity.

Similar species: Fowler's toad, *Bufo fowleri,* is very similar in appearance to the American toad and often hybridizes with it. It is more common in coastal sections.

Spring Peeper, *Hyla crucifer,* has a cricket-like nocturnal call that is one of the first signs of spring. It is a very small frog, rarely over 3 cm (1¼ in) in head-body length. It is equipped with large adhesive discs on its toes that help it climb into trees and bushes. It is brownish or olive in color with a prominent dark X on its back. From close at hand, the chorus of peepers is almost deafening.

Similar species: Gray tree frog, *Hyla versicolor*, is larger than the spring peeper, often reaching 5 cm (2 in) in length. It is easily recognized by its somewhat rough, mottled, grayish or greenish skin. The skin color makes the frog resemble moss or lichen and therefore provides it with excellent camouflage when it is on tree bark. The undersurfaces of the legs are orange. The tree frog is able to darken and lighten its color to help regulate body temperature.

Leopard Frog, *Rana pipiens,* is one of the region's two spotted frogs. Adults range in head-body length from 5 to 9 cm (2 to 3½ in) with a ground color of brown, tan, or green. The spots are dark brown with white borders, rounded in shape and irregular in size, arranged in two or three lengthwise rows. The leopard frog is often found in moist meadows, sometimes quite far from water. It is reputed to be the best jumper of the native frogs, one individual having jumped a record 112 cm (44 in).

Pickerel Frog, *Rana palustris,* is quite similar in appearance to the leopard frog described previously, except that it is smaller in head-body length, usually between 4.5 cm and 7.5 cm (1¾ to 3 in), and its spots are irregular squares. It also has bright yellow or orange on the concealed surfaces of the hind legs. The pickerel frog has a characteristic odor and secretes a strong poison from its skin glands. (See color plate VII.)

Wood Frog, *Rana sylvatica,* is a small frog usually ranging in body length from about 3 to 7 cm (1¼ to 2¾ in). The color of its skin varies from reddish brown in early spring to light tan in summer, and it is easily recognized by dark mask-like streaks behind the eyes. The coloration varies with the temperature, the darker phase being more heat-absorptive. As its name suggests, the preferred habitat of the wood frog is moist woodlands. (See color plate VII.)

Green Frog, *Rana clamitans,* is larger than the frogs previously described, with an adult head-body length of between 6 and 9 cm (2¼ to 3½ in). Its color is greenish or brownish, with small dark spots on the back and sides; often the head is greenish and the rear of the body brownish. The green frog is probably the most abundant species in the region. One characteristic that distinguishes it from the bullfrog described below is a ridge down either side of the back. Unlike the species previously described, it is an aquatic frog, almost always being found in shallow fresh water or within jumping distance of it. It is very alert and difficult to catch. (See color plate VII.)

If threatened by a snake, the green frog, as well as several other species, assumes an unusual defense posture: it lowers its head, fills up its lungs, and lifts its body off the ground by extending its fore and hind legs. Apparently it is more difficult for a snake to swallow the frog in this position.

Variant forms: Blue and, more rarely, yellow forms of the green frog are found. These unusual body colors result from an absence of either the blue or the yellow pigment that together give the frog its normal green color.

Bullfrog, *Rana catesbeiana,* is the giant of native frogs, sometimes reaching a body length of over 20 cm (8 in). In coloration and habitat it resembles the smaller green frog just described, but lacks the two dark ridges down its back.

Bullfrogs consume substantial amounts of food. Their diet, like that of other frogs, is primarily insects, but they also eat other frogs, small turtles, mice, rats, and bats. Probably as a result of their large food requirements, bullfrogs are aggressive and territorial. I once saw a bullfrog attack a water snake, and I have myself been bitten on the finger by a large specimen I had captured. Because the bullfrog, like other native frogs, lacks teeth, however, both the snake and I escaped unharmed.

The call of the bullfrog is a sonorous foghorn-like note that can carry up to several hundred meters on a still evening.

Reptiles
of Southern New England

THE REPTILES are far more suited to a terrestrial environment than are the amphibians. Chief among their adaptations for living on land is a much more highly developed and efficient respiratory system, in which their lungs are ventilated by muscular movement. Without the need to absorb oxygen and water through their skins, the reptiles have evolved an impervious leathery skin that is covered by protective scales. Unlike the amphibians, all of the reptiles that lay eggs (some species of snakes hatch their eggs internally and the young emerge directly) produce eggs that are encased in limy or leathery skins to hold in the moisture, and the eggs are laid on land. Another difference from the amphibians is that the young of the reptiles closely resemble the adults both in physiology and in appearance.

Like amphibians, the reptiles have evolved into very diverse forms. Probably the lizard most closely resembles the ancestral reptilian prototype, while both the snakes and the turtles represent radical departures from the early forms. The snake evolved from the lizard quite recently in geologic time, the atrophy of its legs and elongation of its body allowing it to assume a slithering means of locomotion that is well suited for movement over rough ground. On some primitive species such as the boa constrictor, the tiny vestigial hind legs may still be seen.

Far more radical in its departure from the reptilian norm was the evolution of the turtle. The development of the cumbersome shell from the scaly skin has provided the turtles with a large measure of protection, but the internal rearrangements, such as a backbone fused to the shell, a huge set of ribs to support its extra weight, and a different means of breathing, has made the turtle so highly specialized that it has become an evolutionary dead end. For over 200 million years turtle evolution has consisted only of other turtles.

All reptiles are carnivorous; some of the land turtles also include plant material in their diets. Reptiles have teeth, though in the turtles they have become modified into a sharp beak-like structure.

In snakes a flexible jaw has evolved that allows them to swallow their prey whole. Some of the constricting species throw a coil or two around their victims to smother them; in the poisonous species the salivary glands have evolved into poison glands.

Many people are unreasonably frightened by snakes, even small ones. But whether this is some innate fear or whether it is learned is not clear. Particularly repulsive to many people is the feeding behavior of snakes, but we should remember that snakes—unlike the familiar and much-loved house cat—will kill only when hungry (or as the last measure of defense) and attempt to dispatch their prey with as much speed and efficiency as possible.

Snakes are believed to be among the most efficient rodent killers in all of nature; and, as such, they perform a valuable service to man in his continuing attempts to control these grain-eating and disease-carrying creatures. In fact, one expert figured that every milk snake, a species often living around barns, had an economic value of at least ten dollars as a rodent exterminator.

Though the reptiles are better adapted for a terrestrial existence than the amphibians, they are not nearly as common in New England as they are in warmer and drier parts of the country. There is a total of ten species of turtles native to New England (excluding five marine species that are sometimes seen in offshore waters) and fourteen species of snakes. One species of lizard, the five-lined skink, may still occasionally be found in southwestern Connecticut, though it appears to be extinct in Massachusetts and Rhode Island.

Several of the common species of snakes do well in captivity. Though they are clean and easy to care for, snakes remain inactive most of the time and have a rather limited repertoire of behaviors. All demand warmth and at least some dryness, and they all need drinking water. More difficult is providing snakes with live food, especially during the winter. Since there are certain general requirements for keeping snakes, as well as specialized requirements for the different species, you should consult the references at the end of Part VIII before attempting to keep snakes.

Keeping turtles in captivity is far more difficult. Most do very poorly and eventually die unless they receive expert care. Because of the alarming decline in the numbers of native land turtles, it is especially important that these species be left in their natural habitats.

Connecticut and Massachusetts have active herpetological societies. More information about the care and habits of both reptiles and amphibians may be obtained through membership in these organizations. The addresses of each are given in the resource list at the end of this book.

Common Turtles

Snapping Turtle, *Chelydra serpentina*, was described by one expert as a turtle with a long tail and a short temper. It is a very dark turtle with a large head, a rough upper shell, and a small undershell. It grows to be the largest native turtle, adults ranging in shell length from about 20 to a record of 45 cm (8 to 18 in). The snapping turtle may be found in any permanent body of fresh water and occasionally in brackish water.

Luckily for people who wade in ponds where it lives, the turtle is usually inoffensive when stepped upon, but on land it is vicious in its defense, striking with lightning-like rapidity at any moving object that comes within range. Recent studies have shown, however, that the diet of the snapping turtle is largely water plants. The widely held belief that they are destructive of young waterfowl has not been borne out by careful investigations.

The snapper is edible. In earlier times it was the custom in the country to keep a snapping turtle in the rain barrel, where it grew fat and tender to be killed later for food. One such turtle reached a weight of 86 pounds.

Similar species: The musk turtle, *Sternotherus odoratus*, is a dark-colored turtle that has a small undershell like the snapper, but a smooth upper shell. It is much smaller than the snapper, usually reaching only about 10 cm (4 in) in shell length. It is identified by two yellow lines along each side of the head and the disagreeable odor it gives off when captured.

Painted Turtle, *Chrysemys picta*, is a common aquatic

turtle with a shell length of about 11 to 15 cm (4½ to 6 in) in the adult stage. The shell is smooth and black with reddish or yellowish markings around the margins of the plates, but these shell colors are likely to be obscured if the water in which the turtle lives is acidic. The head is black with yellow spots. Painted turtles are often seen sunning themselves on logs or rocks along the water's edge. They are an alert species that dive at the first indication of danger. (See color plate, VIII.)

Spotted Turtle, *Clemmys guttata,* is a small turtle up to about 11 cm (4½ in) in length, which is easily recognized by the scattered yellow spots on the shell and the orange or yellow spots on the head. The spotted turtle lives near water but is occasionally seen some distance from it. Because of its terrestrial proclivities it is far easier to capture than the painted turtle, and as a result has become scarce in many parts of the region.

Box Turtle, *Terrapene carolina,* is a terrestrial species, up, to 15 cm (6 in) in length, that is easily recognized by its high-domed usually yellowish shell. The box turtle is well adapted for terrestrial life; the high dome of the shell provides a fluid reservoir that acts as a buffer against temperature changes and supplies the animal with water. The undershell is hinged, enabling the turtle to close up so tightly that it is impossible to fit a knife blade between the upper and lower shells—an adaptation that prevents most predators from eating it. They are common in central Connecticut and in the Cape Cod area of Massachusetts. (See color plate VIII.)

Similar species: Blanding's turtle, *Emydoidea blandingi,* has a somewhat domed shell and a hinged undershell that can close, though not so tightly as the box turtle. Its black shell is speckled with yellow and its head is black above and yellow below. It is essentially aquatic but may be found on land. Its main range is in the Midwest, but it occurs in our area as a small disjunct colony only in a part of eastern Massachusetts and southeastern New Hampshire. The wood turtle, *Clemmys insculpta,* is another terrestial turtle. It is larger than the box turtle, sometimes reaching 23 cm (9 in) in shell length, and may be identified by its sculptured shell, each plate of which is pyramidal in shape. (See color plate VIII.)

Common Snakes

Red-bellied Snake, *Storeria occipitomaculata,* is a secretive little snake rarely exceeding 25 cm (10 in) in length. It is brown, dark gray, or black above but has a bright usually coral-red belly. It lives under leaves and logs and is almost never casually encountered.

Similar species: Ringneck snake, *Diadophis punctatus,* is usually a bluish-black or dark gray color, 25 to 38 cm (10 to 15 in) long, with a yellow ring around its neck and a yellow belly. Like the red-bellied snake, it hides under rocks and rotting logs. The northern brown or DeKay's snake, *Storeria dekayi,* is another small species, usually between 22 and 33 cm (9 to 13 in), that remains hidden most of the time. It is brown with two parallel rows of dark spots down the back. It is often found even in urban areas.

Garter Snake, *Thamnophis sirtalis (Natrix sirtalis),* is the most familiar and abundant snake in the region. It is extremely variable in coloration and pattern, normally bearing three yellowish stripes down the back and sides, but often seen with a checkered skin. It is usually less than 76 cm (30 in), though larger specimens have been found. It is common in a wide variety of habitats. When captured, the garter snake often discharges an unpleasant-smelling substance from glands near the tail.

Similar species: The ribbon snake, *Thamnophis sauritus (Natrix sauritus),* also bears three bright yellow stripes on a dark background, but is much more slender in shape. It is agile, fast moving, and difficult to capture, and is most commonly found near streams and other watercourses.

Variant form: A blue form of the ribbon snake is sometimes found.

Water Snake, *Natrix sipedon,* is common around swamps, marshes, ponds, and rivers. It is a stout dark-colored snake, though younger specimens are usually cross-banded and frequently reddish colored. When it is captured, the snake has an ugly disposition, biting and discharging foul-smelling musk. Though formerly thought to be destructive to fish populations in the ponds and rivers where they live, it is now believed that water snakes actually improve the fish population by culling out sick and less vigorous individuals. (See color plate VIII.)

Hognose Snake, *Heterodon platyrhinos,* is a harmless snake with a dramatic defense behavior. When confronted by an enemy, the snake flattens its head and neck like a cobra, hisses, inflates its body with air, and may strike without biting. If this performance doesn't work, the snake may then roll over and play dead. The hognose snake is medium-sized, ranging in length from 46 to 76 cm (18 to 30 in), variably colored and patterned, though usually spotted. Its most easily recognizable feature is its turned-up nose. Hognose snakes have been reported throughout the region but are common only in the sandy areas of Cape Cod and in central Connecticut.

Black Racer, *Coluber constrictor,* is the black snake most often seen in the region. Adults are large, usually between 90 and 150 cm (36 to 60 in). The black racer is an alert, fast-moving snake, difficult to capture and difficult to maintain in captivity.

Similar species: The black rat snake, *Elaphe obsoleta,* is the giant of the southern New England snakes. Adults range in length from about 100 to 240 cm (3½ to 9 ft). Like the black racer, it is shiny black in color, but it is less active and more docile. The black rat snake is of great value as a rodent catcher. It is found only in parts of Connecticut and in southwestern Massachusetts.

Milk Snake, *Lampropeltis triangulum,* is a handsomely marked snake with black-bordered brown or russet-red saddles on a gray background. It is a medium-sized snake, usually ranging in length from 60 to 90 cm (24 to 36 in). Milk snakes usually remain hidden from view but occasionally are seen around farms, where they hunt for voles and mice. Though milk snakes bear little resemblance to copperheads, they are often mistaken for them and killed. (See color plate VIII.)

Copperhead, *Agkistrodon contortrix,* is occasionally found on the basalt ridges of the Connecticut Valley Lowland and in other habitat blocks in Connecticut and southwestern Massachusetts, but rarely elsewhere in the region. A full description is on page 25. (See color plate VIII.)

Timber Rattlesnake, *Crotalus horridus,* is a rare snake, perhaps close to extinction in the region. A full description is on page 25.

Introduction to Inland Birds
of Southern New England

PEOPLE who become interested in New England birds will find themselves members of a large and enthusiastic fraternity. More people study birds than any other branch of natural history, and there are probably more knowledgeable birders in southern New England than in any other area of comparable population in the United States.

Such widespread interest is easily understood. The birds themselves are a fascinating group of animals. They are abroad in the daytime; many species are brightly colored or distinctively marked. They are plentiful; their variety is challenging but not unmanageable; the chance of sighting rare or unusual species always exists.

Learning to recognize the various species, moreover, is only a beginning. There is enough in the study of the various aspects of bird behavior—feeding, nesting, courtship, and migration—to maintain lifelong interest and enjoyment. Broader studies of changes in bird populations and their geographic range can provide valuable information about both the species themselves and the habitat. Studies such as these may also yield information about the ecological effects of changing land use patterns or of environmental deterioration.

The New Englander's long tradition of interest in all aspects of natural history has probably helped to give impetus to birding here. Bird study has been furthered also by the establishment of the influential state Audubon societies and the many local birding clubs.

The activity of this army of birders in southern New England clearly manifests itself in the national state-by-state census of species. In Massachusetts, for example, one of the smallest states in the country, there have been well-documented sightings of over 400 different species. In Rhode Island, which is even smaller, 333 species have been sighted. Giant states such as Texas and California boast a larger number of sighted species, but the number of sightings in the New England states is proportionately far higher. Probably many of these same birds have also visited

171. Great horned owl and young. This large owl is common in southern New England.

other states, but no one has reported seeing them there as yet. It is also probable that very few additional species will be added to the southern New England state lists. In contrast to the number of sightings, the number of species known to breed in these states is much smaller: only 180 in Massachusetts and 141 in Rhode Island.

For the beginning birder, 400 species would seem a large and hopelessly confusing number of possibilities. But, of that total, close to one hundred are sea birds or shore birds that rarely venture inland; at least another hundred are transients, only observed here during their migrations; and many of the rest are rare accidentals or vagrants that have been carried here by storm winds or have otherwise strayed out of their normal ranges. In fact, there are substantially less than a hundred different species that one is likely to see in inland areas outside of the migration season. In comparison with the nearly two thousand species of flowering plants and ferns or the many thousands of insect species native to the region, this variety of birds should be easy to manage.

A book of this size cannot adequately provide illustrations

and descriptions for even the most common inland birds of the region. Nevertheless, this section will give you enough introductory information, including lists of birds by habitat, to enable you to embark on a serious study of birds with the help of a good field guide.

Bird Migration

Of the many aspects of bird behavior, none is more intriguing than migration. Each spring the majority of temperate species embark on a long and hazardous journey from their winter ranges in the warmer parts of the hemisphere northward to their breeding grounds; each fall they fly southward to escape the winter climate with its attendant lack of food.

The fact that the birds migrate is known to every school child. Less well known is the extent of some of the migratory journeys that different species make. The arctic tern, a shore bird which occasionally breeds in New England and whose migration route takes it close to the New England coast, is the record-holder for long distance migration. This species makes a twice yearly journey of some 20,000 kilometers from northern Canada to the Antarctic. Among the New England species, the bobolink, a familiar bird of fields and pastures, migrates to the grasslands of Argentina, a distance of almost 12,000 kilometers. Even the tiny ruby-throated hummingbird travels several thousand kilometers from its summer breeding grounds in this region to its winter range in Mexico. Included in the hummingbird's journey is a nonstop flight of almost 1,000 kilometers across the Gulf of Mexico.

The ability to migrate, like all other aspects of behavior, evolved gradually over time. Young nestlings require far more food than adults. Therefore, in order to be assured of a continuous supply of food during the breeding period, the population density of each species must remain in balance with the carrying capacity of the habitat. Migrating into large tracts of suitable nesting territory each year allows each species to raise and maintain a larger population than would be possible if it remained in the tropics.

Yet the advantages of an enhanced breeding situation are partially offset by the hazards of migration. Under routine weather conditions, the birds probably find the rigors of migration well within their limits of endurance; indeed many birds not only make long nonstop flights over oceans but routinely continue over land for many kilometers before landing. If the birds encounter unfavorable weather conditions, however, such as strong crosswinds which could blow them out to sea or extended foggy periods which confuse their navigation, vast numbers may be lost. The fall migration also coincides with the peak of the Atlantic hurricane season; a single storm could wipe out thousands of birds.

Man-made structures such as tall buildings, lighthouses, television towers, and airport beacons also take their toll. As a result of these hazards—both natural and man-made—probably hundreds of millions of migrating birds each year never reach their destinations.

Different species migrate at different times during the year. In the spring the ducks are among the first to arrive, some reaching New England as early as the first week of March. The main influx of land birds is not until several weeks later, reaching its height about the third week in May.

Bird migration seems to be concentrated along the coasts and up the major river valleys, though many species advance across the land in broad fronts. One of the major migration routes for shore birds and a number of land birds follows the eastern seaboard. In southern New England, a large number of birds turn inland along the Housatonic and Connecticut valleys, while many of those remaining cross Narragansett Bay and fly northward to the Boston area, skirting the sparse woodlands of Cape Cod. At Boston the migrating birds avoid the downtown area and detour through Brookline, Cambridge, Belmont, and the Middlesex Fells, returning to the coast in northern Essex County. The Mount Auburn Cemetery in Cambridge, a large green oasis near the center of the Boston metropolitan area, is noted for its variety and abundance of birds during migration times.

The fall migration is less spectacular. Some inland species begin flying southward as early as the first week of August, while others, mainly waterfowl, do not migrate until the fifteenth of November. By fall, birds such as the scarlet tanager, bobolink, and many of the male warblers have shed their bright breeding plumage for less distinct coloration that makes them more difficult to identify.

Bird Populations and Distribution

Sight records kept over the last hundred years have shown some dramatic fluctuations in populations of southern New England birds. Natural catastrophes such as hurricanes during the migration season or hard freezes and freak snowstorms in the northern part of the winter ranges of some species have undoubtedly contributed to population declines; but certainly the greatest decimation of bird populations in modern times was the result of the appalling slaughter of birds by market and plume hunters during the last part of the nineteenth century. During this time, a number of formerly abundant species were so overhunted both for food and for the adornment of ladies' hats that they came within a hairsbreadth of extinction. Stringent federal laws passed around the turn of the century brought an abrupt stop to this carnage. The laws have since provided total protection to all migratory songbirds as well as carefully regulated hunting seasons on waterfowl. Two species, however, the passenger pigeon and the heath hen, never recovered; both became extinct in the early decades of this century.

Many of the other decimated species were protected in time and have since made a strong comeback, but so small had some of the populations become that it was not until relatively recent times that their numbers increased appreciably. When a tiny population doubles it is still small; when an already large population doubles, the increase is dramatic.

The growing human population and changing patterns of land use also have had effects on bird populations. Once-abundant field birds such as the bobolink and meadowlark have declined in numbers, probably as a direct result of the declining agriculture in southern New England. For this same reason, however, some woodland species have probably increased their numbers. Summer camps and motorboats on lakes have probably resulted in the decline of some water birds, while populations of those species that coexist well with humans, such as the robin, blue jay, and house sparrow, may have increased.

The role of DDT, Chlordane, Aldrin, Lindane, and other persistent pesticides in the decline of bird populations is well documented. As with so many other man-made compounds, there is no naturally occurring enzyme to break them down into simpler, nontoxic compounds. Insect-eating and predatory species concentrate these poisons in their fat deposits until toxic levels are reached. The main effect of these compounds is an interference with calcium metabolism and, as a result, with eggshell formation. Predatory species such as the osprey, bald eagle, and peregrine falcon have suffered serious declines in their numbers, as has a formerly common resident of orchards, the bluebird. Since 1972, when the Environmental Protection Agency banned the general use of these compounds, the osprey has shown modest recovery in its population. Perhaps this augurs well for the other affected species.

One of the greatest bird population explosions of the country has occurred with the herring gull. The numbers of this hitherto obscure coastal species have increased so dramatically that herring gulls now pose a threat at coastal airports; they have been implicated in several plane crashes. A study of gull feeding behavior has linked this population increase to the penchant of this species for feeding at town dumps. As the human population has increased, so has garbage and so has the herring gull population.

Though thorough documentation is lacking, severe weather conditions in the winter ranges and during migration periods, as mentioned earlier, may have been the reasons for several otherwise inexplicable sudden declines in bird population in recent times. Ships sailing through the calm eye of a hurricane have often been covered with small migrating land birds that have landed to rest. On the other hand, long periods of favorable weather conditions during these seasons may result in an increase in the populations of migratory birds.

Though during migration periods the flocks of transient birds sometimes result in very dense populations for a few days, the average population density of breeding birds in unmanaged habitats is surprisingly low. Data from eastern Massachusetts suggest that the population density in unmanaged tracts of the oak forest is only about ten birds per hectare. The population density on agricultural land is about the same, but on abandoned farmland, where the cover is varied, and where bodies of water are near, the number of birds per hectare is higher. Freshwater marshes with their higher degree of productivity will support substantially more birds, usually between fifteen and forty-five per hectare.

By providing nesting boxes, birdhouses, and a variety of food plants, as is done in bird sanctuaries, it is possible to increase the population density in a given area as much as twentyfold. Some suggestions on how homeowners can attract more birds to their backyards are given later in this chapter.

Another interesting phenomenon of bird distribution has been the recent northward range extensions of several species formerly found only in the southern part of the region. Such resident species as cardinals, mockingbirds, and tufted titmice, which only a few years ago barely reached Massachusetts, now range well into New Hampshire.

People who make a serious study of birds should keep records of both the variety and numbers of birds seen on a particular date. When collected from many places and analyzed, this locally gathered information can provide researchers with valuable evidence about bird population trends.

Learning to Recognize Birds

If you have begun your natural history pursuits with a study of the plants, learning to recognize birds will present a new set of problems. Except when nesting, birds are in almost constant motion. They are sharp-eyed and timid; in most cases they will see you before you see them, and except for the few species such as the robin and chickadee that live in civilization, most will leave the area or seek cover upon your approach. Unless a particular bird is nesting in the vicinity, identification must often be made on the basis of a glimpse or two, sometimes with little opportunity for verification. Poor light conditions or heavy foliage compound the problem. But with good binoculars, an understanding of field techniques, and experience in the field it is possible to become skillful at bird recognition in a reasonably short time.

Except for the few species that visit winter feeders and the additional few that live close to human habitation, you will have to identify most birds from afar. Binoculars are therefore a necessity for birding.

Binoculars come in several powers. The most popular birding binoculars are 7 x 35; that is, they have a magnification power of 7 times with a 35-millimeter objective lens. Higher-powered models are harder to hold steady; in lower-powered models the magnification is, of course, less strong. The size of the objective lens is a design factor related to the magnification power and not to the width of the field of view.

Most 7 x 35 binoculars have a width of field—usually expressed in feet per 1,000 yards—of about 350 to 400 feet at 1,000 yards. This number means, for example, that a bird 100 yards away could move a distance of 35 to 40 feet across the field before you would have to move the binoculars. Generally speaking, the higher the power of the binoculars, the narrower the width of field. Binoculars with wide-angle lenses are available but they are more expensive, and for some people the wide view tends to be more distracting than helpful.

There is a bewildering array of binoculars on the market, ranging in price from under fifty dollars to several hundred dollars. The difference in price is almost entirely related to the quality of the optics, yet, surprisingly, many birders find binoculars at the lower end of the price range perfectly adequate for their needs.

It is important, however, to exercise a great deal of care when purchasing binoculars, especially inexpensive ones. There are a number of poorly made binoculars for sale, the purchase of which would amount to money thrown away. Perhaps the best procedure is to choose binoculars on the recommendation of experienced birders, and to buy from a reputable dealer.

Poorly made binoculars can be inferior in several ways. The barrels may be out of alignment, producing eyestrain with continued use; the lenses may be uncoated (coated lenses have a bluish or yellowish cast), cutting down the amount of light transmitted through the barrels; the field of view may be distorted or out of focus around the edges; dark images viewed against a light background may have colored outlines. When buying binoculars you should also check the guarantee and see whether there are return or exchange provisions if you are not satisfied. Fortunately there are several helpful booklets that give pointers on buying binoculars—they are included in the bibliography at the end of Part VIII—but recommendations from experienced birders are probably the best criteria.

Using binoculars requires practice. To keep them steady, rest the eyepieces against the ridge of bone just below the eyebrows, or, if you wear glasses, rest your thumbs against your cheekbone. Steadying your elbows, arms, or shoulder against some rigid object is also helpful.

The most difficult maneuver for beginners, however, is picking up a bird that they have first spotted with the naked eye. Here the best procedure is to find an easily identifiable reference point such as a crotch in the tree or a forking branch, note its position relative to the bird, focus on it, and then move to the bird. Because birds rarely stay still for long, you must be able to do this very quickly, but with practice the process becomes automatic.

As you use your binoculars, you will find it is important to have the sun at your back. Even with the best binoculars, birds are hard to identify on dark days or when the sun is behind them. Birds are usually more active on warm, rainy days, but harder to identify then unless in open habitats.

Although binoculars are enormously helpful in bird identification, they have their limitations. Most serious birders will eventually find the need for a higher-powered instrument, especially if they are viewing birds from some distance—on beaches, marshes, and other open areas. For such distant views a spotting telescope with a tripod or car window mount is the answer. These spotting scopes range in magnification power up to 60x and, like binoculars, also vary in price and quality. The higher-powered models have a much narrower field of view and are therefore more difficult to use, though of course their range is much greater.

FIELD GUIDES

A good field guide is another essential item to accompany you when you look for birds. Except for the most colorful species, it is almost impossible to maintain a clear enough mental image of an unknown bird to identify it at some later time. It is often difficult enough to make a positive identification with a guide in hand. Sometimes, for example, the field marks of closely related species are so similar that you will need several sightings before you can make positive identification.

There are three outstanding guides for birds in this area. All are comprehensive, portable, and accurate. Peterson's *A Field Guide to the Birds* and Robbins, Bruun, and Singer's *Birds of North America*, like most ornithological publications, describe and illustrate the birds in approximate order of their evolution. They begin with the most primitive species, the loons and grebes, and end with the most advanced species, the grosbeaks, finches, and sparrows. Most of the birds described in the earlier sections are shore birds, waterfowl, and predators; the smaller inland songbirds are illustrated in later sections. The third guide, Bull and Farrand's *Audubon Society Field Guide to Birds: Eastern Region*, groups the birds according to color and habitat.

If you are a beginner, you should spend time familiarizing yourself with your guide. With the range maps provided, you can narrow down the possibilities to those species that are probable in your area and learn their field marks. If you must laboriously thumb through the guide every time you encounter an unknown bird, your quarry may be far away before you can take a second look to verify it.

RECOGNIZING BIRDS BY THEIR CALLS

Birds don't sing for joy but to establish and hold breeding territory and to attract a mate. The males of each species have a distinctive call that warns other males that the particular breeding space is already occupied. Of course, different species with their differing food requirements can often coexist peacefully in the same territory.

Many experts need only hear the call of a bird to make a positive identification, but for most people visual recognition comes first. Usually, you will learn to recognize birds by their calls only after you observe the species calling; then the sound and the bird become associated.

You can speed up this process, however, with the help of one of the excellent recordings of bird calls now available. You should try to fix only a few calls in your mind at each sitting; listening to the entire record will leave you hopelessly confused. Also, using your field guide along with the record will help you match the bird to the call. Playing the record at fairly low volumes, about as loud as you would hear the bird calling nearby in the field, will also help you obtain an accurate rendition of the call.

BIRDS' NESTS

The nests of many species are as distinctive as the birds themselves, though birds have a high degree of adaptability and vary their nesting sites and nest-building materials to a substantial degree. Except for hawks and crows and those species that nest in hollow tree trunks, most occupy a nest for one season only. Despite this fact, if you plan to collect disused birds' nests for identification or study, you should obtain a salvage permit from the United States Fish and Wildlife Service, the address of which is given in the list at the end of this book.

Of course the easiest method for identifying birds' nests is to identify the nest maker, but often this is difficult since most birds nest in inaccessible and hidden places, camouflage their nests well, and remain quiet and still when on or near the nest. As a result, birds' nests are much easier to find after the leaves have fallen. A couple of excellent guides are available for identifying birds' nests. If you collect nests, you should make a note of where you found them and whether they were built on a tree, a shrub, or directly on the ground.

OTHER FIELD TECHNIQUES

Though mastering the use of binoculars and field guides are the two most important field techniques in birding, there are several others that should help you add to the list of birds that you see. Probably the most important of these is knowing where to look. As was mentioned in the section on mammals and earlier in the introduction to the wetlands, the places where two different habitats come together are the best places to look for birds. The greater variety of food plants and the varying conditions of cover along habitat borders attract a larger variety of birds than would normally be seen in large unbroken expanses of any one vegetation type.

Another important consideration is quiet and cautious movement. Even high in the trees, birds are acutely aware of ground movements. If you must move closer to a bird in order to get a clear look, move slowly and quietly. A sudden movement or loud noise will usually send your quarry on its way. A seated figure is less threatening to birds; remaining seated in one place and letting the birds come into your vicinity is a comfortable alternative method to stalking them. Light, bright, or contrasting colors in clothing also make you very conspicuous to birds.

Surprisingly enough, people seated in a car are not nearly as threatening to birds as people on foot. For example, you may have noticed crows and other species feeding close to a busy highway, seemingly oblivious of the speeding traffic nearby; yet, many of these same birds would not allow a person on foot within a hundred meters of them without flying away. If you can drive to a vantage point in a good birding area, observing from inside your car will often yield more species than you would see on foot.

A technique recommended by birders is calling birds. One means is by making a kissing or squeaking sound on the back of your hand. Or you may purchase a small wooden bird call with which you can make a variety of squeaking sounds by turning one rosin-covered wooden cylinder within another. These sounds supposedly mimic the sounds of birds in distress and attract other birds to the area to see what is amiss. If you are birding in marshy areas, sometimes it is possible to bring hidden birds to view by clapping your cupped hands together.

THE BEST BIRDING TIMES

Though some birds may be seen at any time of day and at any season of the year, clearly some birding times are better

172. Belted kingfisher. These birds are
most often seen along rivers.

than others. As far as seasons of the year are concerned, the
largest numbers and greatest variety of birds may be observed in May just before the trees leaf out. During this time
the species are adorned in their bright breeding plumage,
making identification easier than in the fall, when many of
the males have molted and assumed their nondescript
winter coloration.

Once the leaves have reached their full size many of the
smaller species, especially those which normally feed near
the tops of the trees, are all but obscured.

As mentioned previously, many of the spring birds are
transients. By summer the number and variety of woodland
birds is much smaller, now limited only to those species that
breed in southern New England and to a population density
determined by the territorial demands of the various
species. Marsh birds and waterfowl remain relatively abundant during the summer.

The time of day will also have an important bearing on the

number of birds you'll find. Birds are most active in the cool hours of early morning when they are hungry after their nightly fast. For this reason, experienced birders often begin their observations before sunrise; the old adage about early birds applies to early birders as well. Birds are less active during the heat of the day but again become more active in the late afternoon.

Because it is almost essential to have the sun at your back for bird identification, it may be helpful to plan your birding itinerary so that you walk in a westerly direction during the morning and an easterly direction during the afternoon, and to save the most open habitats for morning and evening twilight.

Attracting Birds

In addition to seeking out birds in their habitat, you can arrange your own home grounds so that more than the usual number of birds will come to you. On carefully managed land, where shrubs that attract birds have been planted and nesting boxes and birdhouses have been supplied, it is possible to increase the population density of birds many times over. Even in very small properties there are several things a homeowner can do to increase the number of birds that come there.

WINTER FEEDING

Probably the simplest way to attract birds is to maintain a winter feeder. During the time when the dreary New England weather curtails most outdoor activities, maintaining a feeder can be an immensely satisfying natural history pursuit. Tens of thousands of people in the region do feed the birds during the winter; perhaps this has been a factor in the northward range extension of the cardinal and tufted titmouse mentioned earlier. Though as many as thirty-five different species may visit feeders, the average is about six to eight.

A feeding program need not be inordinately expensive. There are many excellent moderately priced bird feeders available. Plans for easy-to-build but equally satisfactory homemade feeders are also available from many different sources. Seed mixtures do vary in price, though you can make a good mixture at home out of seeds bought relatively inexpensively in bulk. Nevertheless, you should remember that if you begin to feed birds, it is essential that you continue to do so daily right through the winter. Unless there are several people maintaining feeders in your neighborhood, birds that come to depend on your feeder for food will be hard-pressed if that food supply is cut off. And it is also important to remember that if you attract a substantial number of birds, they will consume many pounds of food before the winter is over.

Feeders should be located in the sun, out of the prevailing wind, and in places where they are easy to refill. What may be easy to reach when the ground is bare can become a problem in deep snow. Some people attach their feeders to clothesline pulleys so they can reel them in for refilling, or attach them directly to the windowsill.

Feeders should also be located near a shrub or small tree where the birds can land and survey the area for predators before flying to the feeder. Evergreens are useful in this regard, since they supply shelter as well as a perch. Red cedar is especially good: the seeds themselves are food for some birds. Since a number of winter birds prefer to feed on the ground and will eat the seeds spilled from the feeder, you should place the feeder away from hiding places for cats and other predators.

To keep your bird seed purchases within bounds, it is important to protect your feeder from squirrels. Though squirrels are attractive and enjoyable to have around during the winter, they also will consume a huge quantity of bird seed if it is within their reach. If the feeder is on a post, attach a conical squirrel-guard to it to prevent the animals from climbing the post and reaching the seed. Feeders located within jumping distance of a nearby tree are almost sure to be visited by squirrels.

Winter feeding programs should be started early in November. Studies indicate that even where there is an unlimited amount of artificial food available, birds will spend most of the time foraging for natural food, so beginning the feeding program early will not mean that the seed- and insect-eating birds will gorge themselves on store-bought food rather than earning their keep by eating caterpillar cocoons and weed seeds.

A mixture of sunflower seed, which is relatively expensive, and cracked (not ground) corn, which is not, will attract many winter birds. Other birds such as the small finches will be attracted to the more expensive thistle seeds. Millet seed and kafir corn, which make up the bulk of many commercial feed mixes, are not nearly so popular. Some experts recommend adding fine sand or charcoal to the seed mixture for grit.

Beef suet and bacon fat are also excellent winter foods. This may be stuffed in wire holders or placed in open mesh onion bags and attached directly to the trees. Many of the insect-eating species such as chickadees and woodpeckers will feast on suet during the winter.

WATER

In both winter and summer, water is another bird attractor. When there is snow on the ground birds can obtain enough water for drinking, but even during severe weather, birds will bathe if shallow open water is present. During times when the temperature remains below freezing, it may be impractical to try to maintain open water in a birdbath, unless, of course, the ground is bare and there is no nearby source of water for the birds to drink.

Birdbaths should be placed in the open so cats and other predators cannot wait in ambush. As is the case with feeders, a shrub or small tree nearby will provide the birds with a lookout perch where they can land before visiting the birdbath.

A birdbath need not be elaborate. A trash can lid set on a few rocks will work well. Some birds prefer bathing near the ground rather than in a pedestal birdbath, though the latter affords more protection from cats. The splash or drip of water into a birdbath also attracts birds. A dripping hose or even a plastic gallon jug with a small hole in the bottom suspended above the birdbath will probably increase the number of birds using it.

BIRDHOUSES

Though most species prefer to nest in the open air, some will nest in birdhouses if they are provided. These birdhouses can range from elaborate purple martin apartment houses to simple covered nesting shelves, but birds are very particular about their nesting sites. Different species require houses of very definite dimensions, and the height the birdhouse should be placed above the ground also varies according to the species.

Several of the references at the end of Part VIII provide plans for carefully designed but easy-to-build birdhouses that will almost certainly be occupied if the particular species for which they are designed nest in your area.

PLANTINGS TO ATTRACT BIRDS

A great many trees and shrubs produce fruits which are edible by birds and other wildlife. In most cases, the seeds which lie within these fruits are indigestible and pass unscathed through the animal's digestive system, probably to be dropped some distance away. Thus animal and plant have gradually evolved an important sustaining partnership: one receives nourishment; the other, an efficient dispersal of its seeds to new habitats.

Even in a small suburban backyard, the addition of a few of these fruiting trees and shrubs should increase the number and variety of birds that regularly visit there. Moreover, among these plantings are some of the most handsome ornamentals that can be grown in southern New England; their presence in a garden will be as pleasing to humans as their fruits are to the birds.

In the Northeast about 12 percent of the native plants produce fruits that are eaten by birds and other wildlife. Many are common woodland and roadside plants and can be collected from the wild. Almost all are also available at most nurseries, and sometimes conservation organizations like the state Audubon Societies make small plants available at minimal prices.

Following are lists of shrubs and small trees that are especially attractive to birds. As indicated, some have specialized cultural requirements, but like most other flowering plants, they will bloom more profusely and set more fruit in sunny areas. Trees and shrubs that are particularly ornamental are marked with an asterisk; *N* indicates those native to the area, and *I*, those that have been introduced.

Trees Attractive to Birds

Common name *Latin name*	Origin	*Fruiting season*	*Comments*
*Red cedar *Juniperus virginiana*	N	July–Nov.	thrives in full sun; excellent cover
*White pine *Pinus Strobus*	N	Sept.–Oct.	small seeds eaten by many winter birds
*Birch *Betula* spp.	N	Oct.–Dec.	all native species have small seeds eaten by winter birds
*Mulberry *Morus* spp.	N/I	July	some forms very ornamental
*Shadbush *Amelanchier canadensis*	N	June	grows well in wet ground
*Hawthorn *Crataegus* spp.	N	Oct.–Dec.	many fine ornamental varieties
Cherry *Prunus* spp.	N	July–Sept.	all native species produce edible fruit
*Flowering crab *Pyrus* spp.	I	Sept.–Dec.	among the finest ornamentals; zumi crab one of the best for birds
*Mountain ash *Pyrus* spp.	N/I	Sept.–Nov.	fruits best in full sun
*American holly *Ilex opaca*	N	Nov.–March	many varieties; needs sheltered spot in cold areas; male and female plants necessary for fruit set
*Tupelo *Nyssa sylvatica*	N	Oct.–Jan.	grows well near water
*Dogwood *Cornus florida*	N	Oct.–Nov.	fruits best in full sun
*Fringe tree *Chionanthus virginicus*	N	Aug.–Sept.	thrives in moist ground and semishade

Shrubs Attractive to Birds

Common name *Latin name*	Origin	*Fruiting season*	*Comments*
Bayberry *Myrica pennsylvanica*	N	Nov.–Jan.	tolerates poor sandy soil
Blackberry, raspberry *Rubus* spp.	N/I	July–Sept.	not very ornamental but good cover and food
*Rose *Rosa* spp.	N/I	Sept.–March	many species; *R. multiflora* is invasive
*Chokeberry *Pyrus* spp.	N	Sept–Nov.	thrives in wet areas
*Inkberry, winterberry *Ilex* spp.	N	Nov.–April	both thrive in wet areas
Bittersweet *Celastrus scandens*	N	Oct.–April	vine; tends to become invasive
Virginia creeper *Parthenocissus quinquefolia*	N	Oct.–Dec.	vine; fruits best in full sun
Grape *Vitis* spp.	N	Sept.–Oct.	rank-growing vine; fruit attracts many birds
Russian olive *Elaeagnus* spp.	I	Oct.–Dec.	silvery foliage; rapid growing
*Dogwood *Cornus* spp.	N	Sept.–Oct.	all shrub species produce edible fruit
Blueberry *Vaccinium* spp.	N	July–Aug.	excellent summer fruit for birds and humans
Huckleberry *Gaylussacia* spp.	N	July	fruit better for birds than humans
*Honeysuckle *Lonicera* spp.	N/I	June–July	several ornamental varieties; avoid Hall's honeysuckle, *L. japonica,* invasive and impossible to control; Tartarian honeysuckle, *L. tatarica,* one of the best
*Snowberry, coralberry *Symphoricarpos* spp.	N/I	Sept.–March	will grow on dry sites
*Viburnum *Viburnum* spp.	N/I	Nov.–March	many handsome varieties; most prefer moist soils
Elderberry *Sambucus* spp.	N	Sept.–Oct.	thrives in moist soil

Birds by Habitat

Because of their mobility and adaptability, many birds are difficult to classify by habitat. Some species, such as those living in marshes, usually remain in that habitat or close to it, but other species may appear wherever there is food to eat. The following lists, therefore, are offered as a rough guide to help you narrow down the possibilities. *Those species marked with one asterisk are rarely seen in Massachusetts outside of the Connecticut Valley. Those marked with two asterisks are rarely seen except in southern Connecticut and Rhode Island.*

Common Summer Birds
of the Oak Forest Communities

Red-tailed hawk
Red-shouldered hawk
Broad-winged hawk
Ruffed grouse
*Yellow-billed cuckoo
Black-billed cuckoo
Great horned owl
Screech owl
Barred owl
Ruby-throated hummingbird
Common flicker
Hairy woodpecker
Downy woodpecker
**Acadian flycatcher
Great crested flycatcher
Least flycatcher
Eastern wood peewee
Blue jay
Common crow
Black-capped chickadee
Tufted titmouse

White-breasted nuthatch
Woodthrush
Veery
Yellow-throated vireo
Red-eyed vireo
Black-and-white warbler
**Worm-eating warbler
*Golden-winged warbler
*Blue-winged warbler
Black-throated green warbler
**Prairie warbler
Ovenbird
*Yellow-breasted chat
American redstart
Northern oriole
*Orchard oriole
Scarlet tanager
Cardinal
Rose-breasted grosbeak
Rufous-sided towhee
Song sparrow

Common Summer Birds of Farms, Farmland,
Abandoned Farmland, and Open Thickets
(some may also appear in suburban residential areas)

American kestrel
Ring-necked pheasant
Killdeer
American woodcock
Rock dove (pigeon)
Mourning dove
Common nighthawk
Eastern kingbird
Eastern phoebe
Tree swallow
Bank swallow
Barn swallow
Purple martin
Common crow
House wren
**Carolina wren
Mockingbird
Gray catbird
Brown thrasher
American robin

Eastern bluebird
Cedar waxwing
Starling
**White-eyed vireo
Yellow warbler
Chestnut-sided warbler
Common yellowthroat
Bobolink
Eastern meadowlark
House sparrow
Common grackle
Brown-headed cowbird
Indigo bunting
American goldfinch
Rufous-sided towhee
Savannah sparrow
*Grasshopper sparrow
Chipping sparrow
Field sparrow
Song sparrow

Common Summer Birds of Freshwater Marshes,
Ponds, and Other Wetlands

Pied-billed grebe
Great blue heron
Black-crowned night
 heron
Least bittern
American bittern
Canada goose
Mallard
Black duck
Wood duck
Virginia rail
Sora rail

Common gallinule
American coot
Common snipe
Spotted sandpiper
Solitary sandpiper
Greater yellowlegs
Lesser yellowlegs
Pectoral sandpiper
Least sandpiper
Semipalmated sandpiper
Great black-backed gull
Herring gull

Belted kingfisher
Tree swallow
Barn swallow
Long-billed marsh wren
Northern parula warbler
Yellow warbler

Palm warbler
Northern waterthrush
**Louisiana waterthrush
Common yellowthroat
Red-winged blackbird
Swamp sparrow

Common Winter Birds (many will visit feeders)

Mallard
Black duck
Red-tailed hawk
American kestrel
Ring-necked pheasant
Great black-backed gull
Herring gull
Rock dove (pigeon)
Mourning dove
Hairy woodpecker
Downy woodpecker
Blue jay
Common crow
Black-capped chickadee
Tufted titmouse

White-breasted nuthatch
Mockingbird
American robin
Starling
House sparrow
Cardinal
Evening grosbeak
Purple finch
Common redpoll
American goldfinch
Dark-eyed junco
Tree sparrow
White-throated sparrow
Fox sparrow
Song sparrow

FURTHER READING AND LISTENING

Mammals of Southern New England

Burt, William H., and Richard P. Grossenheider. *A Field Guide to the Mammals*. Boston: Houghton Mifflin, 1964. Comprehensive guide to mammal species found north of Mexico. Range maps and skull information included.

Collins, Henry Hill. *Complete Field Guide to American Wildlife*. New York: Harper and Row, 1959. Comprehensive introduction to American wildlife. Not as detailed as guides to specific animal classes.

Godin, Alfred J. *Wild Mammals of New England*. Baltimore: Johns Hopkins University Press, 1977. The definitive work on New England mammals. Range maps, descriptions.

Goodwin, George Gilbert. *The Mammals of Connecticut*. Connecticut Geological and Natural History Survery Bulletin 53. Hartford, Conn.: State Library, 1935. Description of Connecticut's native mammals.

Hall, E. R., and K. R. Kelson. *The Mammals of North America*. 2 vols. New York: Ronald Press, 1959.

Hamilton, W. J., Jr. *American Mammals*. New York: McGraw-Hill, 1939. Standard reference work on American mammals.

Lawrence, Barbara, and Charles P. Lyman. *List of Mammals of Eastern Massachusetts: Concord Field Station* (A Guide to Resources No. 7). Cambridge, Mass.: Museum of Comparative Zoology, Harvard University, 1974. Annotated list of species. Good bibliography.

Murie, Olaus J. *A Field Guide to Animal Tracks*. Boston: Houghton Mifflin, 1954. A guide to tracks, scats, and other signs of mammals and other animals.

Amphibians and Reptiles of Southern New England

Babbitt, Lewis Hall. *The Amphibia of Connecticut*. Connecticut Geological and Natural History Survey Bulletin 57. Hartford, Conn.: State Library, 1937. Descriptive listing of Connecticut's amphibians.

Babcock, Harold L. *Turtles of the Northeastern United States*. New York: Dover, 1971. Another excellent Dover reprint of a long out-of-print work. Superb color plates.

Bishop, Sherman C. *Handbook of Salamanders: The Salamanders of the United States, of Canada, and of Lower California*.

Ithaca, N.Y.: Cornell University, 1941. The definitive work on native salamanders. Identification keys. Detailed accounts and photographs of all species.

Carr, Archie. *Handbook of Turtles of the United States, Canada, and Baja California*. Ithaca, N.Y.: Comstock, 1952. The definitive work on turtles.

Conant, Roger. *A Field Guide to Reptiles and Amphibians*. Boston: Houghton Mifflin, 1958. Excellent guide for amateurs. Colored illustrations, descriptions, and range maps.

Kauffeld, Carl. *Snakes: The Keeper and the Kept*. Garden City, N.Y.: Doubleday, 1969. Excellent book on keeping snakes in the home. Good advice, interesting anecdotes, illustrated.

Lamson, George Herbert. *The Reptiles of Connecticut*. Connecticut Geological and Natural History Survey Bulletin 55. Hartford, Conn.: State Library, 1935. Description of Connecticut's reptiles. Some terminology is out of date.

Lazell, James D., Jr. *Reptiles and Amphibians in Massachusetts*. Lincoln, Mass.: Massachusetts Audubon Society, 1974. Excellent little booklet describing the fifty species of reptiles and amphibians native to Massachusetts. Information on caring for different species in captivity.

Oliver, James. *The Natural History of North American Amphibians and Reptiles*. Princeton, N.J.: Van Nostrand, 1955. Useful nontechnical book of reptile behavior and habits. Photographs and line drawings.

Petersen, Richard C. *The Venomous Snakes of Connecticut*. Geological and Natural History Survey Bulletin 103. Hartford, Conn.: State Library, 1970. Balanced treatment of life history, distribution, and habitat of the rattlesnake and copperhead, New England's only poisonous species.

Smyth, H. Rucker. *Amphibians and Their Ways*. New York: Macmillan, 1962. Excellent introduction to the natural history of amphibians. Discussion of many New England species. Good bibliography.

Voices of the Night: The Calls of Thirty-four Frogs and Toads of the United States and Canada. Ithaca, N.Y.: Cornell University. LP recording of eastern frogs and toads.

Wright, A. H., and A. A. Wright. *Handbook of Frogs and Toads: The Frogs and Toads of the United States and Canada*. Ithaca, N.Y.: Cornell University Press, 1949. The definitive work on native frogs and toads. Semitechnical. Identification keys, range maps, photographs, and detailed descriptions.

Wright, A. H., and A. A. Wright. *Handbook of Snakes*. 2 vols. Ithaca, N.Y.: Comstock, 1957. Life histories, anatomy, and ecology of North American species.

Introduction to Inland Birds of Southern New England

Bent, Arthur Cleveland. *Life Histories of North American Birds*. 20 vols. New York: Dover, 1958. Highly detailed accounts of all North American species.

Birder's Kit. Lincoln, Mass.: Massachusetts Audubon Society. A yearly collection of birding information including a directory of all natural history and bird clubs in the state, schedules of meetings and field trips, lists of good birding localities, checklists, etc. Very useful for beginner or expert.

Bull, John, and John Farrand. *The Audubon Society Field Guide to Birds: Eastern Region Guide*. New York: Knopf, 1977. Color photographs arranged by color and shape for easy identification. Text organized according to habitat.

Dennis, John V. *A Complete Guide to Bird Feeding*. New York: Knopf, 1975. Excellent guide to bird feeding and to the habits of those birds that visit feeders.

Field Guide to Eastern Bird Songs, Bird Songs in Your Garden, Song Birds in the Northern Woods. Boston: Houghton Mifflin. Three of nearly two dozen records produced by Cornell Laboratory of Ornithology of songs of American birds.

Forbush, E. H. *Birds of Massachusetts*. 3 vols. Boston: Commonwealth of Massachusetts, 1925, 1927, 1929. Long out of print but still useful. Comprehensive text with fine paintings by Louis Agassiz Fuertes.

Harrison, Hal H. *A Field Guide to Birds' Nests*. Boston: Houghton Mifflin, 1975. Color photographs and descriptions of birds' nests by species.

Headstrom, Richard. *Whose Nest is That?* Rev. ed. Lincoln, Mass.: Massachusetts Audubon Society, 1965. Easy-to-use key to common bird and mammal nests of southern New England.

Leahy, Christopher. *An Introduction to Massachusetts Birds*. Lincoln, Mass.: Massachusetts Audubon Society, 1975. A booklet illustrating the common birds of Massachusetts by habitat. Interesting bird lore and realistic conservation ideas.

McElroy, Thomas P. *The Habitat Guide to Birding*. New York: Knopf, 1974. A useful introduction to birding. Tells how and where to look for birds. Lists birds by the habitats in which they are most likely to be found. Information on purchasing binoculars.

Peterson, Roger Tory. *A Field Guide to the Birds*. Boston: Houghton Mifflin, 1947. Illustrations of all eastern species. Descriptive text includes field marks and how to distinguish from similar species.

Pettingill, Olin Sewall, Jr. *A Guide to Bird-Finding East of the Mississippi*, 2d ed. New York: Oxford University Press, 1977.

Comprehensive guide to many of the best birding sites in New England and elsewhere.

Pough, Richard H. *Audubon Land Bird Guide* and *Audubon Water Bird Guide*. Garden City, N.Y.: Doubleday, 1949 and 1951. Extensive text on habits and nesting as well as illustrations.

Robbins, C. S., B. Bruun, and H. S. Zim. *Birds of North America*. New York: Golden Press, 1966. Exceptionally fine illustrations by Arthur Singer of all North American species. Short. Descriptions and range maps.

Schutz, Walter. *How to Attract, House, and Feed Birds*. New York: Collier, 1970. Illustrated diagrams of many bird feeders and bird houses. Information on dietary preferences of many species.

"Sounds of Nature" Series, including *Birds of the Forest, Finches, Warblers of Eastern North America*, and others. Recordings produced by Federation of Ontario Naturalists, Toronto, but available in the U.S.

APPENDIXES

USEFUL ADDRESSES

Below are listed the mailing addresses for government and private agencies that publish information on southern New England's geology, scenery, and plant geography.

U.S. Government Agencies

For topographic and geologic maps:

> Distribution Section, U.S. Geological Survey
> 1200 South Eades Street
> Arlington, Virginia 22202

Topographic maps may also be purchased at the U.S. Government Bookstore, John F. Kennedy Building, Boston, Massachusetts 02114, and in many book and sporting goods stores.

For information about maps and aerial photographs:

> Map Information Office
> U.S. Geological Survey
> Washington, D.C. 20242

State indexes of topographic maps and special maps, as well as lists of dealers for topographic maps, are available from this office.

For U.S. Geological Survey and Forest Service publications:

> Superintendent of Documents
> U.S. Government Printing Office
> Washington, D.C. 20402

For salvage permits to collect birds' nests and information about U.S. Wildlife Refuges:

> U.S. Fish and Wildlife Service
> 801 Post Office Building
> Boston, Massachusetts 02108

State Agencies and Private Nonprofit Organizations

Appalachian Mountain Club
5 Joy Street
Boston, Massachusetts 02108

Connecticut Audubon Society
Audubon Center
613 Riverville Road
Greenwich, Connecticut 06833

Connecticut Forest and Park Association
P.O. Box 389
East Hartford, Connecticut 06108

Connecticut Herpetological Society
Mrs. Nancy Ford, Secretary
598 Durham Road
Guilford, Connecticut 06437

Massachusetts Audubon Society
Lincoln, Massachusetts 01773

Massachusetts Herpetological Society
Shelley Taylor, Secretary
52 Prince Street
Brookline, Massachusetts 02146

New England Wildflower Society
Hemenway Road
Framingham, Massachusetts 01701

The Audubon Society of Rhode Island
40 Bowen Street
Providence, Rhode Island 02903

The Trustees of Reservations
224 Adams Street
Milton, Massachusetts 02186

Sierra Club
3 Joy Street
Boston, Massachusetts 02108

Connecticut Geological and Natural History Survey publications:

State Librarian
State Library
Hartford, Connecticut 06115

GUIDES TO NATURAL AREAS

Because this book is intended to be used in any natural area in the region, specific places to visit are not mentioned. The following guides will direct you to many beautiful and interesting natural areas.

Jorgensen, Neil. *A Guide to New England's Landscape*, 2d ed. Chester, Conn.: Pequot Press, 1977. This earlier book of mine lists at the end of each chapter places where specific landscape features may be seen.

AMC Massachusetts–Rhode Island Trail Guide, 3d ed. Boston: Appalachian Mountain Club, 1977. Guide to hikes in the two-state region. Most of those listed for the part of Massachusetts covered by this guide are relatively short and easy.

AMC New England Canoeing Guide. Boston: Appalachian Mountain Club, 1971. Descriptions of every canoeable river in New England. Soon to be superseded by *AMC River Guide*, vol. II, which covers the rivers in central and southern New England. Canoeing is another excellent way to see the countryside.

Connecticut Recreation Guide. Hartford: Connecticut Forest and Park Association, 1969. Excellent little book that catalogs most of the state-owned public lands.

Connecticut Walk Book. Hartford: Connecticut Forest and Park Association, 1968. Complete guide to Connecticut's extensive trail system.

Fisher, Alan. *AMC Guide to Country Walks Near Boston*. Boston: Appalachian Mountain Club, 1977. Interpretive guide to natural areas within reach of public transportation.

Keyarts, Eugene. *Short Walks in Connecticut*. 3 vols. Chester, Conn.: Pequot Press, 1973. Delightful little guides to 125 country walks in Connecticut. Easy-to-follow maps for each walk.

Sadlier, Paul and Ruth. *Fifty Hikes in Massachusetts*. Somersworth, N.H.: New Hampshire Publishing Co., 1975. Informative guide to fifty day hikes. Maps, text, superb photographs.

Sadlier, Paul and Ruth. *Short Walks on Cape Cod and the Vineyard*. Chester, Conn.: Pequot Press, 1976. Fine pocket guide with excellent photographs, maps.

In addition, the state Audubon Societies, the Trustees of Reservations, and the New England Wildflower Society all maintain properties which may be explored by naturalists. Directions to them may be obtained from the headquarters of each organization.

Many southern New England towns have acquired conservation lands that are usually open to the public. Some towns have developed their own trail systems on conservation lands and elsewhere. By visiting the town hall you can usually obtain maps and guides to the conservation lands.

INDEX

Numbers in boldface refer to pages on which plants and animals are described, numbers in italics to pages with illustrations, including maps. For full information on a species, read also the introduction to the section in which it appears.

A

Abies spp.: migration of, 60; *balsamifera*, 41, 312

Acer spp.: migration of, 60; *negundo*, 23, **296**; *pennsylvanicum*, **317**, *317*; *platanoides*, 9; *rubrum*, 8, 92, 105, *131*, **131**, *144*, 275, 276, **279**, 318; *saccharinum*, 279, **288** (range), **288**, 290; *saccharum*, 8, 92, 105, 141, *195*, **195**, 318; *spicatum*, **318**

Acorus Calamus, **258**, *259*

Actaea spp., 95; *pachypoda*, **170**, *170*; *rubra*, 171

Adiantum pedatum, 95, *186*, **187**

Agkistrodon contortrix, **25**, *28* (range), 375, pl. VIII

Alder, 269, **270**, 327, 328; migration of, 60

Alnus spp., 269, **270**, 327, 328; migration of, 60

Amanita verna, 24

Amaranthus spp., 211, 215

Ambrosia spp., 215; *trifida*, 298

Ambystoma spp.: *maculatum*, **366**, pl. VII; *opacum*, **366**

Amelanchier spp., **272**; *canadensis*, **272**, 273, 393

Amphibians, 362-69; keeping, 365; frogs and toads, 367-69; salamanders, 365-66; pl. VII

Andromeda glaucophylla, **303**, *304*

Andropogon scoparius, 129, 217-18

Anemone: rue, **169**; wood, **169**, pl. I

Anemone quinquefolia, **169**, pl. I

Anemonella thalictroides, **169**

Angle of repose, 75

Anomaly, 11-18

Anthracnose fungus, 289

Aquilegia canadensis, 95

Aralia spp.: *hispia*, **173**; *nudicaulis*, *172*, *172*; *racemosa*, **173**

Arbutus, trailing, 95, *158*, **158**, 245, pl. I

Arctostaphylos Uva-ursi, 238, **245**, *246*

Arethusa, **263**, 308, pl. II

Arethusa bulbosa, **263**, 308, pl. II

Arisaema spp., **284**

Arrowhead, *253*, **256**, 257

Arrow-wood, 148, *149*, 328

Asclepias spp., 216

Ash: black, **279**, *280* (range), *281*, 318; green, **296**; red, 280, **296**; white, 8, 92, 141, *146*, **146**, 197, 224, 296, 318, 327

Aspen: big-toothed, **220**, 221; quaking, 8, 92, 106, **220**, *221*, 221

Asplenium spp., 95; *platyneuron*, 95n, 151, 179; *trichomanes*, 179

Aster: wild, 95, 216; wood, *172*, *172*

Aster spp., 95, *172*, 216; *divaricatus*, *172*, *172*

Athyrium spp.: *Filix-femina*, **181**, *184*, *336*; *pycnocarpon*, 179; *thelypteroides*, 179

Azalea, 95; mountain, 142, **148**, pl. V; pink, 142, **148**; white swamp, 273, **282**, *283*, 303

B

Baneberry, 95; red, **171**; white, **170**, *170*

Basswood, 91, 92, *193*, *193*, 318

Bayberry, 394

Bearberry, 238, **245**, *246*

Beaver, **353**

Beech, American, 8, 92, 105, 141, 197, **316**, 322-24; migration of, 61

Bellwort, **164**

Betula spp., 393; ice damage to, 56; migration of, 60; *lenta*, 8, 92, 105, 111, 134, **136**, *136*, 318; *lutea*, 105,

L

Labrador tea, 303, *304*
Ladies' tresses, common, 265, *265*
Lady's slipper, pink, 95, **165**, *165*, pl. II
Lampropeltis triangulum, 375, pl. VIII
Land use, 214-19; clues to, 207-13
Laportea spp., 24; *canadensis,* **322**
Larch, 41, **312**, *313*
Larix laricina, 41, **312**, *313*
Latitude: effect on mesoclimate, 49
Latrodectus spp.: *mactans,* **32**; *variolus,* **32**
Laurel: bog, **303**, *304*; mountain, 95, **141**, 152-54, *153*, 303, 320, pl. V; sheep, 105, **132**, *133*, 245, 303
Leatherleaf, **268**, 271, **271**, 299, 303
Leatherwood, **198**
Ledum groenlandicum, **303**, *304*
Lemna spp., *253*, **258**
Levees, natural, 286
Liliaceae, 161-64
Lilies, 161-64
Lilium spp.: *canadense,* 161, *266*, **266**; *philadelphicum,* 95, **161**, pl. III; *superbum,* **266**, pl. IV; *tigrinum,* **266**
Lily: bluebead, **321**; Canada, 161, *266*, **266**; tiger, **266**; Turk's cap, **266**, pl. IV; wood, 95, **161**, pl. III
Lindera Benzoin, 95, **198**, 274, 320, **327**, pl. V
Liquidambar styraciflua, 42, *281*, **281**
Liriodendron tulipifera, 91, 92, *194*, *194* (range), **195**
Little bluestem, 129, 217-18
Liverworts, 277-78
Loam, 89
Lobelia spp.: *cardinalis,* 267, **328**, pl. IV; *inflata,* 211
Local species (plants), 12-16
Locust: black, 212, **222**, 223; shipmast, **223**
Lonicera spp., 394; *canadensis,* **320**
Loosestrife, purple, 216, **258**
Low slope community, 143-49, *144*
Lycopodium spp.: *annotinum,* 190; *clavatum,* *189*; *complanatum,*

188, *189*; *lucidulum,* **190**; *obscurum,* **189**, *189*; *tristachyum,* **189**
Lygodium palmatum, 13, *14*, 95, 331
Lynx rufus, 344
Lythrum Salicaria, 216, **258**

M

Macroclimate, 46-47
Magnolia, sweetbay, 12, *13*, 42
Magnolia virginiana, 12, *13*, 42
Maianthemum canadense, 95, **161**, *162*, 277
Mammals, 340-62; carnivorous 356-62; diurnal, 345-50; food trails of, 342-43; habitat of, 341; keeping, 344; nocturnal, 350-56. *See also* Tracking mammals
Maple: migration of, 60; mountain, **318**; Norway, 9; red, 8, 92, 105, *131*, **131**, *144*, 275, 276, **279**, 318; silver, 279, *288* (range), **288**, *290*; striped, **317**, *317*; sugar, 8, 92, 105, 141, *195*, **195**, 318
Marble, 69, 191
Maritime cold front, 51
Marmota monax, *349*, **350**
Marsh community, 252-61, *253*
Marsh marigold, 16, 95, **328**, pl. I
Marsh pink, **261**
Matteuccia Struthiopteris, *335*, **336**
Mayflower. *See* Trailing arbutus
Meadowsweet, **272**
Medeola virginiana, 95, 168, 329, **329**
Mephitis mephitis, 344, **360**
Mesoclimate, 46-56
Microclimate, 76-88; effect of trees on, 79-80
Midslope community, 134-42, *135*
Migration, bird, 378-79
Migration, forest, 56-62
Milkweed, 216
Mink, **360**
Mitchella repens, 95, **168**, *168*
Mixed mesophytic community, 190-98; distribution of, *192*; ferns of (chart), 178-79
Monotropa uniflora, *160*
Morning glory, wild, 216
Morus spp., 393

FIELD NOTES

FIELD NOTES

FIELD NOTES

FIELD NOTES

FIELD NOTES

FIELD NOTES

FIELD NOTES